Jordan

**Anthony Ham
Paul Greenway**

LONELY PLANET PUBLICATIONS
Melbourne • Oakland • London • Paris

JORDAN

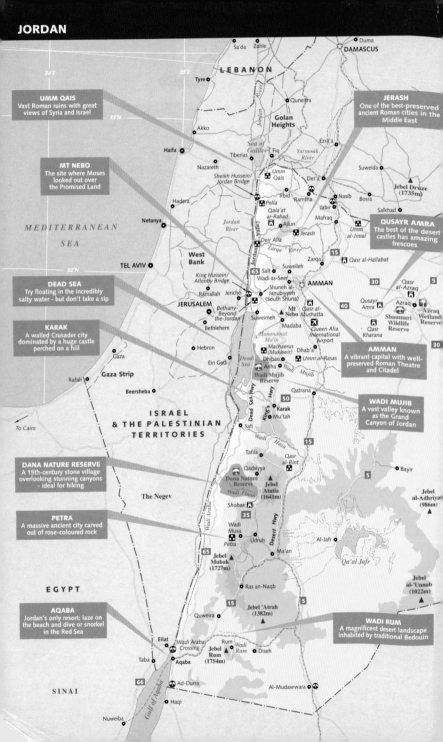

UMM QAIS
Vast Roman ruins with great views of Syria and Israel

MT NEBO
The site where Moses looked out over the Promised Land

DEAD SEA
Try floating in the incredibly salty water - but don't take a sip

KARAK
A walled Crusader city dominated by a huge castle perched on a hill

DANA NATURE RESERVE
A 15th-century stone village overlooking stunning canyons - ideal for hiking

PETRA
A massive ancient city carved out of rose-coloured rock

AQABA
Jordan's only resort; laze on the beach and dive or snorkel in the Red Sea

JERASH
One of the best-preserved ancient Roman cities in the Middle East

QUSAYR AMRA
The best of the desert castles has amazing frescoes

AMMAN
A vibrant capital with well-preserved Roman Theatre and Citadel

WADI MUJIB
A vast valley known as the Grand Canyon of Jordan

WADI RUM
A magnificent desert landscape inhabited by traditional Bedouin

LEBANON

DAMASCUS

Golan Heights

MEDITERRANEAN SEA

Sea of Galilee

Yarmouk River

West Bank

Jordan River

TEL AVIV

JERUSALEM

AMMAN

ISRAEL & THE PALESTINIAN TERRITORIES

Gaza Strip

To Cairo

The Negev

EGYPT

SINAI

Gulf of Aqaba

Sa'da · Zahle · Duma

Tyre · Quneitra · Ezra'a

Akko · Tiberias · Fiq · Suweida · Jebel Druze (1735m)

Haifa · Nazareth · Umm Qais · Der'a · Bosra · Salkhad

Hadera · Sheikh Hussein/ Jordan Bridge · Irbid · Ramtha · Nasib · Jabir · Mafraq

Netanya · Pella · Qala'at ar-Rabad · Ajlun · Jerash · Umm al-Jimal · Qasr al-Hallabat

Deir Alla · *Zarqa River* · Zarqa · 15

Ramallah · Salt · Suweileh · Qasr al-Azraq

Jericho · Wadi as-Seer · 65 · Shuneh al-Janubiyyeh (South Shuna) · Qusayr Amra · Azraq · Azraq Wetland Reserve

Bethany-Beyond-the-Jordan · Mt Nebo · Qasr al-Mushatta · Shaumari Wildlife Reserve

Bethlehem · Suweimeh · Madaba · Queen Alia International Airport · Qasr Kharana

Hebron · *Hammamat Ma'in* · Machaerus (Mukawir) · Dhab'a · Umm ar-Rasas

Ein Gedi · Dhiban · 30

Gaza · *Dead Sea* · Ariha · *Wadi Mujib* · Wadi Mujib Reserve · Qatrana

Rafah · Beersheba · Safi · Karak · Mu'tah · 50

Tafila · *Wadi Hasa* · 15 · Bayir

Qasr al-Bint · 5

Qadsiyya · Dana Nature Reserve · Jebel Atata (1641m) · Jebel al-Adhriya' (986m)

Wadi Araba · Shobak · 35

Wadi Musa · Petra · Udruh · Ma'an · Al-Jafr · *Qa'al Jafr*

65 · Jebel Mubak (1727m) · Jebel al-'Unnab (1022m)

Ras an-Naqb

15 · Jebel 'Atrah (1382m) · 5

Quweira · WADI RUM

Eilat · Wadi Araba Crossing · Rum · *Wadi Rum* · Diseh

Taba · Aqaba · Jebel Rum (1754m) · Al-Mudawwara

66 · Ad-Durra

Haqi

Nuweiba

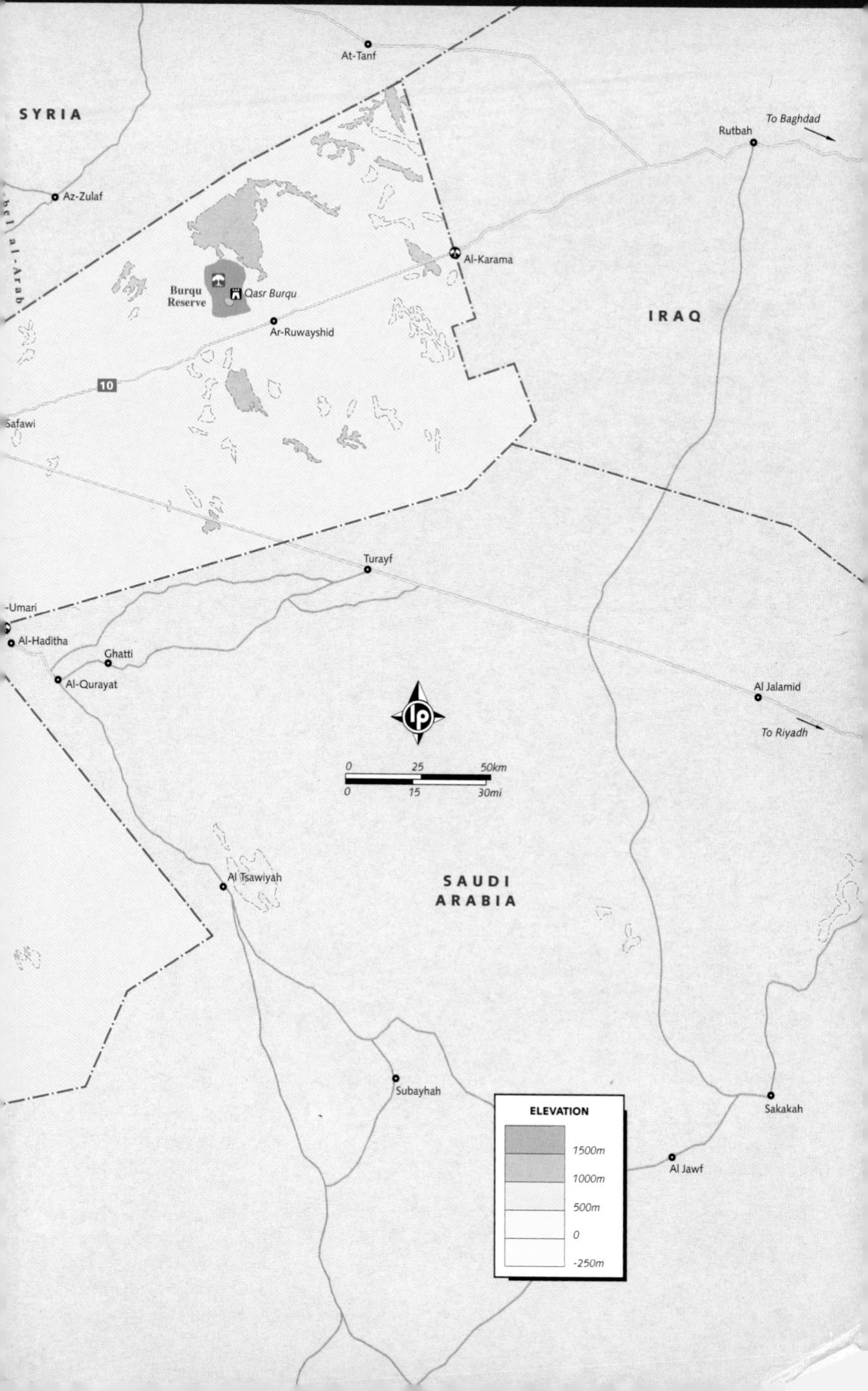

SYRIA

At-Tanf

Rutbah

To Baghdad

Az-Zulaf

Al-Karama

IRAQ

Burqu
Reserve

Qasr Burqu

Ar-Ruwayshid

10

Safawi

Turayf

-Umari

Al-Haditha

Ghatti

Al-Jalamid

Al-Qurayat

To Riyadh

SAUDI
ARABIA

Al Tsawiyah

| 0 | 25 | 50km |
| 0 | 15 | 30mi |

Subayhah

Sakakah

ELEVATION

1500m

1000m

500m

0

-250m

Al Jawf

Jordan
5th edition – April 2003
First published – October 1987

Published by
Lonely Planet Publications Pty Ltd ABN. 36 005 607 983
90 Maribyrnong St, Footscray, Victoria 3011, Australia

Lonely Planet Offices
Australia Locked Bag 1, Footscray, Victoria 3011
USA 150 Linden St, Oakland, CA 94607
UK 10a Spring Place, London NW5 3BH
France 1 rue du Dahomey, 75011 Paris

Photographs
Many of the images in this guide are available for licensing from
Lonely Planet Images.
w www.lonelyplanetimages.com

Front cover photograph
The Khazneh (Treasury), in Petra, is believed to have hidden pirate
treasures (Paul David Hellander)

ISBN 1 74059 165 8

Printed by The Bookmaker International Ltd
Printed in China

**Although the authors
and Lonely Planet try
to make the informa-
tion as accurate as
possible, we accept
no responsibility for
any loss, injury or
inconvenience sus-
tained by anyone
using this book.**

Contents – Text

Contents – Maps

CHAPTER INDEX MAP

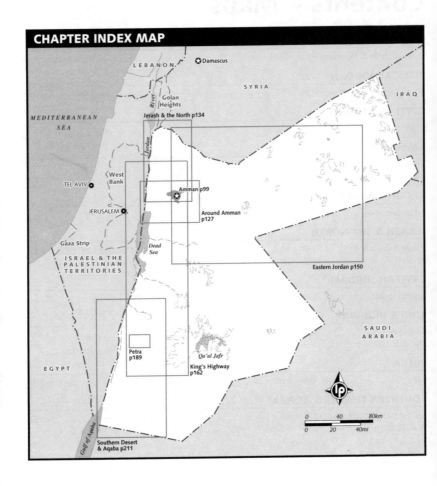

The Authors

Anthony Ham

Anthony worked as a refugee lawyer for three years, during which time he completed a masters degree in Middle Eastern politics. After tiring of daily battles with a mean-spirited Australian government, he set out to see the world and restore his faith in humanity. Sitting on the running boards of a train in Thailand, he decided to become a writer and ever since has been travelling throughout the Arab world, India and Africa. Whenever circumstances permit he heads for the Sahara Desert, and now lives in Madrid. For Lonely Planet, Anthony has worked on *Middle East, Africa, Iran, India, North India, West Africa, Jordan* and his most satisfying project, writing the first edition of *Libya*.

Paul Greenway

Paul caught his first tropical disease in 1985 and has had the travel bug ever since. Gratefully plucked from the blandness and security of the Australian Public Service, he is now a full-time traveller and writer. Paul has contributed to several Lonely Planet guides, such as *South India* and *Indonesia*, and has written guides to a diverse number of countries, such as *Mongolia, Iran* and *Bali & Lombok*.

During the rare times he is not travelling (or writing, reading and dreaming about it), Paul tries to write and record some tuneless ditties, eats and breathes Australian Rules football, and will do anything (like going to Mongolia and Iran) to avoid settling down.

Damien Simonis

With a degree in languages and several years' reporting and sub-editing on several Australian newspapers (including the *Australian* and the *Age*), Sydney-born Damien left the country in 1989. He has lived, worked and travelled extensively throughout Europe, the Middle East and North Africa. Since 1992, Lonely Planet has kept him busy with *Jordan & Syria, Egypt & the Sudan, Morocco, North Africa, Italy, the Canary Islands, Spain* and *Barcelona*. He now lives in London.

FROM ANTHONY

As always in the Arab world, I made many new friends in Jordan and so many people gave their assistance without asking anything in return.

Special thanks must go to Fayez al-Kayyali, Ra'ed Agrabawi and Dr Suheil Twal for their friendship and invaluable insight in Amman. Thanks also to the following for their patience, information and the warmth of their welcome: Ahmad al-Omari at the Umm Qais museum; Nowa Nasser at the Jordan Tourism Board in Amman; Deeb Hussein for his avuncular help in Pella; Ahmed Mansour in Irbid; Charl al-Twal and Osamah Twal in Madaba; Hayat for her charming tour around Hammamat Ma'in; Zac and Jan for feeding me so well in Amman – sorry that illness prevented me making it back to say goodbye; Jihad al-Sawalqa for being such an inspirational host in Dana and for sending me the information as promised; Jihad Amarat at the visitor centre in Petra; Sabah at Wadi Rum visitor centre; Attayak Ali, Difallah Ateeg and Osama Musa in Wadi Rum; Mater Saqer in the Public Information Office of UNRWA; and the urbane Mazhar and soulman Khalil (Dreads) at Books@café, Amman. Finally, a very special thank you to Ruth who was hugely generous with her assistance as she is to all travellers who visit Jordan.

Back home, a massive thank you to my family and friends for their patience, understanding and warmth despite my long absences, especially to Jan, Ron, Lisa, Greg, my very special nieces Alexandra and Greta, Rachael, and Damien and Quetta for such a chilled wedding in Vanuatu on the way home – I hope you all know how much I miss you. In the LP office, grateful thanks to Virginia Maxwell for her Jordan insights, and Brigitte Ellemor and Meredith Mail for their support during days of upheaval.

And in my new home in Madrid, thanks to Don Timson for his invaluable assistance; and to the very special Marina Lopez Garcia for lighting up my world and for not laughing too often at my Spanish.

This Book

Anthony Ham updated Jordan for this fifth edition. He built on the work of Paul Greenway and Damien Simonis, who researched the previous editions.

From the Publisher

This book was commissioned by Lynne Preston and produced in Lonely Planet's Melbourne office. Huw Fowles was the project manager. Editing and proofing was done by Kate James and Peter Cruttenden, with assistance from Will Gourlay. Sally Morgan co-ordinated the design and James Hardy designed the cover. Maps were produced by Leanne Peake and Valentina Kremenchutskaya, with final map corrections from Chris Thomas, Julie Sheridan and Amanda Sierp. Adriana Mammarella and Kate McDonald did the layout checks. Thanks go to Hunor Csutoros and James Ellis for the climate charts, Nick Stebbing for script assistance and Quentin Frayne for the language chapter. Thanks also to Amy Schmidt in Amman who helped with updating research.

THANKS
Many thanks to the travellers who used the last edition and wrote to us with helpful hints, advice and interesting anecdotes. Your names appear in the back of this book.

Foreword

ABOUT LONELY PLANET GUIDEBOOKS

The story begins with a classic travel adventure: Tony and Maureen Wheeler's 1972 journey across Europe and Asia to Australia. There was no useful information about the overland trail then, so Tony and Maureen published the first Lonely Planet guidebook to meet a growing need.

From a kitchen table, Lonely Planet has grown to become the largest independent travel publisher in the world, with offices in Melbourne (Australia), Oakland (USA), London (UK) and Paris (France).

Today Lonely Planet guidebooks cover the globe. There is an ever-growing list of books and information in a variety of media. Some things haven't changed. The main aim is still to make it possible for adventurous travellers to get out there – to explore and better understand the world.

At Lonely Planet we believe travellers can make a positive contribution to the countries they visit – if they respect their host communities and spend their money wisely. Since 1986 a percentage of the income from each book has been donated to aid projects and human rights campaigns, and, more recently, to wildlife conservation.

Although inclusion in a guidebook usually implies a recommendation we cannot list every good place. Exclusion does not necessarily imply criticism. In fact there are a number of reasons why we might exclude a place – sometimes it is simply inappropriate to encourage an influx of travellers.

UPDATES & READER FEEDBACK

Things change – prices go up, schedules change, good places go bad and bad places go bankrupt. Nothing stays the same. So, if you find things better or worse, recently opened or long-since closed, please tell us and help make the next edition even more accurate and useful.

Lonely Planet thoroughly updates each guidebook as often as possible – usually every two years, although for some destinations the gap can be longer. Between editions, up-to-date information is available in our free, monthly email bulletin *Comet* (w www.lonelyplanet.com/newsletters). You can also check out the *Thorn Tree* bulletin board and *Postcards* section of our website, which carry unverified, but fascinating, reports from travellers.

Tell us about it! We genuinely value your feedback. A well-travelled team at Lonely Planet reads and acknowledges every email and letter we receive and ensures that every morsel of information finds its way to the relevant authors, editors and cartographers.

Everyone who writes to us will find their name listed in the next edition of the appropriate guidebook. The very best contributions will be rewarded with a free guidebook.

We may edit, reproduce and incorporate your comments in Lonely Planet products such as guidebooks, websites and digital products, so let us know if you don't want your comments reproduced or your name acknowledged.

How to contact Lonely Planet:
Online: e talk2us@lonelyplanet.com.au, w www.lonelyplanet.com
Australia: Locked Bag 1, Footscray, Victoria 3011
UK: 10a Spring Place, London NW5 3BH
USA: 150 Linden St, Oakland, CA 94607

Introduction

The highlight of Jordan, and one of the most spectacular sights in the entire Middle East, is the magical ancient Nabataean city of Petra. Carved out of the rock in the 6th century BC, the rose-coloured city is remarkably well preserved and has delighted ancient travellers, writers and painters – and more recently the producers of the film *Indiana Jones and the Last Crusade*.

And yet there's so much more to see in Jordan. There are enough attractions – landscapes, desert castles and forts, nature reserves, ruined cities and cafés – to keep most visitors happy for at least two weeks. Adventure tourism is increasingly popular, with everything available from the sedate plodding of camels through the desert areas or horse trekking, to the more strenuous pursuits of serious hiking and rock climbing.

Jordan is home to the Bedouin, many of whom still live a traditional lifestyle in the desert. You'll see men wearing full-flowing robes and leading herds of goats and sheep across the modern highways. Visitors may spend a lot of time enjoying the endless cups of tea and coffee offered by these hospitable people.

This friendliness is found at every level. Unlike some countries in the region, Jordan welcomes visitors with open arms. Visas are normally available on arrival, travelling is reasonably cheap and often good value, and there's a wide range of hotels in most major towns and tourist sites. Don't miss an opportunity to try the local cuisine, whether it be sitting down to a formal banquet or squatting around a communal bowl of rice and meat with a Bedouin family in their desert tent. Alternatively, Western food is easy to find in the larger towns.

The capital, Amman, is a modern, surprisingly cosmopolitan city built on many small hills or *jebels*. It is home to good museums, art galleries, a wonderful amphitheatre, friendly locals, some excellent hotels and restaurants, and a vibrant nightlife if you know where to look.

Aqaba is Jordan's resort town, much visited by Jordanians and Saudis, and offers the country's only diving and snorkelling sites and swimming beaches. Other attractions are the ancient ruined cities of Jerash and Umm Qais and the windswept desert castles of the east, while the incredible red sandy jebels of Wadi Rum and plunging canyons of Dana Nature Reserve always impress. The Dead Sea is the lowest point on earth, and swimming – or more correctly,

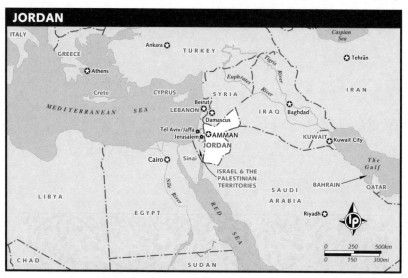

floating – in the salty water is a unique experience. The area is slowly being developed for tourism, as are the natural thermal springs and waterfalls at Hammamat Ma'in.

Jordan is easy to get around independently because English is widely spoken and the country is compact; it's possible to see everything on day trips from only four towns. Most attractions are accessible by public transport, and renting a car, or chartering a taxi, is straightforward.

It's squeezed between Iraq, Saudi Arabia, Israel and the Palestinian Territories, but Jordan is probably the safest and most stable country in the region. It has until recently had one leader for over 45 years; Islamic extremism and militancy are extremely rare.

Many people come to Jordan on a side trip from Israel – through one of three open borders – or as a stopover along a fascinating jaunt between Turkey and Egypt, via Syria. But Jordan is simple to reach from Europe by air, and with connecting flights from the USA, Canada, Australia and New Zealand now easier to arrange, it's never been a better time to visit. Jordan is certainly worth an exclusive trip; it's definitely worth more than the few days most travellers allow.

Facts about Jordan

HISTORY

Although the modern state of Jordan is a creation of the 20th century, it can claim to have hosted some of the oldest civilisations in the world. The region was never strong enough to form an empire itself, and it was for the most part a collection of city states, but its strategic position ensured that all the great early civilisations passed through. The Egyptians, Assyrians, Babylonians, Hittites, Greeks, Romans, Arabs, Turks and Crusaders all helped to shape the region. They traded, built cities and fought their wars here, leaving behind rich cultural influences.

Today Jordan is a nation at the crossroads of ancient customs and modern development. Yet its rich and eclectic history lives on, particularly in the Bedouins and their stories of the desert.

Ancient History

Evidence of human habitation in the area dates back about 500,000 years, but little is known until the Neolithic Age. Archaeological finds from Jericho (on the other side of the Jordan River, in the Palestinian Territories) and Al-Beidha (near Petra), positively dated at around 9000 BC, have revealed extensive villages where inhabitants lived in mud and stone houses, bred domestic animals, made pottery and used sophisticated agricultural methods.

The Chalcolithic (or Copper) Age (4500–3000 BC) saw the beginning of copper smelting. The remains of buildings and implements used for copper smelting can be found at Khirbat Finan (in the Dana Nature Reserve). Sheep and goats were reared and crops such as olives, wheat and barley were introduced. Materials such as basalt and mud were used for buildings, and irrigation systems were first implemented.

During the Bronze Age crafts, such as pottery and jewellery-making became common. Permanent settlements were established at the Citadel (in modern-day Amman) and in the southern desert regions. Foreigners introduced the idea of mixing copper and tin to create bronze, a hardier material for making domestic implements and weapons.

The Early Bronze Age (3000–2100 BC) saw occupation of the Jordan Valley by the

Canaanites, a Semitic tribe. They grew crops such as wheat and olives, raised sheep and goats, and used sophisticated methods of irrigation. Along with other tribes in the area, the Canaanites discovered the virtue of building defensive walls against invaders. During the Middle Bronze Age (2100–1500 BC) trade was developed with neighbouring powers in Syria, Palestine and Egypt. The Late Bronze Age (1500–1200 BC) saw the decline of Egyptian influence and created opportunities for nearby tribes, such as the Hebrew-speaking people who later became known as the Israelites.

During the Iron Age (1200–330 BC), Jordan was divided into three: the Edomites settled in the south; the Moabites near Wadi Mujib; and the Ammonites on the edge of the Arabian Desert with a capital at Rabbath Ammon (present-day Amman). This is the period, detailed in the Bible, that saw the rule of the great Israelite kings David and Solomon. By David's death in 960 BC, he ruled the principalities of Edom, Moab and Ammon and, at the time of Solomon's rise to the throne, Israel entered its golden age with great advancements in trade. However, by about 850 BC, the time of Ahab, the seventh king of Israel, the now-divided empire was defeated by Mesha, king of Moab, who recorded his victories on the famous Mesha Stele in the Moabite capital of Dhiban (see the boxed text 'A Stele at Twice the Price' in the King's Highway chapter).

The Greeks, Nabataeans, Romans & Byzantines

In 333 BC, Alexander the Great stormed through Jordan on his way to Egypt. After his death in 323 BC, Alexander's empire was parcelled up among his generals: Ptolemy I gained Egypt, Jordan and parts of Syria, while Seleucus established the Seleucid dynasty in Babylonia. Many people in Jordan now spoke Greek, and cities were renamed accordingly (eg, Amman became Philadelphia). In 198 BC, the Seleucid ruler Antiochus III defeated Ptolemy V, and took control of western Jordan. Around this time, the Jews gradually re-established themselves and by 141 BC controlled much of northern Jordan.

In southern Jordan, the Nabataeans rose to prominence with the establishment of their major city, Petra. Originally a nomadic tribe, their strength lay in the control of trade routes and almost exclusive knowledge of desert strongpoints and water supplies. Heavy duties exacted on goods transported on the trade routes, and protection money to keep bandits at bay, made them comparatively wealthy.

Attacks against the Nabataeans by the Roman general Pompey in 64 BC were unsuccessful, but further attacks by Herod the Great were more harmful and by his death in 4 BC the Nabataeans were much reduced in stature.

The Sassanians (or Sassanids) from Persia (modern-day Iran) briefly occupied parts of eastern Jordan in about AD 260, while the Byzantines occupied the rest. Under Byzantine occupation, Christianity became the official religion of Jordan as the Byzantine emperor Constantine had converted to Christianity in the early 4th century AD. This was a period of prosperity and stability. Many churches were constructed (often over the remains of ancient temples) and were usually decorated with elaborate mosaics.

In the early 7th century, the Sassanians again reoccupied parts of Jordan. Although the Byzantine emperor Heraclius forced them into a peace agreement in Syria in 628, it was the beginning of the end for Byzantine rule in the region.

The Advent of Islam

After the Prophet Mohammed's death in 632, his followers began to exert power in the region. They lost their first battle against the Byzantines at Mu'tah (near Karak) in 629, but defeated them in 636 under Khaled ibn al-Walid at the Battle of Yarmouk. Islam quickly became the dominant religion and Arabic the major language of the region. The capital of their empire was in the holy city of Medina (in modern-day Saudi Arabia).

In 661 Ali, the fourth caliph (see Religion later in this chapter) was succeeded by the Syrian governor, Mu'awiya, who established the Umayyad dynasty, based in Damascus.

The Umayyads' rich architectural legacy included the Umayyad Mosque in Damascus, and the Mosque of Omar and the Dome of the Rock in Jerusalem. In eastern Jordan, the Umayyads' great love of the desert led to

the construction of the 'desert castles'. (See Desert Castles in the Eastern Jordan chapter.)

In 747 an earthquake devastated much of Jordan, weakening the Umayyads' hold on power and they were overthrown by the Abbasids in 750. The Abbasids followed a stricter form of Islam, and were far less tolerant of Christianity than the Umayyads. Based in distant Baghdad, the Abbasids were perpetually fighting the Fatimid dynasty in Egypt and Seljuks from Turkey; as a result, Jordan was virtually ignored.

In 969 the Cairo-based Fatimids wrested control of Palestine, Trans-Jordan (Jordan's original name) and southern Syria from the Abbasids. In 1037 the Seljuk Turks took over what remained of the Abbasid territory and within the next 50 years also took over Trans-Jordan.

The Crusaders

In 1095 Pope Urban II sought a 'holy war' as revenge for the ongoing destruction of churches and to protect pilgrim routes to the Holy Land. The Crusaders captured Jerusalem in 1099, slaughtering countless inhabitants and causing devastation.

The Crusaders took control of most of Jordan by about 1115, and built fortresses (which can still be seen today) at Karak, Shobak and on Pharaoh's Island, just offshore from Aqaba. As a minority, their hold was always tenuous, and only survived because the Muslim states remained weak and divided until the late 12th century.

In the 12th century, Nur ad-Din (literally 'Light of the Faith'), son of a Turkish tribal ruler, was able to unite all of Syria, and most Arabs in the region, to defeat the Crusaders in Egypt. His campaign was completed by Saladin (Salah ad-Din – 'Righteousness of the Faith'), who overthrew the Fatimid rulers in Egypt, recaptured Palestine and occupied most of the Crusader strongholds in Jordan. The Damascus-based Ayyubids, members of Saladin's family, parcelled up his empire on his death in 1193, and the Crusaders recaptured much of their former territory along the coast. The main remnant of Ayyubid rule in Jordan is the magnificent Qala'at ar-Rabad at Ajlun.

The Mamluks, the name given to a vast group of boys taken from foreign lands to serve as slaves and soldiers for the Ayyubids, gained so much power that they eventually overthrew their masters in 1250. From their bases in Cairo and Damascus they defeated the first wave of rampaging Mongolian forces in 1258, invaded Jordan and finally expelled the Crusaders. The Mamluks rebuilt the castles at Karak, Shobak and Ajlun, which they used as lookouts and as a series of staging posts for carrier pigeons transporting messages. The Mongols under Tamerlane then destroyed much of the Mamluk Empire around 1400.

The Ottoman Turks

The Ottoman Turks took Constantinople in 1453, and defeated the Mamluks in Jordan in 1516. The Ottomans concentrated on other cities, such as the holy city of Jerusalem and the commercial centre of Damascus, and Jordan again declined in importance. However, four centuries later the Ottomans did build the Hejaz Railway linking Damascus with the holy city of Medina, via Amman (see the boxed text 'The Hejaz Railway' in the Getting There & Away chapter).

The dynasty declined in power after the incursions, and brief occupation of Jordan, by the Egyptians in the 1830s. The Egyptians were eventually defeated by the Ottomans with the unexpected assistance of several European powers.

WWI

During WWI Jordan was the scene of fierce fighting between the Ottoman Turks, who had German backing, and the British, based in Suez (Egypt). By the end of 1917 British and Empire troops occupied Jerusalem and, a year later, the rest of Syria. Their successes would not have been possible without the aid of the Arabs, loosely formed into an army under Emir Faisal, who was Sherif (ruler) of Mecca and had taken up the reins of the Arab nationalist movement in 1914. The enigmatic British colonel TE Lawrence, known as Lawrence of Arabia (see the boxed text 'Lawrence of Arabia' in the Southern Desert & Aqaba chapter), helped coordinate the Arab Revolt and secure supplies from the Allies.

In June 1916 the Arabs joined the British drive to oust the Turks, following British assurances that they would be helped in their fight to establish an independent Arab state. This was one month after the British and French had concluded the secret Sykes-Picot Agreement, whereby 'Syria' (modern-day Syria and Lebanon) was to be placed under French control and 'Palestine' (a vaguely defined area including modern Israel, the Palestinian Territories and Jordan) would go to the British.

This betrayal was heightened by the 1917 Balfour Declaration which stated that:

His Majesty's Government view with favour the establishment in Palestine of a National Home for the Jewish people, and will use their best endeavours to facilitate the achievement of this object.

After WWI

At the end of the war, Arab forces controlled most of modern Saudi Arabia, Jordan and parts of southern Syria. The principal Arab leader, Emir Faisal, set up an independent government in Damascus at the end of 1918, a move at first welcomed by the Allies. His demand at the 1919 Paris Peace Conference for independence throughout the Arab world was not so kindly greeted.

The British later came to an agreement with Faisal, giving him Iraq and having his elder brother, Abdullah, proclaimed ruler of the territory known as Trans-Jordan (formerly part of the Ottoman province of Syria), lying between Iraq and the East Bank of the Jordan River.

Abdullah made Amman his capital. Britain recognised the territory as an independent state under its protection in 1923, and a small defence force, the Arab Legion, was set up under British officers – the best known of whom was Major JB Glubb (Glubb Pasha). A series of treaties after 1928 led to full independence in 1946, when Abdullah was proclaimed king.

The Palestinian Dilemma

The Balfour Declaration, and subsequent attempts to make the Jewish national home a reality, was destined for trouble from the start. Arabs were outraged by the implication that they were the 'intruders' and the minority group in Palestine, where they accounted for about 90% of the population.

Persecution of Jews under Hitler in the 1930s accelerated the rate of Jewish immigration to Palestine and violence between Jews and Arabs increased. In 1939 a White Paper was drawn up calling for the creation of a bi-national state. This was rejected by both sides, however, and during WWII both sides cooperated with the British.

After the war, the conflict reached its high point. In 1947, the UN voted for the partition of Palestine and on 14 May 1948 the State of Israel was proclaimed. The British Mandate finished, but as troops withdrew from the area, Arab armies marched into Palestine. Highly trained Israeli forces proved too strong for the ill-equipped Arab volunteers and by mid-1949 armistices had been signed.

King Abdullah harboured dreams of a 'Greater Syria' to include all the modern states of Syria, Lebanon, Jordan and what is now Israel and the Palestinian Territories in a single Arab state (later to include Iraq, as well). For this, he was suspected by his Arab neighbours of pursuing different goals from them in their fight with the state of Israel.

At the end of hostilities, Jordanian troops were in control of East Jerusalem and the West Bank. In response to the establishment of an Egyptian-backed Arab Government in Gaza in September 1948, King Abdullah proclaimed himself King of All Palestine. In April 1950 he formally annexed the territory, despite paying lip service to Arab declarations backing Palestinian independence and expressly ruling out territorial annexations. The new Hashemite Kingdom of Jordan won immediate recognition from the governments of Britain and the US. However, the first wave of Palestinian refugees virtually doubled Jordan's population.

King Abdullah was assassinated outside Al-Aqsa Mosque in Jerusalem in July 1951. His son Talal ruled for a year, before his grandson Hussein was proclaimed king, finally ascending to the throne in 1953. In 1956, Hussein sacked Glubb Pasha (by then Chief of Staff of the Jordanian Army). After elections that year, the newly formed Jordanian government broke ties with the UK, and the last British troops left Jordan by mid-1957. Hussein then staged a coup against his government, partly because it had tried to open a dialogue with the Soviet Union.

With the (temporary) union of Egypt and Syria in 1958, King Hussein feared for his own position and tried a federation with his Hashemite cousins in Iraq. This lasted less than a year because the Iraqi monarchy was overthrown, and British troops were sent in to Jordan to protect Hussein.

In February 1960, Jordan offered a form of citizenship to all Palestinian Arab refugees and, in defiance of the wishes of the other Arab states for an independent Palestine, insisted that its annexation of Palestinian territory be recognised. Despite Jordan's opposition, the Palestine Liberation Organization (PLO) was formed in 1964, with the blessing of the Arab League, to represent the Palestinian people. The Palestine National Council (PNC) was established within the PLO as its executive body – the closest thing to a Palestinian government.

At about the same time, an organisation called the Palestine National Liberation Movement (also known as Al-Fatah) was established. One of the stated aims of both the PLO and Al-Fatah was to train guerrilas for raids on Israel. Al-Fatah emerged from a power struggle for control of the guerrilla organisations as the dominant force within the PLO, and its leader, Yasser Arafat, became chair of the executive committee of the PLO in 1969.

The Six Day War

With aid from the USA and a boom in tourism – mainly in Jerusalem's old city – the early 1960s saw Jordan's position improve dramatically. Things changed with the outbreak of the Six Day War.

The build-up to the war had seen increasing Palestinian guerrilla raids into Israel from Syria. The Syrians stepped up the raids once President Nasser of Egypt promised support in the event of an Israeli attack. When the Syrians announced that Israel was massing troops in preparation for an assault, Egypt responded by asking the UN to withdraw its Emergency Force from the Egypt–Israel border, which it did. Nasser then closed the Straits of Tiran (the entrance to the Red Sea), effectively sealing the port of Eilat. Five days later, Jordan and Egypt signed a mutual defence pact.

On 5 June 1967, the Israelis dispatched a pre-dawn raid that wiped out the Egyptian Air Force on the ground, and in the following days decimated Egyptian troops in the Sinai and Jordanian troops on the West Bank, and stormed up the Golan Heights in Syria.

The outcome for Jordan was disastrous: it lost the whole of the West Bank and its part of Jerusalem, which together supplied Jordan with its two principal sources of income

Palestinian Refugees in Jordan

No country has absorbed more Palestinian refugees than Jordan. As of December 2002, more than 1.6 million Palestinians were registered as refugees in Jordan by the United Nations or 32.8% of the population. The figure is surpassed only by the Gaza Strip (74.4%) and the West Bank (33.9%).

The stereotype of helpless refugees is only one part of the story. Most of the refugees have become an integral part of Jordanian life with many succeeding in business, politics and cultural pursuits. In the aftermath of the 1990 Iraqi invasion of Kuwait, as many as 500,000 Palestinian refugees entered Jordan. Although they placed a huge strain upon already creaking infrastructure, they also brought with them an estimated US$500 million, sparking a booming economy.

Nonetheless, around 280,000 refugees (18% of the total refugee population in Jordan) are housed in 10 camps administered by the United Nations Relief and Works Agency (UNRWA), which remains responsible for all health, education and relief programmes. The first four camps were set up after 1948 with the remaining six established after the 1967 war. As of December 2002, the largest camps were those at Baqa'a (with 78,163 inhabitants), 20km north of Amman, the Amman New Camp (49,034), Marqa (40,349) and Jebel al-Hussein (27,831), with large camps also at Zarqa (the country's first), Jerash and Irbid. As the period of separation from their homeland grew to a longer-term concern for refugees, their original tent shelters were replaced with more permanent structures.

The UNRWA health services have moved beyond the initial focus on first aid to more established medical services administered through 24 health centres that are active in immunisations, family planning, postnatal care, preventive medicine and outpatient treatment, although there are no hospitals. They are also responsible for sanitation in the camps.

The UNRWA runs one of the largest school systems in the Middle East with 184 schools in Jordan alone teaching double-shift classes (due to limited space) for 140,000 students up to Grade 10 level. The UNRWA also facilitates university scholarships.

The relief side of the UN operation is targeted primarily at special hardship cases and poverty alleviation, with special emphasis on women's programmes, rehabilitation for people with a disability and microfinance for disadvantaged individuals.

For more information on the work of UNRWA in Jordan, contact the **UNRWA Public Information Office** (☎ 06-5607194, ext 166, fax 5685476; e m.saqer@unrwa.org; Mustapha bin Abdullah St, Shmeisani, Amman). For more general information about Palestinians in Jordan, contact the Jordanian **Department of Palestinian Affairs** (part of the Ministry of Foreign Affairs; ☎ 06-5666172).

(agriculture and tourism), and resulted in yet another wave of Palestinian refugees.

Black September

After the 1967 defeat, the Palestinians became more militant and, although there was tacit agreement with the Jordanian government that they could operate freely out of their bases in the Jordan Valley, they also expected immunity from Jordan's laws. It was not long before the inevitable showdown took place.

By 1968, Palestinian *fedayeen* (guerrilla) fighters acted as a state within a state, openly defying and humiliating Jordanian soldiers. In June 1970, things deteriorated into sporadic conflict, with King Hussein's motorcade coming under direct fire from militants and a Palestinian faction holding 68 Western hostages in an Amman hotel.

On 6 September 1970, the rogue Popular Front for the Liberation of Palestine (PFLP) hijacked Swissair and TWA flights to an airstrip in Jordan's remote desert. Six days later another hijacked plane arrived before all three were spectacularly blown up in front of the world's TV cameras. On 16 September, martial law was imposed and bloody fighting between Palestinian militants and the Jordanian army broke out across Amman and Jordan. At first the rebels enjoyed a measure of success with a liberated zone set up around Irbid. At the height of the fighting, Yasser Arafat was spirited out of Amman disguised as a Kuwaiti sheikh in order to attend an Arab League summit in Cairo. A fragile ceasefire was signed, but not before at least 3000 lives had been lost. It was not until midway through 1971 that the final resistance around Ajlun was defeated.

The guerillas were forced to recognise Hussein's authority and the Palestinians had to choose between exile and submission. Most chose exile in Lebanon.

In October 1974, King Hussein reluctantly agreed to an Arab summit declaration that recognised the Palestinian Liberation Organization (PLO) as the sole representative of Palestinians with a right to set up a government in any liberated territory, nullifying Jordan's claims to the West Bank. In July 1988, the king severed all of Jordan's administrative and legal ties with the West Bank.

In November 1989, the first full parliamentary elections since 1967 were held in Jordan, and women were allowed to vote for the first time. Four years later, most of the political parties were legalised and allowed to participate in parliamentary and municipal elections.

Although the Islamic Action Front occupied many of the 80 lower house seats, royalist independents together still constituted a large majority, which continued to assure that King Hussein remained in power.

The Gulf War

Jordan found itself caught in a no-win situation when Iraq (its major trading partner) invaded Kuwait in 1990. Support for Saddam was at fever pitch among Palestinians in Jordan after he promised to link the Kuwait issue to their own and force a showdown.

King Hussein's diplomatic skills were stretched to the fullest when he refused to side against Iraq, largely out of fear of unrest among Jordan's Palestinian populace. This was misunderstood in the West as support for Saddam, but Hussein played the game with typical dexterity. Although tending to side publicly with Baghdad, he maintained efforts to find a peaceful solution and complied, officially at least, with the UN embargo on trade with Iraq. This last step won him the sympathy of Western financial bodies and, although US and Saudi aid was temporarily cut, along with Saudi oil, loans and help were forthcoming from other quarters, particularly Japan and Europe.

For the third time in 45 years, Jordan experienced a massive refugee inflow.

Peace with Israel

With the signing of the PLO–Israeli declaration of principles in September 1993, which set in motion the process of establishing an autonomous Palestinian authority in the Occupied Territories, the territorial question was virtually removed as an obstacle to peace between Jordan and Israel.

Compared with Syria, Jordan had long displayed greater willingness to countenance peace with Israel. On 26 October 1994 Jordan and Israel signed a peace treaty that provided for the dropping of all economic barriers between the two countries and close cooperation on security, water and other issues.

The clause in the treaty recognising the 'special role of the Hashemite Kingdom of Jordan in the Muslim holy shrines in Jerusalem' sounded alarm bells in Palestinian circles. The treaty made Jordan very unpopular with the region's governments and people alike, as well as severely straining relations with other countries such as Syria and Libya.

The King is Dead, Long Live the King

By the time of his death in February 1999, King Hussein was well on his way to becoming one of the great peacemakers of history. From his frantic efforts at diplomacy to avert the 1991 Gulf War to his peace agreement with Israel in 1994, the urbane and articulate king of a country in one of the world's toughest neighbourhoods came to be seen as a beacon of moderateness and stability in a region known for neither attribute. This reputation was secured in 1997 when a Jordanian soldier shot and killed seven Israeli schoolgirls in northern Jordan. King Hussein personally attended the funeral in a public display of grief and solidarity with the Israeli families.

Like all great figures of history, King Hussein has also become a figure of legend. When the first king of Jordan, King Abdullah, was assassinated at Al-Aqsa Mosque in Jerusalem in July 1951, his grandson Hussein was by his side. By some accounts, he was hit in the chest by a bullet, miraculously deflected by a medal worn on his uniform. On succeeding to the throne on 2 May 1953 at the age of 18, the youthful, British-educated Hussein was known more for his love of pretty women and fast cars than any great political skill. He went on to marry four times and sired 11 children.

The Royal Women of Jordan

When Queen Noor met her future husband, King Hussein, she was simply known as Lisa Najeeb Halaby, a Washington DC–born architect and urban planner fresh out of Princeton. Born into a distinguished Arab–American family (her father served under the administration of John F Kennedy), she met King Hussein while working on a project for the Royal Jordanian airline. After a much scrutinised whirlwind romance they married in a traditional Islamic ceremony in 1978. The fairy-tale romance, however, was not without its detractors. Many Jordanians were uneasy about an American joining their revered royal family (the Hashemite family line can be traced back to the Prophet Mohammed).

Adopting the name Queen Noor (Light of Hussein) upon her conversion to Islam, Jordan's new queen effectively signalled the beginning of a new era; one which placed the country squarely at the cross-roads of ancient culture and modern life. Throughout her tenure she has campaigned for a number of humanitarian and environmental causes (including the late Princess Diana's much-favoured Landmine Survivors Network). Arguably her greatest accomplishments, however, have been in the area of women's rights. She founded, among other organisations, the Women and Development Project, and was the one-time honorary president of the General Federation of Jordanian Women, which established the National Information Center for Women, the first of its kind in the Arab world. The Noor Al Hussein Foundation also encompasses a range of issues, including education, children's welfare and community improvement. Since her husband's death, Queen Noor has scaled back her public presence, although more recently she has been a vocal supporter of Afghani women's rights.

For more information on Queen Noor visit **W** www.noor.gov.jo.

Since the ascension of King Abdullah and his wife Queen Rania, parts of the media have been unable to resist offhand newspaper headlines such as 'Battle of the Queens'. Not unlike Queen Noor, Queen Rania has assumed a prominent public position on a number of issues. Born in Kuwait to a notable Jordanian family of Palestinian origin, and educated at the American University of Cairo, she married King Abdullah bin Al-Hussein in 1993. As Jordan's new first lady she too has become a public supporter of a variety of issues, both in Jordan and abroad, regarding the rights of women. She is the honorary president of the Arab Women Labor Affairs Committee. More recently she headed the Second Arab Women's Summit, which brought together Arab first ladies committed to the advancement of women across the Arab world. She has also been a tireless support of children and youth rights, recently joining the Unicef Global Leadership Initiative.

For more information on Queen Rania, visit **W** www.queenrania.jo.

Anastasia Safioleas

His first marriage was to the beautiful Dina bint Abedelhamid. After one year of marriage and the birth of a daughter, Princess Alia, they divorced. In 1961, Hussein married Antoinette Gardner, a British army officer's daughter who took the name Princess Muna upon converting to Islam. They had two sons, Prince Abdullah and Prince Feisal, followed by two daughters, Princess Zein and Princess Aisha. In 1972 the couple divorced. That same year Hussein married Alia Toukan. They had a daughter, Princess Haya, and a son, Prince Ali, as well as an adopted daughter, Abeer Muhaisin. Tragedy struck the family in 1977, however, when Queen Alia was killed in a helicopter crash. The following year, King Hussein married his fourth and final wife, American-born Lisa Halaby, who took the name Queen Noor.

They had two sons, Prince Hamzah and Prince Hashim, and two daughters, Princess Iman and Princess Raiyah.

While King Hussein was active on the world's political stage, his loyalty to his people was also well regarded. In a role emulated by his son decades later, Hussein would disguise himself as a taxi driver and ask passengers what they really thought of the king. In November 1958, Hussein, a trained pilot, flew his air force plane towards Europe for a vacation only to be intercepted by two Syrian fighter planes who sought to force him down. He escaped back to Jordan, adding to his already growing legend.

And yet King Hussein also struggled to maintain his credibility among the majority Palestinian population of his kingdom. Numerous assassination attempts, fuelled by

The Royal Handshake

Like any royal family worth its salt, Jordan's Hashemites were not immune from squabbles over the royal succession. While King Hussein was in the USA for cancer treatment, the widely respected elder statesman of Jordanian diplomacy, Hassan bin Talal (Hussein's brother and Crown Prince for 34 years), was in charge. Just before his death in February 1999, Hussein returned to Jordan, stripped Hassan of power and unexpectedly announced that Hussein's son from a previous marriage, Abdullah bin Hussein, would be the new king.

While the public appearance was of a smooth transition and happy families, all was not well behind the scenes. Soon after the succession was finalised, reports began to surface from within the palace that Abdullah had agreed to become king only for a limited time, after which the more charismatic but youthful Crown Prince Hamzah would take the throne. In 2002, unofficial reports suggested that Abdullah had changed his mind and decided to remain as king. Queen Noor, who retains her title of 'Queen', has been surprisingly absent from Jordan since Hussein's death: neither she nor Prince Hamzah were at Abdullah's enthronement ceremony.

accusations that the king had been carrying out secret negotiations with the Israelis and was on the payroll of the CIA after 1957, dogged the early years of his reign. His belief that he was the true representative of the Palestinian people brought him frequently into conflict with an increasingly militant Palestinian movement. It was not until his later years, after he renounced all claims to the Palestinian leadership and to the West Bank, that the rift was officially healed. Even then, his 1994 peace treaty with Israel was branded by some Palestinians as a betrayal and this uneasy relationship remained largely unresolved at the time of his death. After an official mourning period, Hussein's son was enthroned as King Abdullah II on 9 June 1999. Prince Hamzah, the 18-year-old son of Queen Noor and King Hussein, is the very popular crown prince.

King Abdullah II

Abdullah was born on 30 January 1962 to Princess Muna, King Hussein's second (British) wife. He studied in the USA and, like his father, attended Sandhurst in the UK and other military academies in the USA. He was promoted to lieutenant in the Jordanian Army at 22, and became head of Jordan's Special Forces in 1998 after he was involved in the successful (and televised) capture of two assassins.

Abdullah is a keen sportsman, pilot and rally driver; he enjoys Western food and speaks perfect English. He is married to Queen Rania, a glamorous Palestinian dedicated to children's and women's charities, and has three young children, Prince Hussein, Princess Iman and Princess Salma.

Despite such a lofty upbringing, the young king is not without a mischievous streak. In the great tradition of The Thousand and One Nights, Abdullah has been known to disguise himself as an ordinary citizen to carry out secret checks on the performance of government services and to see what is really happening in his kingdom. These have included numerous incognito visits to hospitals where the king was not amused to find that the service was far from adequate.

Since mid-1999, Abdullah has visited important leaders in the region, including Jordan's old foes, Syria and Libya. He also went to Paris, Washington and London to ensure financial support from major Western allies, and successfully obtained US$300 million in aid from the USA. Throughout the Al-Aqsa intifada in the Palestinian Territories, Abdullah has been one of the voices of moderation within the Arab world, preferring diplomacy as a means of bringing about a peace settlement. This stance has won him much respect in international circles. He has, however, come under attack from many Palestinians and other Arabs for maintaining relations with Israel and being ineffectual in his attempts to bring about a solution to the conflict. Although he has proven to be adept at following in his father's footsteps, it remains to be seen whether Abdullah's diplomatic skills are as enduring, or as ultimately effective, as Hussein's. At home, his drive to stamp out corruption has helped to maintain his popularity. Concerns remain, however; in 2002 human rights activists claimed that freedom of expression was being restricted, with all demonstrations in support of the Palestinians being strictly controlled by the government.

GEOGRAPHY

Jordan encompasses 91,860 sq km – it's slightly smaller than Portugal or the US state of Virginia. When King Hussein renounced claims to the West Bank (5600 sq km) in 1988, the country reverted back to the same boundaries as the former Trans-Jordan.

Jordan can easily be divided into three major regions: the Jordan Valley, the East Bank plateau, and the desert. Distances are short – it's only 430km from Ramtha, on the Syrian border in the north, to Aqaba, in the far south. From Aqaba to the capital, Amman, it's 335km.

Jordan Valley

The dominant physical feature of western Jordan is the fertile valley of the Jordan River. Forming part of the Great Rift Valley of Africa, it rises just over the Lebanese border and continues the entire length of Jordan from the Syrian border in the north, past the salty depression of the Dead Sea, and south down to Aqaba and the Red Sea. The 251km-long river is fed from the Sea of Galilee (Lake Tiberias), the Yarmouk River and the valley streams of the high plateaus to the east and west.

The Dead Sea (see the boxed text 'The Dead Sea' in the Around Amman chapter) is the lowest point on earth, and the highly saline soils of this central area of the Jordan Valley support little vegetation.

East Bank Plateau

The East Bank plateau is broken up only by gorges cut by Wadi Zarqa, Wadi Mujib and Wadi Hasa (a wadi is a valley formed by an often dry watercourse; some wadis begin to flow again when there has been substantial rainfall). Most of the plateau sits at between 600m and 900m above sea level.

This area contains the main centres of population: Amman, Irbid, Zarqa and Karak. It also contains the sites of major interest to visitors: Jerash, Karak, Madaba and Petra. The plateau ends at Ras an-Naqb, from where a fairly rapid drop leads down to the Red Sea, and the port of Aqaba.

The Desert

About 80% of Jordan is desert, mostly in the south and east. The volcanic basalt of the north (the bottom end of the area known as the Hauran in Syria) gives way to the south's sandstone and granite, which sometimes produces amazing sights. The area known as Wadi Rum is one of the most fantastic desert landscapes in the world, and boasts Jebel Rum (1754m), the highest peak in Jordan.

CLIMATE

For a small country, Jordan has an extraordinary range of climates. The weather in the Jordan Valley is extremely oppressive in summer – it feels like you're trapped in an airless oven. Daily temperatures are in excess of 36°C and have been recorded as high as 49°C. Rainfall is low: less than 200mm annually.

Average daytime maximum temperatures in Amman range from 12.6°C in January to 32.5°C in August. Snow in Amman is not unheard of, and even Petra gets the occasional fall. The area around Aqaba has much warmer, drier weather, with average daytime maximum temperatures of around 20°C in January and 38°C in August.

The climate in the desert is extreme: summer temperatures can reach into the high 40s, yet there are days in winter when cold winds howl down from central Asia. Rainfall is negligible, with less than 50mm per year.

Weather forecasts for Amman and the rest of the country are listed in the English-language newspapers published in Amman.

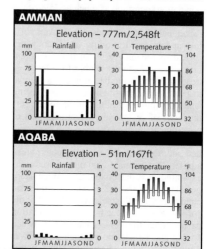

ECOLOGY & ENVIRONMENT

According to the international Environmental Sustainability Index for 2002, Jordan ranked the highest of any Arab country at 53rd out of 142 nations, higher than Belgium and eight places behind the United States. In 1995, the Jordanian Parliament passed the Law of the Protection of the Environment to set up regulators and funding streams as part of a generally impressive (but recent) commitment by the Jordanian government to environmental protection. This includes the refusal of mining licences in protected areas on environmental grounds.

Jordan is not, however, without its environmental problems, most notably a lack of water, caused by a growing population, rising living standards in the cities, heavy exploitation for agriculture, and wastage. Other important issues include air pollution, waste management, erosion (a problem caused by steeply graded agricultural land) and desertification.

Water

Jordan has one of the lowest water-per-capita ratios in the world – 200 cubic metres of renewable water per capita per year, expected to fall to 90 cubic metres by 2025. By some estimates, Jordan will run out of water within 20 years. Jordan uses about 30% more water than it receives from natural sources.

One major problem is simply mismanagement: Jordan's farmers (around 5% of the population) consume as much as 75% of the water (often inefficiently). According to one report, half the water consumed in Amman is lost in leakage. Rationing has been widespread in recent years. Current treatment plants are sometimes unable to effectively treat algae and some bacteria, and a scandal in 1998 about foul-smelling and foul-tasting water in Amman resulted in the forced resignations of several high-level members of government.

Jordan's only sources of water are the Jordan and Yarmouk Rivers, and subterranean aquifers that are already in many cases over-exploited (see the boxed text 'What Happened to the Wetlands?' in the Eastern Jordan chapter). In 1964, Israel diverted most of the Jordan River to feed its own irrigation canals. Since the 1994 peace treaty between Jordan and Israel, under which Jordan was permitted to extract 50 million cubic metres

per year from Lake Tiberias, disputes have arisen over whether Jordan is getting its fair share. In 1998 Jordan had to beg ingloriously for water from Syria (an old foe).

Both Jordan and Israel have recently allocated millions of dollars to water projects. The joint Syrian–Jordanian Wihdeh Dam on the Yarmouk River is a major project being built in conjunction with Jordan's neighbours. Another idea is the construction of a series of desalination plants, hydroelectric power stations and canals that would link the Red Sea with the Dead Sea (see the boxed text 'The Dead Sea' in the Around Amman chapter for details).

To make matters worse, Jordan has endured droughts for five consecutive years: the one in 1998/9 was the worst in 50 years, and cost an estimated US$200 million in lost and damaged agriculture and livestock. During this period there was also a fall of between 10% and 30% in the country's cereal production. Although the winter rains in 2001–02 eased the effects of the drought, water storage levels remain critically low at around 30% of capacity.

Effects of Tourism

While a substantial recent increase in the number of tourists has brought in badly needed foreign currency, most funds are used to build more hotels, roads and tourist facilities – at the expense of the environment.

The Royal Society for the Conservation of Nature (RSCN) has been at the forefront of attempts to foster ecotourism projects (see the boxed text 'Royal Society for the Conservation of Nature' under National Parks & Reserves later in this chapter). Its impressive efforts are most evident at Dana Nature Reserve, Wadi Rum Protected Area, Wadi Mujib Reserve and the reserves at Azraq and Shaumari in the east of the country. At places such as these, environmentally sustainable tourism is slowly taking hold as a means of redressing the excesses of the past. At the springs of Hammamat Ma'in, a luxury resort complex with a high entrance fee is being used to discourage large numbers of visitors.

Tourism has also caused a rapid increase in pollution from cars and industries and demand for precious water, as well as damage to unique sites such as Jerash and Petra (see the boxed text 'Petra & Tourism' in the Petra chapter). Other problems are vandalism at archaeological sites, damage to artwork from flash photography, and rubbish left at hot springs and baths.

Marine Life

The reefs off the coast at Aqaba are a treasure trove of marine life, but every year thousands of tonnes of phosphates are dumped at the port at Aqaba. The Dead Sea is also slowly dying (see the boxed text 'The Dead Sea' in the Around Amman chapter.)

Desertification

Like most countries in the region, Jordan has a serious problem with desertification (the seemingly unstoppable spread of the desert to previously fertile, inhabited and environmentally sensitive areas). According to the RSCN, millions of hectares of fertile land in Jordan have become infertile and uninhabitable desert. This means there are now fewer pastures for livestock and crops, reduced land for native animals and plants, and an unhealthy and unattractive landscape for the Jordanian people (and tourists).

Desertification is usually caused by human factors such as overgrazing, deforestation and overuse of off-road vehicles, as well as wind erosion and drought.

Useful Organisations

For further information on the ecology and environment of Jordan, contact the following organisations:

Jordan Royal Ecological Diving Society (JREDS; ☎ Aqaba 03-2022995, ☎/fax Amman 06-5679142, |e| jreds@nets.com.jo)
Royal Society for the Conservation of Nature (☎ 06-5350456, fax 5347411, |e| tourism@rscn.org.jo, |w| www.rscn.org.jo) PO Box 6354, Amman 11183

FLORA

Jordan boasts over 2500 species of wild plants and flowers (including about 20 species of orchid), but due to desertification, urban sprawl and pollution at least 10 have become extinct over the past 100 years.

Spring is the best time to see wildflowers, and Wadi as-Seer, near Amman, is especially beautiful. The pine forests of the north give way to the cultivated slopes of the Jordan Valley where cedar, olive and eucalyptus trees are dominant. In a very few areas, such as the Dana Nature Reserve, acacia trees thrive. In the deserts, cacti are about the only plants that grow, unless there is heavy rain.

The national flower of Jordan is the Black Iris. One of the best places to see this flower is on the eastern walls of the Jordan Valley, particularly around Pella and Wadi as-Seer.

FAUNA

Jordan is not renowned for the quantity and variety of its wildlife, and visitors will count themselves very fortunate to see anything more than a few domesticated goats and camels. The eastern and southern deserts are home to desert and red foxes, sand rats, mountain and desert hares, wolves, Asiatic jackals, and several species of rodent, namely the jerboa (with long legs for jumping), shrew and jerbil.

In Shaumari Reserve, a number of formerly prevalent species are being reared for possible reintroduction to the wild; see the boxed text 'Saving the Arabian Oryx' in the Eastern Jordan chapter.

The Jordan Valley, and the forested and sparsely inhabited hills of northern Jordan, are home to ill-tempered wild boar, marbled polecats, stone martens, jungle cats, crested porcupines and ibexes, as well as species of mongoose, hyrax and hedgehog. In the few wet and swampy areas, such as the Jordan Valley and Azraq wetlands, there are small populations of otters.

For information about underwater wonders in the Gulf of Aqaba, refer to 'Diving & Snorkelling' in the Facts for the Visitor and Southern Desert & Aqaba chapters.

Birdlife

About 365 species of bird have been recorded in Jordan. Commonly seen around the eastern and southern desert regions are the many species of vulture, eagle and partridge. Other desert species in the east of the country include Temminck's horned lark, desert lark, hoopoe lark, desert wheatear and the trumpeter finch. For a desert region, Dana Nature Reserve boasts an extraordinary number of bird species, including warbler, partridge, vulture and falcon. In eastern Jordan, the Azraq Wetlands Reserve and the Burqu area attract a large number of migratory water bird species, such as heron and egret. Around the Dead Sea, the Dead Sea sparrow, the sand partridge and quaintly

Jordan's National Bird

The Sinai finch (*Carpodacus synoicus*) is Jordan's national bird. It thrives in the few areas where water can be found, such as the Jordan Valley, but has learnt to adapt to drier and rockier areas of southern Jordan. The bird was first found in Petra in the early 20th century, but now also lives in the Dana Nature Reserve and Wadi Mujib Reserve, as well as the Sinai peninsula of Egypt (after which it was named). The male is a distinctive pink, but the female is grey or brown. Adults are small (about 16cm long), and the female produces up to five eggs a year.

named Tristam's grackle can be seen. In the northern hills, warblers and Palestine sunbirds can be seen, while in the rocky terrain off the King's Highway, species include the griffon vulture, Bonelli's eagle, Hume's tawny owl, blackstart, house bunting and the fan-tailed raven. Aqaba has a variety of migratory birds, but little has been done to protect them, and their habitats are being eroded by development and desertification.

The RSCN (see Useful Organisations under Ecology & Environment earlier in this chapter) can organise birdwatching tours.

Endangered Species

About 20 species of mammal have become extinct in the past 100 years. Some were hunted and poached (especially after WWII, when weapons were more common), including species of lion, cheetah, gazelle, Syrian brown bear, onager (wild ass) and Arabian leopard. (The last known leopard was killed in the area now known as Dana Nature Reserve in 1986, although there have been unsubstantiated sightings since.)

The reasons for the number of extinct species – and the continuing threat to animals and birds include poor land management, such as deforestation, and the pumping of water from vital areas such as the Jordan River, Dead Sea and the Azraq wetlands; urban sprawl; weak environmental laws; unremitting use of pesticides, especially near water sources in the Jordan Valley; hunting; air and water pollution; and overgrazing.

Officially endangered are the Northern Middle East wolf and South Arabian grey wolf (both are often shot to protect livestock); lynx (always popular with hunters); striped hyena; Persian squirrel; and the Persian, dorcas, goitred and mountain gazelles. A successful breeding programme by the RSCN for the Nubian ibex (hunted to near extinction in the wild) began in the Wadi Mujib Reserve in 1989 with some being reintroduced into the wild.

Endangered birds include the marbled duck; imperial and less spotted eagles; houbara bustard; and lesser kestrel. The killifish, unique to the Azraq Wetlands, has recently been saved from extinction but its situation remains precarious (see the boxed text 'What Happened to the Wetlands?' in the Eastern Jordan chapter).

Animal species such as the Arabian oryx and onager have been successfully reintroduced to Jordan after becoming extinct, and are being bred in captivity. (See Shaumari Reserve in the Eastern Jordan chapter.)

NATIONAL PARKS & RESERVES

Nearly 25 years ago the Jordanian government established 12 protected areas, totalling about 1200 sq km. While environmental agencies waited for funds and battled with bureaucracy, some potential reserves were abandoned because they had suffered appalling ecological damage. Less than 1% of Jordanian territory is covered by forest or woodland.

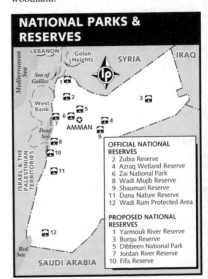

NATIONAL PARKS & RESERVES

OFFICIAL NATIONAL RESERVES
2 Zubia Reserve
4 Azraq Wetland Reserve
6 Zai National Park
8 Wadi Mujib Reserve
9 Shaumari Reserve
11 Dana Nature Reserve
12 Wadi Rum Protected Area

PROPOSED NATIONAL RESERVES
1 Yarmouk River Reserve
3 Burqu Reserve
5 Dibbeen National Park
7 Jordan River Reserve
10 Fifa Reserve

Royal Society for the Conservation of Nature (RSCN)

Established in 1966, the RSCN is Jordan's major environmental agency. It aims to protect the local environment in seven official reserves and hopes to establish several more. It is also heavily involved in saving animal, plant and bird species from extinction, and has successfully reintroduced species such as the Arabian oryx and two species of ostrich.

Other activities include conducting public awareness programmes among Jordanians, especially children; sponsoring environmental clubs throughout the country; training guides; promoting eco-tourism; fighting against poaching and hunting; lobbying against mining; and promoting programmes such as the Wadi Dana Project, in which people are involved in maintaining their culture and heritage.

An urban nature reserve and centre promoting environmental causes and hosting cultural activities was set to open in Amman in June 2003; contact the RSCN for details.

The RSCN publishes the excellent *Al-Reem* magazine (JD2.500; free to members with membership costing JD15 per year) every three months in Arabic and English; a three-issue subscription costs JD6. You can also 'adopt' an animal from an endangered species, for JD40 to JD60 per year. For contact details, see Useful Organisations under Ecology & Environment earlier in this chapter.

The limited resources of the RSCN are used to maintain and develop the six reserves listed below. These represent about 1% of Jordan's total land area – a small percentage compared with the land allocated in Saudi Arabia (9%) and the USA (11%).

Azraq Wetland Reserve (12 sq km) This new reserve is home to about 300 species of bird, plus a few buffalos, semi-wild horses, jackals and jerbils. There are hotels nearby. Walks on designated trails are permitted. See the Eastern Jordan chapter for details.

Dana Nature Reserve (320 sq km) This spectacular reserve is home to a diverse ecosystem, including about 600 species of plants, about 200 species of birds, and over 40 species of mammals. Pre-set tents are available, and there are hotels in nearby Dana village. Short walks and long-distance hiking are possible with the permission of the RSCN. See the King's Highway chapter for details.

Shaumari Reserve (22 sq km) This small reserve is more like a zoo and is specifically for reintroduced Arabian oryxes; blue-necked and red-necked ostriches; subgutu rosa and dorcas gazelles; and onagers. Nearly 250 bird species have also been identified. There are hotels in nearby Azraq. See the Eastern Jordan chapter for details.

Wadi Mujib Reserve (212 sq km) This vast reserve is mainly used for the captive breeding of Nubian ibexes. Camping and hiking are allowed in designated areas with permission from the RSCN. See the King's Highway chapter for details.

Wadi Rum Protected Area (540 sq km) This stunning and popular area is now fully under the RSCN's control. Camping and trails are limited to those areas approved by the RSCN. See the Southern Desert & Aqaba chapter for details.

Zai National Park This is a small and dense pine forest, close to Amman, with great views. See the Around Amman chapter for details.

Zubia Reserve (12 sq km) This small and disappointing reserve was established to protect native fauna, including roe deer, but it's not set up for tourism. See the Jerash & the North chapter for details.

In addition, the RSCN and the Jordanian government hope to create five new protected areas (their exact names are not confirmed at this stage):

Burqu Reserve (400 sq km) After the debacle in the Azraq wetlands (see the boxed text 'What Happened to the Wetlands?' in the Eastern Jordan chapter), the desert lake at Burqu needs urgent protection. See the Eastern Jordan chapter for more details.

Dibbeen National Park (8 sq km) One of the last pine forests left in Jordan, it's home to endangered species such as the Persian squirrel. See the Jerash & the North chapter for more details.

Fifa Reserve (27 sq km) This area alongside the Dead Sea has rare subtropical vegetation, and is home to migratory water birds

Jordan River Reserve (5 sq km) Based around the Tell al-Kharrar religious site (see the Around Amman chapter for details), this is the only section of the Jordan River that has not been ecologically damaged in some way

Yarmouk River Reserve (30 sq km) Because of its close proximity to the border of Israel and the Palestinian Territories, this area has remained undeveloped and is home to many natural features of the forest including water birds, endangered gazelle and otter

GOVERNMENT & POLITICS

Jordan is officially called the Hashemite Kingdom of Jordan (HKJ), or Al-Mamlakah al-Urdunniyah al-Hashimiyah in Arabic. The Hashemites were named after Hashem, the great-grandfather of the Prophet Mohammed, from whom King Abdullah (the founder of modern Jordan) claimed descent.

The 1952 constitution states that Jordan is a hereditary constitutional monarchy with three levels of power. The first level is the king, who is vested with a wide range of powers, eg, he appoints judges, approves amendments to the constitution, declares war and is Commander of the Armed Forces. He approves and signs all laws, although his power of veto can be overridden by a two-thirds majority of both houses of the National Assembly.

The second level, the 80-member lower house, is elected by all citizens (men and women) of Jordan over the age of 18, but the prime minister, president and 40 members of the Senate are appointed by the king. Collectively, the bicameral National Assembly is known as the Majlis al-Umma. The prime minister, or the king through the prime minister, appoints council of Ministers who are subject to the approval of parliament. The council is responsible for general policy and the various government departments.

At the next level, some minor powers are granted to the 305 local councils throughout the country. Jordan now has 22 registered parties, including a communist party and the Islamic Action Front (IAF), which is the largest and most powerful. The IAF has connections with the fundamentalist Muslim Brotherhood (which is outlawed in some neighbouring countries), and the IAF's opposition to the peace treaty with Israel causes disquiet. In fact, elections are sometimes boycotted by the IAF and other parties because of the Jordanian government's relationship with Israel.

For administrative purposes, Jordan is divided into 12 *muhafazat* (governorates): Irbid, Ajlun, Jerash, Balqa (west of Amman), Amman, Mafraq, Zarqa, Madaba, Karak, Tafila, Ma'an and Aqaba.

Voting is not compulsory, but 72% of all voters turned out for the 1995 municipal elections.

ECONOMY

Jordan has very few natural resources capable of generating vital foreign currency through exports. Jordan is also squeezed between several countries experiencing recent political turmoil, which has resulted in massive numbers of refugees fleeing to Jordan. Moreover, political sanctions have recently been put into place against Iraq, an important trading partner. However, considering that Trans-Jordan (as it was known) in 1948 was a country of about 400,000 mostly poor Bedouin, the transformation in the past 50 years or so has been remarkable.

Like most countries in the region, Jordan suffers from high unemployment (officially 15% but possibly double that), unsettled refugees, poverty and unpredictable climatic conditions. It also relies very heavily on foreign aid, and has one of the highest foreign debts per capita in the world – currently about 100% of the gross domestic product (GDP). This foreign debt is a result of unrestrained increases in population, forcing increased expenditure on infrastructure; poor financial management by the government; and an arms build-up in the region.

Currently, about 30% of the government's expenditure is used to pay off this debt. Since becoming king, Abdullah II has been visiting Western allies to ensure that the foreign aid continues, and to ask for the easing and eradication of the burden of debt. He has been successful in the former but not the latter.

Gulf War

Jordan was one of the main economic victims of the Gulf War in 1990–91, but it managed to weather the storm far better than expected. One UN assessment put the total cost to Jordan of the war from mid-1990 to mid-1991 at more than US$8 billion. The UN naval blockade of Aqaba, which was aimed at enforcing UN sanctions against Iraq, cost Jordan around US$300 million a year in lost revenue between 1991 and 1994.

A quarter of Jordan's prewar trade had been with Iraq, and for a while Jordan was obliged to seek other sources of oil (80% of which was being delivered from Baghdad prior to the war). Later, Amman was allowed to take Iraqi oil as direct debt repayment, but only as long as no cash changed hands.

Until the Gulf War, an important source of income had been remittances from Jordanians and Palestinians working in the Gulf States. By early 1992, most had left, and as many as 500,000 settled in Jordan. The loss of remittances was initially seen as a blow, but the 'returnees' brought US$500 million home with them, and actually helped unleash an unprecedented boom, stimulating economic growth to a huge 11% in 1992.

Agriculture

Agriculture, which makes up 6% to 7% of Jordan's GDP, is concentrated in the Jordan Valley, where ambitious irrigation schemes, like the King Abdullah Canal and several dam projects, make cultivation possible on thousands of hectares. Indeed around 80% of Jordan's agriculture is watered by irrigation with just 20% rain fed. Modern methods ('plasticulture' and greenhouses) have greatly increased productivity, and Jordan exports much of its fruit, vegetables and cereals. On the highlands forming the eastern edge of the Jordan Valley, crops such as tobacco, wheat, barley and beans are grown, as well as olives, tomatoes and watermelons.

Scarce water supplies, however, are a constant threat. In 2000 and 2001, the Jordanian Government told farmers and irrigators in the Jordan Valley not to plant the summer crops (because the necessary water would have strained resources) and paid compensation (in the form of leases) for lost income. Despite the rains, the system of compensation and fallow lands was continued for 2002. Jordan is home to about three million sheep and goats, but there is simply not enough pasture to feed them, so a lot of feed is now imported. The authorities are trying to encourage farmers to earn an income in some other way, while closing some pastoral lands to alleviate overgrazing and the subsequent problem of desertification.

Two possible answers to the problem are to introduce other types of feed, such as spineless cacti, which require little water, and to recycle sewerage as a water source for irrigation.

Industry

Industry accounts for about 26% of Jordan's GDP. Phosphate mining, carried out from

vast reserves at Wadi Hasa and Shidiya (near Ma'an), is a major export, as is potash from near the Dead Sea. Mining companies are hoping to mine areas of the Dana Nature Reserve, which are rich in copper, but the Jordanian government has not yet granted any mining licences. Local manufacturing ranges from cement and batteries to toys, beer and matches.

Oil has yet to be found in commercially viable quantities, and the government is placing greater hope in natural gas. Big reserves were found in the northeast of the country in 1987–88, and now meet about 17% of Jordan's energy needs.

As a way of encouraging foreign investment, the Jordanian government has introduced a reduced corporate tax rate, and provided other incentives, but the interest shown from overseas investors so far has been lower than the government hoped for.

Tourism

Tourists first started to trickle into Trans-Jordan in the 1920s, but only since the 1994 peace agreement with Israel has tourism been regarded by the government as a significant contribution to the Jordanian economy.

Tourism now accounts for about 10% of GDP, and is the second-largest source of foreign currency (after industry). Tourism generates a total annual income of about US$696 million, and employs about 15,000 people. In 2001, 1.48 million people visited Jordan – up from 858,000 only seven years before – of whom 960,000 were Arab visitors. However, about 60% of visitors are from neighbouring countries, stay with friends and families, and do not spend much money. In fact, about 10% of all visiting Arabs come to Jordan solely for the high-quality and low-cost medical care.

In the aftermath of the September 11 attacks, the number of tourists visiting Jordan from non-Muslim countries fell sharply, a situation exacerbated by the escalation in hostilities between Israelis and Palestinians just across the border. Although Jordan remained calm and there are very few reports of hostility towards foreigners, Jordan's tourism industry continues to suffer from the instability of its neighbours and stereotypes about the safety of Muslim countries.

Jordan is small and tourists do not generally stay for very long. As an example, the average tourist stays 18 nights in Israel and the Palestinian Territories, and eight in Egypt, but only four in Jordan. The total number of tourists to Jordan also fluctuates wildly, depending on regional politics. Any war or political strife in the Middle East, regardless of the distance from Jordan, means a significant drop in tourist numbers. The open border with Israel and the Palestinian Territories means that many Israelis come, but often only on day trips to Aqaba or Petra.

Tourism is fairly one-dimensional, and still tends to focus on Jordan's archaeological marvels. To encourage more tourists to come, and to stay longer than a few days, the authorities are trying to promote events such as the Jerash Festival, and Christian pilgrimages. Adventure tourism is also starting to take off with hiking, climbing, diving and desert safaris among the most popular – see Activities in the Facts for the Visitor chapter.

Foreign governments have accepted the importance of tourism to the Jordanian economy. The Japanese recently announced an offer of technical assistance and soft loans to develop a tourist precinct in central Amman (see the boxed text 'Giving Downtown a Facelift' in the Amman chapter for details).

POPULATION & PEOPLE

The population of Jordan stood at about 5.3 million in 2001, a substantial increase from just 586,000 in 1958. More than 1.5 million people were registered as refugees (primarily from the wars of 1948 and 1967) with the United Nations Relief & Works Agency (UNRWA). In an effort to reduce the expected population of eight million in 2024, the Jordanian National Population Commission is hoping to dramatically reduce the birth rate, through the promotion of family planning, to 2.1 children per family. In 1990 the fertility rate stood at 5.6 children, with the figure reduced to 3.5 by 2001.

Approximately 1.8 million people live in the capital, Amman, and a further 700,000 live in neighbouring Zarqa and suburbs. About 80% live in urban centres. The majority (98%) of Jordanians are Arab; over 60% are Palestinian Arabs. There are also small communities of Circassians, Chechens, Armenians and Western expatriates.

The Bedouin were originally desert dwellers and form the majority of the indigenous population, but today not more than 40,000 Bedouin can be considered truly nomadic (see the boxed text 'The Bedouin' in the Southern Desert & Aqaba chapter).

Arabs

Arabs are descended from various tribes that migrated to the area from all directions over the centuries.

Palestinians About 60% of the population is made up of Palestinians who fled, mostly from the West Bank, during the wars of 1948 and 1967 and after the Gulf War in 1990–91.

All Palestinians have been granted the right to Jordanian citizenship, and many have exercised that option. Palestinians play an important part in the political, cultural and economic life of Jordan, and although many occupy high positions in government and business, they continue to dream of a return to an independent Palestine. This is partly why so many continue to live in difficult conditions in the 30 or more refugee camps that dot the landscape. (See the boxed text 'Palestinian Refugees in Jordan' earlier in this chapter.)

Circassians & Chechens

The Circassians fled persecution in Russia in the late 19th century to settle in the Jordan Valley, becoming prosperous farmers. There are now about 30,000 Circassians – living mainly in Wadi as-Seer and Na'ur (both near Amman) – but intermarriage has made them virtually indistinguishable from Arabs.

Historically and ethnically related to the Circassians is the small (about 4000) Shiite community of Chechens, the only other recognised ethnic minority in Jordan.

EDUCATION

Jordan is one of the better-educated Arab countries; about 87% of Jordanians are literate, and about 97% of children attend primary school. There are government, private and missionary schools, but about 70% of pupils attend the government schools. UN agencies run schools for refugee children. School is compulsory for children from the ages of five to 14.

Of the seven state-owned universities, the largest are the University of Jordan (w www .ju.edu.jo) in northern Amman, Yarmouk University (w www.yu.edu.jo) in Irbid, and Mu'tah University (w www.mutah.edu.jo)

south of Karak. There are also 13 private universities, including the American University of the Middle East, which has a campus near Amman. Although the universities are attended by about 100,000 students, these include a large number of foreign students from the Palestinian Territories and elsewhere in the Middle East, so the demand for spaces from Jordanian students still exceeds supply.

ARTS

Despite the region's rich tradition of music, literature and arts, the comparatively modern nation of Jordan could not boast much in the way of distinctive arts and literature until the last 25 years. Jordan's emergence as a centre of contemporary arts was recognised by Unesco, which named Amman as its Arab Cultural Capital for 2002.

Music & Dance

Arab music reflects a synthesis of indigenous and Western influences. Popular music, which differs little from that of neighbouring Arab countries, takes some time to get used to, and for many its attraction remains a mystery. Others, however, are eventually caught up in its particular magic – which is probably a good thing, because you'll be hearing it in one form or another wherever you go.

The Bedouin have long had their own musical traditions that are simple but mesmerising. The sound of men chanting at a distant wedding, drifting across the desert on a still night, is haunting. Up close, the musical aspects of the festivities are clearly rooted in ancient traditions. A row of men will, arm in arm, gently sway backwards and forwards engaged in what appears to be an almost trance-like chant. They are singing to a lone, veiled woman who dances before them with restrained but unmistakable sensuality.

The music in the streets of Amman today, however, has precious little to do with timeless desert traditions. The most common and popular style of music focuses on a star performer backed by anything from a small quartet to a full-blown orchestra. The kind of orchestras that back these singers are a curious mix of East and West, although the sounds that emanate from them are anything but Western. Western-style instruments such as violins, the piano and many of the wind and percussion instruments predominate, next to local instruments such as the *oud* (lute).

The Performing Arts Center in Amman was established in 1987 under the auspices of the Queen Noor Foundation to 'develop the value and understanding of contemporary music and dance by local Jordanians'. The subsequent interest in modern music and dance resulted in the very first Western musical – *The Wizard of Oz* – performed in Jordan in Arabic, and the opening of the Theatre Arts School with over 50 students being trained in theatre, music, dance and writing. Foreign governments, and NGOs such as the British Council in Amman, continue to sponsor all forms of art in Jordan.

Among the younger generation of modern Jordanian pop stars is the female performer Rania Kurdi.

Literature

Classical Literature & Poetry The Quran itself is considered the finest example of classical Arabic writing.

Al-Mu'allaqaat, which predates the Quran and the advent of Islam, is a widely celebrated collection of early Arab poetry. Prior to Islam, a poet was regarded by Arabs as having knowledge forbidden to ordinary people, supposedly acquired from the demon. Al-Mu'allaqaat means 'the suspended', and refers to traditions according to which the poems were hung for public view, possibly on the walls of the Kaaba in Mecca.

As the Middle Ages drew to a close, and the Arab world came to be dominated by other forces (most notably the Ottoman Turks), Arabic literature also faded, stagnating in a classicist rut dominated by a complex and burdensome poetical inheritance until well into the 19th century.

One of the few classical Jordanian poets was Mustafa Wahbi al-Tal, also known as Irar. Born in Irbid in 1899, he was renowned for his incisive and humorous poems about Arab nationalism and anti-colonialism.

Contemporary Literature & Poetry

Modern literary genres such as the novel have only fairly recently taken off in Jordan, largely due to increased contact with Europe as well as a reawakening of Arab 'national' consciousness in the wake of the Ottoman Empire's stagnation.

Egyptians (such as the Nobel Prize winner Naguib Mahfouz), Lebanese and, to a lesser extent, Palestinians, seem to dominate Middle Eastern literature, but there are now a number of renowned Jordanian writers and poets. Ramadan al-Rawashdeh has published collections of short stories, including *The Night*. His novel *Al-Hamrawi* won the Naguib Mahfouz Arabic Novel Prize, and more recently he published *The Shepherds' Songs*. Mounis al-Razzaz, who died in 2002, was regarded by many as the driving force behind contemporary Jordanian literature. His works spoke of wider turmoil in the Arab world, most notably in his satirical final work *Sweetest Night*, as well as the transition of Amman from a small village to a modern metropolis. Rifka Doudeen, one of an emerging number of female authors, has published a collection of short stories called *Justifiable Agony*, and a novel, *The Outcast*. Another popular Jordanian writer is Yousef Dhamra.

Other writers to watch out for are: young short-story writer Basma Nsour; Hashim Gharaybeh; novelist and playwright Mefleh al-Adwan, who won the coveted Unesco prize for creative writing in France in 2001; Raga Abu Gazaleh; Jamal Naji; Abdel Raouf Shamoun; and poets Ibrahim Naserallah and Abdullah Mansour.

Many Jordanian writers and poets are Palestinians who often graphically relate first-hand experiences of the Arab–Israeli conflicts. Taher al-Edwan's *The Fact of Time,* telling the story of a Palestinian family fleeing to Amman in 1948, is regarded as an important Jordanian novel.

Very few of these titles are available in languages other than Arabic, but the best places to look for an English translation are the bookshops listed in the Amman chapter and in the Aqaba section of the Southern Desert & Aqaba chapter.

Painting

That Islam frowns on the depiction of living beings does not mean that everyone took the hint. Long-standing artistic traditions in Asia Minor, Persia and further east – including Spain and other parts of Europe – held by the Muslims could not be completely swept away, and depictions of living creatures

---

Contemporary Art

One of the first Jordanian painters to gain any international recognition was the redoubtable Fahrenasa Zeid (the great-great aunt of King Abdullah II), who exhibited works in the galleries of Europe and the USA in the 1910s and 1920s. However, it really wasn't until the creation of the Jordan Artists' Association in 1978, and the opening of the country's first art gallery (the Jordan National Gallery of Fine Arts) two years later, that contemporary art in Jordan was taken seriously.

Many Jordanian artists are Palestinians who fled the West Bank during the two wars with Israel: Adnan Yahya specialises in gut-wrenching paintings of Palestinian persecution; Ahmad Nawash is famous for his distinctive stick figures in pastel colours; and another famous Palestinian-Jordanian painter is Ibrahim abu-Rubb.

Other popular contemporary Jordanian painters include: Suha Shoman, Yaser Duweik, Ali Jabri, Ahmad al-Safareeni, Mohanna Durra (an internationally renowned Jordanian cubist and abstract painter), Ahmed al-Khateeb and Rafiq Lahham. Lahham is a pioneer of modern Jordanian art. His work incorporates traditional Islamic architectural forms, reflecting the built environment of the Middle East. He uses an eclectic mix of styles, with some of his most appealing work incorporating Kufic script along with abstract elements and a striking use of colour. A new female artist is Samar Haddadin, whose paintings and drawings capture religious harmony. Other female artists of renown include Karima ben Othman, Basma Nimry, Clara Khreis, Rula Shukairy, Riham Ghassib, Ghada Dahdaleh and Mukaram Haghandouga. The Jordanian sculptor, Larissa Najjar, specialises in sandstone sculptures with different colours and unusual designs. Also renowned for their sculptures are Samaa Tabaa and Margaret Tadros.

Works by these and other Jordanian artists can be seen in the numerous art galleries and cultural centres of Amman, particularly the excellent Darat al-Funun and Jordan National Gallery of Fine Arts, as well as galleries in Madaba, Salt and Fuheis.

continued. While the greatest riches of this kind are to be found in illustrated manuscripts mostly coming from Turkey, parts of Iraq and further east, good examples can still be seen in Jordan today.

The 7th-century Umayyad rulers, who comprised the first real dynasty after the demise of the Prophet Mohammed, left behind a series of so-called 'desert castles' across the eastern desert of Jordan; traces of frescoes can be found on the walls of most of these – but none so extraordinary as those in Qusayr Amra. (See the boxed text 'The Frescoes of Qusayr Amra' in the Eastern Jordan chapter.)

The boxed text 'Making Mosaics' in the Madaba section of the King's Highway chapter has information about the ancient (and contemporary) art of mosaics.

Handicrafts

Jewellery Excavations show that jewellery made from copper and gold was worn as far back as the 8th century BC.

Throughout the region, jewellery was used for dowries (these days the practice is less common) and as an indicator of wealth, and many believed that some types of jewellery had healing powers or brought good luck. Silver has also been supplanted in popularity by gold, most of which is imported from overseas.

The Bedouin make traditional silver jewellery with old coins, or precious or semi-precious stones, such as red agate. Popular among Jordanians are bracelets, mostly made of gold, called *mabroomeh*; chokers; and necklaces called *hjab* and *kirdan*, often made with precious stones or decorated with inscriptions from the Quran. Rings are often elaborate, and are also worn by men.

Weaving Always an important part of the Bedouin lifestyle, weaving was used to furnish tents, create saddlebags and make ornaments. Today, 2000 or more Palestinian and Bedouin women are involved in the manufacture of *mafrash* rugs, carpets, *idel* bags and other goods under the guidance of several Jordanian charity organisations. (See Shopping in the Facts for the Visitor chapter, and the boxed text 'The Bani Hamida Story' in the King's Highway chapter.)

Home-made looms are still used for simple items, but workshops in the village are now more common. Weavers use sheep and goat wool, dyed the dark colours preferred by the Bedouin. While some natural dyes from the Jordan Valley are used, most dyes are chemically based and imported.

Traditional Dress Traditional women's clothes (predominantly Bedouin and Palestinian) are elaborate, and vary considerably from one end of Jordan to another. However, unless you're invited to a traditional ceremony or a special event you're unlikely to see many traditional costumes in Jordan.

In Ma'an, which has always had close ties with Syria (because of the Hejaz Railway), women's dresses are colourful, while in Jerash and Ajlun, the long men's and women's *shirsh* features an embroidered neckline, cuffs and sleeves. In Karak and Salt, men and women often wear a woollen belt called an *ub*. Materials such as *dubeit* (black cotton) can be imported from Syria, but synthetics from Asia are now common.

SOCIETY & CONDUCT

Jordan is a typically Arab country, with very hospitable people. Jordanians are usually willing to forgive foreigners who innocently break the numerous points of etiquette, although an effort to respect local customs will invariably be appreciated; see Social Graces in the Facts for the Visitor chapter to get an idea of how to avoid giving offence. Proactive efforts – such as offering sweets and wishing people '*eid mubarak*' during the festival of Eid al-Adha – will especially endear you to your hosts.

Traditional Culture

Welcome! You could be forgiven for thinking that 'welcome' is the first word of English learned by Jordanians. At every turn you'll hear it, and it seems to leave as many travellers perplexed as enchanted. Behind this simple word and makeshift translation lies a whole series of social codes.

One of the most common greetings in Arabic is *ahlan wa sahlan*. The root words means 'people' or 'family' *(ahl)* and 'ease' *(sahl)*, so translated loosely the expression means 'be as one of the family and at your ease'. It's a nice thought, and one that ends up simply as 'welcome' in English. Among Arabs, it's used to mean anything from 'hello' to 'you're welcome' (after thanks).

There is, however, a lot more to it. The Arab traditions of hospitality and kindness are based on the harsh realities of life in the desert and have been virtually codified in social behaviour. As a rule, strangers were given shelter and food as a matter of course (see the boxed text 'The Bedouin' in the Southern Desert & Aqaba chapter).

Accepting an offer to join people in a meal or a cup of tea or coffee can be a wonderful way to learn more about the country you're travelling in (and its people). Some visitors may feel bad accepting what is often very generous treatment; offering small gifts or mementos can be a good way around this.

Sometimes people will insist that you join them – but nine times out of 10 this is not the case. Rather than curtly saying 'no', the way to avoid any kind of invitation that you feel disinclined to accept is to refuse politely with your right hand over your heart – you may have to do it several times. Adding something noncommittal like 'perhaps another time, *in sha'Allah*' (if God wills it) is a perfectly suitable, ambiguous and, most importantly, inoffensive way to turn down unwanted offers.

In the Home Many families, especially in smaller towns and rural areas, remain traditional in terms of divisions within the house. Should you be invited into one, it's worth bearing a few things in mind. As a rule various parts of the house are reserved for men, and others for women. This becomes particularly apparent when guests are present.

Given that the most likely reason for you being in someone's home is to eat, remember that meals are generally eaten on the floor, everyone gathered around several trays of food shared by all. Single men invited to eat or stay over at a house will be taken to a room reserved for men, or perhaps a mixed dining area. Depending on how conservative your hosts are, you may be directly served by the women or simply observe them bringing food and drink to the men, who then deal with you, the guest. (See the boxed text 'Body Language' later in this chapter for more details on appropriate behaviour.)

Foreign women will more often than not be treated as an honorary 'male'. In the case of a couple, a foreign woman may be wel-

Body Language

Arabs gesticulate a lot in conversation, and some things can be said without uttering a word. Jordanians often say 'no' by raising the eyebrows and lifting the head up and back. This is often accompanied by a 'tsk tsk' noise, which can be a little disconcerting if you're not used to it.

Shaking the head from side to side means 'I don't understand'. Stretching out the hand as if to open a door and giving it a quick flick of the wrist is equivalent to 'what do you want?', 'where are you going?' or 'what is your problem?'.

If an official holds out a hand and draws a line across the palm with the index finger of the other hand, they're asking to see your passport, bus ticket or other document.

A foreign man asking directions should not be surprised to be taken by the hand and led along by another man; it's quite natural. Women should obviously be more circumspect about such an action from a Jordanian man.

A right hand over your heart means 'no, thanks'. When you've had enough tea, put your hand over the cup, and say *da'iman* (always).

As the left hand is associated with toilet duties it's considered unclean, so always use your right hand when giving or receiving something.

come to sneak off to hang around with the Jordanian women and then come back to see how the 'men's world' is getting on. In this way, a foreign woman can find herself in the unique position of being able to get an impression of home life for both sexes.

More traditional families are often quite hierarchical at meal times. The grandparents and male head of the house may eat in one circle, the latter's wife and the older children and other women in the family in another, and the small children in yet another. Usually, outsiders eat with the head of the household.

Women in Jordan

Compared to some neighbouring countries, particularly Saudi Arabia, women in Jordan enjoy more freedom and privileges: they have access to a full education (in 2002, the number of girls in primary and secondary schools was almost identical to the number of boys); they can vote (a few women have become members of parliament); many work in male-dominated industries and businesses; and they can drive cars. In 2001, the legal age of marriage was lifted from 15 years old for women and 16 for men to 18 for both, although Islamic judges are still permitted to sanction underage marriages.

In recent years Jordanian women have made great progress in male-dominated professions. Jordan gained its first female MP (Toujan Faisal) in the early 1990s, first female taxi driver in 1997, first female mayor in Ajlun in 1995, first female judge in 1996, first ambassador to the European Union in 2001 and the first director of Jordan Radio in 1999. Yet the rise of a few women to senior positions has yet to be matched by across-the-board equality. The highest levels of in- equality remain in the media and the political arena; not a single woman was elected to the lower house in 1997. Less than 1% of judges are women with just 12 female judges in 2002. In 1991, 14% of the labour force was made up of women; by 2001, this had risen to 20%.

Jordan is secular, and freedom of religion is part of the constitution. Unlike some neighbouring Muslim countries, polygamy (by men) is rare though legal; segregation is uncommon (except in some homes and restaurants, and all mosques); divorce is allowed for women (but it still carries a stigma); there are no official restrictions about dress codes; and female infanticide and female circumcision are extremely rare.

Arranged marriages and dowries are still common, but parents do not often enforce a wedding against their daughter's wish. A woman's 'honour' is still valued in traditional societies, and sex before marriage can still be dealt with harshly by other members of a woman's family. According to a recent report, 'honour crimes' make up a staggering 25% of all solved murders in Jordan (around 25 Jordanian women annually), and the (mostly male) judges and juries are not unsympathetic to the (male) murderers. Much of the problem stems from the legal sanction offered by Article 340 of the legal code which states that when a man is in a 'state of fury' he cannot be convicted of a crime, the rationale being that the woman is responsible for inciting the man's fury. Despite government pressure and petitions carrying over 15,000 signatures, Jordan's all-male lower house refused to repeal the article in 2000.

Women in more traditional societies are starting to gain some financial independence, prestige and self-respect through a number of Jordanian charity organisations (mentioned in the Shopping section of the Facts for the Visitor chapter).

Impact of Tourism

Although there have been some official studies about the impact of tourism on Jordan's environment, it is only recently that the damage from tourism to the environment and traditional lifestyles of Jordanians, particularly the Bedouin, have been taken seriously. As in most other traditional societies, unrestrained tourism from Western countries can create a dichotomy between the host and visiting cultures, often exacerbated by thoughtless Westerners who, for example, drink alcohol in public or wear skimpy clothes. In places such as Wadi Musa (Petra) – a traditional Bedouin community which has been inundated with tourists since 1994 – this clash of cultures has been particularly pronounced (see Dangers & Annoyances in the Facts for the Visitor chapter and the boxed text 'Warning' in the Petra chapter for more details).

Vast differences between the cultures of the West and Jordan can cause many problems: there is resentment from locals who have little or no opportunity for improvement; social values change as young Jordanians pick up unattractive habits from the West, eg, swearing, drinking alcohol and taking drugs; and education suffers as the youth flock to tourist areas in search of a fast buck.

Also, the cost of housing and rent in places like Wadi Musa and Aqaba is often high, so locals cannot afford to live where they like; and land is sometimes bought by richer Jordanians solely for speculative purposes. Prices for fruit, meat and vegetables are often high in tourist areas, because of the demand for these goods from upmarket, big-spending hotels.

Treatment of Animals

Most visitors to Jordan will witness what they regard as maltreatment of animals – whether it's shepherds whipping their beasts, overloaded camels plodding through the desert or donkeys struggling up hundreds of steps in Petra. These sorts of activities may seem cruel by Western standards, but the owners rely heavily on their animals to make a living, and are normally sensible enough to keep them healthy.

The Jordanian government, with the aid of several NGOs, has started educating children, especially in poorer regions, about the treatment of animals. In addition, children are being taught about the importance of preserving their environment.

One of the very few animal hospitals and agencies working for animal rights is the Princess Alia Horse Clinic, affiliated with the Brooke Hospital for Animals, in Petra – see the boxed text 'Brooke Hospital for Animals' in the Petra chapter.

RELIGION

Although the population is overwhelmingly Islamic, Jordan is officially secular, and freedom of religion is a statute right of the Jordanian constitution.

Islam

Islam is the predominant religion in Jordan. Muslims are called to prayer five times a day and no matter where you might be, there always seems to be a mosque within earshot. The midday prayers on Friday, when the sheikh of the mosque delivers his weekly sermon, or *khutba*, are considered the most important.

While Islam shares its roots with the other great monotheistic faiths – Judaism and Christianity – that sprang from the harsh and unforgiving soil of the Middle East, it is considerably younger than both. The holy book of Islam is the Quran. Its pages carry many references to the earlier prophets of both the older religions: Abraham (known in the Quran as Ibrahim), Noah (Nuh), Moses (Musa) and others – but there the similarities end. Jesus is seen as another in a long line of prophets that ends definitively with Mohammed.

The Quran is believed to be the word of God, communicated to Mohammed directly in a series of revelations in the early 7th century. For Muslims, Islam is the apogee of the monotheistic faiths from which it derives so much. Muslims traditionally attribute a place of great respect to Christians and Jews, whom they consider *Ahl al-kitab*, the 'People of the Book'.

Mohammed, born into a trading family of the Arabian city of Mecca (in present-day Saudi Arabia) in 570, began receiving revelations in 610, and after a time began imparting the content of Allah's message to the inhabitants of Mecca. The essence of it was a call to submit to God's will (*islam* means submission), but not all locals were terribly taken with the idea.

Mohammed gathered quite a following in his campaign against the idolaters of Mecca, and his movement especially appealed to the poorer levels of society. The powerful families became increasingly outraged, and by 622 had made life sufficiently unpleasant for Mohammed and his followers; they fled to Medina, an oasis town some 300km to the north and now Islam's second most holy city. This migration – the Hejira – marks the beginning of the Islamic calendar, year 1 AH or AD 622.

In Medina, Mohammed continued to preach. Soon he and his followers clashed with the rulers of Mecca, led by the powerful Quraysh tribe. By 630, his followers returned to take Mecca. In the two years before his death, many of the surrounding tribes swore allegiance to him and the new faith.

Mecca became the symbolic centre of the Islamic religion, containing as it did the Kaaba, which houses the black stone that had long formed the object of pagan pilgrimage and later was said to have been given to Ibrahim by the Archangel Gabriel. Mohammed determined that Muslims ('those who submit') should always face Mecca when praying outside the city.

Upon Mohammed's death in 632, the Arab tribes conquered all of what makes up modern Jordan, Syria, Iraq, Lebanon, Israel and the Palestinian Territories. By 644, they had taken Egypt and spread into North Africa, and in the following decades crossed into Spain and, for a while, deep into France.

The initial conquests were carried out under successive caliphs, or Companions of Mohammed, of whom there were four. In turn, the caliphs were followed by the Umayyad dynasty, based in Damascus, and the Abbasids, based in Baghdad. For more information see the History section earlier in this chapter.

In order to live a devout life, a Muslim is expected to carry out at least the Five Pillars of Islam:

Haj The pinnacle of a devout Muslim's life is the pilgrimage to the holy sites in and around Mecca. Ideally, the pilgrim should go to Mecca in the last month of the year, Zuul-Hijja, and join Muslims from all over the world in the pilgrimage and subsequent feast. The returned pilgrim can be addressed as Haj, and in simpler villages at least, it is not uncommon to see the word Al-Haj and simple scenes painted on the walls of houses showing that its inhabitants have made the pilgrimage.

Sala Sometimes written *salat*, this is the obligation of prayer, done ideally five or six times a day when the muezzins call upon the faithful to pray. Although Muslims can pray anywhere, a strong sense of community makes joining together in a *masjid* (mosque) preferable to most.

Shahada This is the profession of the faith, the basic tenet of Islam: 'There is no God but Allah and Mohammed is his prophet' (*La il-laha illa Allah Mohammed rasul Allah*). It's commonly heard as part of the call to prayer, and at other events such as births and deaths. The first half of the sentence has virtually become an exclamation good for any time of life or situation. People can often be heard muttering it to themselves, as if seeking a little strength to get through the trials of the day.

Sawm Ramadan, the ninth month of the Muslim calendar, commemorates the revelation of the Quran to Mohammed. In a demonstration of the Muslims' renewal of faith, they are asked to abstain from sex, and from letting anything (including cigarettes) pass their lips from dawn to dusk every day of the month. For more information about Ramadan, see Public Holidays & Special Events in the Facts for the Visitor chapter.

Zakat Giving alms to the poor was, from the start, an essential part of Islamic social teaching and, in some parts of the Muslim world, was later developed into various forms of tax as a way of redistributing funds to the needy. The moral obligation towards one's poorer neighbours continues to be emphasised at a personal level, and it's not unusual to find notices, exhorting people to give, posted up outside mosques.

About 92% of the population are Sunni Muslims, and there is a tiny Shiite population.

Sunnis & Shiites In its early days, Islam suffered a major schism that divided the faith into two streams, the Sunnis and Shiites. The power struggle between Ali (the last of the four caliphs and Mohammed's son-in-law) and the Umayyad dynasty in Damascus lay at the heart of the rift that tore asunder the new faith's followers.

The succession to the caliphate had from the first been marked by intrigue. Ali, the father of Mohammed's sole male heirs, lost his struggle and was assassinated, paving the way to the caliphate for the Umayyad leader Mu'awiya. The latter was related to Ali's predecessor, Othman, in whose murder some believed Ali was implicated.

Those who recognised Mu'awiya as caliph (which were the majority) came to be known as the Sunnis, and would become the orthodox bedrock of Islam. The Shiites, on the other hand, recognise only the successors of Ali. Most of them are known as Twelvers, because they believe in 12 imams (religious leaders), the last of whom has been lost from sight, but will appear some day to create an empire of the true faith.

The Sunnis divided into four schools of religious thought, each lending more or less importance to various aspects of doctrine.

Islamic Customs When a baby is born, the first words uttered to it are the call to prayer. A week later this is followed by a ceremony in which the baby's head is shaved and an animal is sacrificed. The major event of a boy's childhood is circumcision, which normally takes place sometime between the ages of seven and 12.

Marriage ceremonies are colourful and noisy affairs. One of the customs is for all the males to drive around the streets in convoy making as much ballyhoo as possible. The marriage ceremony usually takes place in either the mosque or the home of the bride or groom. After that the partying goes on until the early hours of the morning, often until sunrise.

Before praying, Muslims must follow certain rituals. They must wash their hands, arms, feet, head and neck in running water. All mosques have a small area set aside for this purpose. If they're not in a mosque and there is no water available, clean sand suffices, and where there is no sand, they must still go through the motions of washing.

Then they must cover their head, face Mecca (all mosques are oriented so that the mihrab, or prayer niche, faces the right way) and follow a set pattern of gestures and genuflections. Outside mosques, Muslims can pray anywhere, and you regularly see them praying by the side of the road; many keep a small prayer rug handy for such times.

In everyday life, Muslims are prohibited from drinking alcohol and eating pork (as the pig is considered unclean), and must refrain from fraud, usury, slander and gambling.

Christianity

Statistics on the number of Christians in Jordan are wildly contradictory. They are believed to account for 5% to 6% of Jordan's population. Most live in Karak, Madaba, Salt, Fuheis, Ajlun and Amman – all with a bewildering array of churches representing the three major branches of Christianity in Jordan: Orthodox, Catholic and (to a far lesser extent) Protestant.

About two-thirds of Christians in Jordan are Greek Orthodox. This church has its liturgy in Arabic, and is the mother church of the Jacobites (Syrian Orthodox), who broke away in the 6th century, and the Greek Catholics, who split off in the 16th century. Coptic Orthodox Christians, with a pope and most coreligionists in Egypt, are also represented in Jordan.

The other third are Greek Catholics, or Melchites, under the authority of the patriarch who resides in Damascus. This church observes a Byzantine tradition of married clergy being in charge of rural parishes, while diocesan clergy are celibate.

BIBLICAL JORDAN

 Bethlehem was the birthplace of Jesus Christ, but was Christianity born at the River Jordan? Christianity was certainly the dominant religion in Jordan from the late 4th century to the early 7th century, and today's Islamic Jordan celebrates its strong ties with Christianity, with accounts of Moses, Jesus *and* the Prophet Mohammed all relating to Jordan. There are numerous sites of relevance to Christians to be found throughout the country (100 sites alone are mentioned in the Bible), and following the significant discovery in 1994 of Bethany-Beyond-the-Jordan (Tell al-Kharrar, the site where Jesus is widely believed to have been baptised by John the Baptist) on the east banks of the Jordan River, ever-increasing numbers of pilgrims continue to descend upon Jordan to visit these remarkable landmarks.

Major Biblical Sites

'Ain Musa or Ayoun ('Ain) Musa Then Moses raised his arm and struck the rock twice with his staff. Water gushed out, and the community and their livestock drank. (Numbers 20:11)

The exact location of where Moses struck the rock is open to debate: it's either 'Ain Musa (near Wadi Musa), or Ayoun ('Ain) Musa, near Mt Nebo. See the Petra and King's Highway chapters, respectively.

Bethany-Beyond-the-Jordan (Tell al-Kharrar) Then Jesus came from the Galilee to the Jordan to be baptised by John. (Matthew 3:13)

As early as 1899 works along the east bank of the Jordan River revealed ancient remains. In 1931, numerous small dwellings were also

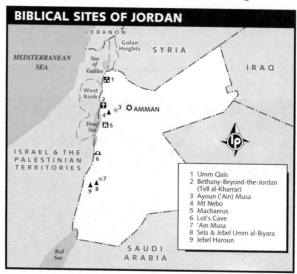

BIBLICAL SITES OF JORDAN

1 Umm Qais
2 Bethany-Beyond-the-Jordan (Tell al-Kharrar)
3 Ayoun ('Ain) Musa
4 Mt Nebo
5 Machaerus
6 Lot's Cave
7 'Ain Musa
8 Sela & Jebel Umm al-Biyara
9 Jebel Haroun

Insert: Detail of the Siyagha mosaic, Moses Memorial Church, Mt Nebo. (Illustration by Valerie Tellini)

uncovered. It wasn't until works were carried out by archaeologists and activists clearning landmines (following the 1994 peace treaty with Israel) that the remains of churches, caves, extensive wells and water channels, as well as several baptism pools, were found. After much debate, scholars declared the area in the South Jordan Valley as indeed the site of John the Baptist's mission, and where Jesus Christ was baptised. Events culminated with Pope John Paul II conducting a massive open-air mass at the site in the spring of 2000.

In addition to the celebrated baptism, Bethany-Beyond-the-Jordan is where Jesus 'went back across the Jordan to the place where John had been baptising to escape persecution from Jerusalem' (John 10:40). Many also believe that it was from here that Elijah ascended to heaven in a whirlwind (2 Kings 2:11). See Bethany-Beyond-the-Jordan in the Around Amman chapter.

Dead Sea ...while the water flowing down to the Sea of the Arabah was completely cut off...(Joshua 3:16)

The Sea of Arabah, also known as the Salt Sea, is mentioned several times in the Bible. See the Around Amman chapter.

Jebel Haroun Aaron will be gathered to his people: he will die there. Moses did as the Lord commanded: they went up to Mount Hor in the sight of the whole community. (Numbers 20:26-27)

Mt Hor is believed to be Jebel Haroun in Petra. It's also a holy place for Muslims. See Hiking in the Petra chapter.

Jebel Umm al-Biyara He [the Judaean king, Amaziah] was the one who defeated ten thousand Edomites in the Valley of the Salt and captured Sela in battle... (2 Kings 14:7)

The ruins on top of Umm al-Biyara mountain in Petra are deemed to be the ancient settlement of Sela. See Hiking in the Petra chapter.

Lot's Cave He and his two daughters...settled in the mountains...and lived in a cave. (Genesis 19:30)

PATRICK HORTON

Left: Shrine built over Aaron's Tomb (Jebel Haroun)

The cave where Lot and his daughters lived for years after Lot's wife turned into a pillar of salt is thought to be just off the Dead Sea Highway, not far from Safi. Nearby is believed to be the site of Sodom. See Around Karak in the King's Highway chapter.

Machaerus The King was sad, but because of his oaths and his dinner guests he gave orders that her request be granted, and had John beheaded in the prison. (Matthew 14:9-12)

John the Baptist had denounced Herod Antipas' marriage to his brother's wife, Herodias, as Jewish law forbade a man marrying his brother's wife while he lived. Overcome by his stepdaughter Salome's skill as a dancer the king promised to grant her anything she wished. To take revenge on the Baptist, Herodias told her daughter to ask for his head on a platter. So, at the request of Salome, John was killed at Herod's castle, Machaerus. Provocative Salome has inspired painters and writers alike over the centuries. See Mukawir in the King's Highway chapter.

Mt Nebo Go up unto...Mount Nebo in Moab, across from Jericho, and view Canaan, the land I am giving the Israelites as their own possession. There on the mountain that you have climbed you will die. (Deuteronomy 32:49-50).

Right: The Siyagha mosaic at the Moses Memorial Church, Mt Nebo.

VALERIE TELLINI

Mt Nebo is a particularly holy place because it is where Moses died – although his tomb has never been found. (See Mt Nebo in the King's Highway chapter.) According to the Bible, Moses viewed the Holy Land from Mt Nebo before he died. By standing on the site of the Moses Memorial Church, visitors today can enjoy the same vista Moses enjoyed across the Jordan Valley and Dead Sea towards the hills of Jerusalem.

Umm Qais When he [Jesus] arrived at the other side in the region of the Gadarenes, two demon-possessed men coming from the tombs met him. (Matthew 8:28-34)

Umm Qais was known as Gadara in the Bible, and in other ancient scriptures. See the Jerash & the North chapter.

ANDERS BLOMQVIST

Left: A carved face on a marble slab at the Roman ruins of Gadara, now Umm Qais

Facts for the Visitor

SUGGESTED ITINERARIES

One week is the minimum required to truly explore Jordan on any form of transport; two weeks is ideal and in one month you could see almost everything covered by this book. Even if you use public transport most of the time, it's still worth hiring or chartering a vehicle for a few days to visit remote places.

Public Transport

Using any form of public transport (and occasionally hitching when public transport is infrequent or nonexistent), the following itineraries are well worth considering:

Three Days
Amman/Jerash (one day) and Petra (two)
One Week
Amman (one); Jerash and Umm Qais (one); Madaba & Karak (one); Petra (two); Wadi Rum (one); and Aqaba (one)
Two Weeks
Amman (two); Jerash and Umm Qais (one); desert castles (one); Dead Sea (one); Madaba and Mukawir (Macchaerus; one); Karak (one); Dana Nature Reserve (one); Petra (three); Wadi Rum (two); and Aqaba (one).
One Month
Follow the schedule listed above for two weeks, with one or two extra days in each place, and allow yourself extra time to dive/snorkel in Aqaba; trek/ rock climb in Wadi Rum, Petra and Dana Nature Reserve; visit one or two national reserves; and spend time making your way down the King's Highway, including a visit to Shobak castle.

Rented Car or Chartered Taxi

Renting a private car is a popular option (see Car & Motorcycle in the Getting Around chapter for more information). However, it's not cheap and can be impractical if you spend a few days at sites like Petra and Jerash, which can only be explored on foot. Chartering a service (public) taxi or private taxi with a driver is potentially better value because the taxi can be chartered one hour or one day at a time.

The following suggested itineraries do not include visits to Amman, Madaba, Dead Sea, Wadi Rum, Aqaba, Petra and Jerash because they are all easy to reach by public transport.

Three Days
Day 1: North of Amman – Ajlun, Dibbeen National Park, Umm Qais, Al-Himma (Mukheiba), Pella and Deir Alla
Day 2: Amman to Karak, via the King's Highway – Madaba, Mt Nebo, Mukawir and Wadi Mujib
Day 3: Karak to Amman, via the Dead Sea Highway – Dana Nature Reserve, Shobak castle and the Dead Sea
One Week
It's easy to see Jordan's major sites by rented car or chartered taxi in one week. Follow the schedules listed above for three days, and allow extra time to visit places near Petra, Wadi Rum and Aqaba. Alternatively, add an extra day to visit the desert castles, Umm al-Jimal and one or two national reserves.
Two weeks
In two weeks you could see most of the places covered in this book, including Petra and Wadi Rum

Day Trips

Just about anywhere in Jordan can be visited on a day trip from Amman; even Aqaba is only 3½ hours away by car. Any place to the north, west and east of Amman, and anywhere as far south as Karak, can easily be visited on a day trip from the capital. The major sites such as Petra, Wadi Rum and Aqaba should only be visited in a day trip if you have very limited time.

By public transport, it's easy to visit in one day: Madaba and Mt Nebo; Karak; Jerash and Ajlun; Pella and the Dead Sea; Irbid and Umm Qais; or Wadi as-Seer, Salt and Fuheis.

By private car or chartered taxi, the following places can be visited, albeit very briefly, in one day:

- Madaba, Mt Nebo, Machaerus, Hammamat Ma'in and (at a stretch) Karak
- Desert Castles in eastern Jordan and Umm al-Jimal
- Salt, Fuheis, Wadi as-Seer, the Dead Sea, Bethany and Pella
- Jerash, Dibbeen National Park, Ajlun and Umm Qais

PLANNING
When to Go

The best time to visit Jordan is in spring (March to May) and autumn (September to November), when the daytime temperatures aren't going to knock you flat and the winds aren't too cold (see Climate in the Facts about Jordan chapter for more information).

If you visit in summer be well prepared, and come with a hat, sunscreen and protec-tive clothing. At this time the entire country boils, nowhere more than around Wadi Rum and the eastern desert. The humidity can also become quite suffocating, especially along the Jordan River.

Highlights

Archaeological Sites
Petra (p 186)
Petra is the greatest site in Jordan, and one of the most spectacular in the whole of the Middle East, with highlights including the Treasury, Monastery and Royal Tombs. Allow at least two days.

Jerash (p 133)
This remarkably well-preserved Roman city, sec-ond only to Petra as a 'must-see', is easily acces-sible from Amman, and can be visited along with other sites, such as Ajlun and/or Umm Qais

Karak (p 176)
Arguably the most interesting of Jordan's Cru-sader castles, Karak is rich in history and the set-ting is truly superb

Umm Qais (p 143)
These ruins of another ancient city offer won-derful views over the Jordan Valley to Israel and the Palestinian Territories and Syria

Mt Nebo (p 169)
The site where Moses looked out over the Promised Land has great religious significance as well as fine views over the Dead Sea and beyond

Qusayr Amra (p 157)
This baths complex in the deserts of eastern Jor-dan reflects the cultural heritage of the Umay-yads in an evocative and remote setting

Museums & Galleries
National Archaeological Museum (p 109)
The main museum overlooking the capital is compact and informative, and located in the ruins of the ancient Citadel

Museum of Jordanian Heritage (p 142)
Probably the best museum in Jordan, it's in the vibrant Yarmouk University in Irbid

Darat al-Funun (p 110)
A short walk from Downtown Amman, this art gallery has various interesting exhibitions and a charming outdoor café

Landscapes & Natural Features
Wadi Rum (p 211)
Wadi Rum offers the most stunning desert land-scapes in Jordan. Camping, hiking and jeep tours are currently allowed. It is acknowledged as one of the world's foremost desert climbing areas.

Dana Nature Reserve (p 182)
Plunging canyons, diverse ecosystems and the 15th-century stone village of Dana make for a memorable stay

Wadi Mujib (p 174)
This vast valley, known as the Grand Canyon of Jordan, stretches from the Dead Sea Highway to the King's Highway and beyond

The Dead Sea (p 130)
Floating in the Dead Sea is high on novelty value and there's enough salt, sea and mud for an en-joyable day trip from Amman

Activities
Diving & Snorkelling (p 234)
The waters south of Aqaba have enough coral and marine life to satisfy most divers and the best can also be enjoyed by snorkellers

Hiking & Rock Climbing (p 218)
Anyone with some fitness and experience can enjoy trekking and rock climbing among the hills of Wadi Rum or the gorges of Dana. Guides are usually necessary.

For Something a Bit Different...
Jeep Tours (p 218)
Bedouin drivers offer trips around remarkable Wadi Rum in 4WDs

Archaeological Digs (p 70)
Anyone with a specific interest, and plenty of time, can join an archaeological dig

Camel Treks (p 218)
For a taste of the Bedouin lifestyle, camel treks can be organised from Wadi Rum to Wadi Musa (near Petra) and Aqaba

The tourist authorities usually plan festivals (such as the Jerash Festival) for the July/ August period.

Winter is not a complete washout. It can be bitterly cold throughout most of the country, but once you come off the high plateaus and head down to Aqaba and the Red Sea, it becomes very pleasant. In fact, Aqaba is quite a hit with deep-frozen northern Europeans during winter.

Ramadan is a time when visitors should not eat, drink or smoke in public during the day for one month, so it's not the best time to visit. Eid al-Fitr, the great celebration after the end of Ramadan, can last several days. Although this is a fun time to visit, it's best to stay put for a few days because buses are heavily booked, service taxis and private taxis are less frequent and hotel rooms are sometimes hard to find, especially in Aqaba. See Public Holidays & Special Events later in this chapter for more information about travelling around Jordan during Ramadan.

Maps

For most visitors, the maps in this guidebook will be more than sufficient, but if you're doing some hiking or intensive exploration, a detailed map of Jordan is a good idea.

The most accurate map of the country (available in Jordan) is the colourful *Map of Jordan,* published by Luma Khalaf. The same company also publishes the *Street Map of Amman*, which is available in some hotels and is surprisingly detailed. The Royal Geographic Centre of Jordan publishes a series of decent maps that are available at major bookshops in the country. Its map of Amman, called *Today's Amman*, is excellent, as is the hiking map of Petra, but the ones for Jerash, Madaba, Karak and Aqaba are less useful. The Jordan Tourism Board's *Map of Jordan* is also worth getting hold of.

Several detailed maps should be available in your own country: Bartholomew's *Israel with Jordan* is OK, but it includes Israel and the Palestinian Territories at the expense of eastern Jordan; *Jordan* by Kümmerly & Frey is good, and probably the best if you're driving around Jordan; and the third edition of GEO Project's *Jordan* (1:730,000) also includes an excellent map of Amman.

What to Bring

For most travellers, the backpack remains the best option, and the only one if you end up having to do any walking. On the down side, they do not afford the greatest protection to valuable belongings.

A few handy items are: a Swiss army knife, torch (flashlight), a few metres of nylon cord (for a clothesline), pegs, a universal sink plug, an adaptor for electrical items (if necessary), earplugs (useful if you're staying near mosques), medical and sewing kits, padlocks, a towel, short-wave radio, sleeping sheet and/or bag if you're camping or staying overnight in Wadi Rum.

If you're going in winter, make sure you have plenty of warm clothes and a windproof and waterproof jacket, because some parts of Jordan, particularly the north, can get surprisingly miserable at this time of year. The southern desert region can also get cold at night at any time of the year.

Tampons are not always readily available. You should also bring your own contraceptives and any special medications. Other toiletries are easily found. See Health later in this chapter for a list of medical items worth bringing.

RESPONSIBLE TOURISM

About 20 years ago, Jordan started to appreciate the economic importance of tourism, but only recently have the Jordanian government and foreign non-governmental organisations (NGOs) fully realised the impact on the environment from mass tourism. For example, the cumulative effects of the extraordinary number of people visiting the fragile ancient city of Petra every day are threatening the future of Petra – which is also a vital source of revenue for the government. (The boxed text 'Petra & Tourism' in the Petra chapter has more information.)

The environmental problems of Jordan may seem insurmountable, but there is a lot we can all do to minimise our impact:

Leave it as you found it For as long as outsiders have been searching for, and stumbling over, the ancient monuments of Jordan, they have also been chipping bits off, or leaving their contributions engraved upon them. When visiting historical and archaeological sites, please consider how important it is to leave things alone.
Don't litter Discarded rubbish is strewn all across the countryside. Some of the refuse – eg, plastic

bottles – is recycled in many ways, so don't be too quick to point an accusing finger at the locals. However, please resist the local tendency to ditch rubbish out of the car or bus window.

Do as requested Please follow instructions and regulations, eg, don't touch the coral off the coast of Aqaba and don't go to areas of national reserves which are off limits.

For more details about the impact of tourism, see Ecology & Environment and Society & Conduct in the Facts about Jordan chapter.

TOURIST OFFICES
Local Tourist Offices

The main tourist office in Amman is located on the ground floor of the **Ministry of Tourism and Antiquities** *(☎ 06-4646264 or ☎ 4642311; southwest of 3rd Circle; open 8am-11pm daily)* in Jebel Amman. The staff are friendly and speak good English.

Smaller tourist offices are located at Madaba, Aqaba, Karak, Jerash, Petra and Wadi Rum. A new innovation in Jordan is the number of visitor centres springing up. There is one at the desert castle of Qusayr Amra in eastern Jordan and at most of the major sites.

One scheme to encourage tourists is 'Passgate', a programme akin to a domestic passport for travellers. It costs US$10 and involves getting a number of stamps whenever you visit a major tourist site, entitling you to discounts at participating (and usually upmarket) dealers. Contact any tourist office or ⒠ info@passgate-intl.com for details.

The Jordan Tourism Board (JTB) publishes an array of excellent brochures in English, German, Spanish, Italian and French, and sometimes you can even find one in Japanese. The brochures about Amman, the desert castles, Umm Qais, Jerash, Petra, Karak, Mt Nebo, Madaba, Ajlun, Wadi Rum, Aqaba and Petra are all informative, pocket-sized and free. Pick one up from a JTB office overseas or from any tourist office in Jordan.

Tourist Offices Abroad

After evaluating the importance of tourism to the Jordanian economy, the Jordan Tourism Board has recently spread its network to include offices in several countries:

France (☎ 01-45 61 92 58, fax 42 25 66 40, ⒠ jordanie@worldnet.fr) 32 rue de Ponthieu, 75008 Paris

Germany (☎ 69-9231 8870, fax 9231 8879, ⒠ jordan@adam-partner.de) Postfach 160 120, 60064 Frankfurt

UK (☎ 020-7371 6496, fax 7603 2424, ⒠ debbieflynn@jordantourismboard.co.uk) Lee House, 2nd Floor, 109 Hammersmith Rd, London, W14 0QH

USA (☎ 202-243 7404, fax 243 7406, ⒠ seejordan@aol.com) Suite 770, 2000 North 14th St, Arlington, Virginia 22201

There are also JTB offices in Amsterdam, Barcelona, Brussels, Jeddah and Madrid.

The **JTB office** in Amman *(☎ 06-5678294, fax 5678295; ⒠ jtb@nets.com.jo; ⒲ www.see -jordan.com.jo)* is upstairs in the shopping complex adjacent to the Ammon Hotel (see Places to Stay in the Amman chapter). If you cannot visit a JTB office overseas, it's best to email the Amman office from wherever you are.

Information is sometimes available from Royal Jordanian airline offices (such as those in Amsterdam, Berlin, Chicago, Frankfurt, London, Los Angeles, Montreal, New York, Paris, Rome and Sydney). Also try the Jordanian embassies and consulates listed later in this chapter.

VISAS & DOCUMENTS
Passport

Everyone requires a valid passport to travel to Jordan. Check that your passport is valid for at least six months after you arrive in Jordan; otherwise you may not be granted a visa. Keep an eye on the number of pages you have left in the passport. If it's nearly full get a new one before leaving home.

Always carry your passport with you when travelling around sensitive areas such as near the border of Israel and the Palestinian Territories – which means most of the Jordan Valley and anywhere along the Dead Sea Highway. Checkpoints are common near all borders, and passport checks are often required.

Visas

Visas are required by all foreigners entering Jordan. Tourist visas are valid for three months (ie, you must enter the country within three months of the date of issue) for stays of up to two weeks from the date of entry, but can be easily extended for stays of up to three months (see Visa Extensions later in this chapter).

Travelling To/From Israel and the Palestinian Territories

Most countries in the Middle East and North Africa (with the exception of Jordan, Egypt and Morocco) will not grant visas, or allow entry, to anyone who has *any* evidence of visiting Israel, or the Palestine Territories (which includes the West Bank). This includes Israeli exit stamps from any of the three borders with Jordan (ie, from Eilat, King Hussein Bridge and Sheikh Hussein Bridge); Israeli exit stamps or Egyptian entry stamps at Rafah and Taba, both on the border; and any Jordanian entry stamps at the border of Israel and the Palestinian Territories. Travellers have even been turned away from Syria's border with Jordan for having unexplained periods of time in their passport, such as three weeks in Jordan without any evidence of a Jordanian visa extension.

Even if you do things in a convoluted fashion – eg, visit Israel and the Palestinian Territories from Egypt, return to Egypt and go to Jordan on the ferry – you run a good chance of acquiring unwanted evidence in your passport. Even if the Israelis do not stamp you in or out, the Egyptians may well do so (at Rafah at least). And then if you apply for a Syrian visa, or attempt to cross the Jordan/Syria border, without a Jordanian entry stamp you'll probably be denied a visa or entry.

The only foolproof method is to visit the countries that will not accept evidence of a visit to Israel and the Palestinian Territories *before* going there, and then go to countries, such as Egypt and Jordan, which will accept Israeli visas/stamps – and later get a new passport. If you have dual citizenship, try to get two passports, but keep them separate and make sure you get the correct visas and stamps in the right passport.

If none of the above is possible or feasible, cross the border from Jordan to Israel and the Palestinian Territories at the King Hussein Bridge and go back to Jordan the same way. To be sure, leave and re-enter Jordan within the time limit specified on your Jordanian visa (ie, within 14 days of your original visa or within the duration of any extension). But make sure you ask for all Jordanian and Israeli stamps to be placed on a separate piece of paper. People who have crossed from Jordan to the West Bank in small groups have asked for stamps on separate pieces of paper, but have still been caught out; for some reason, Israeli immigration officials may not stamp the first two or three passports, but then they'll stamp the next few – so it's best to cross individually or in groups of two.

If you get an Israeli or Jordanian exit or entry stamp in your passport, there's little you can do. If you report that your passport is 'lost' to your embassy in any country in the Middle East, it may be met with extreme cynicism, and even rejection. And some countries may also be highly sceptical, and even refuse you a visa or entry, if you have a brand new, unused passport issued in the Middle East.

The easiest way to get a visa is on arrival in the country. Visas are issued with a minimum of fuss at the border or airport on arrival (JD10). Note that visas are not issued at the King Hussein Bridge if you plan to enter from Israel and the Palestinian Territories. At the airport immigration counters, look for the yellow 'Visa' sign to make sure you join the appropriate queue. There are moneychangers adjacent to the counters, but no ATMs.

Visas can also be obtained from Jordanian consulates or embassies outside the country. The cost is usually around US\$20/40 for a single/multiple entry visa, they are issued within 24 hours and no more than two photos are required. In the Middle East, visas are available from Jordanian embassies in Turkey, Lebanon, Syria, Israel (avoid this if you wish to travel elsewhere in the region), Egypt, Iraq, Yemen and the Gulf States. See Jordanian Embassies & Consulates later in this chapter for the location of other Jordanian diplomatic missions.

The only reason to apply for a visa from a Jordanian consulate or embassy is if you wish to obtain a multiple-entry visa, as these are not issued at the border, or if you plan to arrive via the King Hussein Bridge.

One exception worth knowing about is that if you arrive in Aqaba by sea from Nuweiba (Egypt), your visa may be free because Aqaba has been designated as a Special Economic Zone set up for free trade. The situation regarding such visas was unclear at the time of writing. Before you get too excited, you'll still have to pay the JD10 visa fee when you leave Jordan or re-enter Aqaba, although some officials claimed that the visa remained free if you spent sufficient (but unspecified) time in Aqaba. There

Getting Other Visas in Jordan

Jordan is generally not a good place to get visas for neighbouring countries other than Egypt. See Embassies & Consulates in Jordan later in this chapter for addresses.

Egypt

The easiest place to obtain Egyptian visas is from the consulate in Aqaba, where you'll need one passport photo, one to two hours and JD12/15 for a single-/multiple-entry tourist visa. The consulate is open from 8am to 3pm Sunday to Thursday.

In Amman, the relatively chaotic Egyptian embassy is open 9am to noon Sunday to Thursday for visa applications. You'll need JD15/19 for a single/multiple entry visa, one photo and you can usually pick up your visa around 3pm the same afternoon.

Most nationalities are issued a visa on arrival in Egypt, including at Nuweiba for those arriving by ferry from Aqaba (the Egyptians sometimes demand payment in US dollars); however, it's very important to check whether the visa issued at the Egyptian embassy or consulate, or on arrival at Nuweiba, is for all of Egypt – or just the Sinai peninsula (ie, as far as Sharm el-Sheikh). Some visitors have been caught, so check with the Egyptian consulate in Aqaba or embassy in Amman beforehand.

Iraq

Iraqi visas are now possible, if difficult to obtain. If you make your application at the Iraqi embassy on Al-Kulliyah al-Islamiyah St in Jebel Amman, you will wait until four other tourists (preferably of the same nationality) also make an application. Groups of a minimum of five people can then obtain their visas, although your visit will be strictly supervised (and you will probably be escorted) during your time in Iraq. If you're travelling on a US passport, you can probably forget it. Visas cost US$100 and require two photos.

Israel and the Palestinian Territories

Staff at the heavily fortified Israeli embassy actively discourage visa applications as visas are available at most border crossings and many nationalities do not require them. At the King Hussein

---

were also reports that if you entered from another border crossing and asked for a special 'Aqaba visa', your visa would be free if you went to Aqaba within 48 hours of arrival in the country. Failure to do this will incur the JD10 visa fee and a fine.

Visa Extensions A single-entry visa is valid for 14 days after arrival in Jordan, and is stamped with a reminder to visit the police within that period if you wish to stay longer than 14 days. Failure to do so will result in a fine of at least JD1 per day for every day you have overstayed.

One visa extension of two or three months is easy to obtain, and often in less than 30 minutes. Extensions are technically possible in major provincial capitals such as Aqaba, Irbid and Karak, but are best done in Amman (see Visa Extensions in the Amman chapter for details). An extension costs nothing, and no photos are needed.

If you want another extension, wish to reside in Jordan, or there is something unusual about your visa (eg, a curious number of Israeli stamps), you may be sent to the **Directorate of Residence, Borders & Foreigners** (☎ 196, ext 3392; Suleiman an-Nabulsi St, Amman; open 8am-2pm Sat-Thur) for further checking and paperwork. Take service taxi No 6 or 7 from Downtown.

Travel Insurance

A travel insurance policy to cover theft, loss and medical problems is a good idea. Some policies offer varied-rate, medical-expense options; the higher ones are chiefly for countries such as the USA, which have extremely high medical costs. There is a wide variety of policies available, so check the small print.

Some policies specifically exclude 'dangerous activities', which can include scuba diving, motorcycling and even trekking. A

Getting Other Visas in Jordan

Bridge, three-month Israeli visas are available, while visas of just one month's duration are available at Sheikh Hussein Bridge and the Wadi Araba/Rabin crossing.

Lebanon

Lebanon has followed Syria's example and virtually stopped issuing visas to travellers who aren't resident in Jordan. They do, however, point out that there is also no point issuing visas as they are readily available at Lebanese entry points. If you want to try for a visa in Amman, the embassy is open from 8am to 11am Sunday to Thursday, and you need to take along a photocopy of your passport details, two passport photos and JD15. Remember that if you are travelling to Lebanon via Syria, you will need to obtain your Syrian visa *before* you arrive in Jordan.

Saudi Arabia

The only visas currently issued to tourists seem to be transit visas, which sometimes allow you to travel along the Tapline (Trans Arabia Pipeline) in three days, but sometimes only lets you fly in and out, and spend a day in Riyadh. Ask at the Saudi consulate close to 1st Circle in Amman for prevailing conditions and prices.

Syria

If you intend to travel to Syria, make sure you have a Syrian visa before you arrive in Jordan. It is imperative to note that only foreign residents in Jordan (ie, expatriate workers and diplomats) can be issued a Syrian visa at the embassy in Amman. Some readers have received a Syrian visa after obtaining a letter of recommendation (in Arabic) from their embassy in Amman, but this is definitely more the exception than the rule and should never be counted on.

Other than in extremely rare cases, visas are not available at the Syria/Jordan border.

You will be refused a Syrian visa, and entry to Syria, if there is any indication in your passport of entry to Israel and the Palestinian Territories – see the 'Travelling To/From Israel and the Palestinian Territories' boxed text earlier in this chapter for more information. The embassy is open 9am to 11am daily except Friday.

---

locally acquired motorbike licence is not valid under some policies.

You may prefer a policy that pays doctors or hospitals directly rather than making you pay on the spot and claim later. If you have to claim later make sure you keep all documentation. Some policies ask you to call back (reverse charges) to a centre in your home country where an immediate assessment of your problem is made.

Check that the policy covers ambulances and emergency flights home.

Driving Licence

An International Driving Permit may be required if you intend to drive anywhere in Jordan, although most car rental companies accept your national driving licence instead.

Student Cards

The policy with regard to student cards was being inconsistently applied at the time of research. Officially, student discounts of 50% are available at most tourist sites, including Petra, but officials in many places stand firm against allowing the discount. Note that the card must be an International Student Identity Card (ISIC) and not just your university ID card. At the time of research the Jordanian government was undecided as to whether the discounts would continue beyond 2002.

Photocopies

All important documents (passport data page and visa page, credit cards, travel insurance policy, air/bus/train tickets, driving licence, etc) should be photocopied before you leave home. Leave one copy with someone at home and keep another with you, separate from the originals.

Another option for storing details of your vital travel documents before you leave is Lonely Planet's online Travel Vault. Storing details of your important documents in the vault is safer than carrying photocopies. Your password-protected travel vault is accessible online any time. Create your own free travel vault at w www.ekno.lonelyplanet.com.

EMBASSIES & CONSULATES
Jordanian Embassies & Consulates

All of the following are embassies unless otherwise indicated:

Australia (☎ 02-6295 9951) 20 Roebuck St, Red Hill, ACT 2603

Canada (☎ 613-238 8090) 100 Bronson Ave, Suite 701, Ottawa, Ontario ON K1R 6G8

Egypt (☎ 02-748 5566, fax 760 1027) 6 Al-Shaheed Basem al-Khatib, Doqqi, Cairo

France (☎ 01 46 24 23 78) 80 Blvd Maurice Barres, 92200 Neuilly-Seine, Paris

Germany (☎ 030-36 99 60 0) Heerstrasse 201, 13595 Berlin (there's also a consulate in Hanover)

Israel (☎ 03-751 7722, fax 751 7712) Rehov Abbe Hillel Silver 14, Ramat Gan 52506

Lebanon (☎ 05-922 500, fax 922 502) Rue Elias Helou, Baabda, Beirut

Netherlands (☎ 70-416 7200, fax 416 7209) Badhuisweg 79, 2587 CD, The Hague

Syria (☎ 11-333 4642, fax 333 6741) Al-Jala'a Ave, Damascus

Turkey (☎ 0312-440 2054, fax 440 4327) Mesnevi Ded Korkut Sokak 18, Çankaya, Ankara

Your Own Embassy

It's important to realise what your own embassy can and cannot do to help you if you get into trouble.

Generally speaking, it won't be much help in emergencies if the trouble you're in is remotely your own fault. Remember that you're bound by the laws of the country you're in. Your embassy will not be sympathetic if you end up in jail after committing a crime locally, even if such actions are legal in your own country.

In genuine emergencies you might get some assistance, but only if other channels have been exhausted. For example, if you need to get home urgently, a free ticket home is exceedingly unlikely – the embassy would expect you to have insurance. If you have all your money and documents stolen, it might assist with getting a new passport, but a loan for onward travel is out of the question.

Consulate: (☎ 0212-230 1221, 241 4331) Kalipci, Sokak 119/6, Tesvikiye, İstanbul

UK (☎ 020-7937 3685) 6 Upper Phillimore Gardens, London, W8 7HB

USA (☎ 202-966 2664, e hkjembassydc@aol .com) 3504 International Drive NW, Washington DC 20008

Consulate: (☎ 212-832 0119) 866 Second Ave, 4th Floor, New York, NY 10017

Embassies & Consulates in Jordan

Foreign embassies and consulates are in Amman (Egypt also has a consulate in Aqaba). In general, the offices are open from 9am to 11am Sunday to Thursday for visa applications and again from 1pm to 3pm for collecting your visa. The area code is ☎ 06 unless stated otherwise.

Australia
Embassy: (☎ 5807000, fax 5807001, e ausemb@nets.com.jo) 3 Youssef Abu Shahhout St, Deir Ghbar

Canada
Embassy: (☎ 5666124) Abdul Hameed Shoman St, Shmeisani

Egypt
Embassy: (☎ 5605175, fax 5604082) 22 Qurtubah St, between 4th & 5th Circles
Consulate: (☎ 2016171) Cnr Al-Istiqlal & Al-Akhatal Sts, Aqaba

France
Embassy: (☎ 4641273, fax 4659606) Mutanabi St, Jebel Amman

Germany
Embassy: (☎ 5930367, fax 5685887) 31 Benghazi St, between 4th and 5th Circles, Jebel Amman

Iraq
Embassy: (☎ 4623175, fax 4619172) Near 1st Circle, Zahran St, Jebel Amman

Israel
Consulate: (☎ 5524686) Maysaloon St, Rabia

Lebanon
Embassy: (☎ 5922911, fax 5929113) Al-Neel St, Abdoun, near the UK embassy

Netherlands
Embassy: (☎ 5930525) 4th Circle, Alico Building, across from the Prime Ministry

New Zealand
Consulate: (☎ 4636720, fax 4634349) 4th floor, Khalas Bldg, 99 Al-Malek al-Hussein St, Downtown

Saudi Arabia
Consulate: (☎ 5920154, fax 5921154) 1st Circle, Jebel Amman

Syria
Embassy: (☎ 4641076, fax 4651945) Afghani St, between 3rd and 4th Circles, Jebel Amman

UK
Embassy: (☎ 5923100, fax 5913759) Wadi Abdoun, Abdoun
USA
Embassy: (☎ 5920101, fax 5820123) 20 Al-Umaywiyeen St, Abdoun

CUSTOMS

The usual goods are prohibited, eg, drugs and weapons, as are 'immoral films, tapes (cassettes) and magazines' – but customs inspectors are not tough on this unless the stuff is pornographic.

Duty-free allowances for 'non-residents' (tourists) are: 200 cigarettes or 25 cigars or 200g of tobacco; two bottles of wine or one bottle of spirits; and a 'reasonable amount of perfume for personal use'.

Jordan has no restrictions on the import and export of either Jordanian or foreign currency.

MONEY
Currency

The currency in Jordan is the dinar (JD) – it's known as the *jay-dee* among hip young locals – which is made up of 1000 fils. You will sometimes hear *piastre* or *qirsh*, which are both 10 fils (10 qirsh equals 100 fils). Often when a price is quoted, the ending will be omitted, so if you're told that something is 25, it's a matter of working out whether it's 25 fils, 25 piastre or 25 dinars! Although it sounds confusing, most Jordanians wouldn't dream of ripping off a foreigner, so ask for clarification.

Coins are 50, 100, 250 and 500 fils, and one dinar. The value of the coins is written in English; the numerals are in Arabic only. Each denomination can have two different versions, often a different shape (circular or octagonal), colour (gold, silver or both) and name (eg, '500 fils' or 'half-dinar'). Some taxi drivers, and occasional unscrupulous merchants, sometimes use the confusing array of coins as a way to short-change foreigners, so take care.

Notes come in denominations of JD0.500, 1, 5, 10 and 20. For everyday use, the JD5 note is about as large as you want, but even finding change for a JD3.500 meal from a JD5 note can cause minor chaos in some restaurants. Try to change larger notes as often as possible at larger restaurants, and when paying your hotel bill.

Exchange Rates

The current exchange rates for most major foreign currencies are printed in the business sections of the English-language newspapers, the *Jordan Times* and the *Star*.

country	unit		dinar
Australia	A$1	=	JD0.401
Canada	C$1	=	JD0.454
Egypt	E£1	=	JD0.155
euro	€1	=	JD0.749
Japan	¥100	=	JD0.601
New Zealand	NZ$1	=	JD0.374
Switzerland	Sfr1	=	JD0.517
Syria	S£10	=	JD0.144
UK	UK£1	=	JD1.151
USA	US$1	=	JD0.714

Exchanging Money

Changing money is very easy in Jordan, and most major currencies are accepted in cash and travellers cheques. US dollars are the most accepted, followed by UK pounds and euros; you'll get nowhere with Australian or New Zealand dollars.

Jordanian currency can sometimes be bought before leaving your home country, or in neighbouring countries (especially Syria), and there are no restrictions about the amount of dinars that can be brought into Jordan. It's possible to change dinars back into some foreign currencies in Jordan, but you'll need to show receipts to prove that you changed your currency into dinars at a bank in Jordan.

As a rule, the most widely recognised travellers cheques are American Express (Amex). Some banks, such as the Union Bank, which is an agent of sorts for Amex, will change nothing else – but will still charge a hefty JD7 fee per transaction.

Syrian, Lebanese, Egyptian, Israeli and Iraqi currency can all be changed in Amman, usually at reasonable rates, though you may have to shop around. Egyptian and Israeli currency is also easily changed in Aqaba. It's a good idea to talk to travellers arriving from across the border you're about to cross; you can find out the in-country rates, so you know how much to change.

Cash and travellers cheques can be changed in large hotels (for guests and the public), but rates are always lower than those offered by the banks and money-changers. Some shops will accept travellers cheques as payment, but the commission charged by the banks (and hence passed on to you, the purchaser) is prohibitive.

Banks There are banks all over Amman, and several in every major town throughout Jordan. All banks will change cash, and most change travellers cheques – but beware of commissions (from JD3 per transaction to 10% of the amount changed for travellers cheques).

Banks seem to offer slightly better rates than moneychangers for cash, but the difference is not worth worrying about unless you're going to change a huge amount. One irritating demand made by some banks is to see the sales receipts for the cheques before changing them – directly contradicting the standard instructions to keep them separate. Sometimes they will relent and sometimes they won't.

There are small branches of some major banks at the borders and at the airports. Some banks are fussy about the older US dollar notes, and may not even accept them.

Moneychangers Generally, moneychangers offer slightly lower rates than banks for cash. In theory, they do not charge commission on travellers cheques but in practice many do, so shop around. Moneychanger offices are smaller and easier to use than banks, and are open for far longer – usually every day from about 9am to 9pm. They can be found in Amman, Irbid, Wadi Musa (near Petra) and Aqaba. Always check the rates at banks or in the English-language newspapers before changing money.

Credit Cards It is possible to survive in Jordan almost entirely on cash advances, and ATMs abound in all but the smaller towns. This is certainly the easiest way to travel if you know your PIN.

There are no local charges on credit card cash advances but the maximum daily withdrawal amount is JD500, whether over the counter or from an ATM. Whether you can get this much or not will depend on the conditions pertaining to your particular card. All banks have large signs (in English) outside indicating which credit cards they accept.

Visa, which is the most widely accepted card for cash advances and ATMs, is accepted at most branches of the Housing Bank, Arab Bank, Bank of Jordan, Cairo-Amman Bank, Arab Banking Corporation, Jordan Arab Investment Bank, Jordan Islamic Bank and the Jordan Investment & Finance Bank.

MasterCard is accepted at most branches of the Arab Bank, Jordan National Bank, British Bank of the Middle East, Jordan Gulf Bank and Bank of Jordan. Other cards, such as Cirrus and Plus, are also accepted by some of the local banks and ATMs (eg, Jordan National Bank and HSBC).

The emergency numbers to contact in Amman should you lose your credit card are: **American Express** (☎ 06-5607014); **Visa** (☎ 06-5680554); **Diners Club** (☎ 06-5675850); and **MasterCard** (☎ 06-4655863). If an ATM swallows your card call ☎ 06-5669123 (Amman).

Most major credit cards are accepted at top-end hotels and restaurants, travel agents, larger souvenir shops and bookshops. However, always be sure to ask if any commission is being added on top of your purchase price. This can sometimes be as much as 5%; if so, it may be better to get a cash advance and pay with the paper stuff.

International Transfers Some major banks (eg, the Arab Bank and Jordan National Bank) can arrange the international transfer of money. The Cairo-Amman Bank is part of the international service offered by Western Union. The US-based Money-Gram company has agreements for a 'swift transfer service' (only in US dollars) with the Jordan Islamic, Union, Jordan National and Jordan Gulf Banks. However, fees are high, so obtaining a cash advance with a credit card – and even changing travellers cheques at a bank (despite the commission) – is probably better.

Security

Money is about the most precious stuff you'll have on your trip, so it's worth looking after. Although theft is not a real problem in Jordan, it's always wise to take basic precautions. Always carry your wallet (if you have one) in a front pocket, and don't have too much cash in it. The bulk of your money, travellers cheques and documents are better off in a pouch worn close to the skin. There are many types of pouch and money belt that you can hang around the neck or wear around the waist – most travel equipment shops sell several versions of this sort of thing. The best material in hot places like Jordan is cotton.

It's also sensible to leave some of your money hidden as a separate stash in your luggage (eg, rolled up in a pair of thick socks) in case you find yourself in deep trouble at some point.

Costs

Jordan is not the cheapest country in the area to travel around, but it is possible to get by on a really tight budget and, if you spend wisely, good value can be found all over the country.

The most basic accommodation will cost from as low as JD1.500 for a bed in a shared room or on the roof, but most decent budget places will cost about JD5/8/11 for singles/doubles/triples.

Accommodation costs in the mid-range and top-end categories tend to vary more than budget options. As a general rule, mid-range singles/doubles cost from JD12/20 up to JD25/35, while top-end doubles start from JD65 and can go as high as JD190.

Snacks like felafel and shwarma (see Food later in this chapter) cost 300 to 500 fils; other decent budget meals, about JD1.

In any mid-range restaurant, expect to pay JD1 for a starter and from JD1.500 to JD2.500 for most main courses, with a three-course meal and drinks easily making it up to JD5 per person. If you're splashing out at one of Amman's better restaurants, don't expect too much change from JD15 per person, and more if you have a bottle of wine.

A cup of tea normally costs about 250 fils; Turkish coffee, from 500 fils. A large 1.5L bottle of mineral water is about 500 fils, and a 650ml bottle of Amstel beer starts from JD1.500 in a local bar. Public transport is cheap – less than 500 fils per hour of travel in a public bus or minibus, and about JD1 per hour in a more comfortable, long-distance private bus.

One of the biggest sightseeing expenses in Jordan is the entrance fee to Petra (up to JD26 for two days, depending on the season), but it's still great value. At other sites such as Jerash, entrance can cost as much as JD5 in high season. To encourage more tourists, 50% discounts are often available during low season (the dates of which

change depending on the prevailing conditions). Most other sites cost between 500 fils and JD2.

If you stay in a shared room or sleep on the roof at the cheapest possible hotel, eat nothing but felafel and shwarma and use public transport and/or hitch exclusively, it's possible to get by on about JD10/8 per day, though JD12/10 is more reasonable. If you add the cost of occasional chartered taxis, souvenirs, a splurge every now and then on a slap-up meal or a mid-range hotel, and the entrance fee to Petra, the cost per day for a budget-minded traveller is about JD15/12. For JD30/25, you could live comfortably.

Tipping & Bargaining

Tips of 10% are generally expected in better restaurants. Elsewhere, rounding up the bill to the nearest 250 fils or with loose change is appreciated by underpaid staff. Hotels in the mid-range and top-end categories usually add a service charge of about 13%, plus a 'government tax' of another 10%, thereby adding considerably to the final bill.

As in most countries in the region, many prices are negotiable, except public transport (which is set by the government), food in grocery shops, and meals and drinks in restaurants where prices are listed on a menu. Bargaining, especially when souvenir hunting, is essential, but shopkeepers are less likely than their Syrian and Egyptian counterparts to shift a long way from their original asking prices.

POST & COMMUNICATIONS
Postal Rates

Normal-sized letters to the USA and Australia cost 400 fils, and postcards cost 300 fils. To Europe, letters are 300 fils and postcards 200 fils, and to Arab countries they cost 200 fils and 150 fils respectively. Larger letters – rather than parcels – to the UK and Europe cost 300 fils for the first 10g, and 150 fils for every subsequent 10g; to Australia, New Zealand, the USA and Canada, they cost 400 fils for the first 10g, and 200 fils per extra 10g.

Parcel post is ridiculously expensive, so Jordan is not the best place from which to send souvenirs home. To send anything by air to Australia, for example, the first 1kg costs JD13, and each subsequent 1kg, JD7.500. To the UK and Europe, the first

1kg is JD10, and then JD3.500 per extra 1kg; and to the USA and Canada, it costs JD9.900, then JD5.700.

Amman is the best place to send parcels – see Post in the Amman chapter for more information about sending parcels home.

Sending Mail

Stamps are available from all post offices, and from many souvenir shops where postcards are sold. All postcards and normal-sized letters can be dropped in any of the obvious post boxes around most towns. Letters posted from Jordan take up to two weeks to reach Australia and the USA, but often as little as three or four days to the UK and Europe. Every town has a post office, but you're well advised to send things from major places like Amman, Madaba, Karak, Wadi Musa (near Petra) and Aqaba.

Of the international courier companies, **Federal Express** *(FedEx;* ☎ *06-5511460, fax 5531232)* is on Nasser bin Jameel St in Amman, and **DHL** *(*☎ *06-5857136, fax 5827705;* e *info@amm-co.jo.dhl.com)* is behind C-Town Shopping Centre on 7th Circle in Amman. They are typically reliable but expensive (half a kilo costs from JD41/35 to Australia/Europe or the USA, although the per kilo rate decreases dramatically the more you send). DHL also has an office in Aqaba *(*☎ *03-2012039)* on Al-Petra St. There are also a few home-grown versions.

Receiving Mail

The only reliable post restante services are at the main post offices in Amman and Aqaba. If you send anything to a poste restante in another post office it's likely to end up in Amman anyway, so send it there. Note that packages sent to Jordan can end up at the Queen Alia International Airport, where you'll have to battle with the customs department to determine whether any customs duty is applicable.

An alternative is to arrange to receive mail through your hotel, but this only works if you are staying for a long time.

Telephone

The telephone system in Jordan has recently been privatised, and is now run by **Alo** *(*☎ *465 4545, ext 233)*. There are no longer any public telephone offices to make calls from, so visitors must either use a private telephone

agency, call from a hotel or shop, or buy a telephone card for one of the 1000 or more pay phones throughout Jordan.

Pay phones operated by Alo accept phone cards to the value of between JD1 (local calls only) and JD15; they get eaten up rapidly on international calls. Cards can be bought at shops and stalls. The pay phones are widespread (especially around post offices, main squares and major thoroughfares), labelled in English, and easy to use.

All landline telephone numbers in Jordan now have seven digits; those beginning with '0795' or '077' are mobile numbers. The local telephone system is quite reliable. Local calls cost around 100 fils for three minutes and the easiest place to make a call is your hotel. Most shopkeepers and some hotel staff will make their telephones available for about 250 fils, and it costs about the same at a private telephone agency.

Although telephone directories in English and Arabic are published, along with a Yellow Pages in English, finding either anywhere in Jordan can be very difficult. The libraries in the cultural centres and bigger hotels in Amman might have a copy.

Useful telephone numbers are listed below. Those with seven digits are in Amman and require the ☎ 06 area code; the remainder can be dialled from anywhere in the country.

Ambulance	☎ 193 or ☎ 199
Fire Department	☎ 4617101 or
	☎ 199
Highway Police	☎ 5343402
Hotel Complaints	☎ 4613103
Local Directory Assistance	
Amman	☎ 121
Elsewhere in Jordan	☎ 131
International	☎ 0132
Police	☎ 191/192
Price Complaints	☎ 5661176
Public Transport Complaints	☎ 4642311
Queen Alia International Airport	
(Flight Information)	
Royal Jordanian	☎ 4453200
Other airlines	☎ 4452700 or
	☎ 4453250
Tourism Complaints	
(Tourist Police)	☎ 80022228
Traffic Police/Accidents	☎ 4896390 or
	☎ 190

The cost of overseas calls from Jordan varies: the cheapest rates are between 10pm and 8am, and all day Friday and public holidays, when it costs about JD1.250 per minute to Europe, the USA and Canada; and about JD1.750 to Australia and New Zealand. It's most expensive (about 25% more) during Jordanian business hours.

Overseas calls can be made at any pay phone with telephone cards, or from private telephone agencies in the central business districts and around tourist spots. Rates at the private agencies do vary, so shop around if you're making a lengthy long-distance call. Prices from smaller centres like Wadi Rum are exorbitant. Overseas calls from hotels cost substantially more than using a telephone card; it's best to call overseas and then get the recipient to call you back at your hotel.

Jordan is covered by the GSM Cellular Network and mobile telephones can be rented from companies such as **Mobile Zone** (Amman ☎/fax 06-5818294; e thezone@ nets.com.jo) or contact **Fastlink** (☎ 06-551 2010). Rates for signing up can start at JD60 including 20 minutes mobile-to-mobile time or 50 minutes mobile-to-land time. If you have your own phone and purchase a local SIM card, expect to pay around JD25 to get started.

When ringing Jordan from overseas, first dial the international access code in your country, followed by Jordan's international area code of ☎ 962, then the internal area code (see the entry for each town in the relevant chapter) and finally the individual number. Reverse-charge telephone calls are normally not possible, and the Home Country Direct Dial or Canada Direct services are not available.

Fax

The main post offices in Amman and Aqaba can arrange telegrams, telexes and faxes. The cost for a fax depends on the destination and the time it takes to send it, and is charged at the rates mentioned in the preceding Telephone section. Most hotels in the larger towns also send and receive telexes and faxes for guests, but at higher costs than the post office.

Email & Internet Access

Jordan is now truly part of the cyber world, and boasts numerous Internet Service Providers (ISPs).

Internet Centres There are now nearly 100 Internet centres across Jordan, in areas including Amman, Wadi Musa (near Petra), Ma'an, Madaba, Aqaba and Irbid. The most competitive rates, and the highest number of Internet centres, are found outside major universities such as Yarmouk University (Irbid) and the University of Jordan in northern Amman. Costs range from about 750 fils per hour to JD2 per hour. These places are not really 'Internet Cafés' as such, although tea, coffee and soft drinks are often available.

Travelling With Your Computer Travelling with a portable computer is a great way to stay in touch with life back home, but unless you know what you're doing it's fraught with potential problems. If you plan to carry your notebook or palmtop computer with you, remember that the power supply voltage may vary from that at home, and could damage your equipment. The best investment is a universal AC adaptor which will enable you to plug in your appliance anywhere without frying its innards. You may also need a plug adaptor, which is easier to buy before you leave home.

Your PC-card modem may or may not work once you leave your home country – and you won't know for sure until you try. The safest option is to buy a reputable 'global' modem before you leave home, or buy a local PC-card modem if you're spending an extended amount of time in Jordan. Keep in mind that the telephone socket in Jordan will probably be different from that at home, so ensure that you have at least a US RJ-11 telephone adaptor that works with your modem. You can almost always find an adaptor that will convert from RJ-11 to the local variety. For more information on travelling with a portable computer, see w www .teleadapt.com or w www.warrior.com.

Connecting to the Internet from your hotel room is possible, but usually only at top-end and a few mid-range hotels that have direct-dial phones. AOL (w www.aol .com) and Internet Gateway Services are among the international service providers with local access numbers as part of their global roaming services. AT&T doesn't have a Jordan access number.

If you intend to rely on Internet centres, you'll need to carry three pieces of information with you to access your Internet mail account: your incoming (POP or IMAP) mail server name, your account name, and your password. Your ISP or network supervisor will be able to give you these.

A final option to collect mail through Internet centres is to open a Web-based email account such as Hotmail (**w** www.hotmail.com) or Yahoo! Mail (**w** mail.yahoo.com). You can access your mail from anywhere in the world from any net-connected machine using a standard Web browser.

DIGITAL RESOURCES

The World Wide Web is a rich resource for travellers. You can research your trip, hunt down bargain air fares, book hotels, check on weather conditions or chat with locals and other travellers about the best places to visit (or avoid!).

There's no better place to start your web explorations than the Lonely Planet website (**w** www.lonelyplanet.com). Here you'll find succinct summaries on travelling to most places on earth, postcards from other travellers and the Thorn Tree bulletin board, where you can ask questions before you go or dispense advice when you get back. The subWWWay section links you to useful travel resources elsewhere on the Web.

Useful Websites

Websites have an annoying habit of coming and going, but the following should provide a useful starting point for researching your trip to Jordan. More specific websites are listed in the appropriate sections in the book.

AmmanNet Radio station that broadcasts in Arabic live from Amman
  w www.ammannet.net
Aqaba Economic Zone Mostly targeted at investors but some useful information about Aqaba
  w www.aqabazone.com
Baladna Excellent general information, links and chat lines
  w www.baladna.com
Jordan Hotels Association Information and bookings for upmarket hotels
  w www.johotels.com
Jordan News Agency English-language news updated daily by the official government news agency, Petra
  w www.petra.gov.jo
Jordan Tourism Board Reasonable links to range of Jordan-related websites
  w www.see-jordan.com/links.html

Madaba Excellent description of Madaba's attractions and other nearby sites
  w www.madaba.freeservers.com
National Information System Extensive range of information and statistics about Jordan
  w www.nic.gov.jo
Royal Family of Jordan Official website of Jordan's Hashemite royal family
  w www.kingabdullah.gov.jo
RSCN Accessible information about Jordan's environment and ecotourism
  w www.rscn.org.jo
Ruth's Homepage Probably the best website about Jordan, this wonderful window onto Jordanian society is loaded with practical tips
  w www.jordanjubilee.com

BOOKS

Your local bookshop or library is best placed to advise you on the availability of the following recommendations.

Amman has a good range of bookshops with titles in English (and, occasionally, other languages), but none offer a total selection of available titles so you may need to shop around. There are also two excellent bookshops in Aqaba.

Lonely Planet

If you're heading to other countries in the region, Lonely Planet also publishes books devoted to Jordan's neighbours in *Lebanon, Israel & the Palestinian Territories* and *Syria*. Travellers contemplating a longer swing through several countries of the Middle East should check out other Lonely Planet titles, particularly *Middle East* (which also covers Egypt, Syria, Lebanon, Israel and the Palestinian Territories, Turkey, Iran, Iraq, the Gulf States and Yemen), *Turkey*, *Iran*, *Egypt* and *Istanbul to Cairo*. There are also phrasebooks, including (Egyptian) Arabic.

Annie Caulfield's *Kingdom of the Film Stars: Journey into Jordan* is an entertaining, personal account of the author's relationship with a Bedouin man in Jordan. This is part of Journeys, Lonely Planet's travel literature series.

Guidebooks

We hope that you'll rarely need any more information than this guidebook offers, but you may crave more detailed information about specific archaeological sites or tourist attractions, or want to buy a souvenir book as a memento. Guidebooks to places like Petra,

Wadi Rum and Jerash are mentioned in the relevant sections in the rest of this book.

MG Graphic Formula publishes a series of souvenir-cum-guidebooks, such as the general *Jordan: History, Culture & Traditions*, and more specific ones about Jerash and Petra. They're published in English, French, Italian, German and Dutch, and are widely available in Jordan for JD4 to JD6.

The booklets published in English, French and Italian by Al-Kutba in Amman cover Jerash, Amman, Umm Qais, Pella, Madaba and Mt Nebo, the desert castles, Wadi Rum and Umm al-Jimal. They are portable, affordable (JD3 to JD5) and detailed, and available at most major bookshops in Jordan. Another decent pocket-sized guide is *This Way Jordan* by Jack Altman. It has a distinctive yellow cover, and is published by JPM Publications (JD5).

A few private companies publish free booklets for tourists visiting Jordan; they are usually available at tourist offices, mid-range and top-end hotels and some restaurants. The monthly *Jordan Today* is the most ubiquitous and features information about cultural events and entertainment. The Jordan Tourism Board publishes the quarterly *Calendar – Jordan*, which is useful for festivals, exhibitions and other events.

Travel

Most of the early travellers (like many visitors these days) came through Jordan as part of their travels around the Middle East.

In the late 19th century, the archaeologist Selah Merrill set off to explore what is modern Jordan, the area he called *East of the Jordan*. His book is one of the very few written in the 19th century about this area.

Johann Ludwig (also known as Jean Louis) Burckhardt spent many years in the early 19th century travelling extensively through Jordan, Syria and the Holy Land, disguised as a pilgrim and compiling a unique and scholarly travelogue detailing every facet of the culture and society he encountered along the way. The result is *Travels in Syria and the Holy Land*, which mentions his 'discovery' of Petra (see the boxed text "Ibrahim' Burckhardt' in the Petra chapter for details). *Desert Traveller – The Life of Jean Louis Burckhardt* by Katherine Sim is a good biography of this remarkable traveller.

The redoubtable Englishwoman Gertrude Bell wrote a few memoirs including the fairly dated and light-hearted *The Desert and the Sown* about her travels in the region in the early 20th century.

History & Politics

On Jordan's recent history, there is the somewhat gushing *Hussein of Jordan* by James Lunt. A slightly more serious look at Jordanian history is Kamal Salibi's *The Modern History of Jordan*, spanning from the 1920s to the Gulf Wars. A more academic and dry work is Ma'an Abu Nowar's *The History of the Hashemite Kingdom of Jordan*.

For a look at the country in the broader perspective of its position amongst shaky neighbours, *Jordan in the Middle East: 1948–1985* is an insightful collection of essays edited by Joseph Nevo and Ilan Pappé. *King's Highway* by Graeme Nonnan is a potted history of Jordan, based around the country's historical central positioning.

One of the numerous books about King Hussein is *A Life on the Edge: King Hussein* by Roland Dallas.

Among a couple of general recommended histories of the Arabs is the widely acclaimed work *A History of the Arab Peoples* by Albert Hourani. It's as much an attempt to convey a sense of the evolution of Muslim Arab societies as a straightforward history, with extensive treatment of various aspects of social, cultural and religious life.

Contemporary Middle Eastern affairs are treated in *The Modern Middle East*, edited by Albert Hourani, Phillip Khoury and Mary Wilson. Peter Mansfield has written several works, including *A History of the Middle East*. A unique approach to the subject is *The Longman Companion to the Middle East Since 1914* by Ritchie Ovendale, which presents a series of chronologies, biographies and dictionaries of key names and events; it's a handy reference work.

Readers of French might find Joseph Burlot's *La Civilisation Islamique* a manageable introduction to the history not only of the Arab world but of all those countries that have come under the sway of Islam. Dominique and Janine Sourdel's *La Civilisation de l'Islam Classique* is a more thorough work on the Islamic world in its glory days, from the 9th to the 12th centuries.

General

Religion Some understanding of Islam is essential to understanding Jordan's historical context. The Quran itself might seem daunting, but there are several translations around. AJ Arberry's *The Koran Interpreted* and *The Meaning of the Holy Qur'an* by Abdullah Yusuf Ali are among the better ones. One of the more sensitive and accessible recent accounts of Islamic belief and practice is *Islam: A Short History* by Karen Armstrong. For an eloquent and passionate counterpoint to the stereotypes about Islam, try *Covering Islam* by Edward Said.

Culture & Society For a general look at the life of women in Muslim countries, one introduction worth some time is Wiebke Walther's *Women in Islam: From Medieval to Modern Times*. Also one of the better books around in a genre dominated by sensationalist writing is *Nine Parts of Desire: The Hidden World of Islamic Women* by Geraldine Brooks, which includes an account of the author's encounter with Queen Noor. More academic but nonetheless worthwhile is *Gendering the Middle East: Emerging Perspectives*, a diverse collection of writing edited by Deniz Kandiyoti.

Into the Wadi by Michele Drouart is a readable account of an Australian woman's marriage to a Jordanian man and her attempts to gain a greater understanding of Jordanian society.

Photography *High Above Jordan*, is an unexceptional yet officially sanctioned book of aerial photographs by Jane Taylor (JD20). A classy glossy is *Journey Through Jordan* by Mohammed Amin, Duncan Willetts and Sam Wiley. For a rare look at the Jordan long gone, Malise Ruthuen's *Freya Stark in the Levant* provides a selection of the remarkable British writer's photographs from the region. Stark travelled all over the Middle East and left some 50,000 photos, many dating to early last century.

Flora & Fauna Anyone interested in the flora of Jordan should pick up the detailed *Wildflowers of Jordan and Neighbouring Countries* by Dawud MH Al-Eisawi, with beautiful illustrations and photographs (all captioned in English). *The Birds of the Hashemite Kingdom of Jordan* by Ian J Andrews is the definitive work about our feathered friends. *Wild Mammals of HK Jordan* by Adnan Y Dajani, and *Mammals of the Holy Land* by Mazin Q Qumsiyeh, are comprehensive and colourful.

Arts & Architecture *Treasures from an Ancient Land*, by the renowned Arabist Pitor Bienkowski, specialises in the pottery, sculpture and jewellery of Jordan.

If you're serious about looking for quality rugs, kilims and the like, it could pay to first consult *Oriental Rugs – A Buyer's Guide* by Essie Sakhai; or the identically titled book by Lee Allane. Books dealing with the intricate and complex art form of Arabic calligraphy include *Calligraphy and Islamic Culture*, by Annemarie Schimmel. On a less exalted level, Heather Colyer Ross looks into popular art forms in *The Art of Bedouin Jewellery*, a useful asset for those contemplating buying the stuff.

If you're interested in learning more about Muslim religious architecture and its permutations, *The Mosque*, edited by Martin Frishman and Hasan Uddin Khan, is beautifully illustrated and detailed. Also beautifully illustrated is *Islam: Art & Architecture*, edited by Markus Hattstein and Peter Delius, which is weighty and comprehensive.

NEWSPAPERS & MAGAZINES

Jordan maintains a reasonably free media, although the government does flex its muscle about reports that displease it. According to some journalists in the country, pressure is still exercised from time to time on writers and editors, so the bulk of newspapers (in Arabic and English) tend to push an editorial line curiously similar to the government's position. By regional standards, however, the controls are loose.

The *Jordan Times* (200 fils), the daily (except Saturday) English-language newspaper, has good coverage of events in Jordan, elsewhere in the Middle East and worldwide. The *Star* (500 fils), subtitled 'Jordan's Political, Economic and Cultural Weekly', is similar but published only every Tuesday. It also has a double-page supplement in French called *Le Jourdain*.

Both papers list emergency telephone numbers, relevant anywhere in Jordan; telephone numbers for important government departments and pharmacies in Amman, and hospitals throughout Jordan; arrival and departure times for international and domestic flights; and television programmes for the English- and French-language Channel 2.

Of the many local Arabic daily and weekly newspapers printed in Amman, *Ad-Dustour*, *Al-Ra'i* and *Al-Aswaq* are among the more popular.

Some major European daily newspapers, such as the *International Herald Tribune* (surprisingly reasonable value at JD1.250), *The Times* and *Guardian Weekly* (both from the UK) and *Le Monde* from France (JD1.500) are available in bookshops and upmarket hotels in the capital, and at the two major bookshops in Aqaba. These newspapers are generally not more than two days old, but it can cost as much as JD6 for a copy of the hefty *Sunday Times*.

In addition to the environmental *Al-Reem* magazine (see the boxed text 'Royal Society for the Conservation of Nature' in the Facts About Jordan chapter), it's worth looking out for *Crossing Borders*. This free bimonthly youth magazine is a combined Jordanian-Palestinian-Israeli publication. It's available from Books@café (see Bookshops in the Amman chapter for details).

One stylish lifestyle magazine published in Amman is *Living Well*, which contains, among other features, regular restaurant reviews and insights into middle-class Jordan. Current issues of international magazines, such as *Der Spiegel* from Germany, *Time* and *Newsweek*, are available at major bookshops in Amman and Aqaba, but are not cheap.

RADIO & TV

The Jordanian government maintains more control over local radio and television than it does over the newspapers.

Radio Jordan transmits in English on 96.3 kHz FM (98.7 kHz FM in Aqaba), and 90.0 kHz FM in French. Radio Monte Carlo (74.4FM) broadcasts from Paris (via Cyprus) and features news in French and Arabic, and Western music later in the day. There is an Internet radio station at w www .ammannet.net that broadcasts in Arabic live from Amman.

If you have a short-wave radio, **Voice of America** (w *www.voa.gov*), the **BBC World Service** (w *www.bbc.co.uk*) and most major European stations can be picked up easily. The BBC alters its programming every six

months or so, and the British Council in Amman has the latest information.

Jordan TV broadcasts on three channels. Channels 1 and 3 broadcast in Arabic, and Channel 2 airs bad Australian soap operas, worse American sitcoms, locally produced news (all in English) and documentaries in French. Programmes on Channel 2 run every day from about 4pm to midnight.

Uncensored international satellite stations, such as the BBC, CNN, MTV and Al-Jazeera, are found in the homes of most wealthy Jordanians, all rooms in top-end hotels and many mid-range hotels.

PHOTOGRAPHY & VIDEO
Film & Equipment

Most Western brands of print and slide film are available throughout Jordan, but at tourist sites (especially Petra) the prices are horrendous.

In Amman, Madaba or Aqaba, a roll of Kodak 24/36 print film costs from JD2.500/3, although usually it's a dinar or two more; Fuji and lesser-known brands are a little cheaper. There are plenty of professional photo labs in the major towns where developing a roll of 24 prints costs about JD3, and from JD3.500 for 36 prints. Purchasing a roll of 36 slide film costs anywhere between JD4 and JD7, excluding developing. Developing a roll of 36 slide film (mounted) costs about JD7.500 (next day).

Technical Tips

The single biggest factor to take into account is light. Try to work it so that you have your back to any sources of light (sunlight or artificial); the idea is to have light falling onto your subject.

The sun shines strong and hard in Jordan. Taking pictures in the middle of the day is virtually a guarantee of ending up with glary, washed-out results. Where possible, try to exploit the softer light of the early morning and late afternoon, which enhances subtleties in colour and eliminates problems of glare. If you do need to take shots in bright light use a lens filter. As a rule, 100 ASA film is what you'll need most.

Restrictions

Photography in military zones such as 'strategic areas' like bridges and public buildings is forbidden.

Photographing People

If you take pictures of anything suggesting any degree of squalor, even the activity of the marketplace, it can offend some people's sense of pride, although hostility is rare.

A zoom lens is great for taking people shots, usually without being noticed. Some Jordanians, women in particular, object to being photographed, so ask first. Persisting if your snapping is unwelcome can lead to ugly scenes, so exercise caution and common sense. Children will generally line up to be photographed.

Airport Security

All airports in Jordan have X-ray machines for checking luggage. Despite assurances that the machines are safe for camera film, it's better to keep any unexposed film somewhere where it can be easily removed for examination.

Video

Properly used, a video camera can give a fascinating record of your holiday. Often the most interesting things occur when you're actually intent on filming something else.

Video cameras these days have amazingly sensitive microphones, and you might be surprised how much sound is picked up. This can be a problem if there's a lot of ambient noise; filming by the side of a busy road might seem OK when you do it, but viewing it back home you'll get a deafening cacophony of traffic noise. One good rule to follow for beginners is to film in long takes, and don't move the camera around too much. Otherwise, your video could well make your viewers seasick! If your camera has a stabiliser, you can use it to obtain good footage while travelling on various means of transport, even on bumpy roads. And remember, you're on holiday – don't let the video take over your life, and turn your trip into a Cecil B de Mille production.

Make sure you keep the batteries charged, and have the necessary charger, plugs and transformer for Jordan. It's usually worth buying at least a few cassettes duty free to start off your trip, but blank cassettes are available in major towns in Jordan (from JD3.500 up to JD12 for digital).

Finally, remember to follow the same rules regarding people's sensitivities as for still photography – having a video camera shoved in their face is probably even more annoying and offensive for locals than a still camera. Always ask permission first.

TIME

Despite flirting with a single year-round time zone, Jordan has once again gone back to a system of daylight saving time – clocks move forward one hour around the end of March and then back an hour around the end of September or early October.

Between April and September, when it's midday in Jordan the time elsewhere is:

Los Angeles	2am
New York	5am
London	10am
Paris and Rome	11am
Beirut, Damascus and Tel Aviv	noon
Dubai	1pm
Perth and Hong Kong	5pm
Sydney	7pm
Auckland	9pm

There are no time differences within Jordan.

ELECTRICITY

Jordan's electricity supply is 220V, 50 AC. Sockets are almost universally of the European two-pronged variety, although some places use European three-pronged sockets. Power is generated by the two large oil-fired generating plants in Zarqa and Aqaba, and supply is usually reliable and uninterrupted.

WEIGHTS & MEASURES

Jordan uses the metric system. There is a standard conversion table at the back of this guidebook.

LAUNDRY

In Amman and Aqaba there are plenty of places where washing, dry cleaning and ironing can be done. Look for any place with a sign 'Dry Cleaning', or ask at your hotel.

A pair of trousers or a skirt will cost about 500 fils to wash, a shirt or blouse around 400 fils and a T-shirt about 300 fils. It can take as little as 24 hours, but sometimes longer. Ironing costs extra (negotiable) per item. Underwear and socks cost about 200 fils each to wash, but your 'smalls' can be easily washed in your hotel room, where hot water is available and the dry weather ensures quick drying. If you arrange it through your hotel, be prepared to pay JD3 for a 5kg load. In all cases it comes back smelling better and folded more neatly than you could ever have hoped.

TOILETS

Most hotels and restaurants, except those in the budget category, now have Western-style toilets. Otherwise, you'll be using the hole-in-the-floor (squat) variety. These are theoretically more hygienic because only your covered feet come into contact with anything, but in reality toilets in most communal hotel bathrooms, and all public toilets, are grotty, and the sewerage system always seems inadequate.

It does take a little while to master the squatting technique without losing everything from your pockets. There is always a tap and/or hose at a convenient height if you wish to adopt the local habit of using your left hand and water – whether any water comes out is something else again! Toilet paper is rarely offered, except in the mid-range and top-end hotels and restaurants, but is widely available in shops throughout Jordan. Please remember that the little basket usually provided in the toilet is for toilet paper; use it or the toilet's contents will return to you as an overflow on the floor.

A few public toilets in the larger cities are indicated on the maps in this guidebook. These are to be avoided except in cases of emergency.

HEALTH

Travel health depends on your predeparture preparations, your daily health care while travelling and how you handle any medical problem that does develop. While the potential dangers can seem quite frightening, in reality few travellers to Jordan experience anything more than an upset stomach.

Predeparture planning

Immunisations Plan ahead for getting your vaccinations: some of them require more than one injection, while some vaccinations should not be given together. Note that some vaccinations should not be given during pregnancy or to people with allergies – discuss this with your doctor.

It's recommended that you seek medical advice at least six weeks before travel. Be aware that there is often a greater risk of disease with children and during pregnancy.

Medical Kit Check List

The following is a list of items you should consider including in your medical kit – consult your pharmacist for brands available in your country.

☐ **Aspirin or paracetamol (acetaminophen in the USA)** – for pain or fever
☐ **Antihistamine** – for allergies, eg, hay fever; to ease the itch from insect bites or stings; and to prevent motion sickness
☐ **Cold and flu tablets, throat lozenges and nasal decongestant**
☐ **Multivitamins** – consider for long trips, when dietary vitamin intake may be inadequate
☐ **Antibiotics** – consider including these if you're travelling well off the beaten track; see your doctor, as they must be prescribed, and carry the prescription with you
☐ **Loperamide or diphenoxylate** – 'blockers' for diarrhoea
☐ **Prochlorperazine or metaclopramide** – for nausea and vomiting
☐ **Rehydration mixture** – to prevent dehydration, which may occur during bouts of diarrhoea; particularly important when travelling with children
☐ **Insect repellent, sunscreen, lip balm and eye drops**
☐ **Calamine lotion, sting relief spray or aloe vera** – to ease irritation from sunburn and insect bites or stings
☐ **Antifungal cream or powder** – for fungal skin infections and thrush
☐ **Antiseptic (such as povidone-iodine)** – for cuts and grazes
☐ **Bandages, Band-Aids (plasters) and other wound dressings**
☐ **Water purification tablets or iodine**
☐ **Scissors, tweezers and a thermometer** – note that mercury thermometers are prohibited by airlines
☐ **Syringes and needles** – in case you need injections; ask your doctor for a note explaining why you have them

Discuss your requirements with your doctor, but vaccinations you should consider for this trip include the following (for more details about the diseases, see the individual disease entries later in this section). Carry proof of your vaccinations, especially yellow fever; a condition of entry to Jordan is proof of yellow fever vaccination if you're coming from infected areas such as sub-Saharan Africa, and parts of South America.

Diphtheria & Tetanus Vaccinations for these two diseases are usually combined and are recommended for everyone. After an initial course of three injections (usually given in childhood), boosters are necessary every 10 years.

Polio Everyone should keep up to date with this vaccination, which is normally given in childhood. A booster every 10 years maintains immunity.

Hepatitis A Hepatitis A vaccine (eg, Avaxim, Havrix 1440 or VAQTA) provides long-term immunity (possibly for more than 10 years) after an initial injection and a booster at six to 12 months.

Alternatively, an injection of gamma globulin can provide short-term protection against hepatitis A – two to six months, depending on the dose. It's not a vaccine, but a ready-made antibody collected from blood donations. It's reasonably effective and, unlike the vaccine, it's protective immediately, but because it is a blood product, there are current concerns about its long-term safety.

Hepatitis A vaccine is also available in a combined form, Twinrix, with hepatitis B vaccine. Three injections over a six-month period are required, the first two providing substantial protection against hepatitis A.

Typhoid Vaccination against typhoid is recommended if you're travelling for more than a couple of weeks in Jordan. It's now available either as an injection or as capsules to be taken orally.

Hepatitis B Travellers on a long trip, and those for whom sexual contact or needle sharing is a possibility, should consider vaccination against hepatitis B. The US Centers for Disease Control says the level of hepatitis B is high in Jordan. Vaccination generally involves three injections, with a booster available at 12 months. More rapid courses are often available if required.

Health Insurance
Make sure that you have adequate health insurance. See Travel Insurance under Visas & Documents earlier in this chapter for details.

Travel Health Guides
Travel with Children from Lonely Planet includes advice on travel health for younger children. There are also a number of excellent travel health sites on the Internet. From the Lonely Planet home page there are links at **w** www.lonelyplanet.com/weblinks/wl heal.htm to the World Health Organization and the US Centers for Disease Control & Prevention.

Other Preparations
Make sure you're healthy before you start travelling. If you require a particular medication take an adequate supply, as it may not be available in Jordan. Take part of the packaging showing the generic name rather than the brand, which will make getting replacements easier. To avoid any problems, it's a good idea to have a legible prescription or letter from your doctor to show that you legally use the medication.

Basic Rules
Food In Jordan, most restaurants are clean and the chances of getting sick from unhygienic food handling and preparation (as opposed to getting sick simply from a change in diet) are slim. Beware of ice cream that is sold in the street or anywhere it might have been melted and refrozen; if there's any doubt (eg, a power cut in the last day or two), steer well clear. You should avoid shellfish such as mussels, oysters and clams, as well as undercooked meat, particularly in the form of mince. Steaming does not make shellfish safe for eating.

Generally, if a place looks clean and well run, and the vendor looks clean and healthy, then the food is probably safe. Places that are packed with locals will be fine, while empty restaurants are questionable. The food in busy restaurants is cooked and eaten quite quickly with little standing around, and is probably not reheated.

Water Generally, the number one rule for travelling in the region is to be careful of the water, and especially ice. If you don't know for certain that the water is safe, assume the worst. Reputable brands of bottled water or soft drink are generally fine. Milk should be treated with suspicion because it's sometimes unpasteurised, although boiled milk is fine if it's kept hygienically.

Tea or coffee should also be OK, because the water should have been boiled.

Tap water in Jordan is generally safe to drink, but health scares (often only reported after the event) have occurred from time to time so it's better to stick to bottled water. In the Jordan Valley, amoebic dysentery can be a problem. It always pays to add a water purification tablet or two (see later) to the tap water; this way you avoid buying masses of expensive nonbiodegradable plastic bottles of mineral water.

Water Purification The simplest way of purifying water is to boil it thoroughly. Vigorous boiling should be satisfactory.

Consider purchasing a water filter for a long trip. There are two main kinds of filter. Total filters take out all parasites, bacteria and viruses, and make water safe to drink. They're often expensive, but they can be more cost-effective than buying bottled water. Simple filters (which can even be a nylon mesh bag) take out dirt and larger foreign bodies from the water so that chemical solutions work much more effectively; but simple filtering will not remove all dangerous organisms. Remember also that to operate effectively, a water filter must be regularly maintained; a poorly maintained filter can be a breeding ground for germs.

Chlorine tablets will kill many pathogens, but not parasites like giardia and amoebic cysts. Iodine is more effective in purifying water and is available in tablet form. Follow the directions carefully and remember that too much iodine can be harmful.

Medical Problems & Treatment

Self-diagnosis and treatment can be risky, so you should always seek medical help. An embassy, consulate or five-star hotel can usually recommend a local doctor or clinic. Bear in mind that your embassy is *not* an alternative to a good travel insurance policy.

Although we do give drug dosages in this section, they are for emergency use only. Correct diagnosis is vital. In this section we have used the generic names for medications – check with a pharmacist for brands available locally.

Note that antibiotics should ideally be administered only under medical supervision. Take only the recommended dose at the prescribed intervals and use the whole course,

even if the illness seems to be cured earlier. Stop immediately if there are any reactions, and don't use the antibiotic if you're not sure that you have the correct one. Some people are allergic to commonly prescribed antibiotics such as penicillin; carry this information (eg, on a bracelet) when travelling.

There are modern, well-equipped public hospitals in Amman, Irbid, Aqaba and Karak; smaller hospitals in Madaba, Ramtha and Zarqa; and basic health centres in most other towns. Jordan also boasts over 50 private hospitals, which cater primarily to patients from neighbouring countries, who are attracted by the lower medical costs.

Most towns have well-stocked pharmacies, but always check the expiry date of any medicine you buy in Jordan. It's better to bring any unusual or important medical items with you from home, and always bring a copy of a prescription. The telephone numbers for pharmacies (including those open at night) in Amman and Irbid, and for hospitals in Amman, Zarqa, Irbid and Aqaba, are listed in the two English-language newspapers. All doctors (and most pharmacists) who have studied in Jordan speak English because medicine is taught in English at Jordanian universities, and many have studied abroad. Dental surgeries are also fairly modern and well equipped.

Environmental Hazards

Despite the warnings, some visitors get themselves into trouble hiking through the desert in the heat of the day, especially around Wadi Rum. Please read the section below carefully.

Heat Exhaustion Dehydration and salt deficiency can cause heat exhaustion. Take time to acclimatise to high temperatures, drink sufficient liquids and do not do anything too physically demanding. Salt deficiency is characterised by fatigue, lethargy, headaches, giddiness and muscle cramps; salt tablets may help, but adding extra salt to your food is better.

Anhidrotic heat exhaustion is a rare form of heat exhaustion that is caused by an inability to sweat. It tends to affect people who have been in a hot climate for some time, rather than newcomers. It can progress to heatstroke. Treatment involves removal to a cooler climate.

Heatstroke This serious, and occasionally fatal, condition can occur if your body's heat-regulating mechanism breaks down and the body temperature rises to dangerous levels. Long, continuous periods of exposure to high temperatures and insufficient fluids can leave you vulnerable to heatstroke.

The symptoms are feeling unwell, not sweating very much (or at all) and a high body temperature (39°C to 41°C or 102°F to 106°F). Where sweating has ceased, the skin becomes flushed and red. Severe, throbbing headaches and lack of coordination will also occur, and the sufferer may be confused or aggressive. Eventually the victim will become delirious or convulse. Hospitalisation is essential, but in the interim get victims out of the sun, remove their clothing, cover them with a wet sheet or towel and then fan continually. Give fluids if they are conscious.

Hypothermia Too much cold can be just as dangerous as too much heat. In winter – especially around Amman and northern Jordan – and at night any time of the year in the desert, you should always be prepared for cold, wet or windy conditions, even if you're just out walking or hitching.

Hypothermia occurs when the body loses heat faster than it can produce it and the core temperature of the body falls. It's surprisingly easy to progress from very cold to dangerously cold due to a combination of wind, wet clothing, fatigue and hunger, even if the air temperature is above freezing. It's best to dress in layers; silk, wool and some of the new artificial fibres are all good insulating materials. A hat is important, as a lot of heat is lost through the head. A strong, waterproof outer layer (and a 'space' blanket for emergencies) is essential. Carry basic supplies, including food containing simple sugars to generate heat quickly and fluid to drink.

Symptoms of hypothermia are exhaustion, numb skin (particularly toes and fingers), shivering, slurred speech, irrational or violent behaviour, lethargy, stumbling, dizzy spells, muscle cramps and violent bursts of energy. Irrationality may take the form of sufferers claiming they're warm and trying to take off their clothes.

To treat mild hypothermia, first get the person out of the wind and/or rain, remove their clothing if it's wet and replace it with dry, warm clothing. Give them hot liquids – not alcohol – and some high-kilojoule, easily digestible food. Do not rub victims: instead, allow them to slowly warm themselves. This should be enough to treat the early stages of hypothermia. The early treatment of mild hypothermia is the only way to prevent severe hypothermia, which is a critical condition.

Diving, Snorkelling & Swimming Stonefish have a very nasty habit of lying half-submerged in the sand, so wear something on your feet if you're walking into the sea (as opposed to jumping into the deep water from a jetty or boat). If stung by a stonefish, see a doctor immediately. Other nasty creatures to avoid are lionfish which, like the stonefish, have poisonous spikes, and jellyfish, whose sting can be painful. If stung by a jellyfish, douse the rash in vinegar to deactivate any stingers which have not 'fired'. Calamine lotion, antihistamines and analgesics (and urine) may reduce the reaction and relieve the pain. See Cuts & Scratches later in this chapter for information about coral cuts.

It is important to remember that if you dive to any depth, it is dangerous to go to certain altitudes until six hours have elapsed. This includes the road to Petra and most roads out of Aqaba. Deeper dives require an even longer time period.

Aqaba has an excellent hospital where cuts, bites and stings can be treated. Most importantly, it has decompression chambers for the 'bends'.

Prickly Heat Prickly heat is an itchy rash caused by excessive perspiration trapped under the skin. It usually strikes people who have just arrived in a hot climate. Keeping cool, bathing often, drying the skin and using a mild talcum or prickly heat powder or resorting to air-conditioning may help.

Infectious Diseases

Diarrhoea Simple things like a change of water, food or climate can all cause a mild bout of diarrhoea, but a few rushed toilet trips with no other symptoms is not indicative of a major problem.

Dehydration is the main danger with any diarrhoea, particularly in children or the elderly as dehydration can occur quite quickly. Under all circumstances *fluid replacement* is the most important thing to remember. Weak black tea with a little sugar, soda water, or soft drinks allowed to go flat and diluted 50% with clean water are all good. With severe diarrhoea, a rehydrating solution is preferable to replace minerals and salts lost. Commercially available oral rehydration salts (ORS) are very useful; add them to boiled or bottled water. In an emergency you can make up a solution of six teaspoons of sugar and a half teaspoon of salt to a litre of boiled or bottled water. You need to drink at least the same volume of fluid that you're losing in bowel movements and vomiting. Urine is the best guide to the adequacy of replacement – if you have small amounts of concentrated urine, you need to drink more. Keep drinking small amounts often. Stick to a bland diet as you recover.

Gut-paralysing drugs such as loperamide or diphenoxylate can be used to bring relief from the symptoms, although they do not cure the problem. Only use these drugs if you do not have access to toilets, eg, if you *must* travel. Note that these drugs are not recommended for children under 12 years.

In certain situations, antibiotics may be required: diarrhoea with blood or mucus (dysentery), any diarrhoea with fever, profuse watery diarrhoea, persistent diarrhoea not improving after 48 hours and severe diarrhoea. These suggest a more serious cause of diarrhoea, and gut-paralysing drugs should be avoided.

In these situations, a stool test may be necessary to diagnose the cause, so you should seek medical help urgently. Where this is not possible the recommended drugs for bacterial diarrhoea (the most likely cause of severe diarrhoea in travellers) are norfloxacin 400mg twice daily for three days or ciprofloxacin 500mg twice daily for five days. These drugs are not recommended for children or pregnant women. The drug for children is co-trimoxazole, with dosage dependent on weight. A five-day course is given. Ampicillin or amoxycillin may be given to pregnant women, but medical care is necessary.

Two other causes of persistent diarrhoea in travellers are giardiasis and amoebic dysentery. **Giardiasis** is caused by a common parasite, *Giardia lamblia*. Symptoms include stomach cramps, nausea, a bloated stomach, watery, foul-smelling diarrhoea and frequent gas. Giardiasis can appear several weeks after you have been exposed to the parasite. The symptoms may disappear for a few days and then return; this can go on for several weeks.

Amoebic dysentery, caused by the protozoan *Entamoeba histolytica*, is characterised by a gradual onset of low-grade diarrhoea, often with blood and mucus. Cramping abdominal pain and vomiting are less likely than in other types of diarrhoea, and fever may not be present. It will persist until treated and can recur and cause other health problems.

You should seek medical advice if you think you have giardiasis or amoebic dysentery, but where this is not possible, tinidazole or metronidazole are the recommended drugs. Treatment is a 2g single dose of tinidazole or 250mg of metronidazole three times daily for five to 10 days.

Fungal Infections Fungal infections occur more commonly in hot weather and are usually found on the scalp, between the toes ('athlete's foot') or fingers, in the groin and on the body (ringworm). Ringworm (which is a fungal infection, not a worm) is caught from infected animals or other people. Moisture encourages these infections.

To prevent fungal infections wear loose, comfortable clothes, avoid artificial fibres, wash frequently and dry yourself carefully. If you do get an infection, wash the infected area at least daily with a disinfectant or medicated soap and water, and rinse and dry well. Apply an antifungal cream or powder like tolnaftate. Try to expose the infected area to air or sunlight as much as possible and wash all towels and underwear in hot water, change them often and let them dry in the sun.

Hepatitis A common disease worldwide, hepatitis is a general term for inflammation of the liver. There are several different viruses that cause h epatitis, and they differ in the way that they're transmitted. The symptoms are similar in all forms of the illness, and include fever, chills, headache, fatigue, feelings of weakness and aches and pains, followed by loss of appetite, nausea, vomiting, abdominal pain, dark urine, light-coloured faeces, jaundiced (yellow) skin and yellowing of the whites of the eyes. People who have had hepatitis should avoid alcohol for some time after the illness, as the liver needs time to recover.

Hepatitis A is transmitted by contaminated food and drinking water. You should seek medical advice, but there's not much you can do apart from resting, drinking lots of fluids, eating lightly and avoiding fatty foods. Hepatitis E is transmitted in the same way as hepatitis A; it can be particularly serious in pregnant women.

There are almost 300 million chronic carriers of hepatitis B in the world. It's spread via contact with infected blood, blood products or body fluids, for example through sexual contact, unsterilised needles and blood transfusions, or contact with blood via small breaks in the skin. Other risk situations include having a shave, tattoo or body piercing with contaminated equipment. The symptoms of hepatitis B may be more severe than type A and the disease can lead to long-term problems such as chronic liver damage, liver cancer or a long-term carrier state. Hepatitis C and D are spread in the same way as hepatitis B and can also lead to long term complications.

There are vaccines against hepatitis A and B, but there are currently no vaccines against the other types of hepatitis. Following the basic rules about food and water (hepatitis A and E) and avoiding risk situations (hepatitis B, C and D) are important preventative measures.

HIV & AIDS Infection with the human immunodeficiency virus (HIV) may lead to acquired immune deficiency syndrome (AIDS), which is a fatal disease. Any exposure to blood, blood products or body fluids may put the individual at risk. The disease is often transmitted through sexual contact or dirty needles – vaccinations, acupuncture, tattooing and body piercing can be potentially as dangerous as intravenous drug use. HIV/AIDS can also be spread through infected blood transfusions. Some developing countries cannot afford to screen blood used for transfusions, but the medical system in Jordan is fairly developed and doctors are well trained.

If you do need an injection, ask to see the syringe unwrapped in front of you, or take a needle and syringe pack with you. Fear of HIV infection should never preclude treatment for serious medical conditions.

Reliable figures aren't available about the number of people in Jordan with HIV or AIDS, but given the strict taboos in Jordanian society about drugs, homosexuality and promiscuity, the disease is relatively rare. Contracting HIV through a blood transfusion is about as unlikely as in most Western countries, and anyone needing serious surgery will probably be sent home anyway.

Sexually Transmitted Infections HIV/AIDS and hepatitis B can be transmitted through sexual contact – see earlier in this chapter for details. Other STIs include gonorrhoea, herpes and syphilis; sores, blisters or rashes around the genitals and discharges or pain when urinating are common symptoms. In some STIs, such as wart virus or chlamydia, symptoms may be less marked or not observed at all, especially in women. Chlamydia infection can cause infertility in men and women before any symptoms are noticed. Syphilis symptoms eventually disappear completely, but the disease continues and can cause severe problems in later years. While abstinence from sexual contact is the only 100% effective prevention, using condoms is also effective. The treatment of gonorrhoea and syphilis is with antibiotics. The different sexually transmitted diseases each require specific antibiotics.

Typhoid A dangerous gut infection, typhoid is caused by contaminated water and food. Medical help must be sought. In its early stages, sufferers may feel they have a bad cold or flu on the way, as early symptoms are a headache, body aches and a fever which rises a little each day until it's around 40°C (104°F) or more. The victim's pulse is often slow relative to the degree of fever present – unlike a normal fever where the pulse increases. In addition, there may be vomiting, abdominal pain, diarrhoea or constipation.

In the second week, the high fever and slow pulse continue and a few pink spots may appear on the body; trembling, delirium, weakness, weight loss and dehydration may occur. Complications such as pneumonia, perforated bowel or meningitis may ensue.

Cuts, Bites & Stings
See the following Less Common Diseases section for details of rabies, which is passed through animal bites.

Cuts & Scratches Wash well and treat with an antiseptic such as povidone-iodine. Where possible avoid bandages and Band-Aids, which can keep wounds wet. Coral cuts are notoriously slow to heal and if they're not adequately cleaned, small pieces of coral can become embedded in the wound.

Bites & Stings Bee and wasp stings are usually painful rather than dangerous. However, in people who are allergic to them severe breathing difficulties may occur and require urgent medical care. Calamine lotion or a sting relief spray will give relief and ice packs will reduce the pain and swelling. There are some spiders with dangerous bites, but antivenins are usually available. Scorpion stings are notoriously painful and in Jordan can actually be fatal. Scorpions often shelter in shoes or clothing.

Snakes To minimise your chances of being bitten always wear boots, socks and long trousers when walking through undergrowth where snakes may be present. Don't put your hands into holes and crevices, and be careful when collecting firewood.

Snake bites do not cause instantaneous death, and antivenins are usually available. Immediately wrap the bitten limb tightly, as you would for a sprained ankle, and then attach a splint to immobilise it. Keep the victim still and seek medical help. Tourniquets and sucking out the poison are now comprehensively discredited.

Less Common Diseases
The following diseases pose a small risk to travellers, and so are only mentioned in passing. Seek medical advice if you think you may have any of these diseases.

Rabies This fatal viral infection is found in many countries, but is rare in Jordan. Many animals can be infected (such as dogs, cats, bats and monkeys) and it's their saliva which is infectious. Any bite, scratch or even lick from an animal should be cleaned immediately and thoroughly. Scrub with soap and running water, and then apply alcohol or iodine solution. Medical help should be sought promptly to receive a course of injections to prevent the onset of symptoms and possible death.

Tetanus This disease is caused by a germ which lives in soil and in the faeces of horses and other animals. It enters the body via breaks in the skin. The first symptom may be discomfort in swallowing, or stiffening of the jaw and neck; this is followed by painful convulsions of the jaw and whole body. The disease can be fatal, but can be prevented by vaccination.

Women's Health
Gynaecological Problems Antibiotics, synthetic underwear, sweating and contraceptive pills can all lead to fungal vaginal infections, especially when travelling in hot climates. Fungal infections are characterised by a rash, itch and discharge and can be treated with a vinegar or lemon-juice douche, or with yoghurt. Nystatin, miconazole or clotrimazole pessaries or vaginal cream are the usual treatments. Maintaining good personal hygiene and wearing loose-fitting clothes and cotton underwear may help prevent these infections.

Sexually transmitted infections are a major cause of vaginal problems. Symptoms include a smelly discharge, painful intercourse and, sometimes, a burning sensation when urinating. Medical attention should be sought and male sexual partners must also be treated. For more details see the section on Sexually Transmitted Infections earlier in this chapter. Besides abstinence, the best thing is to use condoms.

Pregnancy It is generally fine to travel to Jordan while pregnant, but check your travel plans with your doctor and ask for details of the side effects of any vaccinations as many normally used to prevent serious diseases are not advisable during pregnancy. In addition, some diseases are much more serious (and may increase the risk of a stillborn child) for pregnant women.

SOCIAL GRACES
Etiquette is very important in Jordanian (and Arab) culture, and you'll find that Jordanians will respect you more if you follow these few simple rules:

- Stand when someone important, or another guest, enters the room
- Shake hands with everyone – but only with a Jordanian woman if she offers her hand first

- Do not sit so that the soles of your feet point to anyone
- Never accept any present or service of any kind without first politely refusing twice
- Don't engage in any conversation about sensitive topics (eg, the Jordanian royal family or Judaism) unless you are in private with a person you know well
- An unaccompanied foreign man should not sit next to an unaccompanied Jordanian woman in public transport, unless it's unavoidable
- Remove your shoes when visiting a mosque, or a private house (unless you're specifically told to keep them on)
- Never walk in front of, or interrupt in any way, someone praying towards Mecca
- Foreign couples should not hold hands, or show any signs of affection, in public

Dress

Immodest dress is still a major source of irritation to locals and can often lead to trouble for women.

Do dress appropriately: men can get around in shorts without eliciting much of a response, but women are advised to wear at least knee-length dresses or loose pants and cover the shoulders. Both sexes should always be well covered when entering mosques.

Flouting local sensitivities about dress not only gets the individuals concerned unwanted attention, it also colours the way locals perceive other travellers.

That said, some areas of eastern Amman (such as Shmeisani and Abdoun which are home to trendy nightclubs and cafés) are barely distinguishable from their counterparts in Western cities. There, and only there, will Western women and couples feel comfortable behaving and dressing as they would at home.

WOMEN TRAVELLERS

As a woman travelling alone around Jordan for three weeks, I have found the people only helpful, hospitable and friendly.

K Millar, UK

Attitudes Towards Women

Attitudes to foreign women in Jordan, and throughout much of the Middle East, can be trying to say the least. The reasons for this are complex and, of course, it would be foolish to lump everyone together into the same category. These largely Muslim societies are, by contemporary Western standards, quite conservative when it comes to sex and women, and most men have little or no contact with either before marriage – you'll soon discover that your marital status (whether you're male or female) is a source of considerable interest to pretty much anyone you meet. 'Are you married?' usually figures among the first five standard questions Jordanians put to foreigners.

Western movies and TV also give some men in these countries the impression that all western women are promiscuous and will jump into bed at the drop of a hat.

Safety Precautions

There will probably be times when you have male company that you could well live without. This may go no further than irritating banter or proposals of marriage and even declarations of undying love. Harassment can also take the form of leering, sometimes being followed and occasionally being touched up.

You cannot make this problem go away and, where possible, you should try to ignore it or you'll end up letting a few sad individuals spoil your whole trip. Plenty of women travel through Jordan, often alone, and never encounter serious problems, so please do not become paranoid.

The first rule of thumb is to respect standard Muslim sensibilities about dress – cover the shoulders, upper arms and legs, at least. This is not a magic formula, but it will certainly help. Some women go to the extent of covering their head as well, although this makes little difference, and is not necessary in Jordan. Bear in mind that smaller towns tend to be more conservative than big cities like Amman, and smaller towns are generally more relaxed than tiny villages in the countryside.

Female travellers have reported varying degrees of harassment from local lads on the public beaches in and near Aqaba. Bikinis are permitted on the private beaches run by the hotels and diving centres (where harassment is also common), but elsewhere in Aqaba, and along the Dead Sea (except at the swimming pools at the upmarket hotels), dress conservatively – ie, baggy shorts and loose tops, even when swimming. Never go topless.

Avoid eye contact with any man you don't know (wearing dark glasses can help);

and try to ignore any rude remarks. Some women also find it's not worth summoning up the energy to acknowledge, for example, being brushed up against. This is not to say that you should simply let everything go unremarked, and some behaviour may well warrant a good public scene. You'll be surprised how quickly bystanders will take matters into hand if they feel one of their own has overstepped the mark.

If you have to say anything to ward off an advance, *imshi* (clear off) should do the trick. A wedding ring will add to your respectability in Arab eyes, but a photo of your children and even husband can clinch it – if you don't have any, borrow a picture of your nephew and/or niece.

Particular mention should also be made of Wadi Musa (near Petra): Women should carefully choose their accommodation in this town as we have received many reports of harassment, from peeping toms to serious sexual assault. See the boxed text 'Warning' in the Petra chapter for more details.

Lastly, some advice for single female travellers from single female readers: don't go to any bar unaccompanied; don't sit in the front seat of a chartered private or service taxi; on public transport do sit next to a women if possible; don't venture alone to remote regions of vast archaeological sites such as Petra – including Siq Barid (Little Petra) – and Jerash; always check for peep holes in rooms and bathrooms (particularly cigarette holes in curtains); and always place a chair against your locked hotel room door in case of 'accidental' late-night intrusions.

If you suffer any harassment go to a police station, or a tourist police booth, which can be found at most sites visited by tourists. The tourist police in Jordan *do* take any reports seriously. Should the need arise, do not hesitate to call the nationwide emergency number (☎ 80022228) for tourists, which is staffed by English-speaking police officers.

Restaurants, Bars & Cafés

Some activities, such as sitting in cafés, are usually seen as a male preserve and although it's quite OK for Western women to enter, in some places the stares may make you feel uncomfortable.

A few restaurants have a 'family section' where any local and foreign women, unaccompanied by men, can eat in peace. As a rule, mixed foreign groups have no trouble wherever they sit, including in the tea shops and bars. In some of the local bars and cafés there is only one toilet, so try to avoid using these if only for the inevitable smell and lack of hygiene. A few bars and cafés in Amman where women are welcome are listed in the Amman chapter.

Hotels

In theory, the chances of getting harassed are far greater in budget hotels where there are more local male guests, male hangers-on come and go with little or no control, and mostly male staff are rarely hired for their compassion.

Below is a list of the budget hotels in the major towns which have been recommended by single female travellers:

Amman Farah Hotel; Cliff Hotel; Merryland Hotel; Palace Hotel; Karnak Hotel
Aqaba Al-Naher al-Khaled Hotel; Jordan Flower Hotel; Dweikh Hotel I; Bedouin Garden Village; Mermaid Camp
Azraq Best avoided because a lot of Saudi and Iraqi truck drivers stop in Azraq town, although the mid-range Azraq Lodge is fine
Irbid Al-Ameen al-Kabeer Hotel; Omayed Hotel
Karak There are no particularly safe budget places, so try the mid-priced Al-Mujeb Hotel or Karak Rest House
Madaba Mariam Hotel; Black Iris Hotel; Lulu's Pension B&B
Wadi Musa (near Petra) Al-Anbat Hotel I; Cleopetra Hotel; Mussa Spring Hotel
Wadi Rum Camping alone in the desert would be foolhardy, so it's better to stay at the campground at the Government Rest House (staffed by loads of single local men and never entirely safe)

GAY & LESBIAN TRAVELLERS

Homosexuality is prohibited in Jordan, and conviction can result in imprisonment. The public position on homosexuality is that it doesn't really exist. This is not to say that it doesn't, but Jordan is not an ideal place to 'come out'. There is a very underground gay scene in Amman, so if you're keen to explore it make very discreet enquiries. Public displays of affection by heterosexuals are frowned upon, and the same rules apply to gays and lesbians, although two men or two women holding hands is a normal sign of friendship.

There are a few places in Amman that are gay-friendly, such as the multipurpose Books@café (see Bookshops and Places to Eat in the Amman chapter). Thursday nights at the Irish Pub or the trendy cafés in Abdoun, such as the Blue Fig Café (see Entertainment in the Amman chapter), pull in a young, mixed, but discreet gay and straight crowd.

DISABLED TRAVELLERS

In late 2000, Jordan celebrated its first ever Olympic gold medal by the female athlete Maha Barghouthi in the Sydney Paralympics. Jordanians are very proud of this achievement and it threw the spotlight onto people with disabilities. The benefits of this will take a long time to filter through and for now Jordan is still not a great place for disabled travellers. Although Jordanians are happy to help anyone with a disability, the cities are crowded and the traffic is chaotic, and visiting tourist attractions, such as the vast archaeological sites of Petra and Jerash, involves lots of walking on uneven ground.

The Jordanian government recently legislated that wheelchair access must be added to all new public buildings, but nothing will ever be done to accommodate wheelchairs elsewhere. The only concession to the incapacitated is the horse-drawn carriage (mostly used by weary but able-bodied walkers), which is tolerated as transport for disabled visitors part of the way into Petra. Some travellers with a disability have reported having little difficulty getting around most of Petra on a combination of donkey, horse and carriage.

The Royal Diving Club, south of Aqaba, is a member of the Access to Marine Conservation for All (AMCA) initiative to enable people with disabilities to enjoy scuba diving and snorkelling. The centre's involvement is still in its infancy so contact them (details are in the Southern Desert & Aqaba chapter) or **AMCA** directly in the UK (☎ 020 8294 1515, fax 8850 1918; e a.m.c.a@btopenworld.com).

SENIOR TRAVELLERS

There is no reason why any senior traveller could not travel independently, as long as they take obvious precautions: avoid visiting in the height of summer; don't walk about in the heat of the day; use chartered taxis or rented cars rather than crowded

public transport; and stay in decent hotels on the ground floor (budget hotels are often upstairs, and rarely have lifts). Senior travellers may prefer to join an organised tour from their home country. If you have special needs, be sure to tell the tour operator.

Although the medical system in Jordan is good, bring any medication you need, and prescriptions from home.

TRAVEL WITH CHILDREN

Taking the kids adds another dimension to a trip in Jordan, and of course it's not all fun and games. First, it's a good idea to avoid coming in the summer because the extreme heat could really make your family journey quite unpleasant. With very young children in particular, you'll find yourself having to moderate the pace. Keeping them happy, well fed and clean is the main challenge.

Always take along a bag of small gadgets and a favourite teddy bear or the like to keep junior amused, especially while on public transport. Luckily, you'll rarely have to embark on really long journeys in Jordan, and chartering a taxi or renting a car is easy, so this shouldn't pose too great a problem.

Fresh and powdered milk is available; otherwise, stick to bottled mineral water. Kids already eating solids shouldn't have many problems. Cooked meat dishes, the various dips (such as hummus), rice and the occasional more or less Western-style burger or pizza, along with fruit (washed and peeled) should all be OK as a nutritional basis. Nuts are also a safe, common and cheap source of protein.

With infants, the next problem is cleanliness. It's impractical to carry more than about a half dozen washable nappies with you, but disposable ones are not so easy to come by. As for accommodation, you'll want a private bathroom and hot water.

The good news is that children are as loved in Jordan as anywhere else in the Middle East. Few people bring their young ones to this part of the world, so you'll find that your kids are quite a hit. In that way they can help break the ice and open the doors to contact with local people with whom you might never have exchanged glances.

Some of the more interesting attractions for the kids will be visiting the beaches and snorkelling at Aqaba, exploring castles at Karak, Shobak and Ajlun, riding a camel at

Wadi Rum, floating in the Dead Sea, and walking and enjoying picnics in a few of the national reserves. A list of things to see and do with children in and around Amman is included in the Activities section of the Amman chapter.

For more comprehensive advice about travelling with children, pick up a copy of Lonely Planet's *Travel with Children* by Cathy Lanigan.

USEFUL ORGANISATIONS
Below is a list of some organisations that may be useful; others are listed in the relevant sections throughout this book. All are located in Amman (☎ 06).

Amman Chamber of Commerce	☎ 5666151
Department of Antiquities	☎ 4644714
General Union of Voluntary Societies	☎ 4639555
Jordanian Red Crescent	☎ 4773141
Ministry of Foreign Affairs	☎ 4644361
Ministry of Interior	☎ 5622811
Royal Automobile Club of Jordan	☎ 5850637
Royal Society of Fine Arts	☎ 4630128
UNHCR	☎ 5930395
Unicef	☎ 4629571
WHO	☎ 5684651

DANGERS & ANNOYANCES
Jordan is very safe to visit and travel around; remarkably so considering the turmoil, restrictions and difficulties in other nearby countries. The best general advice for all travellers is to take care – but not to be paranoid. Women who have travelled through places like Turkey will probably find that Jordan is comparatively relaxed and hassle free – but women who have not visited the region before may be annoyed at the leering and possible harassment from local men. Women should be careful at the budget hotels in Wadi Musa (near Petra) – see the boxed text 'Warning' in the Petra chapter.

It is always a good idea to check the prevailing security situation before commencing your journey. In this respect, it's worth checking out the websites of Western governments, including the US Department of State (ⓦ www.travel.state.gov/travel _warnings.html), the UK Foreign and Commonwealth Office (ⓦ www.fco.gov.uk/ travel/) or the Australian Department of Foreign Affairs and Trade (ⓦ www.dfat.gov .au/consular/advice/).

Traffic
The traffic in Amman (especially in Downtown) is appalling, but probably no worse than any other major city in the region. If you're renting a car in Jordan, avoid driving anywhere near Amman. Although most travellers who drive around Jordan encounter few problems, drivers must take special care when driving on the kingdom's roads as the accident rate is high.

For the special challenges faced by pedestrians, see the boxed text 'Crossing the Street in Amman' in the Amman chapter.

Public Disorder
During rare political or economic crises (such as an increase in the price of staple goods), occasional impromptu protests and acts of civil disobedience can occur. There are also frequent demonstrations in support of the Palestinians. These most often take place in Karak, Tafila and Ma'an, and the university areas of Irbid, Mu'tah and northern Amman are sometimes volatile.

Foreigners are never targeted during these protests, but you should avoid becoming involved, and stay away from areas where protests are taking place. The best sources of current information are the English-language newspapers published in Amman; or your embassy or consulate in Jordan.

Theft & Crime
Theft is usually no problem for people who take reasonable care. Leaving your bag under the watchful eye of a member of staff in the office of a bus station or hotel for a few hours should be no cause for concern. Shared rooms in hotels are also quite OK as a rule, but don't take unnecessary risks, and it can be a good idea to keep your luggage secured with a padlock. Be careful very late at night outside nightclubs in Amman patronised by intoxicated, vulnerable and comparatively wealthy foreigners.

The military keep a low profile and you'd be unlikely to experience anything but friendliness, honesty and hospitality from them. It's generally safe to walk around day or night in Amman and other towns, but women should be a little more cautious.

Minefields
Although the risk to travellers is very small, there are a number of minefields that were

laid along the border with Israel and the Palestinian Territories before and during 1967. These are in the Jordan Valley (near Lake Tiberias); north of Aqaba; and in the southern Jordan Valley near the Dead Sea; they have even been known to float into the Dead Sea during flash floods. In 30 years, 470 people (mostly military personnel) have been killed by mines. The minefields are well off the tourist trails, but if you're in these areas please take heed of warnings not to enter – they're there for a good reason.

LEGAL MATTERS

The Jordanian legal system is something of a hybrid. Civil and commercial law is governed by a series of courts working with a mixture of inherited British-style common law and the French code. Religious and family matters are generally covered by Islamic Sharia'a courts, or ecclesiastic equivalents for non-Muslims.

Foreigners would be unlucky to get caught up in the machinations of Jordanian justice. The things to remember are: penalties for drug use of any kind are stiff and apply to foreigners and locals alike; homosexuality is illegal, and penalties are severe; and criticising the king can land you in jail for up to three years! Traffic police generally treat foreign drivers with a degree of good-natured indulgence, so long as there are no major traffic laws broken. However, excessive speeding, drink driving and not wearing a seat belt will land you in trouble. If you do get into strife, there is little your embassy can do for you but contact your relatives and recommend local lawyers.

BUSINESS HOURS

Government departments, including most tourist offices, are open from about 8am to 2pm every day but Friday – and sometimes they also close on Saturday. Visitor centres, especially the one at Petra, generally stay open longer hours. Banks are normally open from 8.30am to 12.30pm, and sometimes again from about 4pm to 6pm, every day but Friday and Saturday. Moneychangers are open every day from about 9am to at least 9pm, but some have restricted hours on Friday. The opening times for post offices vary from one town to another, but tend to be from about 8am to 6pm every day, and until about 2pm on Friday. Some

government departments and banks tend to close about 30 minutes earlier in winter.

Museums and art galleries are often closed for one day every week, but the day off varies from one place to another. Almost all major tourist attractions are open every day; normally during daylight hours.

Smaller shops and businesses are open every day from about 9am to 8pm, but some close for a couple of hours in the middle of the afternoon, and some do not open on Thursday afternoon and Friday. The *souqs* (markets) and street stalls are open every day and, in fact, Friday is often their busiest day.

PUBLIC HOLIDAYS & SPECIAL EVENTS

As the Islamic Hejira calendar is 11 days shorter than the Gregorian calendar, each year Islamic holidays fall 11 days earlier than the previous year. The precise dates are known only shortly before they fall because they depend upon the sighting of the moon. See the Language chapter for a full listing of the Hejira months.

Ramadan

Ramadan is the ninth month of the Muslim calendar, when Muslims fast during daylight hours to fulfil the fourth pillar of Islam (see Religion in the Facts about Jordan chapter for details). During this month, pious Muslims will not allow anything to pass their lips in daylight hours. One is even supposed to avoid swallowing saliva.

Although many Muslims in Jordan do not follow the injunctions to the letter, most conform to some extent. Foreigners are not expected to follow suit, but it's generally impolite to smoke, drink or eat in public during Ramadan.

Business hours during Ramadan tend to become more erratic and usually shorter. In out-of-the-way places, it's hard to find a restaurant that opens before sunset, but elsewhere there'll always be something open. Some places close during all of Ramadan. It's also sometimes difficult dealing with anyone during the day who's hungry, thirsty or craving a cigarette. Out of respect for those fasting during Ramadan, always eat inside or as discreetly as possible.

The evening meal during Ramadan, called *iftar* (breaking the fast), is always something of a celebration. Go to the bigger

Table of Islamic Holidays

Hejira Year	New Year	Prophet's Birthday	Ramadan Begins	Eid al-Fitr	Eid al-Adha
1423	15.03.02	23.05.02	05.11.02	05.12.02	12.02.03
1424	04.03.03	12.05.03	25.10.03	24.11.03	01.02.04
1425	22.02.04	11.05.04	14.10.04	13.11.04	21.01.05
1426	11.02.05	31.04.05	03.10.05	02.11.05	10.01.06
1427	31.01.06	20.04.06	22.09.06	22.10.06	30.12.06

restaurants and wait with fasting crowds for sundown, the moment when food is served – it's quite a lively experience.

While Ramadan can be inconvenient at times for visitors, all tourist attractions remain open and all public transport functions normally throughout the day. Restaurants in hotels will be open for guests and the public, so breakfast and dinner are usually easy enough to arrange.

If you're going to be travelling around during the day, buy some food for lunch (grocery shops will normally stay open during the day), and eat it somewhere discreet. Restaurants catering to tourists will usually still be open, although they may look closed.

Public Holidays

Following the death of King Hussein and the succession of King Abdullah II, the exact number of public holidays, and the dates on which they fall, is slowly changing. King Abdullah's Throne Day (9 June) and his birthday (30 January) will probably replace King Hussein's Throne Day (August 11). King Hussein's Birthday (14 November) will remain a public holiday, however, and the death of King Hussein (7 February) will also probably be a holiday.

During the public holidays listed below, most government offices and banks will close. Most shops, moneychangers and restaurants will remain open, and public transport will still function normally on most public holidays, although most shops will close during Eid al-Fitr and Eid al-Adha.

New Year's Day 1 January
Tree Day (Arbor Day) 15 January
Eid al-Fitr (See Table of Islamic Holidays above) Also known as Eid as-Sagheer (small feast), it starts at the beginning of Shawwal to mark the end of fasting in the preceding month of Ramadan
Arab League Day 22 March
Eid al-Kabir (See Table of Islamic Holidays) This 'big feast' is when Muslims fulfil the fifth pillar of Islam – Haj, or the pilgrimage to Mecca. This period lasts from 10 to 13 Zuul-Hijja.
Eid al-Adha (See Table of Islamic Holidays) This is the commemoration of Allah sparing Ibrahim (Abraham in the Bible) from sacrificing his son, Isaac, and is the end of the Haj. Every year, about 350,000 sheep are sacrificed throughout the Muslim world at this time.
Good Friday March/April
Muslim New Year First Day of Muharram
Labour Day 1 May
Independence Day 25 May
Army Day & Anniversary of the Great Arab Revolt 10 June
Prophet Mohammed's Birthday (See Table of Islamic Holidays) Celebrated on 12 Rabi' al-Awal
King Hussein's Birthday 14 November
Eid al-Isra Wal Mi'raj Another feast which celebrates the nocturnal visit of the Prophet Mohammed to heaven
Christmas Day 25 December

Special Events

Jordan's best-known cultural event is the Jerash Festival of Culture & Arts (see the boxed text 'Jerash Festival' in the Jerash & the North chapter). In summer (mainly August), traditional concerts and plays are sometimes held at the Odeon and Roman Theatre in Amman, and in Salt and Fuheis, near the capital.

For further information about special events in Jordan, contact an overseas branch of the Jordan Tourism Board (see the Tourist Offices Abroad section earlier in this chapter); visit the tourist office in Amman; check out the listings in the English-language newspapers; or look out for some of the tourist booklets mentioned under Guidebooks earlier in this chapter.

ACTIVITIES
Archaeological Digs
Many ancient sites in Jordan are still being excavated and it's possible to join an archaeological dig; note that such work is usually unpaid and you may even have to pay for the privilege.

Plan well ahead if you're interested in working on archaeological excavations. No dig director will welcome an inquiry two weeks before a season begins. Permits and security forms may have to be completed, so allow up to six months for all possible bureaucratic niceties. Much of the work is also seasonal. Opportunities are nonetheless growing as field project leaders realise the advantages of taking on energetic and motivated amateurs.

When you write to dig directors, tell them what you can do. If you have special skills (like photography or drafting), have travelled in the region, or worked on other digs (or similar group projects), let them know. Locals are usually employed to do the basic spade work.

To get an idea of what is going on, and where and when, contact one of the organisations listed below. All are based in Amman (☎ 06).

American Center for Oriental Research (ACOR; ☎ 5346117, fax 5844181) PO Box 2470, Jebel Amman, Amman 11181. ACOR is part of the Archaeological Institute of America (AIA), and prepares an extensive annual listing of fieldwork opportunities in the Middle East. Write to: AIA, 135 William St, New York NY 10038.

British Institute at Amman for Archaeology & History (☎ 5341317, fax 5337197) PO Box 519, Al-Jubeiha, Amman 11941

Department of Antiquities (☎ 4644336, fax 461 5848) 85 Al-Kulliyah Al-Ilmiyah Al-Islamiyah St, Amman

Deutsches Evangelisches Institut für Altertumswissenschaft des Heiligen Landes, Zweigstelle Amman (☎ 5342924, fax 5336924) PO Box 183, Amman 11118

Friends of Archaeology (☎/fax 5930682, e foa@ nets.com.jo, w www.arabia.com/foa) PO Box 2440, Amman 11181. Established in 1960, this Jordanian-run, nonprofit organisation aims to 'protect and preserve the archaeological sites and cultural heritage of Jordan'. FoA operates educational field trips – but for members only.

Institut Français d'Archéologie du Proche Orient (☎ 4640515, fax 4611170) PO Box 5348, Amman, 11181

University of Jordan: Archaeological Department (☎ 5355000, ext 3739)

A number of teams from international universities also undertake projects in Jordan. Some of the better ones worth contacting are:

Australia Universities of Melbourne & Sydney; Australian National University (Canberra)
Canada University of Toronto
France CNRS Lyon & Paris
Germany DAI Berlin, Tübingen & Heidelberg
Holland Universities of Amsterdam & Leiden
UK Universities of Cambridge, London & Edinburgh
USA Chicago, UCLA & Yale

One particularly active programme is run at picturesque Pella, in northwestern Jordan, by the University of Sydney. For details, contact the volunteer co-ordinator at **Pella Volunteers** (☎ 02-9351 4151, fax 9351 6392; e neaf@antiquity.usyd.edu.au) in Australia.

Boats & Other Water Sports
In Aqaba, trips on a glass-bottom boat are fun, although the amount of fish and coral that can be seen is sometimes disappointing and you need at least a couple of hours to get to the better areas. The guys who run these boats are savvy so the bargaining can be intense.

A couple of hotels in Aqaba are well set up for water sports.

Camel Treks
The camel is no longer a common form of transport for Bedouin; most now prefer the ubiquitous pick-up truck – in fact, it's not unusual to see Bedouin transporting a prized camel in this way! For visitors, however, one truly rewarding experience is a camel trek. Enterprising Bedouin are happy to take visitors on three- to six-night camel treks from Wadi Rum to Aqaba or Petra (see Wadi Rum in the Southern Desert & Aqaba chapter for details). Similar trips are possible in a 4WD, but travelling by camel is more charming and environmentally sound, if also more uncomfortable.

Diving & Snorkelling
The coastline between Aqaba and the Saudi border is home to some of the world's better diving spots. Although the diving and snorkelling is generally not as good as it is

at places along the Sinai peninsula in Egypt, there's plenty of coral and colourful marine life. The advantages are that all sites are accessible from a major town (Aqaba), easy to reach for snorkellers and accessible from a jetty or the beach, so a boat is not required (which reduces the cost considerably). Also, visibility in the gulf is usually excellent (as much as 40m, although it's usually closer to 20m), the tides are minimal, the water is shallow, and drop-offs are often found less than 50m from shore.

Diving is possible all year, but January is the coldest month and July and August are the hottest. The best time is early February to early June for water and outside temperatures, visibility and marine life, although March and April are not good because of algae bloom. The other factors to consider are the higher prices and possible lack of decent rooms in Aqaba during winter. Despite the outside temperature in summer, the cold stream in the gulf makes the water temperature bearable.

For specific information about diving and snorkelling activities around Aqaba, see South of Aqaba in the Southern Desert & Aqaba chapter.

Hot Springs

Jordan boasts dozens of thermal hot-water springs, where the water is usually about 35°C to 45°C. The water contains potassium, magnesium and calcium, among other minerals – popular for their apparent health benefits. The most famous and popular is Hammamat Ma'in, near Madaba. Other popular spots around Jordan include Hammamat Burbita and Hammamat Afra, west of the King's Highway near Tafila, and Al-Himma springs in Mukheiba village, very close to the northern border with Israel and the Palestinian Territories.

Women are likely to feel more comfortable at Hammamat Ma'in, which has an area for families and unaccompanied women, and the public baths at Al-Himma, which allocates special times solely for the ladies.

Rock Climbing

Wadi Rum offers some challenging and unique rock climbing, equal to just about anything in Europe. The most accessible and popular climbs are well detailed in the excellent books written by Tony Howard

and Di Taylor (see Books under Hiking later in this chapter). Guides are necessary, and you'll need to bring your own climbing gear. The Wadi Rum section in the Southern Desert & Aqaba chapter has more details.

Swimming

The number of public beaches in Aqaba is slowly diminishing because they're being commandeered by upmarket hotels. The best beaches are now along the coastline south of Aqaba, but most spots have little or no shade, and are not accessible on foot. The beaches run by the upmarket hotels in Aqaba are clean and available to the public for a few dinars.

Most visitors head for the Dead Sea, where swimming is almost impossible because of the incredible buoyancy of the salt water. See The Dead Sea in the Around Amman chapter for more details.

Turkish Baths

If your muscles ache from traipsing around vast archaeological sites like Petra and Jerash and climbing up and down the *jebels* (hills) of Amman, consider a traditional Turkish bath. In Wadi Musa (near Petra) and Aqaba, a steam bath, massage and 'body conditioning' costs about JD8, while in Amman it's worth paying more for a memorable experience.

Women are welcome, but should make a reservation so that female attendants can be organised.

Hiking

Hiking is an increasingly popular pastime in Jordan, with the Dana Nature Reserve, Mukawir, Petra (and surrounds), Wadi Mujib and Wadi Rum among the most rewarding options.

Any hike will take longer, and take more out of you, than you think – walking in sand is not easy, nor is going uphill in the hot sun. Allow yourself plenty of time, and also give yourself time to linger and enjoy the view, chat with passers-by, or simply sit in the shade during the heat of the day.

When to Go The best time for hiking is undoubtedly the middle of spring (mid-March to late April), when it's not too hot, the rains should have finished, the flowers should be in bloom and the wells and springs should be full. At this time, however, Wadi Mujib and some of the wadis in Petra may still be flooded or impassable in places – always check local conditions before setting out. From late September to mid-October is also good; it's dry but not excessively hot.

Rain and floods can occur throughout the months from November to March. This is not a good time to hike or camp in narrow wadis and ravines because flash floods can sweep unheralded out of the hills.

What to Bring If you intend to hike while in Jordan, make sure that you come prepared. A lightweight windproof top is recommended, as is a thin fleece jacket for the evening. Lightweight waterproofs can also be a good idea. Most people walk in lightweight cotton clothes (or the modern equivalent) and trainers are the usual footwear, although some prefer lightweight walking boots, which give more ankle support.

It's not advisable to wear shorts or sleeveless tops – it's inappropriate dress for conservative villages in the countryside, and you may get burnt to a crisp anyway. Don't forget a hat, sunscreen, medical kit, knife, torch (flashlight) and matches. Water purifiers and insect repellent will also be very useful.

Books British climbers Tony Howard and Di Taylor have spent a lot of time exploring the hiking, trekking and rock-climbing possibilities in Jordan. Their books include the detailed *Treks & Climbs in Wadi Rum* (Cicerone Press), the condensed, pocket-sized and more affordable *Walks & Scrambles in Rum*, published by Al-Kutba; and *Jordan – Walks, Treks, Climbs & Canyons* (Cicerone Press). These books are available in major bookshops in Jordan.

Although it can be difficult to find, *Trekking & Canyoning in the Jordanian Dead Sea Rift* by Itai Haviv (Desert Breeze Press) contains numerous trekking and canyoning routes and is worth picking up for those who favour a more strenuous stay in Jordan.

Hiking Agencies Only a tiny fraction of Jordanian travel agencies have experience in organising hiking or trekking expeditions, although most will claim to.

Among those agencies that can be relied upon are:

Petra Moon Tourism Services (☎ 03-2156665, fax 2156666, e eid@petramoon.com, w www .petramoon.com) PO Box 129, Wadi Musa (near Petra)
Royal Society for the Conservation of Nature (☎ 06-5350456, fax 5347411, e tourism@ rscn.org.jo, w www.rscn.org.jo) PO Box 6354, Amman 11183
Zaman Tours & Travel (☎ 03-2157723, fax 2157722, e zamantours@joinnet.com.jo) PO Box 158, Wadi Musa (near Petra)

Responsible Hiking The popularity of hiking is placing some pressure on the natural environment. Please consider the following tips when hiking and help preserve the ecology and beauty of the Jordanian landscape.

Rubbish Carry out all your rubbish. Don't overlook items such as silver paper, orange peel, cigarette butts and plastic wrappers. Empty packaging weighs very little and should be stored in a dedicated rubbish bag. Make an effort to carry out rubbish left by others. Never bury rubbish. Digging disturbs soil and ground cover, and encourages erosion. It may also take years to decompose.

Minimise your waste. Take minimal packaging and no more food than you need. If you can't buy in bulk, unpack small-portion packages and combine their contents in one container before your trip. Take reusable containers or stuff sacks. Don't rely on bought water in plastic bottles. Disposal of these bottles is creating a major problem; use iodine drops or purification tablets instead. Sanitary napkins, tampons and condoms should also be carried out, despite the inconvenience. They burn and decompose poorly.

Human Waste Disposal Contamination of water sources by human faeces can lead to the transmission of hepatitis, typhoid and intestinal parasites such as giardia, amoebas and roundworms. It can also cause severe health risks to local residents and wildlife. Where there's a toilet, please use it. Where there is none, bury your waste. Dig a hole 15cm deep and at least 100m from any watercourse. Consider carrying a lightweight trowel for this purpose. Cover the waste with soil and a rock. Always use your toilet paper sparingly and burn it if possible.

Washing Don't use detergents or toothpaste in or near watercourses, even if they're biodegradable. For personal washing, use biodegradable soap and a water container at least 50m away from the watercourse. Disperse the waste water widely to allow the soil to filter it fully before it finally makes it back to the watercourse. Wash cooking utensils 50m from watercourses using a scourer or sand instead of detergent.

Erosion It is important to stick to existing tracks and avoid short cuts that bypass a switchback. If you blaze a new trail straight down a slope, it will turn into a watercourse with the next heavy rainfall and will eventually cause soil loss and deep scarring. If a well-used track passes through a mud patch, walk through the mud; walking around the edge will increase the size of the patch. Avoid removing the plantlife that keeps topsoil in place.

Fires & Low-Impact Cooking Cutting of wood for fires can cause rapid deforestation. Cook on a light-weight kerosene, alcohol or Shellite (white gas) stove and avoid those powered by disposable butane gas canisters. If you're hiking with a guide and porters, supply stoves for the whole team. Don't surround fires with rocks as this creates a visual scar. Use only dead, fallen wood. Ensure that you fully extinguish a fire after use.

Wildlife Conservation Do not engage in or encourage hunting. Don't buy items made from endangered species. Discourage the presence of wildlife by not leaving food scraps behind you.

Park Regulations Take note of and observe the rules and regulations of the national or state reserve that you are visiting.

COURSES

For those taken enough by the mystery of the Arab world to want to learn something of the language, there are several possibilities, mostly in Amman (refer to the relevant chapters for full contact details of the universities and cultural centres):

British Council (☎ 06-4636147, fax 4656413, e registrar@britishcouncil.org.jo, w www .britcouncil.org/jordan) offers classes (JD140 for 35 hours) in colloquial Jordanian Arabic and MSA with a focus on conversation rather than grammar

Language Centre of the Centre Culturel Français (☎ 06-4612658) runs intensive courses in MSA (taught in French or English) during the summer; a one-month course for several hours a day, five days a week, costs JD75

University of Jordan (☎ 06-5843555, fax 583 2318, e webmaster@ju.edu.jo, w www.ju .edu.jo) offers summer courses in MSA, as well as courses throughout the rest of the year

Yarmouk University (☎ 02-7271100, e web master@yu.edu.jo, w www.yu.edu.jo) Irbid

WORK

Working in Jordan is not really an option for most foreigners passing through, but it is possible for anyone with the right qualifications or interests who has done some planning before leaving home. Your employer in Jordan should be able to deal with the bureaucratic requirements of working permits.

For details of working on archaeological digs in Jordan, see the previous Activities section.

Diving

If you are a qualified diving instructor, you may be able to get some work at one of the diving centres in Aqaba, particularly during the peak season (about September to March). See Diving & Snorkelling in the Southern Desert & Aqaba chapter for contact details.

Language Teaching

Teaching English is the most obvious avenue for travellers. One of the top schools in Amman is run by the **British Council**. The minimum requirements are the RSA Preparatory Certificate (the Diploma is preferred) or equivalent and two years' experience. Most recruiting is done from the UK. For details contact their **head office** (☎ 020-7930 8466; 10 Spring Gardens, London SW1A 2BN) before coming to Jordan. If you're already in Jordan, casual vacancies occasionally arise so it can be worth dropping off your CV, addressed to the Teaching Centre Manager.

The **American Language Center** (☎ 06-5859102, fax 5859101; e info@alc.edu.jo; w www.alc.edu.jo) runs the other top school. Like the British Council, it mainly recruits in its own country.

German, French and Spanish speakers should contact their respective cultural centres in Amman (see Cultural Centres in the Amman chapter for details) about the possibility of teaching these languages.

Volunteer Work

Those hoping to work with Palestinian refugees should contact the public information office of the **United Nations Relief & Works Agency** *(UNRWA; ☎ 06-5607194, ext 166, fax 5685476;* **e** *m.saqer@unrwa.org; Mustapha bin Abdullah St, Shmeisani, Amman)*. There is no organised volunteer programme, but if you are in Jordan for a few months (they prefer longer-term commitments, rather than just a few weeks) and have a particular professional skill in education, relief or health, you may be able to arrange something. Contact them at least three months in advance, detailing your experience and to find out more information.

US citizens may also consider the **Peace Corps** *(**w** www.peacecorps.gov)*, which runs two-year placements in Jordan.

ACCOMMODATION

Jordan has a good range of accommodation options to suit most budgets, although away from the main tourist centres you won't have a lot of choice. This is generally not a problem because Jordan is so compact that most attractions can be easily visited in day trips from the main centres.

Camping

Rooms in cheap hotels are easy to find, and reasonably comfortable; bringing a tent just to save money on accommodation makes little sense. Privacy and safety are the prime concerns for campers, and finding a secluded place to pitch a tent in a densely populated country like Jordan is far from easy.

Some places to discreetly pitch a tent are near Umm Qais, Shaumari Reserve and Ajlun castle. However, the Jordanian authorities prefer that foreigners use designated campsites so always check with the local authorities before setting up. The only campsites where pitching your own tent is allowed are at Aqaba (tents catch the sea breezes in summer) and Dibbeen National Park, although some hotels (eg, the Olive Branch Resort near Jerash and Lulu's Pension in Madaba) allow you to pitch a tent in their grounds. Pre-set tents are also available in Wadi Rum, Dana Nature Reserve and at the Dead Sea Rest House. There are also a couple of camping options south of Aqaba. Camping in national parks or nature reserves requires the permission of the Royal Society for the Conservation of Nature (RSCN). Camping is not permitted inside Petra.

One popular alternative is to 'camp with the Bedouin', ie, share a tent with local Bedouin at Wadi Rum. Facilities are often very basic, but it's a great experience – see Wadi Rum in the Southern Desert & Aqaba chapter for more details.

Hotels

A surprising thing about accommodation in Jordan is that some towns have no hotel at all. Other towns, like Ajlun, offer little or nothing in the budget end of the market. Pre-booking a hotel room is rarely needed – you'll have little trouble finding a hotel in any price range if you just turn up, except in Aqaba at peak times (see the Southern Desert & Aqaba chapter for details).

Most budget and mid-range places charge an extra JD1 to JD2 for breakfast, which is invariably little more than tea/coffee, bread and jam. It's cheaper to buy this sort of food at a grocery store and make your own breakfast, or enjoy a cooked breakfast at a budget-priced restaurant for about the same price.

Breakfast is often included in the price at top-end hotels; many have generous buffet-style breakfasts. Accommodation standards in top-end hotels are all you'd expect from four- or five-star hotels around the world.

There is a telephone number in Amman for **hotel complaints** *(☎ 06-4613103)*.

Budget There are no youth hostels in Jordan. A bed in a shared room (with a shared bathroom) in a cheap hotel will not cost less than JD1.500 and, generally, will be more like JD3 to JD6. Some places, especially those catering to backpackers, allow guests to sleep on the roof – which, in summer, is a good place to be – for about JD2 per person. Private rooms are possible from about JD3/6 for singles/doubles, but anything decent will cost about JD6/10. Prices are negotiable, especially when things are quiet.

Most budget places have 'triples' (rooms with three beds), and often rooms with four beds, so sharing a room with friends, or asking to share a room with another guest, is a way of reducing accommodation costs considerably. Some cheaper places have two accommodation choices: basic rooms with a shared bathroom, and nicer, more expensive ones with a private bathroom.

Especially in Amman, cheap places can be incredibly noisy because of the traffic and the hubbub of cafés and shops below. Try to get a room towards the back of the building. Many budget places are located above shops and cafés, which means climbing several flights of stairs to your room.

Mid-Range There is a reasonable selection of mid-range hotels, with at least one in most towns you're likely to visit, but only in Amman, Wadi Musa (near Petra) and Aqaba will you have much choice. Rooms in mid-range hotels usually have colour TV (sometimes featuring satellite stations such as CNN), fridge, heater (essential in winter) and telephone. For budget travellers, a quiet, clean room with reliable hot water and a private bathroom in a mid-range hotel is sometimes worth a splurge; prices start from about JD15/22 for singles/doubles. Negotiation is always possible, especially if business is quiet or you're staying for several days – so it is sometimes possible to get a nice room in a decent mid-range hotel for a budget price.

Top End There is no shortage of top-end hotels – but only in Amman, Wadi Musa (near Petra), the Dead Sea and Aqaba. They all feature the sort of luxuries you'd expect for the prices. Most guests at these sorts of places are on organised tours; in quieter times negotiation is possible, and surprising bargains are possible when things are quiet. Payment is sometimes required in US dollars, and all major credit cards are accepted. All top-end hotels add a 'service charge' of about 13%, and a 'government tax' of about 10%, to their quoted tariffs.

Rental Accommodation For details of long-term (monthly) rental in Amman, see Places to Stay in the Amman chapter. Short-term rentals are available in Aqaba, where a furnished two-bedroom apartment with a kitchen costs from JD10 per night in the low season and JD20 in the high season. Most apartments in Aqaba can only be rented for a minimum of one week, however, and must be prebooked in the peak season.

FOOD

If you can pay a little more than rock-bottom prices, eating in Jordan can be a wonderful experience. The salads and dips are great and the bread is as good as you'll get in the Middle East – great news for vegetarians. For carnivores, the chicken and meat is similarly good. And, as you'd expect in this part of the world, coffee and tea are a way of life.

Some restaurants have a 'family' section, basically set aside for families and unaccompanied (local and foreign) women. The entrance may not be entirely obvious, so ask the manager where it is. However, foreign women, especially those with male companions, will rarely have any problem eating wherever they choose.

Most restaurants offer knives, forks and spoons to foreigners, but you'll have to use your hands to cope with felafel, shwarma and pastries. If you are offered food from a communal plate in a Jordanian home, and there are no eating implements, always use your right hand.

Grumpy Gourmet is a light-hearted guide, mainly for expatriates and well-off visitors living in Amman. It sometimes runs in local magazines (such as *Living Well* – see Newspapers & Magazines earlier in this chapter) or contact them directly for a copy (e grumpy@grumpygourmet.com) and check out the website at w www.grumpy gourmet.com.

Restaurants

The most common way for a group to eat in any restaurant is to order mezze – a variety of small starters followed by several mains to be shared by all present. Otherwise, simply order one or two starters, bread (which is normally provided free anyway), main course (usually meat) and salad. Some smaller hole-in-the-wall places will specialise in one or two things only, while some just offer chicken or three or four stews.

Some restaurants close on Friday, usually in the evening, but most places frequented by foreigners open every day. A menu in English is usually offered only by restaurants in upmarket hotels, those set up for the tourist trade and outlets of Western fast-food chains. Elsewhere, just ask what's available or point to what other patrons are enjoying. Usually someone in the restaurant will know a bit of English, and 'kebabs', 'chicken', 'salad' and 'soup' are universally understood by restaurant staff.

Before you start ordering, especially at a restaurant frequented by foreigners and where there's no menu in English, ask for the price of each dish.

Starters Hummus is cooked chickpeas ground into a paste and mixed with tahini (a sesame-seed paste), garlic and lemon. Available in virtually every restaurant, it's invariably excellent and generally eaten as a starter with bread. It goes very nicely with any of the meat dishes. *Baba ghanoug* is another dip eaten with bread and is made from mashed eggplant and tahini. Fairly similar is *mutabel*; a vaguely hot red dip is *daqqeh*. Tabouleh is largely a parsley, cracked wheat and tomato-based salad, with a sprinkling of sesame seeds, lemon and garlic. It goes perfectly with hummus in bread.

More solid and tasty starters include *maqlubbeh*, steamed rice topped with grilled slices of eggplant or meat, grilled tomato and pinenuts; and *fareekeh*, a similar dish with cracked wheat. *Fattoush* is pretty much tabouleh with little shreds of deep-fried bread in it. Turkish-style stuffed vine leaves sometimes go by the name of *yalenjeh*.

Snacks The two most popular local versions of 'fast food' are the shwarma and felafel, both well known to anyone who has travelled elsewhere in the region. For both, spicy sauces are optional, and should be treated with caution.

Shwarma is like Greek *gyros* or Turkish *doner*, ie, slices of lamb or chicken from a huge revolving spit, mixed with onions and tomato in bread. The vendor will slice off the meat (usually with a great flourish and much knife sharpening and waving), dip a piece of flat bread in the fat that has dripped off the meat, hold it against the gas flame so it flares, then fill it with meat and fillings.

Felafel is deep-fried balls of chickpea paste with spices, served in a piece of *khobz* (bread) with varying combinations of pickled vegetables or *turshi* (not to everyone's taste), tomato, salad and yogurt.

Bread Arabic unleavened bread, *khobz*, is eaten with absolutely everything and is sometimes called *a'aish* (life) – its common name in Egypt. It's round and flat, and makes a good filler if you're preparing your own food. There's a variety of tastes and textures, but the basic principle remains the same. Tastier than plain old *khobz* is *ka'ik*,

round sesame rings of bread, often sold with a boiled egg from stalls over Jordan. A favourite breakfast staple is bread liberally sprinkled with *zata'* (thyme).

Main Dishes Most main dishes comprise chicken, meat kebabs, or meat and vegetable stews.

Chicken *(farooj)* is often roasted on spits in large ovens out the front of the restaurant. The usual serving is half a chicken *(nuss farooj)*, which comes with bread, a side dish of raw onion, chillies and sometimes olives. Eaten with the optional extras of salad *(salata)* and hummus, it's a great meal.

Kebabs are another favourite, and available everywhere. These are spicy minced lamb pieces pressed onto skewers and grilled over charcoal. *Shish tawouk* is loosely the chicken version of the same thing. Another popular chicken dish is *musakhan*, roast chicken served with onions and pine nuts on *khobz*. Kofta is a delicious and hearty meal of meat, tomatoes and spices.

Stews are usually meat or vegetable, or both, and make a pleasant change from chicken and kebabs. *Fasooliya* is bean stew; *biseela* is made of peas; *batatas* is mostly potato; and *mulukiyyeh* is a spinach stew with chicken or meat pieces. They are usually served with rice *(ruz)* or, more rarely, macaroni *(makarone)*. A local staple is *fuul*, a cheap, and usually tasty, dish of squashed fava beans with chillis, onions and olive oil.

A Bedouin speciality is mensaf. Traditionally served on special occasions, it consists of lamb on a bed of rice and pine nuts, topped with the gaping head of the animal. The fat from the cooking is poured into the rice. Traditionally, the delicacy is the eyes, which are presented to honoured guests (but don't worry if you miss out – there are other choice bits like the tongue!). You can buy a serve of mensaf in better restaurants in the larger cities. It's not cheap, but should be tried at least once. A tangy sauce of cooked yogurt mixed with fat is served with it.

Fish *(samak)* is not widely available, and it's always expensive – even in Aqaba. It is often heavily salted and spiced. *Sayadiya* is boiled fish with lemon juice.

Desserts Jordanians love sugar, and their desserts are assembled accordingly; there are pastry shops in every town selling nothing else. Many of the pastry shops are sit-down places, so you can walk in, make a selection and take a seat – or take some away with you. These pastry shops are often good places for solo women travellers to relax.

The basic formula is pastry drenched in honey, syrup and/or rose water. Many of them, however different they look, fall into the general category of *baklava*. Some tasty treats to try include: *kunafeh*, shredded dough with nuts dunked in syrup; *ma'amoul*, like *kunafeh* but with dates and nuts, and dipped in rose water; *halawat al-jibna*, a soft doughy pastry filled with cream cheese and topped with syrup and ice cream; *isfiniyya*, a coconut slice; *mahalabiyya*, a very sweet dessert made of ground rice, sugar, milk and rose water; and *mushabbak*, a lacework-shaped pastry drenched in syrup.

Vegetarian

Virtually no restaurants in Jordan specialise in vegetarian food, and there are few specific 'vegetarian' dishes. Vegetarians report varying degrees of difficulty in getting by in Jordan. Every restaurant offers a number of different salads at reasonable prices, and two salads with bread often makes a decent meal. Vegetable soups are common, although they may be 'contaminated' with small pieces of meat. Starters such as hummus, and traditional dishes like fuul, are meatless and will become staple foods for vegetarians.

Self-Catering

Buying food for breakfast, lunch or dinner, and eating in your hotel room, is very easy. If you are travelling around during the day, finding a decent restaurant when your stomach starts rumbling is not always easy, so consider taking food with you and enjoying a picnic in the grounds of an ancient castle, or in a park. Almost every town has at least one well-stocked grocery store, and Amman boasts several Western-style supermarkets.

DRINKS

Drinking tea or coffee is a national pastime for locals, and drinking any form of liquid is a preoccupation for most visitors, especially in summer.

Nonalcoholic Drinks

Water Most restaurants offer a jug of free cold (tap) water, but if you prefer mineral water in a sealed plastic bottle, you'll have to pay for it. Small and large bottles of mineral water are easy to buy anywhere in Jordan.

Juices All over Jordan, juice stalls sell freshly squeezed fruit juices *(aseer)*; these stalls are instantly recognisable by the string bags of fruit hanging out the front. Popular juices include lemon, orange, banana, pomegranate and rockmelon, and you can have combinations of any or all of these.

Some stalls put milk in their drinks, which you'd be well advised to stay away from if you have a dodgy stomach. *Sahlab* is a traditional drink, served hot with milk, nuts and cinnamon – delicious, if made properly.

Soft Drinks All the normal international brands are widely available, eg, Coke, Pepsi, 7-Up and Fanta. They come in returnable and recycled glass and plastic bottles. Cans are smaller than bottles, and more expensive because you have to pay for the nonrecyclable can.

Alcoholic Drinks

Alcohol is widely available in bars and from the occasional liquor store in major towns. Before taking alcohol back to your hotel, ask whether the manager (who is probably Muslim) minds. Top-end hotels may not like you bringing alcohol into your room because they prefer guests to drink from the expensive minibar.

Amstel beer is brewed in Jordan under licence from the parent European company, and it's definitely the most widely available (and often the only available) beer. In Amman and Aqaba, beer imported from all over the world – everything from Guinness to Fosters – is available but at prices higher than you'd pay in Ireland or Australia. A bottle of 650ml Amstel beer costs abut JD1 from a liquor store, at least JD1.750 in a dingy bar in Amman and a lot more in a decent pub or nightclub. You may also come across the local Jordanian beer 'Philadelphia', which is OK once you no longer care about taste.

Arak is the indigenous firewater, similar to Greek *ouzo* or Turkish *raki*. Available in shops, bars and restaurants throughout Jordan, it's usually mixed with water and ice and drunk with food – and should be treated with caution. Various other types of hard liquor are available in liquor stores and bars, including all sorts of 'scotch whisky' brewed locally or imported. Any liquor made by a well-known Western company (like Johnnie Walker) is outrageously expensive, so pick up a bottle duty free.

Little wine is produced in Jordan, so brands such as Latroun, St Catherine and Cremisan are imported from the West Bank. Wine costs about JD5/10 for a half/full bottle in a restaurant; less from a liquor store.

ENTERTAINMENT

With the notable exception of eastern Amman, Jordan is not exactly thumping with nightlife. The top-end hotels offer the usual expensive and often dull discos and nightclubs, and occasionally present Arab musicians and belly dancing. The wealthier locals in Amman hang around the restaurants and cafés in Shmeisani or Abdoun, which can be quite busy, but most places shut by about 11pm.

In the evenings, most visitors will probably window shop, stroll around the streets, enjoy a leisurely meal, go to the cinema or watch TV.

Pubs/Bars

The bars in the bigger hotels are more comfortable but more expensive than the dingy bars tucked away in the rabbit warren of alleys around Downtown in Amman. The bars in Amman where women will feel more welcome are listed in the Amman chapter.

Discos/Clubs

Some of the hotels in Amman and Aqaba run nightclubs, but they're nothing to get excited about. Amman has a couple of excellent nightclubs where you can dance the night away. Entrance is usually free but drinks are expensive.

Traditional Music

The various foreign cultural centres in Amman regularly organise musical recitals. Also in Amman, the Royal Cultural Centre occasionally puts on concerts and plays, usually in Arabic; Darat al-Funun art gallery often features recitals of classical and ethnic music; and the Haya Cultural Centre has programmes of music and dance for children. Traditional concerts, plays and dances also feature heavily in the Jerash Festival, and at special events in places like Salt and Fuheis.

Cinemas

In order to show the films quickly, they cut out some parts. Most of the time they're understandable, except for *Indecent Proposal* with the indecent proposal cut out!

J van den Brink, Netherlands

Many popular Western films are eventually given a release in Jordan, although anything considered too risqué in the film is deleted by the censors (but all the sickening violence remains untouched).

Most films at the cheaper cinemas are dubbed into Arabic; the ones at the more expensive places are subtitled in Arabic, so the original language (usually English) is still audible.

Tickets at the cheaper cinemas cost about JD1.500, and starting times are not standardised, nor are they normally known to even the ticket sellers and ushers. Tickets to the better cinemas (all of which are in Amman) are pricey at about JD4, but the quality is far superior to the cheap places. Programmes for the good cinemas in Amman are advertised regularly in the English-language newspapers.

Every year around February, Amman hosts the French Film Festival. Programmes are usually published in 'Le Jourdain', the French-language section of the *Star* newspaper or check the Centre Culturel Français (see Cultural Centres in the Amman chapter).

Cafés

Traditional cafés serve coffee, tea and soft drinks. Some have an unadvertised special section at the back serving as a bar, but it's invariably dingy, and for men only. Few traditional cafés serve food, although more modern Western-style ones sometimes offer simple meals and snacks. In eastern Amman, there are some very trendy cafés that serve meals and/or pastries as well as alcohol. Some also host live music or exhibitions.

Cafés are often great places to watch the world go by, write letters, try the nargileh (water pipe), meet locals and, maybe, play a hand of cards or backgammon. The cafés in Amman that are generally men-only, and those that welcome women, are listed separately. However, any unaccompanied foreign women, with a bit of courage and very modest attire, are usually welcome at most cafés in Jordan.

SPECTATOR SPORTS

Not surprisingly, the most popular sport in the country is football (soccer). The Premier League Championship plays mostly on Friday during winter (from about September to March), and features teams from Amman and most major towns. The fans take the game so seriously that the league was cancelled in 1998 after a referee was beaten up by fans, and the game abandoned. The cancellation was not caused by the horror of the injury to the referee, but by the vehement disagreement about which team should be the 'winner' of the abandoned game. The British embassy also sometimes runs a football competition for women.

Other sports that Jordanians enjoy watching, participating in locally and competing in at overseas events, include judo, table tennis, kite flying, volleyball and horse racing (including long-distance endurance races).

Major sporting events are often held at the massive Sports City, in northern Amman, and at Al-Hasan Sports City, in Irbid. In mid-1999, Jordan hosted the 9th Pan Arab Games, with over 4000 athletes from most Arab countries.

The vast deserts and good roads are ideal for car rallies – such as the 700km Jordan International Rally organised by the Royal Automobile Club of Jordan – and for events such as the Amman–Dead Sea Marathon (about 50km), held every April – see the boxed text 'The Dead Sea Ultra Marathon' in the Around Amman chapter for details.

SHOPPING

Jordan does not boast the best range or prices of souvenirs in the Middle East, so if you're travelling elsewhere in the region, you may want to stock up on mementos in Egypt or Syria (where a lot of souvenirs in Jordan are made anyway). Amman is the best place to shop for souvenirs with everything from unimaginable tourist kitsch to superb and high-quality handicraft boutiques.

Handicrafts

Salt and Fuheis, both near Amman, have several art galleries and handicraft workshops where visitors can buy ceramics, mosaics, paintings and embroidery.

Several chains of shops around Jordan sell high-quality, if pricey, souvenirs made by Jordanians, mostly women. Profits from the sale of all items go to local charities that aim to develop the status of women, or protect the local environment.

Al-Alaydi Jordan Craft Centre Profits go to support poor Jordanian families, including university scholarships. It has an impressive outlet in Amman.

Jordan Design & Trade Centre Run by the Noor Al Hussein Foundation, the centre helps preserve traditional handicraft skills and supports vulnerable women's communities. There are shops in Amman, Madaba, Aqaba and Wadi Musa.

Jordan River Foundation (Bani Hamida) Profits go to support the foundation, which aims to preserve traditional communities of the Jordan River Valley (see the boxed text 'The Bani Hamida Story' in the King's Highway chapter). Shops are located in Amman and Mukawir.

Royal Society for the Conservation of Nature (RSCN) Proceeds from the gift shops go to the RSCN's environmental programmes and to communities such as those of Wadi Dana. RSCN shops can be found in Amman, Azraq, Dana and Wadi Rum.

Other places with a good range of souvenirs are Haret Jdoudna in Madaba, the shops listed under Shopping in the Amman chapter, and Dana village.

Carpets, Rugs & Kilims

While it's still possible to stumble across an aged handmade 'Persian rug' from Iran, chances are it was sewn in an attic above the shop. This is not to say that the carpets are lousy, but it's worth taking a close look at quality. Inspect both sides of the carpet to see how close and strong the sewing is.

Designs generally tend to consist of geometric patterns, although increasingly the tourist market is being catered to with depictions of monuments, animals and the like. Rugs and tapestries made by Bedouin and Palestinian women are popular, but you need to look carefully to make sure that they are actually handmade. Madaba is famous for its traditional rugs.

Gold, Silver & Jewellery

Gold shops are scattered all over the bigger cities of Jordan. As a rule, gold is sold by weight, and all pieces should have a hallmark guaranteeing quality. (A hallmark normally indicates where a piece was assayed, and a date.) Verifying all this is difficult, however, so the best advice is to buy items you're happy with even if you find out at home that the gold content is not as high as you were told by that nice salesman.

The same goes for silver, although its monetary value is in any case somewhat lower. For that reason, it's the most common material used by Bedouin women to make up their striking pieces of jewellery, such as earrings, necklaces and pendants laden with semiprecious stones.

Take most of the talk about 'antique jewellery' with a shaker full of salt, and remember customs regulations about antiques (see Export Restrictions later in this section). Silver is not only used in women's jewellery, but to make carry cases for miniature Qurans and other objects.

Copper & Brassware
From Morocco to Baghdad, you'll find much the same sorts of brass and chased copper objects for sale. The good thing about this stuff is that it's fairly hard to cheat on quality, but check for leaks before buying anything you wish to use (rather than just keep as a souvenir). Most common on the souvenir list are the large decorative trays and tabletops, but other items include traditionally styled Arabic coffeepots and complete coffee sets with small cups.

Instruments
A few stalls in Downtown Amman sell either *ouds* (Arabic lutes) or *darbukkas*, the standard Middle Eastern-style drums. The latter can go quite cheaply, and even the *ouds* are hardly expensive. Such an item's musical value must be considered unlikely to be high – it's the kind of thing you'd buy more to display than to play.

Woodwork
Also popular with foreigners are woodwork items, ranging from simple jewellery boxes to elaborate chess sets and backgammon boards. Better-quality stuff tends to be made of walnut and inlaid with mother-of-pearl. If the mother-of-pearl gives off a strong rainbow-colour effect, you can be almost sure it's the real McCoy. The actual woodwork on many of these items tends to be a little shoddy, even on better-quality items, so inspect the joints and inlay carefully.

Other Souvenirs
The ubiquitous nargileh water pipes are about the most vivid reminder possible of a visit to Jordan. Remember to buy a supply of charcoal to get you going if you intend to use the thing when you return home – a couple of spare tubes would not go astray either. This would have to be about the most awkward souvenir to cart around, however, or post home – and the chances of it surviving either way are not good.

Another simple souvenir that is much easier to carry around is the traditional Arab headcloth, or keffiyah, and *agal* (the black cord used to keep it on your head), so characteristic of the region. The quality of keffiyahs does vary considerably. The elegant flowing ankle-length *jalabiyya* tunic is available at shops all over Jordan.

The non-profit agencies listed earlier in the section specialise in a wide range of attractive textiles in the form of cushions, tablecloths, wall hangings and traditional clothing. Many also sell small mosaic plaques, which can be a nice reminder of Madaba.

The small bottles of coloured sand from Petra and Aqaba are a speciality. The sand is poured into bottles to form intricate patterns, and these are sold for as little as 500 fils.

In Aqaba you may be urged to buy something made from coral but for the sake of the precious marine environment, please don't. In any case, buying anything made of coral is illegal.

Duty Free
There are duty-free shops at the Queen Alia International Airport, and next to the Ammon Hotel in Amman; and small ones at the airports at Marka (in Amman) and Aqaba, and at the three border crossings with Israel.

Export Restrictions
Exporting anything more than 100 years old is illegal, so don't buy any souvenir that is deemed by the salesman as 'antique' – if only because it probably isn't. You may be offered 'ancient' coins around some of the archaeological sites. These may be genuine, but buying them – and taking them home – is highly illegal. If you are unsure about what is an 'antique', contact the **Customs Department** (☎ 06-4623186) in Amman.

Getting There & Away

Most visitors come to Jordan as part of a jaunt around the Middle East. Amman is well connected with most cities in the Middle East and Europe, but no airline has direct flights between Amman and Canada, Australia or New Zealand, and there are very few direct services between Amman and the USA. Schedules for international (and domestic) flights to/from Amman are listed in the English-language newspapers published in the capital. See Newspapers & Magazines in the Facts for the Visitor chapter.

Please note that the information in this chapter is particularly vulnerable to change.

AIR

Jordan is well connected by air with Europe and the rest of the Middle East, but cheap tickets are rare. Always remember to reconfirm your onward or return flight at least 72 hours before departure on international flights.

Airports

The modern **Queen Alia International Airport** (☎ 06-4452000), about 35km south of Amman, is the country's main gateway. There are two terminals, only 100m apart and opposite each other. Terminal 1 is used for most Royal Jordanian flights (with the notable exception of flights to/from Amsterdam) and Terminal 2 is used for all other flights on all other airlines. Both terminals have ATMs that take most major credit cards, as well as foreign exchange counters, a post office and a left luggage counter.

The former military airfield in Marka, northeast of central Amman, is sometimes officially called the Amman Civil Airport. From this airport, there are flights to/from Gaza in the Palestinian Territories and Tel Aviv in Israel. The only other international (and domestic) airport is at Aqaba and some international carriers stop in Aqaba en route to Amman. There are occasional charter flights between Europe and Aqaba.

Tickets

Generally, there is nothing to be gained by buying a ticket direct from the airline. Discounted tickets are released to selected travel agencies and specialist discount

Warning

The information in this chapter is particularly vulnerable to change: Prices for international travel are volatile, routes are introduced and cancelled, schedules change, special deals come and go, and rules and visa requirements are amended. You should check directly with the airline or a travel agent to make sure you understand how a fare (and ticket you may buy) works and be aware of the security requirements for international travel.

The upshot of this is that you should get opinions, quotes and advice from as many airlines and travel agents as possible before you part with your hard-earned cash. The details given in this chapter should be regarded as pointers and are not a substitute for your own careful, up-to-date research.

agencies, and these are usually the cheapest deals going.

One exception is booking on the Internet. Many airlines offer some excellent fares to web surfers. Readers have recommended both w www.connections.be and w www.taxistop.be for discounted tickets to Jordan. Online ticket sales work well if you are doing a simple one-way or return trip on specified dates.

You may find the cheapest flights are advertised by obscure agencies. Most firms are honest and solvent, but there are some rogue fly-by-night outfits around. Paying by credit card generally offers protection, as most card issuers provide refunds if you can prove you didn't get what you paid for. Similar protection can be obtained by buying a ticket from a bonded agency, such as one covered by the Air Travel Organiser's Licence (ATOL) scheme in the UK.

If you purchase a ticket and later want to make changes to your route or get a refund, you need to contact the original travel agency. Airlines issue refunds only to the purchaser of a ticket – usually the travel agency that bought the ticket on your behalf. Many travellers change their routes halfway through their trips, so think carefully before you buy a ticket that is not easily refunded.

Airlines The national airline, **Royal Jordanian** (W www.rja.com.jo), has flights to most major cities in Europe and all over the Middle East. (If you fly with Royal Jordanian, ask them about a free connection to Aqaba.) **Royal Wings** (W www.royalwings.com.jo), a subsidiary of Royal Jordanian, has smaller planes for short Amman–Tel Aviv and Amman–Gaza flights.

Travellers with Special Needs If they're warned early enough, airlines can often make special arrangements for travellers such as wheelchair assistance at airports or vegetarian meals on the flight. Children under two years travel for 10% of the standard fare (or free on some airlines) as long as they don't occupy a seat. They don't get a baggage allowance. 'Skycots', baby food and nappies should be provided by the airline if requested in advance. Children aged between two and 12 can usually occupy a seat for around two-thirds of the full fare, and do get a baggage allowance.

The website W www.everybody.co.uk has an airline directory that provides information on the facilities offered by various airlines to people with disabilities.

Departure Tax The departure tax on all international flights from Amman and Aqaba for foreigners (who are not citizens of a country in the Middle East – they pay nothing) is JD10. Jordanians pay JD25! At Queen Alia airport, the tax must be paid at special counters after you've checked your luggage in, and before you've cleared immigration. If you're in Jordan for less than 72 hours, and depart by air from Queen Alia, you may be exempt from the departure tax, but only if you ask.

The USA There is very little direct traffic between the USA and Jordan, so it's often worthwhile getting a cheap flight to Europe (normally London, Frankfurt or Amsterdam) first, and looking for a cheap deal from there. Alternatively, get a connection in a country near Jordan on a Middle Eastern airline. Saudi Arabian Airlines has flights from New York, via Washington, to Jeddah and Riyadh, and connections to Amman. The cheapest option is probably to fly into Israel and the Palestinian Territories and then cross the border into Jordan by bus or service taxi.

However, this means that your passport will have those disliked Israeli entry stamps – see the boxed text 'Travelling To/From Israel and the Palestinian Territories' in the Facts for the Visitor chapter.

Discount travel agents in the USA are known as consolidators. San Francisco is the ticket consolidator capital of America, although some good deals can be found in Los Angeles, New York and other big cities.

STA Travel (☎ 800-777 0112; W www.statravel.com) has offices throughout the US.

Cheap Tickets (W www.cheaptickets.com) is another recommended agency.

Canada Air Canada and Royal Jordanian offer flights, via London or Frankfurt, to Amman. In the low season, return fares from Montreal start at around C$1950, or C$2200 from Toronto.

Canadian discount air tickets are about 10% higher than those sold in the USA.

Travel CUTS (☎ 800-667-2887; W www.travelcuts.com) is Canada's national student travel agency and has offices in all major cities.

Australia There are no direct flights between Australia and Jordan. One of the cheaper routes to Amman from Melbourne or Sydney is with Qantas Airways or Thai Airways International to Bangkok, and on to Amman with Royal Jordanian. Return low/high season fares start at A$1450/1700. Other airlines flying from Australia include Gulf Air, Emirates and Olympic Airways.

STA Travel (☎ 131 776; W www.statravel.com.au) has offices in all major cities and on many university campuses. **Flight Centre** (☎ 131 600; W www.flightcentre.com.au) also has branches around the country.

New Zealand Flights to Jordan from New Zealand are generally via Frankfurt or Bangkok. From New Zealand, you can expect to pay around NZ$1650 for a return flight to Amman in the low season. **STA Travel** (☎ 0800 874 773; W www.statravel.co.nz) and **Flight Centre** (☎ 0800 243 544; W www.flightcentre.co.nz) have offices in Auckland, Hamilton, Palmerston North, Wellington, Christchurch and Dunedin.

The UK London and other cities in England are well connected with Amman, although some of the cheapest airlines do not fly there directly and require a lengthy (even overnight) stopover. Some of the airlines mentioned below offer 'open jaw' tickets which, for example, allow you to fly in to Amman, but out of Beirut (Lebanon) or Damascus (Syria).

Some of the cheapest flights from the UK to Amman are on Olympic Airways, via Athens; Turkish Airlines, via İstanbul; and Tarom, via Bucharest. Low season return fares start from £320. Royal Jordanian flies between London and Amman every day, once a week via Berlin and once a week via Frankfurt. Expect to pay £420 for a return fare.

Discount air travel is big business in London. Advertisements for many travel agencies appear in the travel pages of the weekend broadsheet newspapers, in *Time Out*, the *Evening Standard* and in the free magazine *TNT*.

STA Travel (☎ 0870 160 6070; w *www .statravel.co.uk*) has branches across the country.

Continental Europe KLM-Royal Dutch Airlines and Lufthansa Airlines offer the most direct flights to Amman, and have excellent connections all around Europe and the UK. Amsterdam and Frankfurt are the two major hubs for air transport in Europe, and home to 'bucket shop' agencies selling discounted fares.

One cheap airline worth considering is Cyprus Airways, which flies to Amman (via Larnaca, Cyprus) from Amsterdam, Berlin, Dresden, Frankfurt, Hamburg, Paris, Milan, Rome, Geneva and Zurich.

From Frankfurt, fares start at US$1250 for a return flight. A recommended agency is **STA Travel** (☎ 030-311 0950; *Goethestrasse 73, 10625 Berlin*), which has branches in major cities across Germany. **Usit Campus** (☎ 01805 788 336; w *www.usit campus .de*), also has several offices in Germany.

As the base for KLM and the home of a multitude of bucket shops, Amsterdam is a popular departure point, with fares to Amman starting at around €1160. Some of the best fares are offered by the student travel agency **NBBS Reiswinkels** (☎ 020-620 50 71). It has seven branches in Amsterdam, and its fares are comparable to those of London bucket shops. NBBS Reiswinkels also has branches in Brussels (Belgium).

In Italy, recommended travel agents include **CTS Viaggi** (☎ 06-462 0431), a student and youth specialist with branches in major cities, and **Passagi** (☎ 06-474 0923). Expect to pay €660 for a return flight to Amman.

Recommended in Paris is **OTU Voyages** (☎ 01 40 29 12 12; w *www.otu.fr*), which has branches across France. Other recommendations include **Voyageurs du Monde** (☎ 01 42 86 16 00; w *www.vdm.com*) and **Nouvelles Frontières** (☎ 08 25 00 08 25; w *www .nouvelles-frontieres.fr*), with branches across the country. Return fares to Amman start at €1100.

The Middle East Jordan is a decent base from which to explore the Middle East, and there are regular flights from Amman (and, to a lesser degree, from Aqaba) all around the region. Flights are not particularly cheap, however, but specials (eg, over the Thursday/ Friday Islamic 'weekend') are sometimes available.

From Amman, there are regular non-stop direct flights to the following (prices are approximate):

destination	airlines	one way/ return (JD)
Abu Dhabi	Gulf Air/ Royal Jordanian	275/350
Bahrain	Gulf Air/ Royal Jordanian	290/300
Beirut	MEA/Royal Jordanian	90/150
Cairo	Egypt Air/ Royal Jordanian	135/150
Damascus	Royal Jordanian/ Syrian Air	55/95
Dhahran	Saudi Arabian	246/330
Doha	Gulf Air/Qatar Airways/ Royal Jordanian	295/300
Dubai	Royal Jordanian/ Emirates	285/365
İstanbul	Royal Jordanian/ Turkish Airlines	210/250
Jeddah	Royal Jordanian/ Saudi Arabian	215/290
Riyadh	Saudi Arabian	275/325

In Amman, the best places to start looking for air tickets are the agencies along Al-Malek Al-Hussein St, near the flyover.

The nearest thing you will find to a discount ticket market in the Middle East is offered by some travel agencies in Israel (particularly in Tel Aviv) and in İstanbul.

In Tel Aviv, try the **Israel Student Travel Association** (ISSTA; ☎ 03-524 6322; 128 Ben Yehuda St). There's also a branch in Jerusalem (☎ 02-625 2799; 1 HaNevi'im St).

In İstanbul there are lots of travel agencies on the northern side of Divan Yolu in Sultanahmet, all of them specialising in budget air tickets. **Orion-Tour** (☎ 212-232 6300; ⓦ www.oriontour.com; Halaskargazi Caddesi 284/3, Marmara Apartimani, Sisli 80220) is highly recommended.

The area around Midan Tahrir in Cairo is teeming with travel agencies, but don't expect any amazing deals. One of the best agencies in Cairo, though it's way down in Ma'adi, is **Egypt Panorama Tours** (☎ 02-350 5880; ⓔ ept@intouch.com) just outside Al-Ma'adi metro station.

LAND

Crossing the border into Jordan from Iraq or Saudi Arabia is nigh impossible, so most travellers come overland from Syria or Israel and the Palestinian Territories (or by ferry from Egypt). However, there are three important things to note:

- *Any* indication of travel to/from Israel and the Palestinian Territories will mean that you cannot enter Syria, Lebanon and most other Middle Eastern countries, although Jordan is OK. See the boxed text 'Travelling To/From Israel and the Palestinian Territories' in the Facts for the Visitor chapter for details.
- All travellers should obtain a visa for Syria before coming to Jordan – see the boxed text 'Getting Other Visas in Jordan' in the Facts for the Visitor chapter
- Jordanian visas are not available at the Israel/ Jordan border at King Hussein Bridge

Most travellers arrive in Jordan by bus if travelling overland, although it's no problem bringing your own car or motorbike. Drivers of cars and riders of motorbikes will need the vehicle's registration papers and liability insurance. Strictly speaking you don't need an International Driving Permit (IDP) to drive in Jordan (your national licence is generally sufficient), but bring one with you to avoid any hassles. You also need a *Carnet de passage en douane*, which is effectively a passport for the vehicle and acts as a temporary waiver of import duty. The *carnet* will also need to specify any expensive spare parts that you're planning to carry

with you, such as a gearbox. This is designed to prevent car-import rackets. Contact your local automobile association for details about all documentation.

At the borders to Jordan (and the ferry terminal in Nuweiba, Egypt) you'll be obliged to take out local insurance of JD35 (valid for one month), plus a nominal 'customs fee' of JD5 for 'foreign car registration'.

Finally, bring a good set of spare parts and some mechanical knowledge, as you will not always be able to get the help you may need. This is especially the case for motorbikes: there are only a few motorbike mechanics in Jordan who are able to deal with anything modern.

See Car & Motorcycle in the Getting Around chapter for more information about driving around Jordan.

Syria

If you want to travel directly between Damascus and Amman, it's worth taking a direct bus or service taxi. Otherwise you may end up spending more time and money once you catch a service taxi to Der'a, organise your own transport across the border, get another lift to Ramtha, perhaps another to Irbid, and then a connection to Amman. The only reason to travel this way is if you want to stop off en route at places such as Ezra'a and Bosra ash-Sham (Syria), or Jerash, Umm Qais and Al-Himma.

Border Crossings The two border crossings between Syria and Jordan are efficient and relatively painless on both sides.

Der'a/Ramtha and Nasib/Jabir are both open for 24 hours every day. The Jordanian sides both have a post office and **tourist office** (open 8am-5pm Sat-Thur, 8am-2pm Fri), moneychangers (open most of the time) where Jordanian dinars and Syrian pounds are changed, and places to eat and drink.

Ramtha is the border most commonly used by foreigners using public transport, and is best for detours to northern Jordan.

Der'a/Ramtha See Ramtha in the Jerash & the North chapter for information about travelling to this border town. From Ramtha, service taxis and minibuses regularly go to the border. If hitching, ask the immigration office on the Jordanian side to flag down a vehicle for a lift to the Syrian border.

Nasib/Jabir Some public transport is now using this border, although Jabir is primarily a crossing for trucks travelling between Amman and Damascus. This crossing is good for a detour to eastern Jordan (eg, Azraq) as the border at Jabir is useful for connections to Zarqa or Mafraq.

Bus Air-conditioned Jordan Express Travel & Tourism (JETT) buses travel between Amman and Damascus (JD5, four to five hours) twice a day in either direction; book at least a day in advance. JETT also has daily buses to Aleppo (JD7.500). JETT's international office is just up from the Abdali bus station in Amman, while the Syrian government bus company, Karnak, has buses from next door. All Damascus services from Amman stop at the Karnak bus station. Afana (also near Abdali bus station) also has an evening bus to Damascus (JD5, 9pm).

Buses are the most comfortable way to cross the border, although you'll have to wait longer than in a shared taxi to complete the formalities. (See Getting There & Away in the Amman chapter for more details.)

Train Services on the Hejaz Railway between Amman and Damascus leave Amman on Monday and Thursday at 8am; they leave Damascus at the same time. Tickets cost JD2.500. The charming old station is on King Abdullah I St, about 2.5km east of the Raghadan station in Amman.

The train may be quaint, but quick it ain't. The trip officially takes eight hours – not counting stops at both sides of the border (allow at least an extra three hours). The **ticket office** (☎ 06-4895413) is really only open from 7am on the morning of departure, although you may find someone around at other times. To get to the station, take a service taxi from Raghadan, or a private taxi (around 800 fils).

Car & Motorcycle If you intend to drive between Jordan and Syria, the better border to cross is at Der'a/Ramtha.

Service Taxi Service taxis – or servees – are slightly faster than buses and run at all hours, although it's harder to find one in the evening. Service taxis take less time to cross the border than trains or buses because there are fewer passengers to process,

The Hejaz Railway

The Hejaz Railway was built between 1900 and 1908 to transport pilgrims from Damascus to the holy city of Medina, reducing the two-month journey by camel and foot to as little as three days. For Jordan, and Amman in particular, this meant an increased boom in trade. The 1462km line was completely funded by donations from Muslims – but lasted less than 10 years.

The trains and railway line were partially destroyed during the Arab Revolt of 1917 during WWI. The line was rebuilt as far south as Ma'an, but is now only used for cargo. The line between Damascus and Amman is still used for passenger services in both directions, and anyone with enough money can charter a carriage between Amman and a nearby town.

and the drivers are experienced in helping passengers with immigration and customs formalities. These taxis are huge, yellow (or white) and American-made.

From Amman, service taxis leave from the eastern or lower end of the Abdali bus station; from Damascus, they leave from next to the Karnak bus station. The trip costs JD6 from Amman, and S£400 from Damascus. Service taxis also travel between Damascus and Irbid (South bus station) in northern Jordan for JD4.500 or S£300.

Iraq
It's very difficult to get an Iraqi visa in Jordan; see the boxed text 'Getting Other Visas in Jordan' in the Facts for the Visitor chapter.

Saudi Arabia
As with Iraq, getting a visa to Saudi Arabia is nigh impossible – see the boxed text 'Getting Other Visas in Jordan' in the Facts for the Visitor chapter for details.

The main land route for public transport into Saudi Arabia is Al-Umari, along the highway south of Azraq. The other two crossing points are Ad-Durra, south of Aqaba, and further east at Al-Mudawwara.

Elsewhere in the Middle East
For many destinations in the Middle East, travellers need time, patience – and most importantly – the necessary visas. These trips are long, so you're better off flying.

Service taxis go to Kuwait (JD30) and Beirut (JD15), and Hijazi has buses to Dubai (JD45), usually once a week.

JETT has services to the following cities from its international bus office in Amman:

destination	days	one way	hours
Beirut	Sun & Thur	15JD	6
Cairo	Sun & Tues	US$58	24
Doha	daily	44JD	30
Dubai	daily	52JD	36
Kuwait	Fri	30JD	18
Manama	daily	35JD	24

Note that the fare to Cairo must be paid in US dollars, and includes the Aqaba–Nuweiba ferry ticket.

Israel & the West Bank

Since the peace treaty between Jordan and Israel was signed in 1994, three border crossings have opened to foreigners – King Hussein Bridge, Sheikh Hussein Bridge and Wadi Araba.

Border Crossings Before crossing into Jordan from Israel and the Palestinian Territories, there are a few things you need to remember:

- Only change as much money as you need because the commission charged by money-changers is often ridiculously high
- Jordanian visas cannot be obtained on arrival at the King Hussein Bridge
- Private vehicles cannot drive across the King Hussein Bridge, but they can be taken across the other borders
- Refer to the boxed text 'Travelling To/From Israel and the Palestinian Territories' in the Facts for the Visitor chapter for information about how deal with the Israeli passport-stamp issue
- Israeli visas of one month's duration are issued at the Wadi Araba (Rabin) and Sheikh Hussein Bridge crossings, but those issued at the King Hussein Bridge are usually for three months

On both sides of all three borders, there are moneychanging facilities, places to eat and drink, and duty-free shops. On the Jordanian side of all three borders, there is a **post office** and **tourist information counter** *(both open 8am-2pm daily, closed on Friday)*.

King Hussein (Jisr al-Malek Hussein)/ Allenby Bridge Only 40km from Amman and 30km from Jerusalem, this border crossing point *(open 8am-6pm Sun-Thur, 8am-2pm Fri & Sat)* offers travellers the most direct route between the two cities. Transport doesn't run during the Jewish Shabbat between sunset Friday and sunset Saturday.

Due to the ongoing intifada and Israeli army action in the Palestinian Territories, no Jordanian buses were crossing King Hussein Bridge at the time of research. Instead they were using other crossings to avoid the West Bank. There are service taxis from Amman's Abdali bus station to (but not across) King Hussein Bridge (JD1.500, 45 minutes) throughout the day and a daily JETT bus (JD6.500). The historic oddity of this crossing has remained enshrined in the fact that, on leaving Jordan, you're not really considered to be leaving Jordan. Prior to 1988, Jordan laid claim to the West Bank as its own territory, and somehow this idea has remained in the approach to visas. If you wish to return to Jordan from the Palestinian Territories on your current Jordanian visa, you need only keep the stamped exit slip and present it on returning by the same crossing (it won't work at the other crossings). Going the other way, however, the Israeli exit tax is a hefty 150NIS (and rising all the time), supposedly because you're paying to leave Israel *and* the Palestinian Territories.

It's a common way to exit, but not enter, Jordan, because Jordanian visas are not issued at this border – so get a Jordanian visa at an embassy/consulate beforehand, or use another border crossing.

The ride to the Israeli and Palestinian Territories side, although extremely short, can seem to last an eternity with repeated stops for passport and bag checks. At the time of research, it was not possible to walk, hitch or take a private car across. Service taxis (around JD1) shuttle between the two borders. There are moneychanging facilities on your way to the exit.

Crossing the border can take up to three hours; avoid 11am to 3pm when delays are more common. Note that if you're entering Jordan this way and intend to return to Israel, you must keep the entrance form given to you by the Jordanians – they may well insist on you prolonging your stay in Jordan if you cannot present it.

To get to Jerusalem from the border, take a *sherut* (Israeli shared taxi) to Damascus Gate or a cheaper bus to Jericho and then a *sherut* to Damascus Gate. Much of the public transport in the West Bank was not running when we were there.

Wadi Araba This handy crossing *(formerly Arava, now Rabin to the Israelis; open 6.30am-10pm Sun-Thur, 8am-8pm Fri & Sat)* in the south of the country links Aqaba to Eilat (Israel and the Palestinian Territories). Get there early (before opening time, if possible) to beat the vehicles that start rolling up at 7am. If you're coming down from Jerusalem and you want to skip Eilat, ask the driver to let you out at the turn-off for the border, a short walk away.

If you're crossing from Jordan, central Eilat is only 2km away. Buses run between the Wadi Araba crossing and the Taba crossing into Egypt, via Eilat's central bus station.

Sheikh Hussein Bridge (Jisr Sheikh Hussein) The northernmost crossing *(Jordan Bridge to the Israelis; open 6.30am-10pm Sun-Thur, 8am-8pm Fri & Sat)* links northern Jordan with Beit She'an in Galilee. It's handy if you wish to visit northern Jordan, and it's the closest crossing to Jerusalem and Amman that will issue Jordanian visas on arrival.

From Irbid, regular service taxis leave the West bus station for the border (750 fils, 45 minutes). From the bridge it's a 2km walk (or hitch) to the Israeli side, from where you have to take a taxi to the Beit She'an bus station for onward connections inside Israel and the Palestinian Territories.

If you're coming from Israel, take a bus to Tiberias, and change at Beit She'an (6km from the border). From there, take another bus to the Israeli border (allow enough time because there are only a handful of buses per day). After passport formalities, a compulsory bus takes you to the Jordanian side.

From the Jordanian side, either wait for a minibus or shared taxi to Irbid (from where there are regular connections to Amman), go to Shuneh ash-Shamaliyyeh (North Shuna) by private or service taxi, or walk (3km) to the main road and flag down a minibus or service taxi.

Bus Several cities in Jordan are now regularly linked to cities in Israel and the Palestinian Territories. Travelling by bus directly between Amman and Tel Aviv will save you the hassle of getting to/from the borders, but it's more expensive than crossing independently, and you'll have to wait for all passengers to clear customs and immigration.

From Amman, Trust International Transport has buses (from its office at 7th Circle) to Tel Aviv (JD21, Sunday to Friday) and also to Haifa (JD18) and Nazareth (JD18). Departures are at 8.30am. Trust also offers services most days from Irbid and Aqaba for the same price.

Car & Motorcycle If you're driving from Israel, use the border crossings at Sheikh Hussein Bridge or Wadi Araba/Rabin (it is not possible to drive over the King Hussein Bridge).

Departure Tax
Almost all foreign tourists leaving Jordan by land must pay a departure tax of JD5. If you are in the country for less than 72 hours, you are usually exempt from departure tax.

SEA
There are two boat services to Nuweiba in Egypt from the passenger terminal just south of Aqaba. With both services, departure times can be subject to change so it's worth calling the **passenger terminal** *(☎ 03-2013240)* on the morning of the day you wish to travel to check the departure time. For noon departures, you should always get there by around 10.30am.

The fast boat, which leaves most days at noon, takes about an hour and costs US$30; children between the ages of five and 12 pay US$18, while those under five pay US$12. It's more expensive (US$45) to come the other way due to government taxes.

There is also a slower ferry service (which doubles as a car ferry) that officially leaves at noon but often leaves quite a few hours later. Some days it doesn't leave at all. If it does, it should take three hours but it usually takes longer. There was talk of another service at 6pm, but this is only during exceptionally busy times (like the haj). The cost is US$22, or US$13/8 for children over/under five. A car in either direction costs an extra US$110.

Tickets in either direction must be paid for in US dollars, which can be bought from the bank inside the terminal building. It's not possible to buy return tickets – if you want to return the same way, you must buy two one-way tickets. Beware of buying ferry tickets in Amman because you may be charged for nonexistent 1st-class seats – buy the tickets in Aqaba.

People of most nationalities can obtain tourist visas on arrival at Nuweiba, but it's best to check this with the Egyptian embassy in Amman or the consulate in Aqaba; travellers from some countries (notably Eastern Europe) have been refused entry onto the ferry at Aqaba because they had no Egyptian visa. It is imperative to note that if you wish to travel further than Sharm el-Sheikh you need a visa for Egypt, rather than a visa just for the Sinai peninsula (see the boxed text 'Getting Other Visas in Jordan' in the Facts for the Visitor chapter).

The worst time for travelling is just after the haj, when Aqaba fills up with hajis (pilgrims) returning home from Mecca to Egypt – the delays and confusion are an introduction to the bureaucratic frustrations that may await in Egypt.

There are money exchange facilities at the terminals at Nuweiba and Aqaba, primarily for buying visas on arrival. Only change enough cash (avoid travellers cheques, which attract hefty commissions) to last until you reach a decent bank or moneychanger.

There has also been talk of a weekly catamaran trip between Aqaba and Sharm el-Sheikh (officially US$90, three hours), known as the 'Fly the Sea' service, but this wasn't operating at the time of research.

Departure Tax
The departure tax on the ferry from Aqaba to Nuweiba is JD5 and is not included in your ticket price.

ORGANISED TOURS
Organised tours take all the hassle out of travelling on your own, but limit your inde-

pendence and are more expensive. See Organised Tours in the Getting Around chapter for details of companies within Jordan that organise tours.

Overland Buses & Trucks
Overland companies offer long-distance, budget-priced trips around Jordan or include Jordan in their trips around the Middle East. UK-based companies include **Dragoman** (☎ 01728-861 133, fax 861 127; e brox@dragoman.co.uk; w www.dragoman .co.uk), **Exodus** (☎ 020-8675 5550; w www .exodustravels.co.uk) and **New Frontier Expeditions** (☎ 016-2686 3443).

Tour Groups
The following groups run organised tours to Jordan:

Australia
Adventure World (☎ 02-9956 7766)
Ya'lla Tours (☎ 03-9523 1988, fax 9523 1934, e yallamel@yallatours.com.au)

UK & Europe
Idris Tours (e f.eykenduyn@planet.nl) Specialises in small group hiking, archaeological and eco tours
Imaginative Traveller (☎ 020-8742 8612, fax 8742 3045, w www.imaginative-traveller.com)
Jasmine Tours (☎ 020-7675 8886, fax 7673 1204, e info@jasmin-tours.co.uk)
Tribes (Fair Trade Travel; ☎ 017-2868 5971, fax 2868 5973, e info@tribes.co.uk)

USA
Journeys Unlimited (☎ 212-366 6678, w www.journeys-intl.com)

Israel
Desert Eco Tours (☎ 972-8 6344259, fax 8 6370104, w www.desertecotours.com) Specialises in camel, hiking and 4WD tours

Getting Around

Jordan is so small that it's possible to drive from the Syrian border in the north to the Saudi border in the south in little more than five hours. There is only one domestic flight (Amman to Aqaba) and no internal public train service, so the main forms of public transport are public buses and minibuses, private buses, service taxis and private taxis.

Where public transport is limited or nonexistent, hitching is a common way of getting around. Hiring a car is a popular if more expensive alternative. Chartering a service taxi (white) or private taxi (yellow) is another alternative, and having a driver will take the hassle out of driving, although the cost will vary depending on your bargaining skills and the distance.

AIR

Since only 430km separates Ramtha in the north from Aqaba in the south, Jordan has only one internal flight, between Amman and Aqaba. It's operated by Royal Wings, a subsidiary of Royal Jordanian. See Aqaba in the Southern Desert & Aqaba chapter for details. See the *Jordan Times* for schedules for this daily flight (and international flights).

There is no departure tax on domestic flights within Jordan.

BUS & MINIBUS

Public minibuses and, to a lesser extent, public buses are the normal form of transport for locals and visitors. They usually leave from obvious bus/minibus stations, although sometimes minibuses leave from other specific spots (indicated on the maps). Buses and minibuses can be hailed from anywhere along the route (although you'll have to stand if there are no seats left). Private buses leave from outside their booking offices.

While private buses are normally labelled in English, this is not the case with most public buses and minibuses, which also don't stand under English-language destination signs. Bus/minibus stations are normally fairly chaotic, so you'll invariably have to ask directions to the correct bus or minibus. Jordanians are happy to help, and simply asking 'Amman?' or 'Karak?' is all that is usually necessary – always double-check with other passengers when embarking.

Tickets for public buses and minibuses are normally bought on the bus. For private buses, tickets are usually bought from an office at the departure point. Tickets for private buses should be bought at least a day in advance; on public buses and minibuses it's every man, woman, child and goat for themselves. Private buses are quicker than public buses and minibuses because they travel directly from one destination to another along the quickest route, and don't take detours or stop to pick up passengers.

There are no set rules about men and women sitting next to each other. Unaccompanied men and women can sit next to each other, but some seat-shuffling often takes place to ensure that unaccompanied foreign men or women do not sit next to members of the opposite sex that they do not know.

Private Bus

It's often worth paying extra for a comfortable and air-conditioned private bus, especially between Amman and Aqaba.

Hijazi runs a regular service between Amman and Irbid, and other private buses travel between Amman and Aqaba. The best two companies are Jordan Express Travel & Tourism (known simply as JETT) and Trust International Transport. Both offer pretty much the same standard of bus, and have similar prices. JETT has several services a day between Amman and Aqaba, as well as services to Petra, Hammamat Ma'in and the King Hussein Bridge (for the border to Israel and the Palestinian Territories). Trust has several services a day between Amman and Aqaba.

Public Bus & Minibus

Large public buses are not as common as minibuses. The correct fares for both are nearly always posted in Arabic somewhere inside the front of the vehicle. Ask the other passengers what to pay. Sometimes you will have to pay the full fare even if you're not going the full distance.

Public buses and minibuses normally only leave when full, so waiting is often required. Standing is not normally allowed (there's little room anyway), but they'll sometimes pick up extra passengers along the way.

DISTANCE CHART (KM)

	Ajlun	Amman	Aqaba	Azraq	Irbid	Jerash	Karak	King Hussein Bridge	Ma'an	Madaba	Ramtha	Tafila	Wadi Musa (Petra)
Ajlun	---												
Amman	73	---											
Aqaba	396	328	---										
Azraq	155	103	415	---									
Irbid	32	89	408	143	---								
Jerash	22	51	370	132	38	---							
Karak	182	118	252	205	202	164	---						
King Hussein Bridge	78	56	367	152	109	89	151	---					
Ma'an	279	212	116	289	294	255	154	252	---				
Madaba	95	32	325	119	115	77	86	64	296	---			
Ramtha	57	94	410	141	28	40	205	130	296	118	---		
Tafila	242	179	189	266	267	229	63	215	90	151	296	---	
Wadi Musa (Petra)	297	230	97	317	313	275	142	268	45	228	316	81	---

TRAIN

There is no internal passenger train service in Jordan. The Hejaz Railway is an international passenger service between Amman (Jordan) and Damascus (Syria), and does not stop anywhere inside Jordan – see Syria under Land in the Getting There & Away chapter for details.

TAXI

Jordan has thousands upon thousands of service taxis (white) and private taxis (yellow). The service taxi – known sometimes as a servees – is a common form of transport that runs along set routes within many towns, and between most towns, as well as between Jordan and the neighbouring countries of Iraq, Syria and Saudi Arabia (see the Getting There & Away chapter for more information).

Service taxis and private taxis (which go wherever you want them to go) can be chartered. Hiring a service taxi for a day is usually cheaper than renting a car, but a long-distance trip in a private taxi will probably cost more than renting a car.

If the taxi driver doesn't speak English, use the Arabic script in this guidebook or ask a local who does speak English to write down the destination(s) in Arabic. A pocket calculator will help with negotiating charter costs and determining normal fares.

Service Taxi

Service taxis are usually battered Peugeot 504 or 505 station wagons with seven seats, or battered Mercedes sedans with five seats. They are always white, and usually have writing and numbers (in Arabic) indicating their route.

Because of the limited number of seats, it usually doesn't take long for one to fill up. They cost up to twice as much as a minibus, and about 50% more than a public bus, but are quicker because they stop less often along the way to pick up passengers. However, they're not always as comfortable as a bus or minibus, especially if you have to squeeze in with someone you don't know.

The seven-seaters normally have room for one passenger in the front (obviously the prized seat and the one lone women travellers should wait for), and two rows of three passengers behind the driver. Try to avoid the airless and bumpy seats right at the back.

The five-seaters normally squeeze two passengers in the front and three in the back. To avoid waiting for passengers, or to give yourself extra room, you can always pay for an extra seat. Women should always do this to avoid sitting next to a local man. If chartering a taxi, single females should always sit in the back.

Chartering a service taxi along a set route (eg, Aqaba to Ma'an) will always be cheaper than chartering a private taxi (yellow). To find out the cost of chartering a service taxi, only one person should approach the driver and ask the cost *per person* of a fare in the shared service taxi, and simply multiply this fare by five or seven, depending on the taxi size. For longer distances, the price is far more negotiable.

Private Taxi

Private yellow taxis can be chartered for any long-distance trip, but are more expensive than service taxis. For indirect routes, longer trips and stopovers, drivers of private taxis are more amenable than service taxis, and all fares are very negotiable.

CAR & MOTORCYCLE

You need courage to drive in Jordan. The people are exceptionally friendly, welcoming, hospitable and courteous, but their driving is quite appalling, selfish and takes no account of any other driver.

MJ & EM Bissett, UK

Visitors from any country where road rules are obeyed may be shocked by the traffic in Jordan, especially in Amman. But anyone who has driven elsewhere in the Middle East may find the traffic comparatively sedate. Indeed, provided that you can avoid driving in Amman, you're unlikely to encounter too many difficulties if you take reasonable care.

There are three main highways south of Amman:

Desert Highway A boring dual carriageway that detours all major tourist attractions
Dead Sea Highway Hot and uninspiring, this is the quickest way to travel between Amman and Aqaba
King's Highway By far the most interesting – but most difficult and time consuming – is the ancient King's Highway, which goes through most major attractions in Jordan

Trips

It makes little sense to hire a car to travel to places like Petra and Jerash, which need a day or more to be explored properly, and can only be visited on foot; or to Wadi Rum, where a 4WD as well as a local driver is needed. Three days is often the minimum period allowed by rental companies (see Suggested Itineraries in the Facts for the Visitor chapter).

Jordan's Most Scenic Drives

First-time visitors to Jordan are often pleasantly surprised by the country's spectacular scenery, although those that only race along the Desert Highway will wonder what all the fuss is about. The most scenic routes are those between the low-lying Jordan Valley and Dead Sea and the eastern plateau. Among these, the roads from **Umm Qais to Al-Himma** and from **Mt Nebo to Suweimeh** are very picturesque, while **Deir Alla to Salt** is incredibly steep and affords stunning views – cyclists should definitely start the journey in Salt. Also quite beautiful is the last stretch of road from **Madaba to Hammamat Ma'in**. The Dead Sea Highway between **Suweimeh and Safi** has some rewarding vistas.

Just about anywhere along the King's Highway rewards the effort to get there, especially **around Dana**, across **Wadi Mujib** and, to a lesser extent, through **Wadi Hasa**. A number of roads around Wadi Musa and Petra are lovely around sunset, most notably the drive from **Wadi Musa to Tayyibeh**. Although nothing compared to the wonders within Wadi Rum, the road from the **Desert Highway turn-off to Rum village** is enough to get you excited about what lies ahead.

Road Rules

Vehicles drive on the right-hand side of the road in Jordan, at least in theory. The general speed limit inside built-up areas is 50km/h or 70km/h on multilane highways in Amman, and 90km/h to 110km/h on the highways. Note that indicators are seldom used, rules are occasionally obeyed, the ubiquitous horn is a useful warning signal and pedestrians must take their chances. The condition of the roads varies; unsigned speed humps are common, as are shallow ditches across the road, usually at the entrance to a town.

Wearing a seat belt is now compulsory, which is fairly pointless because most seats in most vehicles don't have them – including passenger seats in service taxis and private taxis – and a recent survey suggested that fewer than 30% of Jordanians used them. Traffic police are positioned at intervals along the highways. Police tend to be fairly indulgent towards foreigners so long as they do nothing serious.

Checkpoints

All major roads, especially near the borders, have occasional checkpoints manned by the police, but King Abdullah II has ordered a reduction in the number of military checkpoints along the main highways in an effort to make Jordan more accessible for, and friendly towards, foreign tourists.

Checkpoints are mainly for Jordanian drivers of private vehicles, and for trucks. Buses, minibuses, service taxis and private taxis rarely need to stop; if they do, drivers just quickly show their papers to the police. Sometimes police come into a bus (there's rarely room in a minibus) to check the identification papers of passengers (usually young men). Foreigners are rarely bothered, and if you're asked to show your passport (this is more likely to happen anywhere near a border) it's probably more out of curiosity than anything else.

If you have chartered a private taxi, the driver is often waved through the checkpoint when the policeman sees smiling foreigners, obviously out for a day trip. If you're driving a rented or private vehicle, you may be stopped. Again, there's a good chance you'll be waved on unless the policeman is friendly or bored. You are only likely to be asked serious questions if you seem to be going near the border with Iraq.

Nonetheless, always keep your passport, drivers licence, rental agreement and registration papers handy, especially along the Dead Sea Highway. In recent years rental cars have been used by Palestinian militants to cross into Israel and the Palestinian Territories, so police near the border are unusually vigilant.

Accidents

Despite the small population, and relatively good roads, accidents are alarmingly frequent. In 2001 there were 52,000 road accidents in Jordan with 783 fatalities (an average of 16 for every 10,000 vehicles), with a large number of victims being pedestrians and children. As a result, the Jordanian government has forced the traffic police to become more vigilant.

The roads where accidents are more common are those frequented by long-distance trucks, eg, the short stretch of Highway 65 (south of Aqaba to the Saudi border) and Highways 10 and 40 east of Amman.

In the case of an accident in a rental car, do not move the vehicle. Get a policeman from the local station to attend the scene immediately, obtain a police report (Arabic is OK) and contact the car rental company – not obtaining a police report will normally invalidate your insurance. Depending on where you are, most reputable companies will send someone to the scene within hours. If there's any serious injury to you or someone else, also contact your travel insurance company at home and your embassy/consulate in Amman.

If your own private car is involved in an accident, your driving licence and passport will be held by the police until the case has been finalised in a local court – which may take weeks. If you have an accident and there are serious injuries, contact the police and ring your embassy/consulate.

Telephone numbers for local police stations are mentioned throughout the book, but two emergency numbers (☎ 191 and ☎ 192) are valid for police emergencies anywhere in Jordan, and should be answered by English-speaking staff. In Amman, there are separate numbers for the **Highway Police** (☎ 06-5343402) and **Traffic Police** (☎ 06-4896390 or ☎ 190) – the exact difference between the two, however, is unclear.

Driving Tips

If you're driving around Jordan, read the following carefully:

- Many road signs are in English, but they are sometimes badly transliterated (eg, 'Om Qeis' for Umm Qais). Brown signs are for tourist attractions, blue signs for road names and green signs for anything Islamic, such as a mosque
- Take care when it's raining: water and sand (and sometimes oil) make a lethal combination on the roads
- Before and after most small towns and villages, there are brown signs with the words 'welcome' or 'goodbye' in English – but they rarely indicate in English the *name* of the town or village
- One-way streets and speed humps are often not signposted
- Always watch out for obstacles: pedestrians who walk along the road; cars darting out of side roads; and herds of goats and camels, even on the major highways
- Roundabouts are often large, and all drivers (local and foreign) find them totally confusing
- Petrol stations are not that common, so fill up as often as you can

- Parking in major towns, especially Amman, is a problem, but it's easy to find (and normally free) at major attractions like Jerash, Petra and Madaba
- Most roads (and even the highways) are dangerous at night because white lines are not common, obstacles (eg, herds of camels) are still roaming about, and some cars have no headlights or put them permanently on high beam

Rental

Renting a car can be expensive, but if you can split the costs, it's a great way of seeing a lot of Jordan quickly and easily. There's nowhere in the country to rent a motorbike.

There are many rental agencies in Amman, a few in Aqaba and one or two at Terminal 2 in the Queen Alia airport. Any car rental agency in a small town, or even a city like Irbid, is usually just an office with one guy, one desk, one telephone and one car for hire (usually his!). Avoid these smaller agencies unless a local friend can do the negotiating and driving. It's best to stick with the big international companies, or some of the larger local agencies.

Expect to pay from JD15 to JD25 per day for the smallest, cheapest sedan in Aqaba or Amman – plus insurance and petrol. This usually includes free unlimited kilometres – undoubtedly a better deal than accepting a cheaper set rate with a charge per kilometre.

Discounts of about 5% are available for weekly rentals; anything longer than one week should come with a discount. Cars can be booked, collected and paid for in Amman or Aqaba and dropped off in the other city, but the rental companies charge up to JD35 for this service. Companies need a credit card for a deposit, but payment can be also made with cash; most major credit cards are accepted.

To ensure that you don't break down in the middle of nowhere, you should always rent a car less than three years old – most reputable compa ies won't offer anything else. Most rental cars have air-conditioning, which is a godsend in summer and vital along dusty tracks. Cars with automatic transmission are more expensive, but anyone not used to driving on the right-hand side of the road should consider renting an automatic rather than a manual. Always carry a decent road map – these are not provided by rental agencies. Child-restraining seats are available for an extra fee.

Some agencies are closed on Friday and public holidays. If so, prearrange collection and delivery to avoid longer rental periods. Check the car with a staff member for bumps, scratches and obvious defects, and check brakes, tyres, etc, before driving off.

Finally, there is a myriad of complicated conditions and charges to remember and consider:

- Most agencies only rent to drivers over 21 years old; some stipulate that drivers must be at least 26 years
- Some offer free delivery and collection within the same city, but only during working hours
- Most agencies accept your licence from your home country, but only if you've been driving for more than one year. It's worth bringing along an International Driving Permit just in case. The agency will also need to see your passport for extra identification
- Rental is often for a minimum of three days, sometimes two and barely ever for one day. Very rarely will any agency give a refund if you return the car early
- Rented cars cannot be driven outside Jordan

Insurance

All rental companies offer insurance, but this is usually included in the price they will quote to you. Always ask. In case of an accident, you'll have to pay an excess of about JD200 to JD300. To avoid this, major rental agencies offer a Collision Damage Waiver (CDW) fee from about JD7 per day for normal cars, which will absolve you of all accident costs – definitely worth considering.

Insurance offered by major companies usually includes Personal Accident Insurance and Theft Protection, which may be covered by your travel insurance policy from home. Always read the conditions of the contract carefully before signing – an English translation should always be provided.

If you're driving into Jordan in a private vehicle, compulsory third-party insurance must be purchased at the border for about JD35 (valid for one month). You also pay a nominal customs fee of JD5 for 'foreign car registration'.

4WDs

Four-wheel drives are only necessary if you're going to out-of-the-way places in the deserts, such as Burqu. However, 4WDs should only be hired – and driven – by someone who is experienced; driving in the desert where there are no signs, and getting bogged in sand in 45°C heat, is no fun as well as being dangerous.

Four-wheel drive vehicles can be rented from reputable agencies in Aqaba and Amman, but are far more expensive than normal sedans; at least JD65 per day. Insurance is also higher (from about JD12 per day). Also, companies only offer 100 to 200 free kilometres; you then pay extra for each kilometre.

To get around Wadi Rum, you'll need to charter a 4WD jeep with a local driver.

Petrol & Repairs

Benzin 'adi (regular) petrol costs 300 fils per litre, and the less frequently available *mumtaz, khas* (super) costs 370 fils. Remember to check with your rental company as to which petrol your car requires; most take super. Best of luck if you're looking for unleaded. *Khal min ar-rasas* (unleaded petrol) costs about 350 fils per litre, but is only reliably available in Amman and even then at only a few stations – look for the 'unleaded petrol' signs in English at stations in the more upmarket suburbs, eg, around 6th, 7th and 8th Circles, or ask a rental company. Any other stations in Jordan which claim to sell 'unleaded petrol' are probably just giving you leaded petrol at the unleaded price. Diesel is available at about 150 fils per litre.

Petrol stations are obvious, but the only sign in English is 'Jordan Petroleum Refinery Co Ltd' (the state-run monopoly). Stations can be found on the outskirts of major towns, and at some junctions, although you may have to ask at a few if you're looking for super. Along the Desert Highway, there are plenty of stations. There are fewer along the King's Highway, and *very* few along the Dead Sea Highway.

Garages with reputable mechanics can be found on the outskirts of most towns. They can handle most repairs, at negotiable prices, but check with your rental company before getting anything done.

Motorcyclists should be aware that there are precious few mechanics in Jordan able to deal with the average modern motorcycle and its problems.

BICYCLE

Cycling is a popular option, but not necessarily always a fun one. March to May and September to November are the best times to get on your bike.

The disadvantages are: the stifling heat in summer; the few places to stop along the highways; the unpredictable traffic, with drivers not being used to cyclists; the steep streets in some cities, such as Amman and Karak; the paucity of spare parts because so few locals ride bikes; and mischievous children throwing stones at unwary cyclists.

There is no way to cycle along the King's Highway without getting stoned. We read it in your guidebook before leaving, but thought that kids would not stone three male adults with beards and long trousers who are looking angry. We were wrong. And there are not only *some* groups of kids who try to stone you, but basically it's becoming a *major hobby for all male children* between three and 20... Cycle in the morning when children are at school and plan to spend plenty of time discussing and waiting; you probably won't do more than 40km a day.

Bernhard Gerber, Switzerland

The good news, however, is the road system is satisfactory and the roads are generally smooth, while the cities and tourist attractions are well signposted in English.

With some preparation, and an occasional lift in a bus, cyclists can have a great time. Most major sights are conveniently placed less than a day's ride apart heading south from the Syrian border – ie, Irbid–Amman–Madaba–Karak–Dana–Petra–Ma'an–Wadi Rum–Aqaba. All these places have accommodation of some kind and restaurants, so there's no need to carry tents, sleeping bags and cooking equipment. Other attractions can be easily visited on day trips, by bike or public transport, from places such as Amman, Irbid, Madaba, Karak and Ma'an. The King's Highway is the most scenic route, but also the most difficult. The Desert Highway is boring and the traffic is heavy, while the Dead Sea Highway has extremely few stops, and is always hot. Two stretches along the King's Highway where you may want to take public transport are across the extremely wide and steep Wadi Mujib valley between Madaba and Karak, and between the turn-off to Wadi Rum and Aqaba, which is very steep, has appalling traffic and plenty of treacherous turns. Some of the steepest climbs are those from the Jordan Valley up onto the eastern plateau in the north.

The most scenic route between Amman and Aqaba is:

Day 1 Amman to Ariha – 91km (seven hours)
Day 2 Ariha to Wadi Hasa – 66km (five hours)
Day 3 Wadi Hasa to Dana Nature Reserve – 65km (six hours)
Day 4 Dana Nature Reserve to Wadi Musa – 48km (four hours)
Day 5 Wadi Musa to 20km south of the turn-off to Wadi Rum – 106km (seven hours)
Day 6 Wadi Rum to Aqaba – 50km (three hours)

What to Bring

Bicycles can travel by air. Some travellers take them to pieces and put them in a bike bag or box; others wheel the bike to the check-in desk where it should be treated as a piece of baggage. The pedals may have to be removed and the handlebars turned sideways so that the bike takes up less space in the hold. Check with the airline well in advance, preferably before you pay for your ticket.

Spare parts are not common in Jordan, so carry a spare tyre, extra chain links, spokes, two inner tubes, repair kit and tool kit with spanner set. Also bring a low gear set for the hills, a couple of water containers and confine your panniers to a maximum of 15kg.

HITCHING
Getting a Ride

Hitching is never entirely safe in any country in the world. Travellers who choose to hitch should understand that they are taking a small, but potentially serious, risk. People who choose to hitch will be safer if they travel in pairs and let someone know where they are planning to go.

Despite this general advice, hitching is definitely feasible in Jordan. The traffic varies a lot from place to place, but you generally don't have to wait long for a lift on main routes. There's no need to hitch around Jordan simply to save money, because public transport to most places is frequent, and always cheap. But hitching is often necessary to avoid chartering expensive taxis where public transport is limited or nonexistent, eg, parts of the King's Highway and to the desert castles east of Amman.

For the Desert Highway, take a bus to Queen Alia International Airport and disembark at the turn-off to the airport. For anywhere north and east of Amman, take a minibus from Abdali bus station to the roundabout in Suweileh, from where several roads branch out to Jerash, Azraq, Irbid and Salt. Avoid hitching too close to the borders with Israel and Iraq, and always carry your passport.

Always start hitching early, and avoid 1pm to 4pm when it's often too hot, and traffic is reduced while many locals enjoy a siesta. Also, don't start hitching after about 4pm unless it's a short trip on a road with frequent traffic, because hitching after dark increases the risk. The best places to look for lifts are junctions, tourist attractions (eg, lookouts) or shops where cars often stop. Police stationed at major junctions and checkpoints are often happy to wave down drivers and cajole them into giving you a lift.

To indicate that you're looking for a lift, simply raise your index finger in the direction you're heading. On a large truck, you may be asked for a fare; in a private vehicle, you probably won't need to pay anything. However, to avoid a possibly unpleasant situation, ask beforehand if payment is expected and, if so, how much the driver wants. Otherwise, just offer a small amount when you get out – it will often be refused.

Finally, a few general tips. Don't look too scruffy; don't hitch in groups of more than two; women should be very careful, and look for lifts with families, or in a car with another local or foreign female; trucks on some steep and windy roads (eg, between the Wadi Rum turn-off and Aqaba) can be painfully slow; and make sure you carry a hat and lots of water.

Picking up Hitchhikers

If you have chartered a service taxi or private taxi you are under no obligation to pick up any hitchhikers, but if you're driving a private or rented car, the pressure to pick up people along the way can be intense. You can, of course, simply drive past the locals alongside the road waving their arms frantically, but if you stop at a checkpoint, petrol station, lookout or shop you may often be approached for a lift (single female drivers should not pick up male hitchhikers). If you don't want an extra passenger, make excuses about lengthy detours, long stopovers and late arrivals – this may not always work, however, because the passenger(s) may also like to visit a few remote castles on the way.

On major highways, such as the Desert Highway (where there's plenty of public transport), the obligation to pick up passengers is far less. However, on remote stretches where public transport is limited or nonexistent, eg, across the Wadi Mujib valley, you should try to pick up a few passengers.

One advantage about picking up a hitchhiker is the chance to meet a local, and readers have often been invited to a home in return for a lift. Although you may be charged, you should never charge a local for a lift. They will assume that any foreign hitchhiker can afford to pay for transport, and that any foreigner driving a private or rental car doesn't need the extra money.

LOCAL TRANSPORT
Bus
The two largest cities, Amman and Irbid, have efficient and cheap public bus networks, but they're unlikely to be of much use to visitors. These buses cater to locals travelling to and from their homes in the suburbs, so they rarely go anywhere useful to the visitor. Also, none of the public buses have destination signs in English (although some have 'English' numbers), there are no schedules or timetables available and local bus stations are often chaotic. Service taxis are more common throughout Jordan, and the private taxis are still cheap by Western standards.

Service Taxi
Major cities, such as Amman and Irbid, are well served by service taxis that run along set routes within each city, and often go to (or past) places of interest to visitors. As with intercity service taxis, the route is listed in Arabic on the driver's door and drivers wait until they are full before departing.

Private Taxi
The other common mode of transport for visitors is the yellow private taxi. Some travellers avoid using private taxis on principle, but after climbing up and down the *jebels* (hills) of Amman, or staggering around in the infernal summer heat of Aqaba, you'll be glad to fork out the dinar equivalent of less than US$2 for a comfortable, air-conditioned ride across town.

Yellow private taxis are very common in major towns like Amman, Irbid, Jerash,

Ma'an, Madaba, Wadi Musa (Petra) and Aqaba, and important transport junctions like Shuneh al-Janubiyyeh (South Shuna) and Tafila. There is no standard method of payment: in Amman, all taxis are metered, but foreigners occasionally need to persuade the driver to use it; in Wadi Musa, taxis are not metered and the standard fare anywhere local is JD1; and elsewhere, taxis are not metered and fares are negotiable, especially in Aqaba where drivers can be unscrupulous.

ORGANISED TOURS
Many visitors to Jordan come on organised tours, prearranged from their own country. (Organised Tours in the Getting There & Away chapter has more information about foreign companies that offer tours to and around Jordan.)

Most travel agencies in Jordan simply sell airline tickets and/or serve as ground operators for major foreign tour companies. They don't offer organised tours on a regular basis, but will if you provide the itinerary and find the passengers – in which case it's cheaper to arrange everything yourself.

If you're travelling independently, and on a tight budget, jumping on an irregular and budget-priced organised tour to a remote place like the desert castles of eastern Jordan is far easier, and often cheaper, than doing it yourself. Ask at your hotel.

The local agencies listed below are recommended:

Alia Tours (☎ 06-5620501, fax 5620503, ⓦ www.aliatours.com.jo)
Archaeological Adventure Travel & Tourism (☎ 03-2157892, fax 2157891, ⓔ a-a@index.com.jo)
Atlas Travel & Tourist Agency (☎ 06-4624262, fax 4610198, ⓦ www.atlastours.net) Also offers watersports and side trips to Israel, Syria and Lebanon
Discovery (☎ 06-5697998, fax 5698183, ⓔ discovery@nets.com.jo)
Golden Crown Tours (☎ 06-5511200, fax 551 1202) Also specialises in archaeological, religious and adventure tours
International Traders (☎ 06-5607014, fax 566 9905, ⓔ sahar@traders.com.jo) Highly recommended, this company is also the representative for American Express in Amman and Aqaba
Jordan Eco-Tours (☎ 06-5524534, fax 06-5536964)

Near East Resources (☎ 06-5861431, fax 5712815, w www.ner-jordan.com)

Petra Moon Tourism Services (☎ 03-2156665, fax 2156666, w www.petramoon.com) A good agency which also offers an interesting range of treks in remote areas, such as Petra and Dana Nature Reserve

Petra Travel & Tourism (☎ 06-5667028, fax 5681402)

Royal Society for the Conservation of Nature (RSCN, ☎ 06-5350456, fax 5347411, w www.rscn.org.jo) Conservation society worth contacting for eco-tours, especially around Dana Nature Reserve, Wadi Rum and Wadi Mujib

Royal Tours (☎ 06-5857154, fax 5856845, e rtours@rja.com.jo) Part of the Royal Jordanian group, and good for stopover packages for those flying with Royal Jordanian

Sahar Tours (☎ 06-4622054, fax 4645054, w www.sahartours.net)

Universal General Tourist Services (☎ 03-203 1078, fax 2031079, e rock@firstnet.com.jo) Can organise German-speaking guides, and specialises in southern Jordan

Zaman Tours & Travel (☎ 03-2157723, fax 215 7722, e zamantours@joinnet.com.jo) Arranges adventure tours, camping, camel treks and hiking

Amman

عمان

AMMAN

☎ 06 pop • 1.8 million

Amman is a modern Arab city rather than a great, ancient metropolis of the Orient; it has never rivalled Damascus or Cairo as a grand Islamic city of antiquity. For those arriving from Syria or Egypt it can, depending on your perspective, feel either refreshingly or disappointingly modern and Westernised. Its obvious tourist attractions – the Roman Theatre, Odeon and Citadel – can be easily visited in a few hours.

But if you scrape below the surface, Amman has lots to offer the visitor, not least the balance it strikes between the demands of the past and the next generation's vision for the future. Residents talk openly of two Ammans, although in truth there are many. Eastern Amman (which includes Downtown) is home to the urbanised poor; it's conservative, more Islamic in its sympathies, and has vast Palestinian refugee camps on its fringe. Western Amman is a world apart, with leafy residential districts, trendy cafés and bars, impressive art galleries, and young men and women walking openly arm in arm. The up-market district of Shmeisani is referred to by locals as 'shiny Amman' while the Abdoun area sometimes, and not without a little irony, goes by the label of 'Paris'. While that's stretching it a little, it is nonetheless impossible to gain a full understanding of Amman without visiting both areas.

The city has undergone a massive transformation in recent years, and its character has been indelibly altered by the arrival of Palestinian refugees, most significantly in 1990 and 1991 when as many as 500,000 flooded into the city as a result of the Iraqi invasion of Kuwait and the subsequent Gulf War. Many of these new arrivals were highly educated and pushed the boundaries of a cultural life that had been kept under close rein by Islamic conservatives. Along with a young generation of Jordanians, these Palestinians have helped to make Amman a tolerant and outward-looking city.

Don't come to Amman looking for medieval *souqs* and bazaars, or the wonderful mosques of Islam's grand architectural heritage. Do come to Amman to catch a glimpse of a thoroughly modern Arab city, embracing an international and culturally

Highlights

- **Citadel** – walk around the ruins of ancient Amman, visit the impressive National Archaeological Museum, and admire the views of the modern city

- **Roman Theatre** – sit and watch Jordanians come and go from high in Amman's most spectacular ancient monument, and visit the nearby Odeon

- **Darat al-Funun** – enjoy this tranquil place with contemporary art, traditional architecture and one of the nicest cafés in Jordan

- **Nightlife** – join the hip young locals in the cool cafés and wine bars of Shmeisani and Abdoun

diverse vision of the future. Whether you're in the urbane suburbs of the west, or the earthy, chaotic Downtown district, the welcome you receive is sure to be warm.

HISTORY

Excavations in and around Amman have turned up finds from as early as 3500 BC, with most earlier inhabitants living on Jebel al-Qala'a (the site of the Citadel). There has been a town on this site since at least the Bronze Age; objects dated to this time show that the town was involved in trade with Greece, Syria, Cyprus and Mesopotamia.

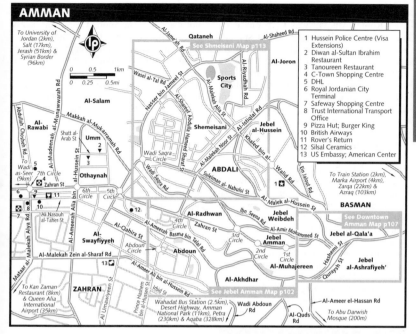

AMMAN

To University of
Jordan (2km),
Salt (17km),
Jerash (51km) &
Syrian Border
(96km)

Qataneh
Al-Jame'ah Rd
Al-Shaheed Rd

Al-Joron

1 Hussein Police Centre (Visa
   Extensions)
2 Diwan al-Sultan Ibrahim
   Restaurant
3 Tanoureen Restaurant
4 C-Town Shopping Centre
5 DHL
6 Royal Jordanian City
   Terminal
7 Safeway Shopping Centre
8 Trust International Transport
   Office
9 Pizza Hut; Burger King
10 British Airways
11 Rover's Return
12 Silsal Ceramics
13 US Embassy; American Center

See Shmeisani Map p113

Sports
City

Al-Salam

Makkah al-Mukarramah Rd

Umm
Othaynah

Shemeisani

Jebel
al-Hussein

ABDALI

BASMAN

To Train Station (2km),
Marka Airport (4km),
Zarqa (22km) &
Azraq (103km)

Al-Radhwan

Jebel
Weibdeh

Jebel
Amman

Jebel al-Qala'a

See Downtown
Amman Map p107

Al-Swayfiyyeh

Abdoun

Al-Muhajereen

Jebel
al-Ashrafiyeh'

ZAHRAN

Al-Akhdhar

See Jebel Amman Map p102

To Kan Zaman
Restaurant (8km),
& Queen Alia
International
Airport (35km)

Wahadat Bus Station (2.5km),
Desert Highway, Amman
National Park (11km), Petra
(230km) & Aqaba (328km)

Wadi Abdoun
Rd

Al-Quds
Rd

To Abu Darwish
Mosque (200m)

Al-Ameer el-Hassan Rd

Biblical references indicate that by 1200 BC Rabbath Ammon, or Great City of the Ammonites in the Old Testament, was the capital of the Ammonites. King David sent Joab at the head of the Israelite armies to besiege Rabbath, after being insulted by the Ammonite king Nahash. After taking the town, David burnt many inhabitants alive in a brick kiln. Rabbath continued to flourish and supplied David with weapons for his ongoing wars. His successor Solomon erected a shrine in Jerusalem to the Ammonite god Molech. From here on, the only biblical references to Rabbath are prophecies of its destruction at the hands of the Babylonians.

The history of Amman between then (circa 585 BC) and the time of the Ptolemies of Egypt is unclear. Ptolemy Philadelphus (283–246 BC) rebuilt the city during his reign, and it was named Philadelphia after him. The Ptolemy dynasty was succeeded by the Seleucids and, briefly, by the Nabataeans, before Amman was taken by Herod around 30 BC, and fell under the sway of Rome. The city, which even before Herod's arrival had felt Rome's influence as a member of the Decapolis (see the boxed text 'The Decapolis'), was totally replanned in typically grand Roman style. It became an important centre along the trade route between the Red Sea and Syria.

Philadelphia was the seat of Christian bishops in the early Byzantine period, but the city declined and fell to the Sassanians (from Persia) in about AD 614. At the time of the Muslim invasion in about AD 636, the town – by then named Amman – was again thriving as a staging post on the caravan trade route. From about the 10th century, however, the city declined, and it was reduced to a prison town for exiled princes.

Amman was nothing more than a sad little village when a colony of Circassians resettled there in 1878. In 1900, it was estimated to have just 2000 residents. It boomed temporarily in the early 20th century when it became a stopover on the new Hejaz Railway between Damascus and Medina (Saudi Arabia). In 1921 it became the centre of Trans-Jordan when Emir Abdullah made it his headquarters. In 1948, many Palestinians settled in and around Amman and, two years later, it was officially declared the capital of the Hashemite kingdom.

AMMAN

ORIENTATION

Like Rome, Amman was born on seven major *jebels* (hills), but today it spreads across 19 – many of which are over 800m above sea level. As such, it's not really a city to explore on foot, apart from within the Downtown area – known by locals as *il-balad*. A straight road is almost unheard of, so it can get confusing at times.

The only way to make any sense of Amman in a short time is to pick out the major landmarks on the *jebels*. The main hill is Jebel Amman, home to some embassies, a few hotels and trendy restaurants. The traffic roundabouts (some now replaced with tunnels and major intersections) on Jebel Amman are numbered west of Downtown from 1st Circle to 8th Circle. If you're travelling in a taxi, street names will mean little so ask for the nearest 'circle' and walk from there, or give the driver a nearby landmark (like an embassy or hotel).

Jebel al-Hussein, northwest of Downtown, has the Housing Bank Centre; its mossy, terraced facade sticks out a mile. This also marks the start of the upmarket

The Decapolis

The Roman commercial cities of what is now Jordan, Syria, Israel and the Palestinian Territories first became known collectively as the Decapolis in the 1st century AD. Despite the etymology of the word, it seems that the Decapolis consisted of more than 10 cities, and possibly as many as 18. No one knows for certain the reason behind such a grouping. In all likelihood the association of the cities served a double function: to unite the Roman possessions and to enhance commerce. In Jordan, the main Decapolis cities were Philadelphia (Amman), Gadara (Umm Qais), Gerasa (Jerash), Pella and possibly Abila.

The cities were linked by paved roads that allowed wagons and chariots to circulate rapidly; at Umm Qais and Jerash, the ruts carved by these wagons can still be seen in the stones of the city streets. The cities flourished during the period of Roman dominance in the east, but fell into decline with the dawn of the Umayyad dynasty, which was based in Damascus. Afterwards, the choice of Baghdad as the centre of the Muslim world dealt the Decapolis a final blow.

Shmeisani area, which stretches out to the north as far as the Sports City. It has plenty of restaurants, shops, top-end hotels and a few nightclubs. Another trendy area is Abdoun, a few hills south of Shmeisani and home to super-cool cafés.

Closer to Downtown is the Abdali area, home to the Abdali bus station and topped by the distinctive blue dome of the King Abdullah Mosque.

Books & Maps

Jordan Today is a free monthly booklet that includes embassies, airlines, travel agencies, car rental companies and other helpful information in English, as well as news of upcoming events. *Calendar – Jordan* is similar. To track down a copy, ask at one of the tourist offices or at your hotel. They're also on display in some restaurants.

Other useful booklets include the pocket guide published by Al-Kutba (JD3 to JD5), although its appeal is more for historical information about the city and surrounds. It's available in some bookshops around town.

The maps in this guidebook should be sufficient for most visitors. If you plan to stay for some time and intend to visit places in the remote suburbs, the *Street Map of Amman* published by Luma Khalaf is detailed and worth picking up. It shows just about every street in the city and also pinpoints many businesses (who fund the map through their advertising), embassies and other helpful buildings. It doesn't, however, cover the area west of the Roman Theatre. The map is available from some hotels around Amman and, usually, from International Traders on Al-Shareef Abdulla Hameed Sharaf St in Shmeisani.

INFORMATION
Tourist Offices

The place to head for information is the ground floor office of the **Ministry of Tourism and Antiquities** (☎ 4642311, fax 4646264; Al-Mutanabbi St), southwest of the 3rd Circle in Jebel Amman. The staff are friendly, speak good English and the office (though not the rest of the ministry) is open 8am to 11pm daily. This is also the centre for the tourist police. If you wish to lodge a tourism-related complaint, call ☎ 80022228 (free if calling from a nonmobile or public telephone).

If you're after brochures and more information about Jordan's tourist attractions than the daily events on offer in Amman, it may be worth contacting the **Jordan Tourism Board** (☎ 5678294; Tunis St). It's next to the Ammon Hotel (see Places to Stay) between 4th and 5th Circles and open 8.30am to 4pm Saturday to Thursday.

Visa Extensions
If you're staying in Jordan for longer than 14 days, you must obtain a visa extension.

The process is simple but involves a little running around. First you will need to get your hotel to write a short letter confirming where you are staying. Your hotel will also need to fill out two copies of a small card (or photocopy) that states all their details. On the back of the card is the application form for an extension, which you must fill out. It's in Arabic but your hotel should be able to help you fill it out and answers can be in English. That done, take the form, letter, photocopies of the front pages of your passport and the Jordanian visa page, and your passport to the relevant police station.

Which police station you visit depends on which area of Amman you're staying; ask your hotel for directions to the relevant office. If you're staying Downtown, go to the first floor of the Al-Madeenah Police Station on Al-Malek Faisal St.

After getting the relevant stamp, take your passport to the Muhajireen Police Station (markaz amn muhajireen) on Al-Ameerah Basma bin Talal Rd west of the Downtown area (see the Jebel Amman map). A taxi there from Downtown should cost around 600 fils or take service taxi No 35 along Quraysh St. A further stamp in your passport should see you with permission to remain in Jordan for an additional three months. Police stations are usually open for extensions from 10am to 3pm Saturday to Thursday, although it's better if you go in the morning. Extensions are granted on the spot and you're unlikely to spend more than 10 minutes in each office.

Money
Changing money is very easy and the Downtown area especially is awash with banks and moneychangers. The American Express representative is **International Traders** (☎ 560 7075; open 8am-6pm Sat-Thur), virtually opposite the Ambassador

Streets & Circles
With its endless one-way streets, narrow lanes and *jebels*, Amman is confusing enough to get around anyway, but the ambiguous names for the streets and circles can challenge the navigational skills of many visitors. We have used the more common names on the maps and in the text, but if street signs, directions given by locals and queries from taxi drivers are confusing you, refer to the list below.

Don't forget that Al-Malek means King, so King Faisal St is sometimes labelled Al-Malek Faisal St. Similarly, Al-Malekah is Queen and Al-Amir (Al-Emir) is Prince. And don't be too surprised that some 'circles' are now called 'squares'.

Streets
Al-Kulliyah al-Islamiyah St – sometimes known as Zahran St
Omar bin al-Khattab St – Mango St
Quraysh St – Saqf Sayl St
Abu Bakr as-Siddiq St – Rainbow St
Suleiman al-Nabulsi St – Police St

Circles
2nd Circle – Wasfi at-Tal Square
3rd Circle – King Talal Square
4th Circle – Abdullah bin Hussein Square
5th Circle – Emir (Prince) Faisal Square
6th Circle – Princess Tharwat Square
Ministry of the Interior Circle – Gamal Abdul Nasser Square

Hotel on Al-Shareef Abdulla Hameed Sharaf St (see the Shmeisani map). It does not change travellers cheques.

The Arab Bank, Jordan Gulf Bank and the Housing Bank for Trade & Finance are among those with widespread ATMs for Visa and MasterCard, while Jordan National Bank and HSBC ATMs allow you to extract dinars from your MasterCard and are Cirrus compatible. The Housing Bank has an ATM in the arrivals hall at Queen Alia airport; you get there after passing through customs so make sure you have some cash to buy your Jordanian visa if necessary.

Many moneychangers are located along Al-Malek Faisal St in Downtown. Sahloul Exchange Co, on the ground floor of the Aicco building, is especially good for travellers cheques.

JEBEL AMMAN

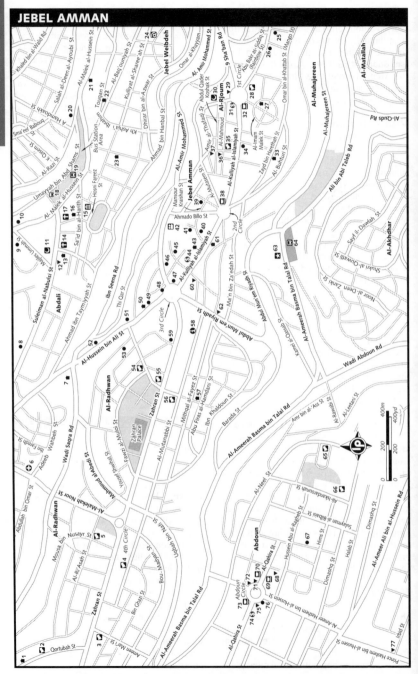

JEBEL AMMAN

PLACES TO STAY
1 Dove Hotel; Irish Pub
7 Radisson SAS Hotel
13 Caravan Hotel
16 Remal Hotel
21 Merryland Hotel
22 Select Hotel
23 Canary Hotel
27 Granada Hotel
33 Shepherd Hotel; L'Entrecote Restaurant
43 Jordan Inter-Continental Hotel; Post Office; Royal Jordanian; Pasha Nightclub; Bookshop
50 Grand Hyatt Amman; JJ Mahoney's
57 Hisham Hotel; Forest Inn Restaurant
61 Carlton Hotel

PLACES TO EAT
12 Snack Box
29 Diplomat Restaurant
36 Fakhr el-Din
37 Grappa
60 Bonita Inn; Las Tapas Latinas
62 Taiwan Tourismo
68 Planet Hollywood
71 McDonalds; Dunkin' Donuts; Baskin Robins
72 Ristorante Casereccio
75 Pizza Hut
77 Blue Fig Café

OTHER
2 Egyptian Embassy
3 Australian Embassy
4 German Embassy
5 Netherlands Embassy
6 Jordan Hospital & Medical Centre
8 Directorate of Residence, Borders & Foreigners
9 Parliament
10 Royal Jordanian Office
11 King Abdullah Mosque; Islamic Museum
14 Coptic Orthodox Church
15 Jordan National Gallery of Fine Arts
17 Greek Orthodox Church
18 Airport Express Bus
19 Abdali Bus Station
20 Gulf Air
24 Internet Cafes
25 Amusement Centre
26 British Council
28 Saudi Arabian Consulate; Sharbain's Bookshop
30 Mosque
31 Bank of Jordan; Firas Car Rental
32 Terrace Cafeteria Petra; Standard Chartered Grindlays
34 Islamic College
35 Iraqi Embassy; Museum of the Political History of HM Late King Abdullah bin al-Hussein; Haboob Grand Stores

38 Hills Café
39 Artisana
40 Al-Alaydi Jordan Craft Centre
41 Al-Burgan
42 Philadelphia Cinemas; Jordan Tower Centre
44 Jordan National Bank
45 Instituto Cervantes
46 Amman Bookshop
47 Jacob's Pharmacy
48 Oriental Souvenirs Store
49 Library; Ministry of Culture
51 Turkish Airlines
52 Emirates
53 Goethe Institut
54 Syrian Embassy
55 Spanish Embassy
56 French Embassy
58 Ministry of Tourism & Antiquities
59 Ministry of Foreign Affairs
63 Muhajireen Police Station
64 Minibuses to Dead Sea & Wadi as-Seer
65 Lebanese Embassy
66 UK Embassy
67 Orthodox Club
69 Caffe Moka; Arab Bank
70 Café de Paris; The Big Fellow Irish Pub; Galleria Cinemas
73 Al-Sanabel
74 Jordan National Bank; Citibank
76 Stallions; Salam Centre

Post

The **Central Post Office** (☎ 4624120; open 7.30am-7pm Sat-Thur) is along Al-Amir Mohammed St in Downtown. The poste restante mail is kept in a box behind a counter at the main entrance. It sometimes opens on Friday until 1.30pm.

There are smaller post offices around town (ask your hotel for the nearest), including at the Jordan Inter-Continental Hotel between 2nd and 3rd Circles, and in the Housing Bank Centre in Shmeisani.

Parcels The **Parcel Post Office** (Omar al-Khayyam St, Downtown; open 8am-2pm Thur-Sat) looks more like a shop, so look out for the weighing machine on the counter in the shop opposite the rear entrance to the Central Post Office. To send a large parcel anywhere, first go to the Parcel Post Office, where it's weighed. Then take it *unwrapped* to the **Customs Office** (open 8am-2pm Thur-Sat) virtually opposite (look for the sign with the word 'Customs' in English on the crest), where a customs declaration must be completed. Then take the parcel back to the Parcel Post Office for packing and paying.

Telephone

There is no central telephone office in Amman. To make a telephone call, use a telephone in your hotel (ask the price and minimum call length before dialling), or one of the numerous payphones operated by Alo (see Post & Communications in the Facts for the Visitor chapter for more information). These can be found on many pavements around town, including most street corners and tourist spots. Telephone cards are available at shops close to telephone booths and grocery stores around town. Long-distance calls can also be made at the obvious private telephone agencies around Downtown, including along Omar al-Khayyam St.

AMMAN

All telephone numbers in Amman now have seven digits. In general, add 5 to the start of all old six-digit numbers starting with 60, 66, 67, 68 and 69; or add 4 to any old number starting with 61, 62, 63, 64 or 65.

Fax
Most of the private telephone agencies around Downtown also offer fax services, as does the Central Post Office. Alternatively, try your hotel.

Email & Internet Access
Amman has plenty of Internet cafés. Among the best and most convenient in Downtown (all charging JD1 per hour) are:

Aicco Internet Café (☎ 4648649, e aicco@go.com.jo) Al-Malek Faisal St. Open 9am to 8pm Saturday to Thursday and some Fridays
Internet Yard (☎ 0795 509569, e dweib@joinnet.com.jo) Al-Amir Mohammed St. Open 24 hours
Yahoo Internet (☎ 464 7215) Al-Jaza'er St, behind Raghadan bus station. Open 9am to midnight Saturday to Thursday and 1pm to midnight Friday

Elsewhere, good places to try include:

Books@café (☎ 4650457, e contact@books-cafe.com) Omar bin al-Khattab St, Jebel Amman. A highly professional set-up (see Places to Eat later in this chapter) with fast connections. JD2 per hour; open 10am-11.30pm daily.
Safeway (e cybertunnel@safeways.com.jo) Nasser bin Jameel St, Shmeisani. JD1 per hour; open 24 hours.

There are also Internet cafés in Jebel Weibdeh (on Kulliyat al-Sharee'ah St), around Abdoun Circle, dotted around Shmeisani and near the University of Jordan.

Photography & Film
There are plenty of places around town that sell film although better places for developing tend to be in Shmeisani or Abdoun. One good place, among many, is **Salam Centre** (☎ 5922755; open 9am-9pm daily), right on Abdoun Circle. In Downtown, there are places on Al-Malek al-Hussein, Hashemi, Al-Malek Talal and Quraysh Sts where you can get passport photos taken immediately.

Travel Agencies
There is a plethora of travel agencies dotted around the city – a crowd of them is strung

along Al-Malek al-Hussein St, not far north of Downtown near the flyover, and along the northwestern end of Al-Shareef Abdulla Hameed Sharaf St in Shmeisani. Although some claim to organise tours within Jordan, the bulk are sales agents for international airline tickets.

Bookshops
Amman has a decent selection of bookshops.

Al-Aulama Bookshop (☎/fax 4636192) 44 Al-Amir Mohammed St, Downtown. This place is good for hard-to-find locally produced (and Lonely Planet) guidebooks, maps and postcards. Open 8am to 8pm Saturday to Thursday.
Amman Bookshop (☎ 4644013) Just down from 3rd Circle on Al-Amir Mohammed St, it has the best range of books and novels in Amman. Open 9am to 2pm and 2.30pm to 6.30pm Saturday to Thursday.
Books@café (☎ 4650457, e contact@books-cafe.com) On Omar bin al-Khattab St, it has a large, if eclectic selection. Open 10am to 11.30pm daily.
Bustami's Library (☎ 4622649) Right in the heart of Downtown on Al-Amir Mohammed St, this is the place to go for largely up-to-date Western magazines and an assortment of newspapers. Open 11am to 6.30pm Saturday to Thursday.
Jordan Inter-Continental (☎ 4641463) The bookshop in this top-end hotel has a good range of books about Jordan although prices are high.
Sharbain's Bookshop (☎ 4638709) On Abu Bakr as-Siddiq St a few metres from 1st Circle, this small shop has a few Western children's books in English. Open 8.30am to 1pm and 2.30pm to 6.30pm Saturday to Thursday.

Many souvenir shops have a selection of books about Jordan and a few maps.

Libraries
The **Amman Central Library** (☎ 4627718; open 9am-5pm Sat-Thur) is near the Roman Theatre on Hashemi St, Downtown. About half of the 1st floor is given to titles in English, and there are some current magazines in English and French on the top floor.

The **Ministry of Culture** has a small library (open from 8am to 2pm daily Saturday to Thursday), just along from the Grand Hyatt Amman on Al-Hussein bin Ali St (see the Jebel Amman map), but there are few English titles.

The Darat al-Funun gallery (see Art Galleries later in this chapter) has terrific art books. The main library at the University of Jordan is your best option for research. There are also libraries at the British Council and in the American, French, Spanish and German cultural centres.

Universities

One of the biggest universities in Jordan is the **University of Jordan** (W www.ju.edu.jo), over 10km northwest of Downtown. It boasts several museums (see Museums later in this chapter) and a huge library. It also offers language courses (see Courses in the Facts for the Visitor chapter), and is a great place to meet young locals. Numerous Internet cafés and Western fast-food outlets are dotted at various points along the main road, just opposite the university. Take any minibus or service taxi to Salt from either Raghadan or Abdali stations – the university is quite easy to spot from the main road.

Cultural Centres

All of the following cultural centres regularly organise film nights and lectures (generally in their own language), exhibitions and concerts (in their own language or Arabic). Tourists are normally welcome at these events, but it's always a good idea to ring the centre first to double-check on the information. You will also find details of functions at the various cultural centres listed in the two local English-language newspapers.

American Center (☎ 5859102) US Embassy, Al-Umawiyeen St, Abdoun. Has a library with US newspapers and magazines. Open 1pm to 4.30pm Saturday to Wednesday and 9am to 4pm Thursday.
British Council (☎ 4636147, fax 4656413, W www .britishcouncil.org/jordan) Abu Bakr as-Siddiq St, southeast of 1st Circle. Has a library with current English newspapers, and a pleasant café. Open noon to 6pm Sunday to Wednesday and 11am to 3.30pm Thursday.
Centre Culturel Français (☎ 4656862) On Kulliyat al-Sharee'ah St by the roundabout at the top of Jebel Weibdeh. Has a useful library. Open 8.30am to 2pm and 4pm to 8pm Saturday to Thursday.
Goethe Institut (☎ 4641993, fax 461 2383, e giam mvw@go.com.jo) 5 Abdul Mun'im al-Rifa'I St, northwest of 3rd Circle. Primarily for German speakers and open 9am to 1pm Sunday to Thursday, 4.30pm to 6.30pm Sunday, Tuesday and Wednesday, and 4.30pm to 6.30pm Monday.
Haya Cultural Centre (☎ 5665195) Ilya Abu Madhi St, Shmeisani. Designed for children, the centre

has a library, playground and museum (see Museums later in this chapter) and the centre regularly organises activities for children. Open 9.30am to 4pm Saturday to Wednesday.
Instituto Cervantes (☎ 4610858, fax 4624049, e cenamm@cervantes.es) Mohammed Hafiz Ma'ath St, behind Amman Surgical Hospital near 3rd Circle. Primarily for Spanish speakers, it has a library. Open 9am to 1pm and 4pm to 7.30pm Sunday to Thursday.
Royal Cultural Centre (☎ 5661026) Queen Alia St, Shmeisani. This large, modern complex hosts concerts and exhibitions. Functions are sometimes advertised in the local English-language newspapers.

Laundries

Several tiny laundries and dry-cleaning services are dotted around Downtown, particularly along Basman and Al-Malek Faisal St and in the laneways between both. Try also Cinema al-Hussein St, Downtown, and, for dry-cleaners, Safeway in Shmeisani.

Toilets

Most public toilets are grotty and you may have to pay 50 fils for the privilege. It's better to use a toilet in a restaurant or museum or ask nicely at any hotel.

Medical Services

Amman has more than 20 hospitals. Among the better ones are:

Islamic Hospital (☎ 5680127) Just off Al-Malek al-Hussein St, Jebel al-Hussein; see the Shmeisani map
Italian Hospital (☎ 4777101) Just off Italian St, southern Downtown; see the Downtown Amman map
Jordan Hospital & Medical Centre (☎ 5607550) Al-Malekah Noor St; see the Jebel Amman map
Palestine Hospital (☎ 5607071) Queen Alia St, Shmeisani; see the Shmeisani map
University Hospital (☎ 5353444) University of Jordan complex, northern Amman

The two English-language newspapers in Amman list the current telephone numbers of these and other hospitals, and of doctors on night duty throughout the capital. The two newspapers also publish a list of pharmacies open after hours. One of the more convenient pharmacies is **Jacob's Pharmacy** (☎ 4644945; open 9am-3pm daily) on 3rd Circle.

AMMAN

Emergency

We hope you won't need to contact any of the following numbers (staff answering these numbers should be able to speak English):

Ambulance	☎ 193
Fire Department	☎ 4617101, ☎ 199
Police	☎ 192, ☎ 191
Traffic Police/Accidents	☎ 4896390, ☎ 190

The main police station in Downtown is **Al-Madeenah Police Station** (☎ 4657788), upstairs on Al-Malek Faisal St opposite the Arab Bank. There are also small tourist police booths at the Citadel and on Hashemi St near the Roman Theatre. For details of lodging a tourism-related complaint, see Tourist Offices in the Facts for the Visitor chapter.

Dangers & Annoyances

The only problem you're likely to encounter is the traffic; if driving, avoid the chaotic Downtown area. The pollution can also affect those with respiratory problems, especially when dust levels are high. Nightclubs frequented by foreigners are more likely to attract pickpockets and bag snatchers, but crime in Amman is extremely rare.

ANCIENT AMMAN

Amman may be a sprawling modern city, but there are some evocative relics of its venerable past. In the heart of the Downtown area, the towering Roman Theatre climbs beautifully up one of Amman's hills and is perfectly complemented by the more compact Odeon. The old Forum is now a pleasantly shady place to sit or stroll while the Citadel affords fine views in addition to offering important signposts to Amman's varied history.

Citadel (Jebel al-Qala'a)

The first inhabitants of the area lived at the highest point of Amman, Jebel al-Qala'a (about 850m above sea level). Artefacts dating from the Bronze Age show that the hill was a fortress and/or agora for thousands of years. The complex is surrounded by 1700m-long **walls**, which were rebuilt many times during the Bronze and Iron Ages, and the Roman, Byzantine and Umayyad periods.

The Citadel's most impressive series of buildings is the **Umayyad Palace**, which stretches out behind the National Archaeological Museum (see Museums later in this chapter). Believed to be the work of Umayyad Arabs and dating from about AD 720, the palace was an extensive complex of royal and residential buildings and was once home to the governor of Amman. Its life span was short – it was destroyed by an earthquake in AD 749 and never fully rebuilt.

Coming from the south, the first major building belonging to the palace complex is the domed **audience hall**. It is the most intact of the buildings on the site and is shaped like a cross because it was built over a Byzantine church. Traces of former elegance remain from the time when it was expressly designed to impress visitors to the royal palace.

Crossing the Street in Amman

When you first arrive in Amman, one of your greatest challenges is likely to be making it safely from one side of the street to the other. This is especially true of the Downtown area, although the faster-moving thoroughfares elsewhere also pose a potential problem. Contrary to what you may think, Amman's drivers have no desire to run you over; they just want to get to their destination as quickly as possible. The installation of more traffic lights has made the situation a little easier, but you'll still have a better chance of survival if you follow a few simple 'rules'. In slow-moving traffic, the name of the game is brinkmanship – whoever yields last will win and a car missing you by inches may scare the hell out of you but is actually a normal and precisely calculated course of events.

Cross wide roads a lane at a time – if you wait for a big gap you'll be there all day. Some travellers have even been known to hail a taxi so that it will block traffic and give them a lane's head start. Make your decision and then don't hesitate – Amman's drivers will make their decisions based on a reasonable assumption of what you'll do next. Above all, have patience; an extra minute's wait is infinitely preferable to a nasty accident. And if all else fails, ask a local to lead you by the hand or at least follow in their slipstream.

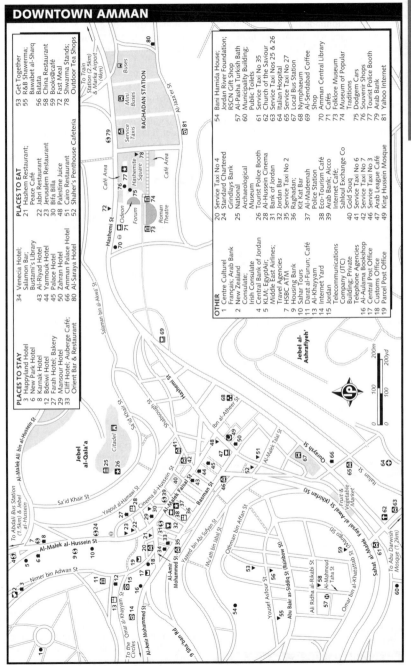

A **courtyard** immediately north of the hall leads to a **colonnaded street**, which was 10m wide, lined with numerous arches and columns, and flanked by residential and administrative buildings. Further to the north is the former **governor's residence**, which includes the **throne room**.

West of the audience hall is the **Umayyad Cistern**, an enormous circular hole with steps down to the bottom, which once supplied water to the palace and surrounding areas. The small disk on the floor in the centre is where a pillar once stood and was used for measuring water levels.

Back towards the museum to the south is the small **Byzantine Basilica**, or church. Little remains as much was destroyed by earthquakes. It dates from the 6th or 7th century AD, and contains a few dusty **mosaics**.

About 100m south of the basilica are the remaining pillars of the **Temple of Hercules**. Once connected to the Forum (see the boxed text 'Tunnel Under Amman'), the temple was built during the reign of Marcus Aurelius (AD 161–180). The only obvious remains are parts of the podium and the columns, which are visible from around town. Nearby is a **lookout** with great views.

There are information boards in English and Spanish at a few places around the Umayyad Palace but, while informative, they can be a little confusing to follow. Guides will probably approach you when you arrive (or you can ask at the tourist police booth or museum) and can really enhance your visit (up to JD5 depending on the length of time and number of people).

Tunnel under Amman

In ancient Roman Philadelphia, royalty considered it beneath them to mingle with the general public unless they had to. To ease their path between the major sites, an underground tunnel was built to connect the Citadel high on the hill with the Nymphaeum and theatre. While modern visitors to Amman might welcome having such access without having to negotiate the streets of Downtown, the tunnel's precise location and state of repair is a closely guarded secret. All the locals know about it, but very few know where it is and some even doubt that it exists. Those that do know aren't telling.

Admission is JD2 for the Citadel and the National Archaeological Museum and no visitors are allowed to enter after 5pm (they often let people in later in summer).

Although it looks close to Downtown, the only access roads are from Al-Malek Ali bin al-Hussein St. It's better to hire a taxi for the trip up (no more than 700 fils from anywhere in Downtown); it's easy to find the way coming down. Alternatively, from the Citadel, it is possible to take the marked path near the tourist police booth and then jump (about 1m) from a wall onto Sa'id Khair St.

Roman Theatre

The restored Roman Theatre *(admission free; open 8am-5pm daily Oct-Apr, 8am-7pm May-Sept)* is the most obvious and impressive remnant of Roman Philadelphia and, for many, the highlight of Amman. It is cut into the northern side of a hill that once served as a necropolis, and has a seating capacity of 6000. It was built on three tiers: the rulers, of course, sat closest to the action, the military had the middle section, and the general public sat way up the top.

The theatre was probably built in the 2nd century AD during the reign of Antoninus Pius (AD 138–161). Theatres often had religious significance, and the small structure built into the rock above the top row of seats is believed to have housed a statue of the goddess Athena, who was prominent in the religious life of the city.

Full restoration began in 1957. Unfortunately, nonoriginal materials were used so the reconstruction is partly inaccurate. In recent years, the theatre has again become a place of entertainment; productions are sometimes put on here in July and August – check with the tourist office or ask at your hotel. The theatre also houses two museums (see Museums later in this chapter).

You may be accosted by guides trying to rope you into a tour (about JD2), which can be useful if you have a specialist interest. More likely, you'll be surrounded by friendly children or other Jordanians keen to practise their English – it's a pleasant place to linger. The best time for photographs is probably the morning, although the views from the top tiers just before sunset are superb. At night the theatre is floodlit, providing a spectacular backdrop to the very modern bustle of Downtown.

Forum

The row of columns immediately in front (north) of the Roman Theatre is all that's left of the Forum, once one of the largest public squares (about 100m by 50m) in Imperial Rome. Built in AD 190, the square was flanked on three sides by columns, and on the fourth side by the Seil Amman stream; almost everything (including the stream, which still runs) is underneath the modern streets. Today, the small park area in front of the theatre is an attractive place to sit.

Odeon

On the eastern side of what was the Forum stands the 500-seat Odeon *(admission free; open 8am-5pm daily Oct-April, 8am-7pm May-Sept)*. Built in the 2nd century AD, it served mainly as a venue for musical performances. The small amphitheatre was probably enclosed with a wooden or temporary tent roof to shield the performers and audience from the elements. It has been nicely restored and, although not as spectacular as the Roman Theatre, it does have a cosy charm.

The Odeon isn't signposted and some visitors walk straight past. The building is to the right (east) as you come out from the Roman Theatre; you enter through a large wooden door. Like the theatre, the Odeon sometimes hosts musical performances in summer.

Nymphaeum

Built in AD 191, the Nymphaeum *(admission free)* was once a large, two-storey complex with fountains, mosaics, stone carvings and possibly a 600 sq m swimming pool – all dedicated to the nymphs (mythical young girls who lived in and around the rivers). Excavations started in earnest in 1993, and restoration will continue for many years. Except for a few columns, an elegant archway and a few alcoves there is still little to see.

The site is easy to find on Quraysh St, not far from the King Hussein Mosque. It's open for as long as the workers are toiling away.

HASHEMITE SQUARE

This square, between the Roman Theatre and the Raghadan station, is the main gathering point for locals (mostly men but also families in the evening and during holidays) in Downtown. They stroll, sip tea, smoke the nargileh and watch the world go by. There are cafés, shwarma stalls, souvenir shops

and even dodgem cars (like any Downtown Amman street really!) for the kids and young at heart. It can be packed on a summer's evening; in winter there's less going on.

MUSEUMS

Amman boasts several good museums, but the best is the National Archaeological Museum in the Citadel.

National Archaeological Museum

This museum *(☎ 4638795; Citadel complex; admission to complex JD2; open 8am-5pm Sat-Thur, 10am-4pm Fri)* is just northwest of the Temple of Hercules in the grounds of the Citadel. It has a collection of items spanning all eras of Jordanian and regional history, ranging from 6000-year-old skulls from Jericho to Umayyad period artwork. It also boasts some examples of the Dead Sea Scrolls found at Qumran in 1952, a copy of the Mesha Stele (see the boxed text 'A Stele at Twice the Price' in the King's Highway chapter) and assorted artefacts from Petra and Jerash.

Most exhibits are well labelled in English and the museum is laid out in easy-to-follow sections devoted to each historic period.

Folklore Museum

This museum *(☎ 4651742; Roman Theatre complex; admission JD1 includes entry to Museum of Popular Traditions; open 9am-7pm Sat-Thur, 10am-4pm Fri May-Sept; 9am-5pm Sat-Thur, 10am-4pm Fri Oct-Apr)* is immediately to the right as you enter the Roman

Theatre. It houses a modest collection of items illustrating traditional Jordanian life. They include a Bedouin goat-hair tent complete with tools; musical instruments such as the single-string *rababa*, a classic Bedouin instrument; woven rugs; some weapons; and various costumes. Captions are in English.

Museum of Popular Traditions

This museum (☎ 4651670; Roman Theatre complex; admission JD1, includes admission to Folklore Museum; open 9am-7pm Sat-Thur, 10am-4pm Fri May-Sept, 9am-5pm Sat-Thur, 10am-4pm Fri Oct-Apr), to the left after you enter the Roman Theatre, has well-presented displays of traditional costumes, jewellery, face masks and utensils. The mosaic collection is mostly from churches in Madaba and dates back to the 6th century.

Museum of Archaeology & Anthropology

If you have an interest in archaeology and/or anthropology, or happen to be at the University of Jordan, this small museum (☎ 535 5000, ext 3412; admission Oct-April/May-Sept JD1/2; open 8am-5pm Sat-Wed) is worth a visit. It has artefacts from around Jordan dating to the Bronze and Iron Ages, as well as the Roman, Greek and Umayyad periods.

To get here, take any minibus or service taxi heading towards Salt from Abdali or Raghadan stations, get off at the entrance to the university and ask directions from there.

Martyr's Memorial & Military Museum

The simple and solemn Martyr's Memorial to Jordan's fallen houses the small but interesting Military Museum (☎ 5664240; admission free; open 9am-4pm Sat-Thur). The museum chronicles Jordan's recent military history, from the Arab Revolt in 1916 (in which 10,000 Arab fighters were killed) through to the Arab–Israeli wars. It does, however, airbrush over many of the controversial aspects of these conflicts – the 1948 and 1967 wars are hardly mentioned and the 1973 war only in passing. The museum is nonetheless interesting and all the exhibits are well displayed and labelled in English.

The memorial is on the road to Zarqa, 1km east of the Sports City junction. The entrance is in the grounds of the Sports City (see the Shmeisani map). Take any minibus

or service taxi towards Zarqa, but check whether it goes past the Sports City (al-medina ar-riyaddiyeh). A private taxi from Downtown should cost less than JD1.500.

Other Museums

If you have the time and interest, there are other museums to check out.

Museum of the Political History of HM Late King Abdullah bin al-Hussein (☎ 462 1151; Al-Kulliyah al-Islamiyah St; open 9am-2pm Sun-Thur) is worth checking out for its coverage of Jordan's political life in the early 20th century It's next to the Iraqi Embassy, west of 1st Circle.

Inside the King Abdullah Mosque, the small **Islamic Museum** (☎ 5672155; Suleiman al-Nabulsi St; admission JD1; open 8am-11am & 12.30pm-2.30pm Sat-Thur, 10am-noon Fri), just up from the Abdali bus station, has some pottery pieces, as well as photographs and personal effects of King Abdullah I. There are also a number of pieces of Muslim art, coins and stone engravings. The entry price also includes access to the mosque.

The Haya Cultural Centre in Shmeisani (see Cultural Centres earlier in this chapter) has the **Children's Heritage & Science Museum** (☎ 5665195; admission free; open 9am-6pm Sat-Thur), which has some interactive displays for kids.

ART GALLERIES

Jordan's traditional and contemporary art can be appreciated by visiting one or two of the excellent galleries around Amman.

Jordan National Gallery of Fine Art

This small gallery (☎ 4630128; Hosni Fareez St; admission JD1; open 9am-5pm Sat-Mon, Wed, Thur) is an excellent place to gain an appreciation of contemporary Jordanian painting, sculpture and pottery. There are also pieces from around the region and it's worth spending an hour or so here. There's an excellent small gift shop and a café.

The gallery is signposted from Suleiman al-Nabulsi St, opposite the King Abdullah Mosque.

Darat al-Funun

Darat al-Funun (☎ 4643251, fax 4643253; e darat@cyberia.com.jo; w www.daratalfunun.org; Nimer bin Adwan St; admission free;

open 10am-7pm Sat-Wed, 10am-8pm Thur) means 'House of Arts' and is a superb complex dedicated to placing contemporary art at the heart of Jordan's cultural life. On the hillside to the north of the Downtown area, Darat al-Funun features a small **art gallery** with works by Jordanian and other Arab artists, an **art library** (which closes an hour earlier than the other sections) and **workshops** for Jordanian and visiting sculptors and painters. A schedule of upcoming exhibitions, lectures, films and public discussion forums is available and current events are advertised in the *Jordan Times* newspaper.

Almost as significant as the centre's artistic endeavours are the architectural features of the site. At the base of the complex, near the entrance, are excavated ruins of a 6th-century **Byzantine church**. Buildings further up the hill are largely restored residences of old Amman dating from the 1920s; it was in one of these that TE Lawrence wrote part of *Seven Pillars of Wisdom*. There is also a café and gardens with superb views over Amman.

It can be difficult to find, and access is easiest on foot. From near the southern end of Al-Malek al-Hussein St, head up the stairs under the 'Riviera Hotel' sign. At the top of the stairs, turn immediately right onto Nimer bin Adwan St and walk uphill for 50m where you need to take the left fork. The entrance gate is on the right after a few metres.

MOSQUES

Amman doesn't boast any truly spectacular mosques. Non-Muslims will feel most comfortable at King Abdullah Mosque.

King Abdullah Mosque

Completed in 1989 as a memorial by the late King Hussein to his grandfather, the unmistakable blue-domed mosque *(Suleiman al-Nabulsi St; admission JD1; open 8am-11am & 12.30pm-2.30pm Sat-Thur, 10am-noon Fri)* can house up to 7000 worship- pers inside, and another 3000 in the courtyard area. This is the only mosque in Amman that openly welcomes non-Muslim visitors, and inside is the small Islamic Museum (see Museums earlier in this chapter for details).

The cavernous, octagonal prayer hall is notable for not having any pillars; the dome is 35m in diameter. The inscriptions quote verses from the Quran. The blue colour of the underside of the dome is said to represent the sky, and the golden lines running down to the base of the dome depict rays of light illuminating the 99 names of Allah. The huge three-ringed chandelier contains more Quranic inscriptions. There is also a small women's section for 500 worshippers, and a much smaller royal enclosure.

Women are required to wear something (which can be borrowed at the mosque) to cover the hair; and of course everyone must remove their shoes before entering the prayer hall.

King Hussein Mosque

Built by King Abdullah I in 1924, and restored in 1987, King Hussein Mosque is in the heart of Downtown on the site of a mosque built in AD 640 by 'Umar, the second caliph of Islam. The mosque is more interesting as a hive of activity than for any architectural splendour; the precinct is a local meeting place and exudes an altogether Arab flavour. Non-Muslims, while generally welcome any time (except during prayer time), may feel intrusive. The area in front of the mosque is almost always crowded with locals chatting, walking, selling and buying. The best place to watch this is the Arab League Café opposite (see Cafés in the Entertainment section later in this chapter).

Abu Darwish Mosque

On top of Jebel al-Ashrafiyeh' is the striking Abu Darwish Mosque. It was built in 1961, and is unmistakable with its alternating layers of black and white stone. The mosque itself is rarely open, and, generally, non-Muslims are not permitted inside. The views on the way up are good. There is also a wonderful view towards the Abu Darwish Mosque high above the King Hussein Mosque from the Arab League Café.

To get to Abu Darwish Mosque, take a No 25 or 26 service taxi from Italian St in Downtown, or charter a taxi. It's a very long and steep climb if you decide to walk.

ACTIVITIES
Swimming

The top-end hotels charge at least JD5 for nonguests to use their swimming pools. Among the cheapest is Manar Hotel (see Places to Stay later in this chapter), which charges non-guests around JD4. **Sports City** *(☎ 5667181)* in northern Amman (see the

Shmeisani map) has an Olympic-sized pool, but nonmembers are charged around JD6, which includes the use of a locker. Women may feel uncomfortable.

Other Activities

The Sports City complex has **tennis courts** (☎ 5682796) for JD1 per hour. This rises to JD2 if you play at night under lights. You will, however, need to provide your own racquet and balls.

The **Bisharat Golf Course** has a nine-hole course, putting greens and even a golf pro. It costs JD15 per day, plus around JD10 for club hire. The club is about 25 minutes' drive south of Downtown, and signposted from the Desert Hwy on the way to Queen Alia airport (see the Around Amman chapter).

For something completely different, gliding is sometimes possible at the **Gliding Club** (☎ 4874587) at the Marka airport east of Amman. The **Royal Racing Club** (☎ 585 0630) holds races (for horses and camels) in spring and summer, and offers horse-riding classes. Details are available from the club, located off the Desert Hwy and on the way to Queen Alia airport.

For the Kids

Children and the young at heart can enjoy **dodgem cars** at Hashemite Square, Downtown *(500 fils; open 9am-10pm daily)*. The **Amusement Centre** next to the British Council on Abu Bakr as-Siddiq St (see the Jebel Amman map) has roller skating, dodgem cars, video games and bowling alleys. **Star Wars** *(open 9am-11pm daily)*, in the Safeway car park in Shmeisani, has video games for 100 fils each. **Luna Park** *(Khaled ibn al-Walid Rd; admission JD1; open 10am-10pm daily)* has a cable car and other attractions for the kids; see the Shmeisani map.

The Haya Cultural Centre in Shmeisani (see Cultural Centres earlier in this chapter) is predominantly for children and has a small playground and museum (see Museums earlier in this chapter). It also organises regular concerts and performances for kids.

There are very few parks in Amman and nothing within walking distance of Downtown. For some open space, tranquillity and greenery, head to **Amman National Park**, just off the Desert Hwy, or go further out to somewhere like **Dibbeen National Park** (detailed in the Jerash & the North chapter).

Turkish Bath

Al-Pasha Turkish Bath *(☎/fax 4633002; open 10am-midnight daily)*, on Al-Mahmoud Taha St in Jebel Amman, is the perfect pampering antidote to the hills and bustle of Amman. Full service (JD13.500) includes steam bath, sauna, Jacuzzi, scrubbing, 40-minute massage and two soft drinks, all done in a superb building architecturally faithful to the tradition of Turkish *hammams*. There are male and female attendants; it's a good idea to book ahead. It's easiest to find if you're coming along Abu Bakr as-Siddiq St from the 1st Circle – it's the fifth street on the right.

ORGANISED TOURS

At least four budget hotels – the Venecia, Bdeiwi, Cliff and Farah – offer day trips from Amman that cost anywhere from JD10 to JD25 depending on the places visited and number of people. Other hotels may also be able to arrange something. Popular destinations include: Madaba, Mt Nebo and the Dead Sea; Jerash, Ajlun and Umm Qais; or the desert castles to the east (particularly worth doing due to the limited public transport on offer). We've received varying reports about the quality of such tours so it's worth asking other travellers before deciding which is currently the best on offer.

One option, which has been recommended by readers, is the tour offered by some hotels (eg, Farah) which leaves Amman at 8.30am and travels to Petra (around 6pm) via Madaba, Wadi al-Mujib, Karak, Shobak and Dana Nature Reserve with a brief amount of time spent at each of the various sites.

SPECIAL EVENTS

Concerts, plays and performances are occasionally held at the Odeon and Roman Theatre in July and August. The Ministry of Tourism office, near 3rd Circle, is the best source of detailed information, but also check out the English-language newspapers. See Special Events in the Facts for the Visitor chapter for more details about events in and near Amman, such as the Jerash Festival.

PLACES TO STAY

Many cheap hotels are in Downtown; there are also a few around Abdali bus station. Many mid-range places are around Abdali and between 1st and 5th Circles; most top-end places are further out in Shmeisani.

SHMEISANI

PLACES TO STAY
10 Ambassador Hotel
13 Regency Palace Hotel
15 Amman Marriott; Champions Bar; National Car Rental
18 Le Meridien; National Car Rental
24 Manar Hotel
33 Ammon Hotel; Jordan Tourism Board

PLACES TO EAT
19 Pizza Hut
20 Burger King

21 Baskin Robbins; Dunkin' Donuts
22 Houstons
23 La Maison Verte
26 KFC; Ata Ali
27 La Terrasse
28 Chilli House; Jabri Restaurant; Canadian Embassy
29 Mama Mia; 30 Something; Milano Restaurant

OTHER
1 Martyr's Memorial; Military Museum
2 United Nations Relief & Works Agency (UNRWA)

3 Safeway Shopping Centre; KFC; Internet Centre; ATMs; Star Wars Video Games; Dry-cleaners; Mövenpick
4 Austrian Airlines
5 Petra Travel & Tourism
6 Budget Car Rental
7 Jordan Design & Trade Centre (Noor Al Hussein Foundation)
8 Federal Express (FedEx)
9 Israeli Consulate
11 International Traders
12 Royal Cultural Centre
14 Palestine Hospital

16 Housing Bank Centre; Post Office; Royal Jordanian Airlines Head Office
17 Luna Park
25 Eurodollar Rent a Car
30 Lufthansa Airlines
31 Haya Cultural Centre; Children's Heritage & Science Museum
32 Air France
34 Islamic Hospital
35 JETT Bus Office (International); Afana; Karnak Buses
36 JETT Bus Office (Domestic)

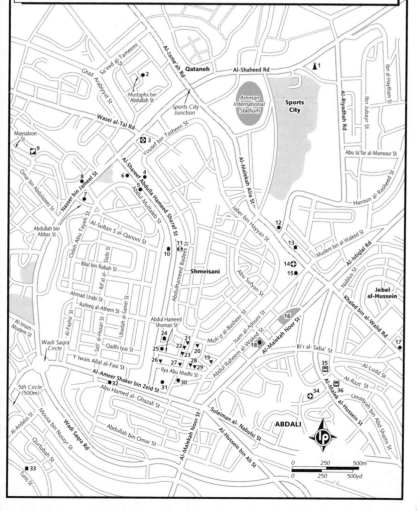

Eastern Travel & Tours has a hotel reservation counter in Terminal 2 of Queen Alia airport, but commissions are high.

PLACES TO STAY – BUDGET

The cheapest places are around the King Hussein Mosque, but these are only for deep sleepers and those for whom price is everything. Many have shops on the ground floor, a tea shop on the second and rooms on the third and fourth floors, so getting to your room involves a lot of climbing. All budget places mentioned here come with shared bathroom facilities unless stated otherwise; all promise hot water and some even deliver.

Downtown

Zahran Hotel (☎ 4625473; Sahat al-Malek Faysal al-Awal St; beds in 4-bed room JD1.500, doubles JD3) is probably the pick of the cheapies around the King Hussein Mosque, but you'll feel as if the muezzin is inside your room. Lone women will definitely feel uncomfortable here. The rooms are basic and showers cost an extra 500 fils.

Cliff Hotel (☎ 4624273, fax 4638078; Al-Amir Mohammed St; dorm beds JD3, singles/doubles JD5/6) is a long-standing backpacker favourite with friendly staff in the heart of Downtown. The rooms are tidy and simple but ask to see a few rooms as some beds are better than others. Showers are usually free. You can also sleep on the roof for JD2 if your room doesn't have a fan.

Farah Hotel (☎ 4651443, fax 4651437; Cinema al-Hussein St; dorm beds JD4, mattress on roof JD2.500, singles/doubles JD7/9) is a backpacker-savvy place which gets consistently good reports from travellers. The rooms are tidy and the staff friendly and eager to help.

Yarmouk Hotel (☎ 4624241; Al-Malek Faisal St; singles/doubles with fan JD5/6), in the heart of the Downtown area, has doubles which are simple but aren't bad value.

Al-Riyad Hotel (☎ 4624260, fax 4625457; Al-Malek Faisal St; doubles with sink & fan JD6) is spelled in numerous ways (such as Reyad Hotel) and is of a similar standard to the Yarmouk. With a mainly Jordanian clientele, there's little English spoken here but plenty of goodwill.

Mansour Hotel (☎ 4621575; Al-Malek Faisal St; singles JD5.500, doubles with fan & shared/private bath JD7.700/8.800) is central

and quieter than most because it's a little back from the busy main road. The rooms are simple but satisfactory, the welcome understated but friendly and there are drinks (but no meals) available.

Venecia Hotel (☎ 4638895; e venicia-h@ hotel@hotmail.com; off Amir Mohammed St; dorm beds JD4, doubles JD6) is a little run-down these days. Most rooms come with a fan and sink and prices may increase by a dinar in summer.

Bdeiwi Hotel (☎ 4643394, fax 4643393; Omar al-Khayyam St; singles/doubles JD5/6, doubles with bath JD8) gets decidedly mixed reviews from travellers but it seems to depend on who's on duty at reception. The rooms are simple but generally clean.

Palace Hotel (☎ 4624326, fax 4650603; Al-Malek Faisal St; singles/doubles with bath JD8/14) is probably the best in the area and worth a little splurge. The rooms at this well-run place are clean, large, and some have balconies with good views over the street.

Karnak Hotel (☎/fax 4638125; Al-Malek al-Hussein St; singles/doubles with fan & bath JD7/10) is excellent value, well run and friendly. The rooms are very comfortable and a few have balconies overlooking the noisy street. Cheaper rates are negotiable for groups and people staying for longer than a few days.

New Park Hotel (☎ 4648145; Al-Malek al-Hussein St; singles/doubles with fan & bath JD10/12) also has a nice feel about it with helpful staff and tidy rooms that come with satellite TV. The rooms at the back are quieter. Meals are available in the cafeteria.

Happyland Hotel (☎ 4639832, fax 462 8550; Al-Malek al-Hussein St; singles/doubles with bath in summer JD5/8, in winter JD4/6) is, like most budget places in Amman, better than its exterior suggests and is actually pretty good value because you get a private bathroom. The rooms are simple and hot water is only available between 7am and noon – at least they're honest about it.

Jebel Amman

The following places are within a short walk of the Abdali bus station and can, therefore, be especially useful for late-night or early-morning departures or arrivals.

Remal Hotel (☎ 4630670, fax 4630670; e sufwat@go.com.jo; off Al-Malek al-Hussein St; singles/doubles JD14/18) is tucked away in a side street and is therefore quieter than most. The rooms are tidy and comfortable and prices are negotiable.

Merryland Hotel (☎/fax 4630370; e mery landhotel@hotmail.com; Al-Malek al-Hussein St; singles/doubles with bath from JD10/16) is excellent value with spotless rooms and friendly staff.

Select Hotel (☎ 4637101, fax 4637102; e sales@amman-select.com; 52 Al-Baq'ouniyah St; singles/doubles JD11/18) is excellent upper-budget value. Its rooms are clean and spacious and come with TV, air-con and spotless bathrooms. Prices include breakfast.

PLACES TO STAY – MID RANGE

Most places listed here have air-conditioning, satellite TV and a fridge in the rooms and all have private bathrooms with hot water. All prices listed here include tax and breakfast unless stated otherwise. Few places are in Downtown, with most around Abdali and between 1st and 5th Circles.

Many offer discounted rates during quiet periods.

Downtown

Al-Saraya Hotel (☎ 4656791, fax 4656792; e sayara-hotel@index.com.jo; Al-Jaza'er St, near eastern end of Raghadan bus station; singles/doubles/triples JD14/18/22), the best mid-range option in Downtown has clean, comfortable and spacious rooms. Among the highlights are Fayez, the friendly owner, and the padded toilet seats in some rooms. The call to prayer from the neighbouring mosque can be quite a shock early in the morning.

Amman Palace Hotel (☎ 4646172, fax 465 6989; Quraysh St; singles/doubles JD24/34 plus 13% tax) is another mid-range option if you want the convenience of being close to the Downtown area. The large rooms are a tad jaded and the hot water can be slow to arrive but it's comfortable nonetheless.

Jebel Amman

Canary Hotel (☎ 4638353, fax 4638353; e canary@go.com.jo; off Kulliyat al-Sharee'ah St; singles/doubles JD18/22) has a welcoming, homy feel. In the leafy Jebel Weibdeh area, it's pleasantly aloof from the chaos of the nearby Abdali bus station. The rooms are more comfortable than luxurious, although the bathrooms sparkle. There is Internet access (JD1.500 per hour) and room rates drop as low as JD15/20 in low season.

Caravan Hotel (☎ 5661195, fax 5661996; e caravan@go.com.jo; Al-Ma'moun St; singles/doubles JD18/24 plus 13% tax), almost opposite the King Abdullah Mosque, is good value with pleasant rooms.

Carlton Hotel (☎ 4654200, fax 4655833; e jcarlton@joinnet.com.jo; Al-Kulliyah al-Islamiyah St; singles/doubles JD35/45), between 2nd and 3rd Circles, is a top-end place with mid-range prices, although they do rise in high season. The rooms are semi-luxurious, the staff friendly and there's a restaurant and café.

Hisham Hotel (☎ 4644028, fax 4647540; e hishamhotel@nets.com.jo; w www.hisham hotel.com; Mithqal al-Fayez St; singles/doubles high season JD30/40, low season JD25/35) is a couple of blocks south of the French Embassy and is an excellent choice. It's a very pleasant place in a leafy part of town, with a personal feel and comfortable rooms. It's popular with journalists and diplomats. Prices are negotiable.

Granada Hotel (☎ 4638031, fax 4622617; Al-Imam Malek St; singles/doubles JD26.400/ 35.200) is another good choice and handily placed near 1st Circle.

Shepherd Hotel (☎/fax 4639197; e she pherdhtl@joinnet.com.jo; Zayd bin Harethah St; singles/doubles/suites JD25/35/60) comes warmly recommended by readers and it's not hard to see why. The rooms are great value and very comfortable.

Dove Hotel (☎ 5697601, fax 5674676; e dove@go.com.jo; Qurtubah St; singles/ doubles JD24/28), between 4th and 5th Circles (see the Jebel Amman map), is one of the best in this price range with nice rooms and excellent service. One added attraction is the Irish pub downstairs (see Entertainment).

Shmeisani

Ammon Hotel (☎ 5680090, fax 5605688; e achte@go.com.jo, 10 Tunis St; singles/ doubles JD25/35) is terrific value with semi-luxurious rooms at mid-range prices. It's in a quiet area and, although prices may rise when business picks up, expect it to remain good value. There's also a bar, restaurant and swimming pool.

Manar Hotel (☎ 5662186, fax 5684329; Al-Shareef Abdulla Hameed Sharaf St; singles/ doubles JD20/25) is excellent value in the Shmeisani area, especially in summer when it's one of the cheapest places in Amman with a swimming pool. It's quiet, some rooms are quite spacious and local telephone calls are free.

Ambassador Hotel (☎ 5605161, fax 568 1101; e ambashtl@go.com.jo; Al-Shareef Abdulla Hameed Sharaf St; singles/doubles JD25/ 35), nearby, is also good. The rooms are very comfortable and it's a professionally run and friendly place.

PLACES TO STAY – TOP END
Amman has its share of four- and five-star hotels. Most are in the Shmeisani district and are not easily accessible by service taxi. Prices include all the luxury bells and whistles you'd expect for these prices, and rates listed here include breakfast and taxes. Many offer discounted and frequently changing rates depending on demand.

Jordan Inter-Continental Hotel (☎ 464 1361, fax 4645217; e ammha@interconti .com; Al-Kulliyah al-Islamiyah St; doubles JD65), midway between 2nd and 3rd Circles, is suitably luxurious and has a shopping arcade and deli.

Grand Hyatt Amman (☎ 4651234, fax 465 1634; e info@ammgh.com.jo; Al-Hussein bin Ali St; doubles around JD90) is similarly good top-end value to the Inter-Continental; rates change on a daily basis. It's quite a complex with seven restaurants, a bookshop, nightclub, expensive boutiques, business centre, exhibition centre and Internet deli (JD3.500 per hour).

Amman Marriott (☎ 5607607, fax 567 0100; e amman@marriott.com; Isam al-Ajlouni St; singles/doubles from JD60/70) is another high-quality place. If you have a spare JD395, try the royal suite which, unlike the other rooms, does include breakfast.

Le Meridien (☎ 5696511, fax 5674261; e meridien@lemeridien-amman.com; Al-Malekah Noor St; doubles from JD160) is only for pop stars, diplomats and people on expense accounts.

Regency Palace Hotel (☎ 5607000, fax 5660013; e regency@nets.com.jo; Queen Alia St; singles/doubles JD110/125) is no longer one of the better-value places around, primarily because of the discounting undertaken by the international five-star hotels.

Radisson SAS Hotel (☎ 5607100, fax 5665160; Al-Hussein bin Ali St; doubles from JD80) has all of the luxuries expected of this international chain.

PLACES TO STAY – RENTALS
The two English-language papers, and notice boards at the cultural centres (see Cultural Centres earlier in this chapter) and at Books@café (see Bookshops earlier in this chapter) are the best places to check for apartments and houses to rent. Alternatively, wander around the nicer areas (just off the road between 1st and 5th Circles, or Shmeisani) and look for signs on residences or shop windows advertising places to rent.

You'll pay at least JD200 per month for a furnished apartment in a reasonable area; a little less if unfurnished. A furnished apartment or small house in a working-class suburb is possible for as little as JD100 per month (usually closer to JD150), but little in this range is advertised so ask around. For this price, don't expect everything to work.

PLACES TO EAT
Amman has a wide range of eating options, with budget places concentrated in Downtown and, to a lesser extent, Jebel Amman, while the more upmarket restaurants serving Arab and international cuisine are concentrated in Shmeisani and Abdoun.

PLACES TO EAT – BUDGET
If money's an issue, your mainstay in Amman will be felafel and shwarma; these are easy to find in Downtown, especially around the Raghadan bus station. There are also a number of budget restaurants; all of the following are in Downtown unless specified.

Palestine Juice (Al-Malek Faisal St; open 7am-11pm daily) is an overflowingly fertile juice stand that serves refreshing carrot or orange juice, or banana with milk for 500 fils (small glass) or JD1 (large).

Hashem Restaurant (Al-Amir Mohammed St; open 24 hrs) is a legendary place which overflows into the alley. It's popular with locals for felafel, hummus and fuul. A filling meal with bread and tea costs less than JD1. As one reader noted: 'nothing but bread, hummus, fuul and felafel, but everything is fresh and dirt cheap. I love this place!'

Jabri Restaurant (☎ 4624108; Al-Malek al-Hussein St; starters from 500 fils, mains from JD1.800; open 8am-8pm Sat-Thur) is easily recognisable by its yellow awning. It's predominantly a pastry place, but the restaurant upstairs is excellent with a spotless dining room and views over the street. The service is attentive and the food also good with highlights including mensaf (JD2.400), shish kebabs (JD2.250), fried half chicken (JD1.800) and a bite-sized cheese or meat pie for 200 fils. A plate of *fuul* for breakfast costs 500 fils. Jabri also has an outlet in Shmeisani.

Cairo Restaurant (☎ 4624527; Al-Malek Talal St; mains from JD1; open 6am-10pm daily) has a pleasant, clean eating area, just off Sahat al-Malek Faysal al-Awal St. A main meal with condiments and drinks shouldn't cost more than JD1.500. The mensaf is also cheaper than elsewhere (JD1.500).

Shahers Penthouse Cafeteria (Sahat al-Malek Faysal al-Awal St; mains from JD2.500; open 9.30am-11pm daily) has a traditionally decorated indoor dining area and an outdoor terrace overlooking the street far below. It's recommended more for its atmosphere than food, although the main dishes (including kebabs, mensaf, *maqlubbeh* and okra) aren't bad. Nargileh costs a steep JD2. Hussein, the resident musician, will happily play the oud or violin to provide a cultured counterpoint to the street noise below.

Bifa Billa (Cinema al-Hussein St; mains from 500 fils; open noon-midnight daily) is one of the best places in Downtown for hamburgers and shwarmas, and they also do excellent milkshakes.

Fast Meal (☎ 4650037; Hashemi St; meals from JD1.250; open 7.15am-2.30am daily) is super clean and close to the Roman Theatre. A tasty burger, chips and a milkshake costs as little as JD1.250.

Get Together (☎ 4617216; e gt_jo@yahoo.com; Abu Bakr as-Siddiq St; mains from JD1.500; open noon-midnight Wed-Mon) is one of the coolest places on the hill overlooking Downtown. The food is good with sandwiches, crepes and salads (including the enigmatically named 'Dirty Minds Salad'), and this chic place carries with it a creative twist – a menu of over 135 board games. The hot drinks are also good.

Batata (☎ 4656768; Abu Bakr as-Siddiq St; small/large/family fries JD0.600/0.750/1.500; open noon-11pm Sat-Thur, 4pm-11pm Fri) satisfies those craving real French fries, which come with a choice of eight sauces (100 fils each). There's also baked potatoes (500 fils) and hot drinks including cappuccino (750 fils) and hot chocolate (500 fils).

R&B Shawerma (☎ 4645347; Abu Bakr as-Siddiq St; shwarmas from 750 fils; open noon-midnight daily) is not your average shwarma place. Shwarmas come in three sizes – six, 10 and 12 inches – and come in Chinese, chicken and cheese varieties. Meals including great fries and a soft drink cost no more than JD2.500.

Snack Box (☎ 5661323; Suleiman al-Nabulsi St; meals JD1.750-2.500; open noon-9pm Sat-Thur), in Jebel Amman, is the best of its kind in Jordan. It has a delicious takeaway menu that includes superb burgers and sandwiches, not to mention Mexican, Chinese, Thai and other international dishes that would leave most restaurants for dead. It's also reasonably priced and everything is freshly prepared while you wait.

If you must, many of the major international fast-food chains have outlets in Amman. Most are open at least from noon to midnight daily.

Pizza Hut, KFC, Burger King, Dunkin Donuts, Chilli House, Baskin Robbins and **McDonalds** are all represented. **Planet Hollywood** (☎ 5930972; open noon-1am daily) also has an outlet behind Abdoun Circle.

PLACES TO EAT – MID RANGE

Books@café (☎ 4650457; Omar bin al-Khattab; mains from JD2.500; open 10am-11.30pm daily) is run by an Italian franchise and they serve genuine Italian pizzas (JD2.500 to JD5) and pasta (from JD2.500). Salads cost JD2.655. The food is excellent, the service discreet and the atmosphere super cool with plenty of hip young Jordanians in attendance. Hot drinks are a steep JD1 to JD1.250 although the 'hot strawberry' may just be worth it. Bottles of wine cost JD11 to JD23 and the beers include Amstel (JD2), Becks (JD2.500), Heineken (JD3), Budweiser (JD3.500) and Corona (JD3.500). On most nights there's some special deal where food and drinks are cheaper; Monday is movie night. On Friday (9am to 1pm) they have a special breakfast feast for JD5, which is excellent value.

Jerusalem Restaurant (Al-Quds; ☎ 463 0168, fax 4649101; Al-Malek al-Hussein St; mains from JD2; open 7am-10pm daily) specialises in sweets and pastries, but has a large restaurant at the back. The menu is in Arabic but most waiters speak English and can order for you. The mensaf (JD2.500) is recommended. It's the sort of place where a tip is expected and usually warranted.

Diplomat Restaurant (☎ 4625592; 1st Circle; starters from 600 fils, mains JD1.500-3.500; open 9.30am-11.30pm daily) does breakfast and a range of European-inspired dishes. Some are disappointing although readers claim the pizzas are better.

Fakhr el-Din (☎ 4652399, fax 4641792; W www.fakhreldin.com; 40 Taha Hussein St; starters JD1-2, main meals JD2-6.500; open 12.30pm-3.30pm & 7.30pm-11.30pm daily) does highly recommended Lebanese food in a classy setting. In addition to the extensive à la carte selections, there's also a menu for JD10 (minimum four people), which is terrific value. Even with 13% tax added to the quoted prices, it's a good place for a splurge. It's about two blocks behind the Iraqi Embassy in Jebel Amman.

Grappa (☎ 4651458, fax 4650295; Abdul Qader Koshak St; starters JD1.900-6.500, mains JD2.500-7.500; open 6pm-1.30am daily) does decent Italian food although it's the setting that is superb. The dining area is tastefully decorated and there is a terrace and beer garden overlooking the valley.

China Restaurant (☎ 4638968; Ali Ridha al-Rikabi St; starters from JD1, mains from JD1.200; open noon-3.30pm & 7pm-11.30pm daily) has a pleasant atmosphere, good Chinese food and willing service. Most of the main dishes are good value and cost around JD2.500, while those craving shark-fin soup should expect to pay JD3.950.

Taiwan Tourismo (☎ 4641093; Mithqal al-Fayez St; starters from JD1.600, mains from JD1.800; open noon-3.30pm & 6.30-midnight daily) is much classier than its name suggests and has over 100 reasonably priced menu items to choose from.

Mama Mia (☎ 5682122; Ilya Abu Madhi St; starters JD1-2, mains JD2-5; open noon-midnight daily) does excellent pasta and pizza. Its bar section, **30 Something** (☎ 5682122; open 6pm-2am daily), often has live music.

Milano Restaurant (☎ 5680670; Ilya Abu Madhi St; starters JD1.700-3.900, mains from JD2.200; open noon-midnight daily) is another pizza and pasta place popular with young locals in the evening.

Ristorante Casereccio (☎ 5934772; Abdoun Circle; mains from JD3; open 1pm-4pm & 7pm-midnight daily) is a decent pizza and pasta place just off the trendy Abdoun Circle.

Blue Fig Café (☎ 5928800, fax 5929988; e bluefig@nets.com.jo; Prince Hashem bin al-Hussein St; starters from JD1.950, mains around JD4; open 8.30am-1am daily) is a super-cool place near Abdoun Circle. It has an extensive and imaginative menu with a delicious range of bread and pizza-type dishes. There's live music on some nights (see Entertainment later in this chapter).

Of the hotel restaurants, the pick is probably **L'Entrecote** (Shepherd Hotel, Zayd bin Harethah St; mains around JD5; open noon-4pm & 7pm-11pm daily), which does French and Swiss dishes including fondue, and the highly recommended **Forest Inn Restaurant** (Hisham Hotel, Mithqal al-Fayez St; mains from JD5, open noon-midnight daily); the latter has a nice outdoor setting in summer and particularly good service.

PLACES TO EAT – TOP END

The classy and expensive places are often in Shmeisani, so unless you're staying there, factor in taxi fares to the total bill for the evening. Remember that most top end places add a whopping 23% tax to the quoted prices. The places listed below are those we consider to be worth the splurge.

Bonita Inn (☎ 4615061, fax 4615060; off Al-Kulliyah al-Islamiyah St near 3rd Circle; starters JD1.750-6, mains from JD5.750; open noon-midnight daily) is a very good choice with European (primarily Spanish) cuisine. The steaks have a city-wide reputation while the paella Valenciana (JD14 for two) is as good as you'll get in Amman. The pastas are surprisingly reasonably priced (from under JD2) and the desserts include tiramisu for JD2. The extensive wine list includes Jordanian, South African, Australian, Chilean, Californian and European selections.

La Terrasse (☎ 5662831, fax 5601675; 11 August St; starters JD1.500-7.500, mains JD3.500-8.500; open 1pm-1am daily) does decent European cuisine in a pleasant setting. The wine list is also extensive with bottles from Jordan and much of the Mediterranean rim. Most nights after 10pm, the stage is given over to live Arab singers and musicians – popular with well-to-do local families.

Houstons (☎ 5620610; off Abdul Hameed Shoman St; starters JD2.900-4.500, mains JD5-9; open noon-midnight daily) is a popular restaurant that gets good reviews from expats. It specialises in Mexican dishes, but it also does top-quality steaks as well as burgers, sandwiches and pasta. The atmosphere is pleasant and the service excellent.

La Maison Verte (☎ 5685746, fax 567 3778; off Abdul Hameed Shoman St; starters JD3.500-9.500, mains JD3.400-11; open 1pm-3.30pm & 7pm-11.30pm daily) is strictly for the well heeled, but diplomats swear that its French cuisine is unparalleled in Amman. It has a classy ambience, excellent service and is the sort of place for a special occasion.

Tannoureen Restaurant (☎ 5515987, fax 5523908; Shatt al-Arab St; starters JD1-3.500, mains JD4.800-8; open 12.30pm-4.30pm & 7.30pm-11.30pm daily) is good for Lebanese food, especially mezzes, but it also does Western dishes such as fillet mignon (JD8) and seafood (around JD8).

Diwan al-Sultan Ibrahim Restaurant (☎ 551 7383; Shatt al-Arab St; starters JD1-5.500, mains JD3.750-8; open noon-midnight daily) comes highly recommended by wealthy locals and expats for quality Arab (and some Western) food. Among the entrees are frogs legs with garlic and coriander (JD5.500), while the deep fried brains (JD2.250) are definitely an acquired taste.

Kan Zaman (☎ 4128391, fax 4128395; lunch/dinner buffet JD6/11; open noon-4pm & 7pm-midnight daily) is a bit of a hike, around 10km south of 8th Circle, but it is one of Amman's longest standing top-end restaurants. Expats in Amman give the food mixed reviews but the vaulted ceilings and historic architecture lend it a lovely ambience. It's part of a tourist complex with handicraft stores (open 8am to midnight daily). Remember, however, to factor in a significant taxi fare (at least JD4 one way).

PATISSERIES & ICE-CREAM PARLOURS

Sweet tooths can find a spiritual home just about anywhere in Amman. In Downtown, the better places include the Jerusalem Restaurant and Jabri Restaurant (see Places to Eat – Budget earlier in this chapter) on Al-Malek al-Hussein St. **Ata Ali** (☎ 581 2310; Al-Shareef Abdulla Hameed Sharaf St; open 7.30am-midnight daily) does excellent sweets and ice creams. **Mövenpick** is among the ice creameries inside the entrance to Safeway in Shmeisani; expect to pay JD1 for two delicious scoops. There are **Baskin Robbins** outlets at Abdoun Circle and in Shmeisani, north off Ilya Abu Madhi St.

SELF-CATERING

Although there are small **grocery stores** throughout the capital, the larger supermarkets are located in the more affluent and remote suburbs. **Safeway** has an outlet (☎ 568 5311; Nasser bin Jameel St; open 24 hrs), around 500m southwest of the Sports City junction, and another just southwest of 7th Circle (☎ 5815558). Also close to 7th Circle is popular **C-Town Shopping Centre** (☎ 581 5558; Zahran St; open 6am-midnight daily). More central is **Haboob Grand Store** (☎ 462 2221; Al-Kulliyah Al-Islamiyah St; open 7am-midnight daily), between 1st and 2nd circles; it sometimes closes on Fridays.

ENTERTAINMENT

There is plenty of nightlife in the evenings in Amman, although little that's salubrious in the Downtown area. The areas of Shmeisani, Abdoun and, to a lesser extent, Jebel Amman have numerous trendy cafés, bars and a few nightclubs that stay open late, some of which have live music.

Bars & Nightclubs

Several bars in Downtown, visited almost exclusively by men, are tucked away in the alleys near the Cliff and Venecia hotels. If you're willing to move beyond Downtown, there are a range of enjoyable options where women will feel much more comfortable.

Mostly Men Strictly for those interested in cheap alcohol over ambience, **Kit Kat Bar** (Basman St; open 6pm-midnight daily) is about as sleazy and dingy as it gets.

Orient Bar and Restaurant (☎ 4636069; off Al-Amir Mohammed St; open 11am-late daily), also known as 'Al-Sharq', is rustic and smoke-filled and serves a range of beers (from JD1.750), spirits (from JD3.500) and the local arak (if you dare) for JD4. Cheap meals are also available with the slowest service in central Amman at no extra cost. If you've had a bit to drink, mind your head on the stairs on the way down.

Auberge Café (see Cafés later in this chapter) has a bar area popular with locals.

Jordan Bar (☎ 0795 796352; off Al-Amir Mohammed St; open 10am-midnight daily) is the place to go if your drinking day starts early. It's a cosy place with an earthy charm that hasn't changed in years. A large Amstel costs JD1.750.

Salamon Bar (☎ 0795 902940; off Al-Amir Mohammed St; open noon-midnight daily), next to the entrance to the Venecia Hotel, is more modern than the others and has beer on tap, but it's tiny and full of smoke. A large Amstel costs JD1.900.

Women Welcome Among the mid-range hotels, Hisham Hotel has a cosy 'English pub' where a pint of draught lager costs about JD2.500.

Las Tapas Latinas at the Bonita Inn (see Places to Eat) is the only salsa bar in Amman. You can get tapas and just about any drink you want, and salsa dance the night away. It opens at 6pm daily but things don't really start to sway until after 8pm.

Rovers' Return (☎ 5814844; Ali Nasouh al-Taher St; open 1pm-late daily) is a popular and fun English pub with a lively atmosphere, although drinks aren't cheap.

Irish Pub, downstairs from the Dove Hotel (see Places to Stay), is a cool place that stays open from 7pm til the last patrons stagger out. It's popular with expats and trendy young locals and the dance floor is often packed, especially on Thursday night when the place rocks. It has Amstel and Tennants on tap as well as the usual spirits and international beers at reasonable prices.

The Big Fellow Irish Pub (☎ 5934766; Abdoun Circle; open noon-2am daily) is another good Irish pub. It's more like a traditional Irish pub than the pub at the Dove Hotel and there are live screenings of international sports events but, as it's run by the Sheraton, prices for food and drinks are higher.

Blue Fig Café (see Places to Eat) is a great place to spend an afternoon or evening, with a chic crowd, pleasant atmosphere, live music on most Saturday nights and occasional exhibitions.

Champions Bar at the Amman Marriott (see Places to Stay) is an upmarket sports bar with an upmarket clientele. It's open from 6pm to midnight.

Some of the larger hotels run modest nightclubs. The Grand Hyatt Amman's **JJ Mahoneys** (cover charge Thur JD5; open 8.30pm-late Mon-Sat) is particularly popular on Thursday night when you'll pay for the privilege of rubbing shoulders with Amman's beautiful people. **Pasha Nightclub** (open 8.30pm-late Mon-Sat) in the Jordan Inter-Continental Hotel is similar.

Cinemas

At least two cinema complexes usually offer recent releases in a not-too-censored form: **Philadelphia** (☎ 4634144), in the basement of the Jordan Tower Centre, just down from 3rd Circle; and **Galleria** (☎ 5934973), on Abdoun Circle (see the Jebel Amman map). Tickets cost about JD4, but the quality of sound, vision and chairs is high. Programmes for these cinemas are advertised in the English-language newspapers.

A few other cinemas show films of the Jackie Chan variety, but these are often dubbed into Arabic and, apart from the violence, are heavily censored. In Downtown, the better ones are **Al-Hussein Cinema** (Cinema al-Hussein St), **Al-Khayyam** (Omar al-Khayyam St) and the **Raghadan** (Basman St).

Darat al-Funun art gallery (see Art Galleries earlier in this chapter) shows films most Thursday evenings. Also in Downtown, **Books@café** (see Bookshops earlier in this chapter) also has film nights for around JD2. The various cultural centres (see Cultural Centres earlier in this chapter) also show films regularly.

Exhibitions & Music

The various foreign cultural centres regularly organise lectures, exhibitions and musical recitals. The **Royal Cultural Centre** also occasionally puts on concerts and plays, usually in Arabic. **Darat al-Funun** often features recitals of classical and traditional music – check with the gallery for a schedule of upcoming events. The **Jordan National Gallery of Fine Arts** sometimes has visiting exhibitions of contemporary art and there's a small exhibition hall downstairs in the **Grand Hyatt**.

Cafés

Some of the cafés in Downtown are great places to watch the world go by, write letters, smoke a nargileh, meet locals and play cards or backgammon. There is a separate list here of ones which are generally men only with scarcely a local woman to be seen, although foreign women with some gumption and very modest attire, especially if accompanied by a male, will be welcome.

Mostly Men In Downtown, **Arab League Café** (Al-Malek Faisal St; open 10am-midnight daily) is a popular male domain with breezes and great views, especially of King Hussein Mosque.

Auberge Café *(Al-Amir Mohammed St; open 10am-midnight daily)* is one floor below the Cliff Hotel and very popular with local men. You'll have to make your way through the tobacco haze to reach the balcony which overlooks the main street and is a good place to smoke a nargileh (JD1). There are no pretensions to luxury but it wears a certain downmarket authenticity as a result.

Peace Café *(☎ 0795 297912; Al-Amir Mohammed St; open 9am-midnight daily)* is reached via a filthy staircase and is fairly basic, but if you can get one of the two balcony tables overlooking the street, you'll have one of the prime vantage points in Downtown.

Women Welcome One of the best places for the uninitiated to try the nargileh is the **Eco-Tourism Café** *(☎ 4652994; Al-Malek Faisal St; tea or coffee 400 fils, nargileh JD1.250; open 10am-11pm Sat-Thur, 1pm-11pm Fri)*. Its 1st-floor balcony is *the* place to pass an afternoon and survey the chaos of the Downtown area down below. Although you won't see any local women here, they're well accustomed to foreign tourists.

Al-Sendabad Coffee Shop *(☎ 4632035; 150m west of Roman Theatre; open 10am-midnight daily)* has great views over the city (though not the theatre) and is kept clean by the friendly staff. It's a great place to smoke the nargileh (JD1), especially on the roof in summer.

Around Hashemite Square and along Hashemi St, a dozen or more cafés can be found. These are decent places for people-watching in this area where the flow of pedestrians never seems to diminish. It's especially lively in summer.

Hills Café *(☎ 0795 631041; 2nd Circle; snacks JD.750-2.500; open 9am-late daily)* is a modern place that serves good sandwiches and cakes, not to mention a range of milkshakes and hot drinks. A nargileh with the famed Bahraini tobacco (aficionados swear by it) costs JD2.

Terrace Cafeteria Petra *(☎ 4612622; 1st Circle; open 8am-midnight)* is a great place to watch the chaos unfold on 1st Circle. There are live oud performances upstairs from 8pm or 9pm (cover charge JD1). A nargileh costs JD1.500.

The place in Amman to be seen at night is anywhere around Abdoun Circle and there are plenty of very cool cafés. You could probably take your pick – fashions change frequently in this part of Amman – but one of the better ones is **Caffe Moka** *(☎ 5926285; Al-Qahira St; open 7.30am-11pm daily)* which serves pastries (from 500 fils) and delicious cakes (from JD1.200), as well as sandwiches and great coffee. The outdoor setting of **Café de Paris** *(☎ 593 4765; Al-Qahira St; open 8am-1pm daily)* is also pleasant, making it a nice place to spend a summer's afternoon.

Across the other side of Abdoun Circle is **Al-Sanabel** *(☎ 5925112; Abdoun Circle; open 8am-12.30am daily)*, a patisserie where the well heeled go to smoke a nargileh (JD2.500).

SPECTATOR SPORTS

Football (soccer) is followed by most locals. The capital's two main teams are Wahadat (generally supported by Palestinians) and Faisaly (supported by other Jordanians). Games are mostly played on Friday at the **Amman International Stadium** near Sports City in Shmeisani.

SHOPPING

Amman is the best place to shop for souvenirs in Jordan. Away from Downtown, there are high-quality handicraft boutiques, many run to benefit women, threatened communities and the environment.

Souvenirs

Al-Alaydi Jordan Craft Centre *(☎/fax 464 4555; e alaydi48@hotmail.com; w www .alaydijordan.1colony.com; off Al-Kulliyah al-Islamiyah St; open 9am-7pm Sat-Thur May-Sept, 9am-6pm Oct-Apr)* is difficult to leave without spending money, with an overwhelming selection spread over a number of floors. Items include jewellery, brass, copper, glassware, ceramics, carpets and other hand-woven or embroidered products. Profits go to support for poor Jordanian families, which includes university scholarships.

Al-Burgan *(☎ 4652585, fax 4652675; e alburgan@go.com.jo; behind Jordan Inter-Continental Hotel; open 9.30am-6.30pm Sat-Thur)* has a smaller selection of items but the staff are knowledgeable and prices are reasonable.

Artisana (*π/fax 4647858; Mansour Kraishan St; open 9.30am-6pm Sat-Thur*), in the same area, is another excellent smaller showroom with reasonable prices.

Bawabet al-Sharq (*π 4637424; e bsharq@nets.jo; w www.bsharq.com; Abu Bakr as-Siddiq St; open 9am-7pm daily*) is a high-quality boutique set up to benefit Jordanian women's groups. The items include handwoven products (cushions, wall hangings and bags) and homewares.

Jordan Design & Trade Centre (*π 569 9141; e jdtc@nets.com.jo; 5 Abdullah bin Abbas St; open 8am-7pm Sat-Thur*) is run by the Noor Al Hussein Foundation, which helps preserve traditional handicraft skills and supports vulnerable women's communities. The centre has a great range of ceramics, embroidered home furnishings, wall hangings, jewellery and rugs.

Jordan River Foundation (*π 4613081, fax 4613083; e showroom@jrf.org.jo; w www.accessme.com/jrd; Bani Hamida House, Fawzi al-Malouf St; open 8.30am-7pm Sat-Thur, 11am-6pm Fri*) has an elegant showroom of homewares with prices to match the quality. There's a showroom for rugs from the Bani Hamida group (see the boxed text 'The Bani Hamida Story' in the King's Highway chapter) on the same site.

Oriental Souvenirs Store (*π 4642820; 3rd Circle; open 8am-7pm Sat-Thur*) is more rustic than the others listed here but it's something of an Aladdin's Cave. It's friendly, family run and recommended.

Proceeds from the **RSCN Gift Shop** (*π 533 7931; Fawzi Al-Malouf St; open 7.30am-4pm Sun-Thur*) go to the Royal Society for the Conservation of Nature (RSCN) with products on offer including jewellery, fruit, herbs, pottery, richly decorated ostrich eggs and a few books.

Silsal Ceramics (*π 5931128; e info@silsal .com; Innabeh St; open 9am-6pm Sat-Thur*) has a small showroom of superb modern pottery with price tags that are surprisingly reasonable. If you're coming along Zahran St from 5th Circle, it's the third small street on the right.

Music
If you're after the latest Western or Arabic CD or DVD, try **Stallions** (*π 5922003; Abdoun Circle; open 10.30am-9.30pm Sat-Thur, 4pm-9pm Fri*).

GETTING THERE & AWAY
For information about international services to/from Amman, see the Getting There & Away chapter.

Air
Amman is the main arrival and departure point for international flights, although some touch down in Aqaba as well.

Royal Jordanian head office (*π 5607300, fax 5672527*) is inconveniently located in the Housing Bank Centre (9th floor) in Shmeisani. There are more convenient offices in the Jordan Inter-Continental Hotel complex (*π 4644266, fax 4642152*) and along Al-Malek al-Hussein St (*π/fax 566 3525*), up from the Abdali bus station. Smaller offices are at the University of Jordan (*π 5346868*) and Queen Alia International Airport (*π 5856835*).

Anyone travelling on Royal Jordanian can check in their bags, pay the departure tax (JD5) and catch a shuttle bus (JD2, buses half-hourly between 8am and 9pm) to Queen Alia International Airport from the Royal Jordanian **city terminal** (*π 5856855, fax 5857136*), but it's inconveniently located on 7th Circle.

The Royal Jordanian subsidiary, **Royal Wings**, has an office (*π 4875201, fax 4875656*) at Marka airport, but it's easier to book and confirm tickets at any Royal Jordanian office in town.

The following international airlines are among those with offices in Amman:

Air France (*π 5666055*) Al-Ameer Shaker bin Zeid St, Shmeisani

Austrian Airlines (*π 5694604*) Al-Shareef Abdulla Hameed Sharaf St, Shmeisani

British Airways (*π 5828801, fax 5862277*) Ali Nasouh al-Taher St, Al-Swayfiyyeh, between 6th and 7th Circles

EgyptAir (*π 4630011*) Zaatarah & Co, Al-Malek al-Hussein St, Downtown

Emirates (*π 4615222*) Al-Hussein bin Ali St, northwest of 3rd Circle

Gulf Air (*π 4653613*) Al-Malek al-Hussein St, Abdali, east of Abdali bus station

KLM Royal Dutch Airlines (*π 4655267*) Al-Malek al-Hussein St, Downtown, near flyover

Lufthansa Airlines (*π 5601744*) Ilya Abu Madhi St, Shmeisani

Middle East Airlines (*π 4636104*) Al-Malek al-Hussein St, Downtown

Turkish Airlines (*π 4659102*) Al-Hussein bin Ali St, near 3rd Circle

AMMAN

Private Bus

Tickets for private buses should be booked at least one day in advance.

Domestic The JETT office (☎ 5664146) is on Al-Malek al-Hussein St, about 500m northwest of the Abdali bus station. Regular services include:

destination	frequency	one-way price (JD)	duration (hrs)
Aqaba	5 daily	4.200	4 to 4½
Petra	3 weekly	6	3½
Hammamat Ma'in	weekly	2.5	2
King Hussein Bridge	daily	6.500	¾

For those with limited time, there is a same-day return trip to Petra for JD28, which includes a guide and food but not the entrance fee. The Petra bus leaves at 6.30am and departs Petra for the return journey at 5pm.

Trust International Transport has six daily buses to Aqaba (JD4, four hours), the first at 7.30am and the last at 6pm. All buses leave from the office (☎ 5813428) inconveniently located at 7th Circle, near the Safeway shopping centre – it's best to charter a taxi to/from Downtown. Trust also has a booking office (☎ 4644627) at the Abdali bus station.

Afana (☎ 4614611) is another private company with hourly departures to Aqaba (JD3) between 7am and 10pm daily from its office next to the JETT International office.

Hijazi (☎ 4638110) has regular buses to Irbid (870 fils, 90 minutes) from Abdali station.

Public Bus & Minibus

At the time of research, the three main bus stations in Amman were Abdali bus station for transport to the north and west, Wahadat bus station for the south, and Raghadan bus station for Amman and nearby towns.

However, the Abdali bus station was due to close some time in 2003, with most of its services having moved to a new station on Amman's northern outskirts in Tabarbor. There was also talk of concentrating services to most tourist destinations from a new-look Raghadan bus station as part of the redevelopment of Downtown Amman. Ask your hotel or the tourist office for more information.

Abdali Station Abdali bus station on Al-Malek al-Hussein Street is a 20-minute walk (uphill) from Downtown; a No 6 or 7 service taxi from Cinema al-Hussein Street goes right by. Regular share taxis depart Abdali for Wahadat bus station (150 fils) throughout the day.

Minibuses take up the top end of the station, then (going downhill) there are the service taxis, private bus company offices and service taxis for King Hussein Bridge and Damascus.

From Abdali, minibuses leave for the following destinations (when full):

destination	cost (fils)	duration (hrs)
Ajlun	500	2
Deir Alla (for Pella)	600	1
Fuheis	150	¾
Irbid	600	2
Jerash	350	1¼
Madaba	270	¾
Ramtha	500	2
Salt	200	¾

Wahadat Station Almost all buses and service taxis headed south leave from Wahadat station, way out in the southern suburbs by Middle East Circle (Duwaar Sharq al-Awsat). To reach the station, take a service taxi or bus No 23 from Abdali station, or service taxi No 27 from Italian St (see the Downtown map). A private taxi will cost around JD1 from Downtown.

From Wahadat, minibuses depart for:

destination	cost (JD)	duration (hrs)
Aqaba	3	5
Karak	0.800	2
Ma'an	1.100	3
Tafila	1	2½

A few times a day, they also go to:

destination	cost (JD)	duration (hrs)
Qadsiyya (for Dana)	1.350	3
Shobak	1.500	2½
Wadi Musa (for Petra)	4	3

Larger buses to Karak and Aqaba leave at least every hour until early in the afternoon. Buses and minibuses also leave regularly for Madaba (270 fils, 45 minutes) but it's more convenient to catch one from Abdali or Raghadan station.

Raghadan Station The chaotic Raghadan station is a few minutes' walk east of the Roman Theatre. It's divided into three sections; the first (when coming from the theatre) is a mass of service taxis going to nearby villages and suburbs of little interest to visitors. A few hundred metres further east, there are minibuses to Madaba (270 fils, 45 minutes), Salt (200 fils, 45 minutes), Wadi as-Seer (200 fils, 30 minutes) and Zarqa (200 fils, 30 minutes). Further east are local buses, also of little use to travellers.

Dead Sea & Wadi as-Seer If you want to go to the Dead Sea, minibuses leave from the small minibus station opposite the Muhajireen Police Station (the corner of Al-Ameerah Basma bin Talal Rd and Ali bin Abi Taleb Rd – see the Jebel Amman map) for Shuneh al-Janubiyyeh (South Shuna; 500 fils, 45 minutes). From South Shuna, you'll probably have to change for Suweimah (200 fils), although occasionally the minibuses go right to the Dead Sea Rest House.

Minibuses leave from the same station for Wadi as-Seer (200 fils, 30 minutes).

Service Taxi

Service taxis are generally faster and take less time to fill, but they're also more expensive. They depart from the same stations as the minibuses and departures are more frequent in the morning.

From Abdali station, there are service taxis to Irbid (JD1), Ramtha (JD1), Salt (450 fils) and the King Hussein Bridge (JD2, 45 minutes).

From Wahadat station, there are semiregular departures to Karak (JD1.400, two hours); Wadi Musa (JD2.750, three hours) for Petra, via Shobak (JD2.250, 2½ hours); Ma'an (JD1.200, three hours); and also infrequently to Aqaba (JD5, five hours).

Car

Listed are some of the more reliable car rental agencies. Charges, conditions and insurance costs (and waiver fees in case of accident) vary considerably so shop around. Many offer discounted rates, especially during low season. Always read the contract carefully before signing. Remember many places require a minimum three days' rental and all require a deposit of up to JD400 payable on pick-up and refunded on return of the car. Most take major credit cards and offer cars no more than three years old.

Budget (☎ 5698131, fax 5673312, e budget@go .com.jo) 125 Al-Shareef Abdulla Hameed Shareef St. Budget charges from JD25 per day including unlimited kilometres and theft insurance.

Eurodollar Rent a Car (☎ 5693399, fax 5687233, e info@eurodollar-jo.com) Al-Shareef Abdulla Hameed Sharaf St. Rates start from JD20 per day, plus JD10 CDW per day with unlimited kilometres.

Firas Car Rental (Alamo Car Rental; ☎ 4612927, fax 4616874, e alamo@nets.com.jo) 1st Circle. Rates are from JD15 per day with unlimited kilometres, and CDW is JD7 per day. Firas is highly recommended.

National Car Rental (☎/fax 5601350, e national car@joinnet.com.jo) Amman Marriott and Le Meridien Hotels in Shmeisani. Charges are from JD25 per day (including CDW). Rates include 200 free kilometres for the first three days (150 fils per additional kilometre) or unlimited kilometres for more than three days' rental.

Nator Car Rental (☎ 4627455) 9th Sha'ban St. Charges start from JD22 with unlimited kilometres, plus JD3 per day for insurance.

Service Taxi Routes

All departure points are listed on the Downtown map.

No 2 From Basman St for 1st and 2nd Circles

No 3 From Basman St for 3rd and 4th Circles

No 4 From the side street near the central post office for Jebel Weibdeh

No 6 From Cinema al-Hussein St for the Ministry of the Interior Circle, past Abdali station and JETT international and domestic offices

No 7 From Cinema al-Hussein St, up Al-Malek al-Hussein St, past Abdali station and King Abdullah Mosque, and along Suleiman al-Nabulsi St

Nos 25 & 26 From behind the Church of the Saviour, Downtown, to the top of Jebel al-Ashrafiyeh' and near Abu Darwish Mosque

No 27 From near the Italian Hospital to Middle East Circle for Wahadat station

No 35 From near the front of the Church of the saviour, passing close to the Muhajireen Police Station

GETTING AROUND
To/From the Airports

Queen Alia International Airport is 35km south of the city. The **Airport Express bus** (☎ 445 1531) runs between the airport and the upper end of Abdali station, passing through the 4th, 5th, 6th and 7th Circles en route. The service (JD1.500, 30 minutes) runs every half hour between 6am and 10pm and every hour after 10pm. From the airport, buses depart from outside the arrivals hall of Terminal 2. With the impending scaling down of the Abdali bus station, the service could shift to either the new station at Tabarbor or the Raghadan bus station.

The only other option is a private taxi, which should cost JD12 to JD15. Although you are within your rights to insist that the driver uses the meter (around JD8), many will simply refuse. With the convenience of the Airport Express, it's difficult to see why you'd need to take a taxi; locals never do.

To get to Marka airport, take a service taxi from Raghadan station (150 fils).

Bus

The local bus system is confusing, with nothing labelled in English. Bus Nos 26, 27, 28, 41 and 43 can be useful for getting to Downtown so hop aboard if you're weary and one passes. If bus travel's your thing, ask around the bus section of Raghadan station to see what's headed your way but you'll need patience. Tickets cost around 50 fils.

Service Taxi

Most fares cost between 100 and 150 fils and you usually pay the full amount regardless of where you get off. After 8pm, the price for all service taxis goes up by 25%.

The cars queue up and usually start at the bottom of a hill – you get into the last car and the whole line rolls back a car space and so on. Always double check that your taxi is going to your destination before climbing in.

Private Taxi

Most drivers of private taxis use the meter as a matter of course, but gently remind them when they don't. You need to be especially careful when you're laden with bags and searching for your hotel or heading out in the evening to an expensive restaurant.

The flagfall is 150 fils. Fares are cheap and worth considering to avoid aching leg muscles; from Downtown to Abdali costs around 500 fils while to Shmeisani shouldn't cost much more than JD1.

Car

See Organised Tours earlier in this chapter for more information on arranging cars and drivers for tours in and around Amman.

If you must drive in Downtown Amman and are fortunate enough to find a parking spot, remember that parking machines operate along many main streets. It costs 150/250 fils for 30 minutes/one hour.

Amman's Taxis

On any given day, Jordan's capital is home to an estimated 16,000 yellow taxis and counting. One will never be far away and they often find you before you find them – hopeful honking at tourists in case they missed the obvious is a favourite pastime. Although Amman inducted its first female taxi driver in 1997, all the others are male. Most drivers are fast and friendly, often more interested in finding out where you're from than keeping an eye on the road. We've had them all, from experienced drivers for whom slowing down is incomprehensible sacrilege to first-day recruits with a very twitchy brake pedal. Some drive as a second job to supplement meagre salaries, and many have studied overseas. Many smoke without asking.

When some drivers spot a tourist laden with bags and obviously just off the plane or bus, they can develop an unscrupulous streak, refusing to switch the meter on, inflating prices and using all manner of persuasion to get you to go to the hotel of *their* choice (where they invariably get a commission) – no, the hotel of your choice hasn't burned down, regardless of what they tell you.

Making the effort to talk with them is illuminating, shedding light on the latest city-wide gossip or scandal to their take on the problems of the Middle East (many are Palestinians with stories to tell). Most work very hard for their money. A good day can yield JD35 (before overheads) in winter, and double that in summer. A bad day will bring as little as JD15 – not much for up to 15 hours' work.

Around Amman

There are a number of worthwhile sites within easy reach of Amman. Salt is an attractive town with good remnants of Ottoman architecture, while Wadi as-Seer combines evocative ruins with beautiful landscapes just outside the bustling capital. Also within striking distance of Amman is the Dead Sea, which is high on the list of must-sees for most visitors to Jordan.

CAVE OF SEVEN SLEEPERS (AHL AL-KAHF) أهل الكهف

The legend of the 'seven sleepers' is mentioned in the Quran and the Bible. It involves several Christian boys who were persecuted, then escaped to a cave and slept there for 309 years. Inside the main cave – also known as Ahl al-Kahf (Cave of the People) – are eight smaller tombs which are sealed, but one can be explored a little with a torch (flashlight) or candle. About 500m west of the cave is a large **Byzantine cemetery**.

Entrance is free and the site is open 8am to 6pm. The cave is next to the main mosque in the village of Rajib, off the road from Amman to Sabah. A bus from Quraysh St goes to about 1km west of the cave, from where you'll have to walk. The best way there is by chartered taxi (at least JD3 one way).

SALT السلط
☎ 05

> In Salt we were invited into two houses...At one house, we had singing in Arabic from the eldest son, and then we had to demonstrate disco-dancing to a cassette of *Saturday Night Fever*, while the whole family stood around clapping. It was most embarrassing!
>
> **Mark Hilton, UK**

The friendly town of Salt is about 30km northwest of Downtown in Amman and set in a steep-sided narrow valley. It was the area's administrative centre under Ottoman rule, but was passed over as the new capital of Trans-Jordan in favour of Amman. Consequently, Salt, which has a large Christian population, has retained much of its charm. Salt was apparently named from the Greek word *saltus* meaning 'forests' (although these are long gone); or from the word *sultana* for the grapes that were once abundant in the region.

Highlights

- **The Dead Sea** – enjoy the buoyancy of floating in the salty water and finish with a mud pack to help improve your skin

- **Salt** – this charming town near Amman boasts fine Ottoman architecture, friendly locals and workshops for arts and crafts

- **Wadi as-Seer** – hike through quiet valleys to the Iraq al-Amir ruins close to Amman

- **Bethany-Beyond-the-Jordan** – visit one of the most important Biblical sites in Jordan, where Jesus is believed to have been baptised

ISRAEL & THE PALESTINIAN TERRITORIES

SYRIA

Around Amman p127

West Bank

Salt p128

AMMAN

Salt is easy to walk around and there are plenty of banks in the central area. The friendly **tourist office** (☎ 3555652; open 8am-3pm Sun-Thur) is upstairs in Beit Mismar on Dayr St.

Things to See & Do

There are some fine examples of decaying **Ottoman architecture**, particularly along the northern end of Dayr St. None of the grand old houses are signposted and most are not open to the public, but some facades are quite elegant. **Beit Muasher** and **Beit Abu Jaber** are among the best. **Beit Mismar**, which houses the tourist office, is built of

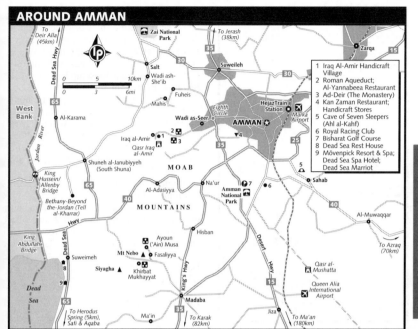

AROUND AMMAN

1 Iraq Al-Amir Handicraft Village
2 Roman Aqueduct; Al-Yannabea Restaurant
3 Ad-Deir (The Monastery)
4 Kan Zaman Restaurant; Handicraft Stores
5 Cave of Seven Sleepers (Ahl al-Kahf)
6 Royal Racing Club
7 Bisharat Golf Course
8 Dead Sea Rest House
9 Mövenpick Resort & Spa; Dead Sea Spa Hotel; Dead Sea Marriot

yellow limestone and dates from the late 19th and early 20th centuries. The simple but appealing facade includes a most attractive door, and there are plans for restoration.

The views from Jebel al-Qala'a are worth the hike up the steep streets.

Salt Archaeological Museum (☎ 355 5651; admission free; open 8am-7pm daily, 8am-4pm winter) is well laid out in a nice Ottoman-era building. Downstairs is glass and pottery spanning the Roman, Byzantine and Islamic eras, mostly from around Salt but also from Deir Alla and Amman. Upstairs are some costumes, models of traditional farming activities and mosaics from the old churches around Salt, as well as some coins. Most exhibits are labelled in English.

The **Salt Cultural Centre** (admission free; open 9am-5pm Sun-Thur) is run primarily for the benefit of locals, but visitors are welcome in the small museum and library. Performances are sometimes held here (ask at the tourist office). Visitors can watch weaving, pottery and other handicrafts being made at the **Salt Handicraft Training Centre** (☎ 3551781; open 8.30am-2.30pm Sun-Thur,

8am-1pm Sat) downstairs from the cultural centre or at the other office about 200m to the south.

The road from the bus station leads into **Wadi ash-She'ib**, a refreshing valley with some **hiking** opportunities as well as interesting **caves**.

Places to Stay & Eat

There is nowhere to stay in Salt; ask at the tourist office to see if this has changed.

The northern end of Maydan St is lined with traditional **cafés**, full of men drinking tea and smoking nargilehs. Basic **restaurants** along the same street serve kebabs.

Al-Salam Restaurant (☎ 3552115; Maydan St; meals JD1.500; open 7am-10.30pm Sat-Thur), opposite the Arab Bank, is one of the best places in town for cheap Arab food.

Canary Restaurant (opposite southern end of Dayr St) is similar to Al-Salam.

Getting There & Away

The bus station is on the main road south of the town centre. There are minibuses to Salt (200 fils, 45 minutes) from Amman's Abdali and Raghadan stations, and occasional

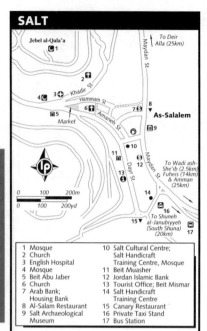

SALT

Jebel al-Qala'a
1

To Deir
Alla (25km)

Maydan St

Khadir St
2
4
3
Hammam St
5
6
7
8
Amaneh St
As-Salalem
Market
9
10
11
12
Day St
13
Maydan St
To Wadi ash-
She'ib (2.5km)
Fuheis (14km)
& Amman
(25km)
14
0   100   200m
0   100   200yd
16
15
To Shuneh
al-Janubiyyeh
(South Shuna)
(20km)
17

1 Mosque	10 Salt Cultural Centre;
2 Church	Salt Handicraft
3 English Hospital	Training Centre, Mosque
4 Mosque	11 Beit Muasher
5 Beit Abu Jaber	12 Jordan Islamic Bank
6 Church	13 Tourist Office; Beit Mismar
7 Arab Bank;	14 Salt Handicraft
Housing Bank	Training Centre
8 Al-Salam Restaurant	15 Canary Restaurant
9 Salt Archaeological	16 Private Taxi Stand
Museum	17 Bus Station

service taxis (450 fils) from Abdali. From Salt, minibuses head down the Jordan Valley to Shuneh al-Janubiyyeh (South Shuna), and to Wadi as-Seer and Fuheis, with which Salt can be combined as a day trip from Amman. Taxis (JD5) can be chartered to Amman.

ZAI NATIONAL PARK

حديقة الزي الوطنية

This small piece of greenery is popular with Jordanians for picnics and has nice views, but there's little reason for a special visit.

If driving to Zai, go to Suweilah, follow the road towards Salt, then bypass Salt and head towards Deir Alla and watch for signs to the park. There is no public transport to the area, so charter a taxi from Salt.

FUHEIS

فحيص

☎ 06

This pleasant village, located at a cool 1050m above sea level, is famous in Jordan for producing fruit and cement, but is of more interest to visitors for its galleries and fine places to eat.

First built in about 2000 BC, Fuheis, which snakes down the hillside, is now an overwhelmingly Christian village. There are numerous **churches**, three of which are just down from the minibus stop. Fuheis has several **galleries** and **workshops** that produce ceramics, mosaics, paintings and embroidery. The largest and most modern gallery is **Riwak al-Balkaa for the Arts** (☎ 4720677). This and other galleries are poorly signposted; ask at the Hakoura Restaurant (see Places to Eat) for directions. Also ask here (or at the tourist office in Amman) about any concerts and exhibitions in Fuheis; they're sometimes held in summer, but are not well advertised.

Hiking in the area is also good; just head down the valley from the bus stop.

At the first roundabout, coming from Salt or Amman, is **Friends Internet 2**, one of a number along the long main street which charge JD1 per hour. There are also banks for changing money, including the Arab Bank, also on the main street, which has an ATM for Visa and MasterCard.

Places to Eat

Fuheis has two excellent restaurants, both easy to spot from the final minibus stop in Al-Rawaq neighbourhood, where the food is excellent, alcohol is served and the atmosphere is charming.

Zuwwadeh Restaurant (☎ 4721528; starters JD1-2, mains JD2-6; open 10am-midnight daily) has shady outdoor tables or a pleasant indoor dining area. The food is fabulous, especially the *fatteh* (fried bread) with hummus, meat or chicken and pine nuts (JD2/4/6 for a small/medium/huge), which is almost worth the trip from Amman on its own. Most nights there are also live oud performances upstairs (after 7pm) and bookings may be necessary.

Hakoura Restaurant (☎ 4729152; starters under JD1, mains JD2.500-5; open 10am-midnight daily) is similarly good and a little cheaper. It's an artistic place with a commitment to traditional hospitality, soulful music and modern art, with some excellent food thrown in.

Getting There & Away

Fuheis is easy to reach by minibus from Abdali bus station in Amman (150 fils, 45 minutes). The town is also regularly connected to Wadi as-Seer and Salt (each 250 fils, around 30 minutes), so you can visit all

King Abdullah Mosque, Amman

Umayyad Palace, Citadel, Amman

Roman Theatre, Amman

Abu Darwish Mosque, Amman

Roman Theatre, Amman

The Dead Sea

three places in one day. If you're eating at one of the restaurants until late, you may need to pre-arrange a chartered taxi back to Amman.

The minibus stop in the older (lower) part of town known as *il-balad* is at a roundabout, close to the two restaurants and a number of churches.

WADI AS-SEER & IRAQ AL-AMIR
عراق الأمير / وادي عسير

The valley was green and restful; the traffic was far away, only the sound of goat bells on a nearby hill, birdsong and the occasional distant cries of children.

Annie Caulfield, *Kingdom of the Film Stars*

The narrow, fertile valley of Wadi as-Seer is quite a contrast to the bare treeless plateau around Amman to the east. Spring (particularly April and May) is the best time to visit, when black iris (the Jordanian national flower) and other colourful flowers are plentiful.

Wadi as-Seer is a largely Circassian village, and now virtually part of western Amman. About 10km down the lovely valley are the Iraq al-Amir 'castle' and caves. Along the way (about 4km past Wadi as-Seer), and next to the sleepy **Al-Yanabeea Restaurant**, is an ancient **Roman aqueduct** on the right. Shortly after, on the left, is a facade cut into the rock, known as **Ad-Deir** (monastery), although it was probably a medieval dovecote (a place to house pigeons).

Iraq al-Amir (Caves of the Prince) are on the right of the road about 6km further past Al-Yanabeea Restaurant if you're coming from Amman. The caves are arranged in two tiers – the upper one forms a long gallery (partially damaged during a mild earthquake in 1999) along the cliff face. The 11 caves were apparently used as cavalry stables, but locals now use them to house their goats and store chaff. The caves themselves are not that interesting, but the views are pleasant. Steps lead up to the caves from the paved road; opposite is the village of Iraq al-Amir and the **Iraq al-Amir Handicraft Village**, which has a small weaving centre supporting 61 women who produce pottery, carpets and paper products. You may need to ask around the village for it to be opened up when the women aren't working.

Qasr Iraq al-Amir
About 700m further down the road, just visible from the caves, are small but impressive ruins of what is thought to have been a villa or minor palace. It's also known as Qasr al-Abad (Palace of the Slave). Mystery surrounds the reason for its construction, and even its precise age, but most scholars believe that Hyrcanus, of the powerful Jewish Tobiad family, started building it in the 2nd century BC. Although never completed, much of the *qasr* has been reconstructed.

The place is unique because it was built from some of the biggest blocks of any ancient structure in the Middle East – the largest is 7m by 3m. The blocks were, however, only 20cm or so thick, making the whole edifice quite flimsy and susceptible to the earthquake which flattened it in AD 362. Today, the setting and the animal carvings on the interior walls are the highlights.

The gate is open every day during daylight hours and admission to the grounds is free. The inside of the *qasr* is locked, so you'll have to find the gatekeeper who'll open it (a tip of around 500 fils is appropriate). If he doesn't show up, ask for the key *(miftah)* at the small shop near the gate.

Getting There & Away
Minibuses leave regularly from the station on Ali bin Abi Taleb St in Amman for Wadi as-Seer village (200 fils, 30 minutes); and less frequently from the Raghadan station in Downtown. From Wadi as-Seer, take another minibus (100 fils) – or walk about 10km, mostly downhill – to the caves; look for the signpost to Iraq al-Amir Handicraft Village, which is virtually opposite the stairs to the caves. From the caves, it's an easy stroll down to the *qasr* (but a little steep back up).

If you're driving, head west from the 8th Circle and follow the main road which twists through Wadi as-Seer village. There are occasional signs to 'Iraq al-Amir'; the *qasr* is at the end of the road down the valley.

SHUNEH AL-JANUBIYYEH
(SOUTH SHUNA) شونا الجنوبية
This nondescript town is simply a junction for public transport to the Dead Sea and north through the Jordan Valley. The town is well connected by minibus with Amman's Dead Sea bus station (450 fils, one hour), as well as with Madaba and Salt.

There are a few cheap **restaurants** in town, as well as places to buy food for a picnic. Because of the limited public transport to places like Bethany (Tell al-Kharrar), chartering a taxi from Shuneh al-Janubiyyeh to visit several sites in a few hours is a good idea, and cheaper than chartering in Amman.

BETHANY-BEYOND-THE-JORDAN (TELL AL-KHARRAR)

تل الخرار

The place where Jesus was baptised by John the Baptist (John 1:28) has recently been opened to the public, although Israelis inevitably lay claim to a similar site just across the border. The site was still being developed when we visited, with an extensive visitor centre nearing completion.

Landscaped paths take you past a number of archaeological excavations, including **water cisterns** dating from the Byzantine and Roman eras; the skeleton of a 3rd-century **prayer hall** with a faded mosaic floor; and the reconstructed arch of a 4th-century **Byzantine church**. The most extensive and intact ruins are those on **Elijah's Hill**, containing three caves, baptismal pools and churches, as well as the **Rhotorius Monastery**, which dates from the Byzantine period and has a mosaic floor with Greek inscriptions. The hill, which is where Elijah is believed to have ascended to heaven, looks down into the reeds of one of the Jordan River's tributaries, said to be the place where Jesus was baptised, and across the Jordan Valley to the city of Jericho in the Palestinian Territories.

There are limited signs throughout the site, but expect this to improve as the development of the site continues.

Getting There & Away

There are signs to the 'Site of Jesus Baptism' along the road from Amman and Madaba to the Dead Sea. Take any minibus to the Dead Sea Rest House (see Getting There & Away in the Amman chapter and Madaba in the King's Highway chapter). About 5km before the Rest House, the road forks; the Dead Sea (and military checkpoint) is to the left, the baptism site to the right. There is no public transport for the 5km to the visitor centre so you'll have to hitch, charter a taxi or walk (take plenty of water). It's a further 750m from the visitor centre to the site proper.

THE DEAD SEA

☎ 05

البحر الميت

Part of the border between Jordan and the Palestinian Territories goes through the Dead Sea, a lake with such high salinity that your body floats – drowning or sinking would be quite a feat. Swimming is also difficult because you're too high in the water to stroke properly, but of course you can always float on your back while reading the newspaper and have your picture taken. The buoyancy you'll experience is the sort of thing that you can only understand once you've been and you'll invariably hear squeals of surprise from people visiting for the first time. While paddling about you'll probably discover cuts you never knew you had (don't shave before visiting), and if any water gets in your eyes, be prepared for a few minutes of agony.

Information

Try to avoid Fridays and public holidays when the Dead Sea Rest House complex is in chaos and public transport is crowded; on any other day there will be few other people around. Always take lots of water as the humidity and heat (over 40°C in summer) can be dehydrating and there's little shade.

After a dip in the Dead Sea, you'll find yourself coated in uncomfortable encrustations of salt that are best washed off as soon as you can. A shower (and shampoo and soap) afterwards is vital. If showers are not available, some readers have recommended bringing a few bottles of water for an abridged version of the same thing. As one reader observed: 'Without showers and clean water it's the same as hell' (Leo Bouwman, Netherlands).

Most visitors (foreigners and Jordanians) head for the run-down **Dead Sea Rest House** complex on the northeastern shore of the lake in Suweimeh. The entrance fee (JD4) provides visitors with access to the Dead Sea (though partially shaded, it's fairly bleak) and showers; a tip for the shower attendant who keeps them clean is appreciated. The beach and showers are open from 6am to sunset daily; swimming is generally not permitted after dark.

At the Rest House, the tables on the rise above the beach are often populated by local men, some with binoculars, so women should try to find a secluded spot as far from them as possible.

The Dead Sea

The Dead Sea – known locally as Al-Bahr al-Mayit or Bahr Lut (Sea of Lot) – is about 65km long and from 6km to 18km wide. Its main source is the Jordan River, but it has no outlet.

The name is apt because the incredibly high salt content (30%) is up to seven times greater than the ocean, so plant and animal life is impossible – 11 species of bacteria survive, but no fish at all. The concentration of salt has nothing to do with the Dead Sea being below sea level; rather it comes about because of the high evaporation rate which has, over the years, led to a build-up of salts.

The level of the Dead Sea has been falling by about 500cm every year for the past 20 years or more, mainly because there is no longer any regular inflow from the stagnant Jordan River, water is diverted from the sea for irrigation, and evaporation is so high. The level has fallen from 392m to 409m below sea level (some experts put the water level at closer to 420m), and about 30% (approximately 300 sq km) of the original area has vanished. Some experts even believe the lake may dry up completely in 50 years. In a bid to reverse the trend, a canal from the Red Sea down to the Dead Sea (known as the Two Seas Canal Project and costing US$6 billion) is planned. The aim is to raise water levels and create enough hydroelectricity along the way to power desalination plants in Jordan and Israel and the Palestinian Territories.

At the southern end of the lake, Jordanians are exploiting the high potash content of the mineral-rich water. Each day, more than one million tonnes of water are pumped into vast evaporation ponds covering some 10,000 hectares. The concentrated potash salts are then refined at processing plants south of Safi. The project is now producing about four million tonnes of potash annually, making Jordan one of the world's largest producers.

The Dead Sea also contains various other minerals. Some are apparently excellent for health and skin. The benefits reportedly include calcium and magnesium, which are good for allergies and bronchial infections; pungent bromine to help with relaxation; iodine to alleviate certain glandular ailments; and bitumen to improve the skin. Most souvenir shops in Jordan stock various 'Dead Sea' creams, lotions, gels and soaps, all of which contain extractions from the lake, thereby exacerbating the environmental damage.

For more information on the dangers to the Dead Sea, contact the **Friends of the Earth – Middle East** (**e** info@foeme.org, **w** www.foeme.org).

Please note that reports have been circulating for some time that the Rest House is to be closed and/or redeveloped, so check with your hotel in Amman or tourist office before setting out.

Even more expensive for accessing the Dead Sea are the upmarket hotels (see Places to Stay later in this chapter) about 5km south of the Rest House where you pay at least JD10, and probably more, for access to their beaches and other facilities, including shower and swimming pool.

Mud Pack Treatment An all-body Dead Sea 'mud pack' is reported to do wonders for your skin. This costs JD1 per person at the Rest House (at the southern end of the beach). Women are strongly advised to apply their own mud (or get the help of a close friend) rather than rely on the all-male staff at the Rest House. Better still, the northern end of the Rest House beach, where the perimeter fence meets the water, is where many locals head for mud which is in abundance, far from prying eyes and free. A mud treatment at one of the luxury hotels listed below will cost much, much more.

Herodus Spring

All along the eastern shore of the Dead Sea are areas where you are free to float, although you'll have no showers and you'll probably have to hitch a ride from near the Rest House unless you have your own transport. The best free place to swim is at the popular, picturesque Herodus Spring, 15km south of the Rest House. It's marked by a bridge and a large military base, and there's a narrow canyon running up towards Hammamat Ma'in where fresh (but undrinkable) water flows – ideal for washing afterwards. The water's edge is a short walk down the hill, under the bridge. There's little privacy; women should dress conservatively.

The Dead Sea Ultra Marathon

For most visitors, the Dead Sea is a place to relax and enjoy the novelty of floating at the world's lowest point or being pampered at an upmarket spa complex. And then for others, there's the Dead Sea Ultra Marathon. Starting at Safeway on 7th Circle in Amman, it involves a 50km run (individually or in a relay) down to the Dead Sea; shorter competitions are also possible. In case you think that this is the preserve of a few mad locals, remember that in 2002 (its 10th year) 730 athletes from 27 countries took part. The race usually takes place in April. If you're keen for a bit of extreme sport, contact the **Amman Road Runners group** (☎ 5930435; **W** www.deadsea marathon.com) or any tourist office for details.

Places to Stay & Eat

There is nowhere to stay cheaply at the Dead Sea (unless you have your own tent), which is why most budget travellers choose to take a day trip from either Amman or, increasingly, Madaba. The only reason to stay is to enjoy the spectacular sunset.

Dead Sea Rest House (☎ 3560110; doubles from JD35; pitch your own tent JD10) offers comfortable but overpriced air-con doubles and bungalows with a sitting room, TV and fridge (but no views). Set meals at the **restaurant** cost JD6 and there are sometimes buffets on Fridays and public holidays.

About 5km south of the Rest House along the Dead Sea Highway are a number of upmarket hotels clustered on a patch of shoreline known as 'Hotel Zone'.

Mövenpick Resort and Spa (☎ 3561111, fax 3561122; **e** resort.deadsea@moevenpick .com; singles/doubles from JD128/156) is the resort to beat, with an ever-expanding area devoted to luxury accommodation, tennis courts, swimming pools, medical centre and its own private beach. It has its own amphitheatre and spa centre offering a range of treatments and massages that represent the ultimate in pampering. There are nine **bars** and **restaurants** (including Asian and Italian).

Dead Sea Spa Hotel (☎ 3561000, fax 356 1012; **e** dssh@nets.com.jo; singles/doubles US$100/120, suites from US$220), about 200m south of the Mövenpick, is also luxurious, though neither as classy nor extensive as its neighbour. It also has a swimming pool.

Dead Sea Marriott is another hotel on the same promontory. It is in its final stages of construction but had yet to open at the time of research.

Getting There & Away

Minibus Some hotels in Amman organise day trips to the Dead Sea so ask around. For details of getting to/from the Dead Sea from the capital, refer to Getting There & Away in the Amman chapter. See Madaba in the King's Highway chapter for details of reaching the Dead Sea from there.

Hitching Hitching back to Amman from the Dead Sea Rest House is relatively easy; Friday and Sunday are the best days, although many cars are full.

Chartered Taxi Taxis can be rented for about JD40 per day from Amman, and for far less from Shuneh al-Janubiyyeh. It's a bit pointless if you're only interested in a long and leisurely bathe at the Rest House, but it does allow you to seek out better (and free) bathing spots along the shore (see Information earlier in this chapter).

DEAD SEA HIGHWAY

The Dead Sea Highway (Highway 65) is the least used of the three main highways crossing Jordan from north to south, but it's a quicker and more interesting alternative to the Desert Highway if you're driving between Amman and Aqaba. Some scenery along the Dead Sea shoreline is superb. Around Safi, however, there are numerous trucks from the nearby potash factory and the southern stretches of the highway are barren and desolate. If you're driving, be aware that there are few petrol stations and places to eat, and there is no access to Petra from the highway, although there is a road to Karak. Much of the highway runs along the border of Israel and the Palestinian Territories, so keep your documents handy, including passport, drivers licence, rental contract and registration card (ruksa) for the car.

From Amman, the road to the highway starts at Al-Quds St and leads past the Dead Sea Rest House at Suweimeh. From Aqaba, follow the signs to the airport.

For details of visiting Lot's Cave near the southern end of the Dead Sea, see Around Karak in the King's Highway chapter.

Jerash & the North

The area to the north of Amman is the most densely populated in Jordan, with the major centres of Irbid and Jerash, as well as dozens of small towns dotted in among the rugged and relatively fertile hills. In this area lie the ruins of the ancient Decapolis cities of Jerash (Gerasa) and Umm Qais (Gadara), and the impressive castle at Ajlun.

Northeast of Irbid, the country flattens out to plains that stretch away into Syria. To the west lies the Jordan Valley, one of the most fertile patches of land in the Middle East.

JERASH
جرش

☎ 02

The ruins at Jerash are one of Jordan's major attractions and have the advantage of being very accessible and compact. Jerash is also one of the best examples in the Middle East of a Roman provincial city, and is remarkably well preserved.

In its heyday, Jerash (known in Roman times as Gerasa) had a population of around 15,000 inhabitants and, although it wasn't on any of the major trade routes, its citizens prospered from the good agricultural land that surrounded it. The ancient city that survives today was the administrative, civic and commercial centre of Jerash. The bulk of the inhabitants lived on the eastern side of Wadi Jerash (now the modern town of Jerash).

History

Although there have been finds to indicate that the site was inhabited in Neolithic times, the city rose to prominence from the time of Alexander the Great (333 BC).

In the wake of the Roman general Pompey's conquest of the region in 64 BC, Gerasa became part of the Roman province of Syria and, soon after, a city of the Decapolis (see the boxed text 'The Decapolis' in the Amman chapter). Over the next two centuries, trade with the Nabataeans flourished and the city grew extremely wealthy. Local agriculture and iron-ore mining in the Ajlun area contributed to the city's wellbeing. A completely new plan was drawn up in the 1st century AD, centred on the typical features of a colonnaded main north–south street intersected by two side streets running east–west.

Highlights

- **Jerash** – a wonderfully preserved Roman provincial city with its superb Oval Plaza, theatres and temples

- **Jerash Festival** – this annual festival showcases cultural performances from around the region against the backdrop of the ancient Roman city

- **Ajlun** – this cool, shady region is great for hiking, and boasts the wonderful Qala'at ar-Rabad

- **Museum of Jordanian Heritage** – arguably Jordan's best museum is in the vibrant Yarmouk University in Irbid

- **Umm Qais** – these remote and interesting ruins offer awesome views over the Jordan Valley, Syria and Israel and the Palestinian Territories

- **Pella** – this ancient site contains traces of all eras of Jordanian history, as well as being a tranquil place to linger

JERASH & THE NORTH

When the emperor, Trajan, annexed the Nabataean kingdom (around AD 106) more wealth found its way to Gerasa. Many of the old buildings were torn down to be replaced by more imposing structures. Construction again flourished when Emperor Hadrian visited in 129. To mark a visit of such importance, the Triumphal Arch (now known

133

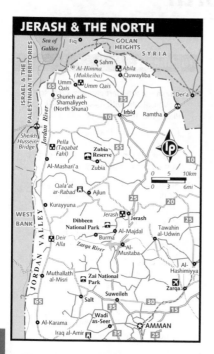

JERASH & THE NORTH

as Hadrian's Arch) at the southern end of the city was constructed.

Gerasa reached its peak at the beginning of the 3rd century, when it was bestowed with the rank of Colony. Its ascendancy was, however, short lived – disturbances such as the destruction of Palmyra (Syria) in 273, the demise of the overland caravans and development of sea trade pushed the city into a slow decline. The only respite came during the reign of Diocletian (around 300), which saw a minor building boom.

By the middle of the 5th century, Christianity was the major religion and the construction of churches proceeded quickly. Under Justinian (527–65) seven churches were built, mostly out of stones from the earlier Roman temples and shrines, but no churches were built after 611.

With the invasion of the Sassanians from Persia (now Iran) in 614, the Muslim conquest in 636 and the devastating earthquake in 747, Gerasa's days of eminence were over and its population shrank to about one-quarter of its former size.

Apart from a brief occupation by a Crusader garrison in the 12th century, the city was completely deserted until the arrival of the Circassians from Russia in 1878, after which the site's archaeological importance was realized and excavations began.

Information

Entrance The entrance to the site is south of the ancient city, close to Hadrian's Arch. The **ticket office** (admission JD2.500; open 7am-5.30pm daily Oct-Apr, 7am-7.30pm May-Sept) is in the complex of souvenir shops and is well signposted from the car park. Although you must enter the site from near Hadrian's Arch, you can leave from near the South Gate, which is more convenient for the bus station. Tickets are also checked at the South Gate.

Next to the South Gate is the **visitor centre** (☎ 6351272), which has informative descriptions of each building in Jerash as well as a good relief map of the ancient city. Allow at least three hours to see everything in Jerash and make sure you take plenty of water, especially in summer.

It's a good idea to visit Jerash before 10am or after 4pm because it's cooler, there will be less glare in your photos and fewer people in the site. Most of the buildings are at their best close to sunset. On the right day you could enjoy dinner before returning for the sound-and-light show. Remember, however, that public transport to Amman is limited after 5pm.

The only toilets at the site are in the Jerash Rest House.

Guides Anyone with a special interest in the history of Jerash may wish to hire a guide (JD5). Guides are available at the ticket checkpoint in front of the South Gate. On most days, guides speaking English, German, Spanish, French, Italian or Greek are available.

Dangers & Annoyances After reports a few years back of foreign women suffering harassment in some of the more remote corners of Jerash, there are now tourist police posted throughout the site.

Books & Maps The free *Jerash* brochure published by the Jordan Tourism Board includes a map, some photos and a recommended walking route. The brochure is available in English, French and German

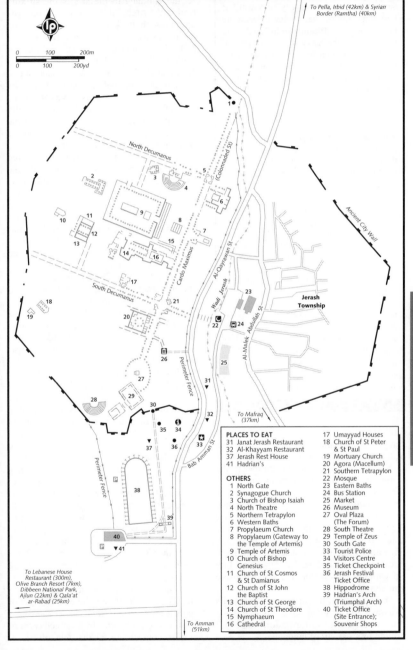

JERASH

To Pella, Irbid (42km) & Syrian Border (Ramtha) (40km)

North Decumanus

Colonnaded St)

Ancient City Wall

Cardo Maximus

South Decumanus

Al-Qayrawan St

Wadi Jerash

Jerash Township

Al-Malek Abdullah St

To Mafraq (37km)

Bab Amman St

To Amman (51km)

To Lebanese House Restaurant (300m), Olive Branch Resort (7km), Dibbeen National Park, Ajlun (22km) & Qala'at ar-Rabad (25km)

PLACES TO EAT
31 Janat Jerash Restaurant
32 Al-Khayyam Restaurant
37 Jerash Rest House
41 Hadrian's

OTHERS
1 North Gate
2 Synagogue Church
3 Church of Bishop Isaiah
4 North Theatre
5 Northern Tetrapylon
6 Western Baths
7 Propylaeum Church
8 Propylaeum (Gateway to the Temple of Artemis)
9 Temple of Artemis
10 Church of Bishop Genesius
11 Church of St Cosmos & St Damianus
12 Church of St John the Baptist
13 Church of St George
14 Church of St Theodore
15 Nymphaeum
16 Cathedral

17 Umayyad Houses
18 Church of St Peter & St Paul
19 Mortuary Church
20 Agora (Macellum)
21 Southern Tetrapylon
22 Mosque
23 Eastern Baths
24 Bus Station
25 Market
26 Museum
27 Oval Plaza (The Forum)
28 South Theatre
29 Temple of Zeus
30 South Gate
33 Tourist Police
34 Visitors Centre
35 Ticket Checkpoint
36 Jerash Festival Ticket Office
38 Hippodrome
39 Hadrian's Arch (Triumphal Arch)
40 Ticket Office (Site Entrance); Souvenir Shops

JERASH & THE NORTH

Jerash Festival

Since 1981, the ancient city of Jerash has hosted the annual Jerash Festival. Events are held in the South Theatre, North Theatre and Oval Plaza in Jerash, as well as the Royal Cultural Centre in Amman, and other places like Umm Qais and Mt Nebo. Special programmes for children are also held at the Haya Cultural Centre in Amman.

The festival is held over 17 days from mid-July to mid-August. It features an eclectic array of performances including plays, poetry readings, opera and musical concerts from around the world. More information is available from the organisers in Amman (☎ 06-5675199, fax 5686198; e jerashfs@go.com.jo). Events are listed in English in the official souvenir newssheet, the *Jerash Daily*, printed in English every day of the festival, and the English-language newspapers published in Amman.

Tickets cost at least JD5 for events in Jerash, and about JD20 for more formal events in Amman and elsewhere. They are available from the Royal and Haya Cultural Centres, and (sometimes) the domestic JETT bus office in Abdali in Amman. JETT also offers one-way and return transport to Jerash during the festival (especially useful when public transport finishes at night). There is also a **Jerash Festival office** for information and buying tickets next to the visitor centre near the South Gate, but it's not open at other times of the year and you'd be well advised to buy your tickets well in advance of arriving in Jerash.

ᘓᘔ ᘓᘔ ᘓᘔ ᘓᘔ ᘓᘔ ᘓᘔ

(and sometimes Italian and Spanish) and can be found at the visitor centre in Jerash or the Jordan Tourism Board in Amman.

Anyone with a particular interest in the history of Jerash should pick up one of the three decent pocket-sized guides: *Jerash: The Roman City*, published by Arabesque; *Jerash: A Unique Example of a Roman City*; or the most comprehensive and readable *Jerash* published by Al-Kutba. All three are available at bookshops in Amman (around JD3 to JD5 each). *Jerash* by Iain Browning is a more detailed and expensive guidebook.

The books on offer at the souvenir stalls in Jerash and Amman have lots of photos (but little useful information) and are printed in a variety of languages.

The Ruins

At the entrance to the site is the striking **Hadrian's Arch**, also known as the **Triumphal Arch**. It's still an imposing structure, but it was twice as high when first built in AD 129 to honour the visiting Emperor Hadrian. The central arch is the highest at 13m and all three once had wooden doors. An unusual feature of the construction is the wreath of carved acanthus leaves above the base of each pillar. The arch was originally erected as a new southern entrance to the city, but the area between the arch and the South Gate was never completed.

Behind the arch is the partially restored **hippodrome**, built sometime between the 1st and 3rd centuries AD. This old sports field (244m by 50m) was once surrounded by seating for up to 15,000 spectators and hosted mainly athletics competitions and chariot races. Recent excavations have unearthed remains of stables, pottery workshops and indications that it was also used for polo by invading Sassanians from Persia during the early 7th century. In summer, **chariot races** (w www.jerashchariots.com) are re-enacted for the benefit of visitors.

About 250m beyond Hadrian's Arch is the **South Gate**, originally one of four along the city wall. It also bears acanthus leaf decoration atop the pillar bases. The gate was built in AD 130.

The **Oval Plaza** or **Forum** is one of the most distinctive images of Jerash. It's unusual because of its oval shape and huge size (90m long and 80m at its widest point). Some historians attribute this to the desire to gracefully link the main north–south axis (*cardo maximus*) with the Temple of Zeus or its predecessor. The Forum was typically a market and a meeting place. The site may also have been a place of sacrifice linked to the temple because of the two altars in the middle; the fountain was added in the 7th century. The 56 reconstructed Ionic columns surrounding the plaza are very impressive, and the centre is paved with limestone.

On the south side of the Forum is the **Temple of Zeus**. It was built in about AD 162 over the remains of an earlier Roman temple. A Byzantine church was later built on the site. The Temple of Zeus once had a flight of stairs leading up to it from a lower sacred enclosure, itself supported by a vaulted corridor built to compensate for the unhelpful local topography. The lower level *temenos* (sacred courtyard) had an altar and served as a holy place of sacrifice. Little remains of the main temple except the perimeter walls.

The **south theatre**, behind the Temple of Zeus, was built between AD 81 and 96 but wasn't opened until the second century AD. It could seat 5000 spectators and can still hold 3000 along 32 rows. The back of the stage was originally two storeys high, and has now been rebuilt to the first level. From the top of the theatre there are superb views of ancient and modern Jerash, particularly the Oval Plaza; just prior to sunset is the best time. The theatre is a testament to the wisdom of the ancients, boasting excellent acoustics as is evident to those attending performances during the Jerash Festival (see the boxed text earlier in this chapter).

Heading northeast from the Forum, the **cardo maximus** (the city's main thoroughfare, also known as the **colonnaded street**) is another highlight. Stretching for 800m from the Forum to the North Gate, it was originally built in the 1st century AD, and rebuilt and redesigned several times since. It is still paved with the original stones, and the ruts worn by thousands of chariots can be clearly seen. Some of the 500 columns that once lined the street were deliberately built at an uneven height to complement the facades of the buildings that once stood behind them.

Just prior to the intersection with the **south decumanus**, and where the columns are taller, is the entrance to the **agora** (which is sometimes referred to as the **macellum**) where the main market was held and people gathered for meetings.

Where the *cardo maximus* joins the south *decumanus* and north *decumanus*, ornamental *tetrapylons* were built. The **southern tetrapylon** consisted of four bases, each supporting four pillars topped by a statue. They are in varying stages of reconstruction; the southeastern one is the most complete. This intersection was made into a circular plaza in the 3rd century.

To the east of the intersection of the *cardo maximus* and south *decumanus* lay the former residential areas now buried beneath the mosque, bus station and modern town. To the west of the intersection are the ruins of some **Umayyad houses**.

About 100m north of the intersection are steps belonging to the 4th-century **cathedral** (probably little more than a modest Byzantine church despite the name). The gate and steps actually cover the remains of an earlier temple to the Nabataean god Dushara.

Next along the main street is the elegant **nymphaeum**, the main ornamental fountain of the city and a temple dedicated to the nymphs. Built in about AD 191, the two-storey construction was elaborately decorated, faced with marble slabs on the lower level and plastered on the upper level. Water used to cascade over the facade into a large pool at the front and the overflow went out through seven carved lions' heads to drains in the street below.

Further along to the west (left) is the **propylaeum**, the gateway to the Temple of Artemis. A stairway, flanked by shops, originally started in the eastern city (now under modern Jerash) and crossed over the *cardo maximus* before finishing here.

Behind the *propylaeum*, and on top of a small hill, is the well-preserved **Temple of Artemis**, dedicated to the goddess of hunting and fertility. The temple was built between AD 150 and 170, and had 12 columns (11 are still standing), but the marble floors and statues have disappeared. Large vaults had to be built to the north and south of the temple to make the courtyard level; the vaults were used to store the temple treasure. After the edict of Theodorius in AD 386 permitting the dismantling of pagan temples, many of the materials were taken away for construction elsewhere. The temple was fortified by the Arabs in the 12th century, but was later substantially destroyed by the Crusaders.

South and west of the temple of Artemis lie the ruins of several **churches**. In all, 15 churches have been uncovered and more are likely to be found. Behind (west of) the cathedral, the **Church of St Theodore**, built in AD 496, has limited remains of mosaics. The **Church of St Cosmos and St Damianus** was dedicated to twin brothers, both doctors. It once had marvellous mosaic tiles, but most are now in the Museum of Popular Tradition in Amman. The **Church of St John the Baptist** was built in about AD 531, but is badly damaged. The **Church of St George**, built in about AD 530, is also destroyed.

At the intersection of the *cardo maximus* and the north *decumanus* is the more intact **northern tetrapylon**, dedicated to the Syrian wife of the emperor Septimus Severus. It was probably built as a gateway to the north theatre; this *tetrapylon* differs from the southern one because it consisted of four arches surmounted by a dome.

Just downhill (to the southeast) is the rubble of the huge **western baths**, measuring about 70m by 50m. Dating from the 2nd century AD, they represent one of the earliest examples of a dome atop a square room. Once an impressive complex of hot- and cold-water baths, they were badly destroyed by various earthquakes.

The **north theatre** is smaller than the south theatre and differs considerably in shape and design. It was built in about AD 165 for government meetings rather than artistic performances, and in 235 it was doubled in size. It has been magnificently restored and still holds about 2000 people. Again, there are good views from the upper tiers.

The *cardo maximus* ends at the comparatively unimpressive **North Gate**. Built in about AD 115, it has not yet been restored as well as its southern counterpart and is probably not worth the detour. It linked the *cardo maximus* with the ancient road to Pella.

Surrounding the ancient city for about 4.5km are remnants of the **city walls**, which were between 2.5m and 3.5m thick when built in the 4th century AD, although most of what remains dates from the Byzantine era. There were also originally 24 towers along the walls.

Museum

Before you finish exploring the ancient city, make sure you visit the small museum (☎ 631 2267; *admission free; open 8.30am-6pm daily Oct-Apr, 8.30am-5pm May-Sept)* just to the east of (and up from) the Oval Plaza. It houses a selection of artefacts from the site, such as pottery, mosaics, jewellery, glass and gold jewellery, as well as coins found in a tomb near Hadrian's Arch. Everything is well labelled in English.

Sound-and-Light Show Between 1 May and 30 September a sound-and-light show (☎ 6351053; *admission free)* is held in the ruins every night except Friday, from 8pm to 9pm, with commentary and historical re-enactments in English (Saturday and Sunday), Arabic (Monday and Tuesday), German (Wednesday) and French (Thursday). Check the schedule with the visitor centre.

There is very little reliable public transport between Jerash and Amman in the evening. Getting there from the capital should be no problem, but you'll probably have to rely on chartered taxis or hitching a ride back to Amman.

Places to Stay & Eat

Surprisingly, there's still no hotel in Jerash, although there are a couple of decent places to stay in Ajlun (see the following). With an early start, you can cover Jerash and Ajlun in a day trip from Amman.

Olive Branch Resort (☎ 6340555, fax 634 0557; [e] olivekh@go.com.jo, [w] www.olive branch.com.jo; singles/doubles JD25/35), around 7km from Jerash off the road to Ajlun, has modern and very comfortable rooms with satellite TV and good bathrooms. You can also camp in your/their tent for JD4/5. The resort has great views, swimming pool (open to nonguests for JD5), a games room with a billiard table and a good **restaurant**. Take the Jerash to Ajlun minibus and get out at the sign; you may be able to hitch the 2km up from the road. Alternatively, charter a taxi from Jerash (JD2).

Jerash Rest House (☎ 6351437; [e] khader@ jerashrest.com; starters JD0.500-1.500, mains JD2.500-3.500; open 9am-6pm) has expensive à la carte meals but if you make the expansive daily buffet (JD5) your main meal for the day, it can be good value.

You'll find cheaper meals outside the site, including at **Al-Khayyam Restaurant** or the **Janat Jerash Restaurant** on Al-Qayrawan St, opposite the visitor centre.

Lebanese House Restaurant (☎ 6351301; meals around JD2.500; open noon-11pm daily), around 500m south of the turn-off to Ajlun, also isn't bad.

For cold drinks, try **Hadrian's** in the car park south of the ticket office; it's open the same hours as the old city and sometimes does snacks. For cheap shwarma and felafel, try around the perimeter of the bus station.

Getting There & Away

Jerash is 51km north of Amman, and the roads are well signed from the capital, especially from the 8th Circle. The entrance to the ancient city is reached via a turn-off about 100m north of the intersection from where the road leads to Ajlun.

From Abdali bus station in Amman, public buses and minibuses (350 fils, 1¼ hours) leave regularly for Jerash.

The minibuses and service taxi station in Jerash is behind the mosque, not far northeast of the visitor centre. Plenty of minibuses travel regularly to Irbid (350 fils, 45 minutes) and Ajlun (300 fils, 30 minutes). If you're still in Jerash after 5pm, be prepared to hitch back to the capital, as most of the buses and minibuses stop running soon after that. Service taxis sometimes leave as late as 8pm (usually later during Jerash Festival and sometimes after the sound-and-light show) but expect a wait. The tourist police are usually happy to cajole a passing motorist into offering a free ride back to Amman. A private taxi one way may cost as much as JD10; you may be able to bargain down to JD7.

AJLUN
عجلون

☎ 02

Ajlun is another popular and easy day trip from Amman, and can be combined with a trip to Jerash. In Ajlun town the **mosque**, just southwest of the main roundabout, has a minaret dating back some 600 years. There are also the remains of **St George's Byzantine Church**, which is signposted north of the roundabout.

The highlight of the trip, however, is unquestionably the towering Qala'at ar-Rabad, just out of town. The area is also popular with locals and the surrounding hills are a few degrees cooler than the rest of Jordan. If possible, visit on a clear day – the views are superb.

Orientation & Information

The castle is about 3km west of the town centre. In the Bonita Ajloun Restaurant, the **tourist office** (☎/fax 6420115) is open from 7am to 1pm Sunday to Thursday. The Housing Bank, just south of the main roundabout, changes money and has an ATM.

Qala'at ar-Rabad

Ar-Rabad Castle (admission in low/high season JD0.500/1; open 8am-5pm daily Oct-Apr, 8am-7pm May-Sept), built atop Mt 'Auf (about 1250m), is a fine example of Islamic military architecture. The castle was built by one of Saladin's generals and nephews, 'Izz ad-Din Usama bin Munqidh, in 1184–8, and was enlarged in 1214 with the addition

of a new gate in the southeastern corner. It once boasted seven towers, and was surrounded by a dry moat over 15m deep.

The castle commands views of the Jordan Valley and three wadis leading into it – the Kufranjah, Rajeb and Al-Yabes – making it an important strategic link in the defensive chain against the Crusaders, and a counterpoint to the Crusader Belvoir Fort in the Sea of Galilee (Lake Tiberias) in Israel. With its hilltop position, Ar-Rabad Castle was one in a chain of beacons and pigeon posts that allowed messages to be transmitted from Damascus to Cairo in one day.

After the Crusader threat subsided, the castle was largely destroyed by Mongol invaders in 1260, only to be almost immediately rebuilt by the Mamluks. In the 17th century an Ottoman garrison was stationed here, after which it was used only by local villagers. The castle was 'rediscovered' by the well-travelled JL Burckhardt, who also stumbled across Petra (see the boxed text 'Ibrahim' Burckhardt' in the Petra chapter). Earthquakes in 1837 and 1927 damaged the castle badly, but its restoration is continuing.

There is a useful explanation in English just inside the main gate, although nothing else is signposted.

The castle is a tough uphill walk (3km) from the town centre, but minibuses very occasionally go to the top for about 100 fils. Alternatively, take a taxi from Ajlun (JD1 one way) or hitch a ride. A return trip by taxi from Ajlun, with about 30 minutes to look around, will cost around JD3.

Places to Stay & Eat

There are two hotels on the road up to the castle; good options if you want to enjoy the sunset. Prices are negotiable at both.

Al-Rabad Castle Hotel (☎ 6420202, fax 4630414; singles/doubles JD24/32 plus 10% tax), about 500m before the castle, is probably the pick of the two. The comfortable rooms come with a balcony and there's an outdoor terrace with great views where meals can be served.

Ajlun Hotel (☎ 6420524, fax 6421580; singles/doubles JD24/32 plus 10% tax) is 400m down the road from the castle and isn't bad. Hot water can be unpredictable.

Bonita Ajloun Restaurant (☎ 6420981; starters JD0.500-1.500, mains JD2.250-3.500 plus 20% tax; open 9.30am-5pm Oct-Apr,

9.30am-11pm May-Sept), 100m down the hill from the castle, has an elegant setting with wonderful views down the valley and towards the castle. Service is also good.

Green Mountain Restaurant, by the main roundabout in Ajlun town, does the usual chicken, hummus, salad and bread for around JD1.500. There are also **shwarma stalls** around the town centre. An alternative is to come prepared to join the locals for a picnic in the surrounding hills. There are **drink stands** next to the castle ticket office.

Getting There & Away

Ajlun is 73km northwest of Amman, and 22km northwest of Jerash. While the castle can be clearly seen from most places in the area, there are few signs from the town centre. If you're driving or walking, take the road (Al-Qala'a St) heading west at the main roundabout in the centre of Ajlun.

From the centre of Ajlun, minibuses travel regularly to Jerash (300 fils, 30 minutes along a scenic road) and Irbid (320 fils, 45 minutes). From Amman (500 fils, two hours), minibuses leave a few times a day from the Abdali bus station; an early start will let you see Ajlun and Jerash in one day, returning to the capital late in the afternoon.

ZUBIA RESERVE

حديقة زوبيا الوطنية

Lost among the forests surrounding Ajlun is the fairly unimpressive Zubia Reserve (13 sq km), also known as Ajlun Nature Reserve and established by the Royal Society for the Conservation of Nature (RSCN) in 1988 to protect native fauna, including the roe deer (of which there are at least 13 in a captive breeding programme).

This reserve is not nearly as well set up for tourists, nor as accessible, as the other RSCN reserves. There is little to do, although some **hiking trails** of 3km to 5km are being developed. Visitors can pitch their own **tents** near the ranger station, and have free access to the basic toilets and showers.

Getting there is an adventure in itself; no public transport goes anywhere close. Minibuses from Irbid (South bus station) and Jerash go to Zubia village, but this is still 5km from the ranger station. It's best to charter a taxi from Jerash or Ajlun. If you're driving, ask lots of directions because the roads are winding, confusing and unsigned.

DIBBEEN NATIONAL PARK

حديقة دبين الوطنية

☎ 02

This large, semiprotected area of forest is good for **hiking** and, especially with locals on weekends, **picnics**. It's also a pleasant drive from Amman. While not spectacular, Dibbeen does have great **views** of the valleys, and is about the coolest place in Jordan during summer.

Hiking

There are some short, marked (but unmapped) trails through the park; hiking them can be an invigorating way to pass a few hours. In the spring, carpets of red crown anemones fill the meadows beneath the pine-forested and sometimes snow-capped hills. Many trails lead through quiet woods and valleys where you may come across farmers tending crops. Most trails are either small vehicle tracks or stony paths, some of which continue beyond the park's boundaries.

Places to Stay & Eat

In the middle of the park is a tourist complex, with a children's playground, places to eat and the **Dibbeen Rest House** (☎ 633 9710, fax 6351146; e khader@dibbinrest .com; doubles/triples JD25/32). The comfortable 'chalets' (which sleep three) have a basic kitchen, large bathroom with hot water, TV and fan; it's worth negotiating. Visitors can pitch their own **tent** in the grounds for JD3 per person, and have access to toilets and hot showers.

The whole complex is quite good and you may have the place to yourself, except on Thursday and Friday when picnicking locals abound. Entrance to the park and complex is free and both are permanently open.

Getting There & Away

Public transport is very limited. From Jerash, the minibus to the villages of Burma or Al-Majdal goes through the park and can drop you off within 1km of the tourist complex entrance – a detour to the complex can be arranged with the driver for an inducement of about JD1. Chartering a taxi from Jerash is the best idea, and will cost about JD4 one way. If you're driving from Jerash, Ajlun or Amman, follow the initial signs close to Jerash and then ask directions to the Rest House – there are few signs.

IRBID

إربد

☎ 02 • pop 500,000

Irbid is a university town and, perhaps as a consequence, is one of the more lively and progressive of Jordan's large towns. In the area around Yarmouk University, south of the city centre, the streets are lined with outdoor restaurants, Internet cafés and pedestrians out strolling, particularly in the late afternoon. The university also hosts arguably Jordan's finest museum, the Museum of Jordanian Heritage.

The area around Irbid has yielded artefacts and graves suggesting that the area has been inhabited since the Bronze Age, although there is little evidence in the town of such antiquity. Jordan's second-largest city is nonetheless a good base from which to explore Umm Qais, Al-Himma and even Jerash, Ajlun and Pella.

Information

Irbid has plenty of **banks** for changing money and many have ATMs from which you can extract dinars from your MasterCard or Visa account. The **police station** is above the market area, and offers great views of the city. The **Royal Jordanian** office (☎ 7242333) is on the corner of King Hussein and Al-Jaish streets.

The **post office,** on King Hussein St (also known locally as Baghdad St), is open from 7am to 5pm Saturday to Thursday and 7am to 1.30pm on Friday. There are literally dozens of **Internet cafés** along the southern end of University St (Shafeeq Rshaidat St) near Yarmouk University; most are open to 3am (some 24 hours) and charge between 750 fils and JD1 per hour. **Malkawi Express** (☎ 7277876) on King Hussein St is a professional photo lab where you can buy Kodak film and develop slide (JD6 for a roll of 36 including mounting) and print (750 fils plus 100 fils for each print) film.

Things to See

There are two museums in the grounds of the vast **Yarmouk University,** which opened in 1977 and now boasts over 22,000 students from across the region. Foreigners are welcome to wander around the university and it's a good place to meet young Jordanians. The university also runs Arabic language courses (see Courses in the Facts for the Visitor chapter).

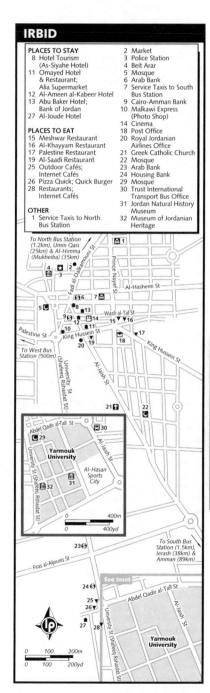

IRBID

PLACES TO STAY
8 Hotel Tourism (As-Siyahe Hotel)
11 Omayed Hotel & Restaurant; Alia Supermarket
12 Al-Ameen al-Kabeer Hotel
13 Abu Baker Hotel; Bank of Jordan
27 Al-Joude Hotel

PLACES TO EAT
15 Meshwar Restaurant
16 Al-Khayyam Restaurant
17 Palestine Restaurant
19 Al-Saadi Restaurant
25 Outdoor Cafés; Internet Cafés
26 Pizza Quick; Quick Burger
28 Restaurants; Internet Cafés

OTHER
1 Service Taxis to North Bus Station
2 Market
3 Police Station
4 Beit Arar
5 Mosque
6 Arab Bank
7 Service Taxis to South Bus Station
9 Cairo-Amman Bank
10 Malkawi Express (Photo Shop)
14 Cinema
18 Post Office
20 Royal Jordanian Airlines Office
21 Greek Catholic Church
22 Mosque
23 Arab Bank
24 Housing Bank
29 Mosque
30 Trust International Transport Bus Office
31 Jordan Natural History Museum
32 Museum of Jordanian Heritage

JERASH & THE NORTH

The **Museum of Jordanian Heritage** (☎ 727 1100, ext 4260; admission free; open 9am-5pm Sun-Thur) is highly recommended and features exhibits of ancient stone implements, coins, pottery and other handicrafts, as well as a reconstructed courtyard typical of northern Jordan. The labels are in English.

Jordan Natural History Museum (☎ 727 1100; admission free; open 8am-5pm Sun-Thur) contains a range of mildly interesting stuffed animals, birds and insects, as well as rocks from the region, but very little is explained in English. The museum is in the huge green hangar.

Beit Arar (off Al-Hashemi St; admission free; open 9am-5pm Sun-Thur) was set up to host cultural events and is located in a superb old house built in the Damascene style. The rooms are set around a courtyard paved with volcanic black stones and there are manuscripts and photo displays of Arar, one of Jordan's finest poets.

Places to Stay

The cheapest hotels are in the city centre in the blocks immediately north of King Hussein (Baghdad) St, all of which have shared bathrooms.

Hotel Tourism (As-Siyahe Hotel; ☎ 724 2633; singles/doubles JD5/7) is fairly basic with simple rooms. There's no hot water.

Al-Ameen al-Kabeer Hotel (☎ 7242384; e al_ameen_hotel@hotmail.com; Al-Jaish St; singles/doubles JD5/8) is probably the best of the cheapies with friendly management and simple but tidy rooms and good bathrooms. Ask for a room with a window.

Abu Baker Hotel (☎ 7242695; Wasfi al-Tal St; dorm beds JD2) is on the second floor of the Bank of Jordan building and has a mostly local (male) clientele. Views over Irbid from some dormitories are superb. There's no lift.

Omayed Hotel (☎/fax 7245955; King Hussein St; singles/doubles with bath & satellite TV JD15.400/19.800) is a cut above the rest in this area in both price and quality, and represents excellent value. The rooms are sunny, clean and most have nice views. The staff are super friendly and it's a good place for women travellers.

Al-Joude Hotel (☎ 7275515, fax 7275517; off University St; singles/doubles/triples with bath, satellite TV & buffet breakfast JD31/37/42, suites JD65) is Irbid's finest with friendly staff, a classy ambience and attractive rooms. There is a **restaurant** (meals from JD2.500), billiard table and the cool downstairs **News Café** where pizza and other snacks are served.

Places to Eat

There are ample choices in the centre of town if your budget extends only to felafel and shwarma. Self-caterers are also looked after with a number of supermarkets, including the excellent **Alia Supermarket** (☎ 724 5987) at street level in the Omayed Hotel.

There are a number of cheap eateries near the post office, including **Meshwar Restaurant**, **Palestine Restaurant** (which doubles as a tea room serving alcohol) and **Al-Khayyam Restaurant**. Most meals in these places start at JD1.500 and they stay open as late as they have customers.

Al-Saadi Restaurant (☎ 7242354; King Hussein St; starters JD0.500-1.500, mains from JD2.500; open 7.30am-9.30pm daily) is one of the better places in the centre with a pleasant dining area and decent service; they also do breakfast (750 fils to JD1.500).

Omayed Restaurant (☎ 7240106; King Hussein St; starters from JD0.500, mains from JD3; open 8am-10.30pm daily) is another good choice with reasonable food and superb views over the city.

There are dozens of **restaurants** to suit most budgets along the southern end of University St. It's a great place in the evening when the street is crowded with young students. Some places serve shwarma on the street as well as sit-down meals inside. When we asked local university students which was their favourite place, most said 'it will change tomorrow' so, rather than recommend particular places, we suggest that you do what the locals do and stroll along the street until you find one that appeals; most have menus with prices posted outside. There are also some fast-food options such as **Pizza Quick** and **Quick Burger**. There are great **cafés** on the main roundabout northwest of the university that stay open late.

Getting There & Away

See the Getting There & Away chapter for details of bus services from Irbid to Syria and Israel and the Palestinian Territories. For the latter, the office of **Trust International Transport** (☎ 7251878) is near Al-Hasan Sports City.

Irbid is 85km north of Amman and easy to reach from just about anywhere in Jordan. There are three main minibus/taxi stations in town.

From the North bus station, there are minibuses to Umm Qais (250 fils, 45 minutes), Mukheiba (for Al-Himma; 350 fils, one hour) and Quwayliba (for the ruins of Abila; 170 fils, 25 minutes).

From the large South bus station (New Amman bus station), air-conditioned Hijazi buses (870 fils, 90 minutes) leave regularly for Amman's Abdali bus station until about 6.30pm. To Amman (Abdali) there are less comfortable buses and minibuses (600 fils, about two hours) and plenty of service taxis (900 fils). Minibuses also leave the South station for Ajlun (320 fils, 45 minutes) and Jerash (350 fils, 45 mins). Buses leave from here for Ramtha (for the Syrian border).

From the West bus station, just off Palestine St, minibuses go to Al-Mashari'a (350 fils, 45 mins) for the ruins at Pella; Sheikh Hussein Bridge (for Israel and the Palestinian Territories; 750 fils, 45 minutes) and other places in the Jordan Valley, such as Shuneh ash-Shamaliyyeh (North Shuna).

Getting Around

Getting between Irbid's various bus stations is easy, with service taxis shuttling between them for around 250 fils. Service taxis and minibuses to the South bus station can be picked up anywhere along Al-Jaish St, or from the service taxi stand on Al-Hashemi St, while for the North station head to Prince Nayef St. A minibus from King Hussein St to the university should cost around 100 fils.

Few of the private yellow taxis use meters. The standard fare for anyone, including locals, for most trips around town is 500 fils and rarely more than JD1.

ABILA (QUWAYLIBA) أبيلا (قويلبا)

Possibly one of the Decapolis cities (see the boxed text 'The Decapolis' in the Amman chapter), the ancient city of Abila (admission free; open daily during daylight hours) was built some time in the Early Bronze Age (about 3000 BC) between two small hills, Tell Abila and Tell Umm-al-Amad.

There is, however, little to see because what was left after the earthquake in AD 747 remains largely unexcavated. Nothing is labelled or set up for visitors, but there

are enough **tombs** and eerie **caves** dotted around the fields to interest archaeology buffs. The **theatre** is fairly obviously carved out of the hill, and there are also some **columns** from the markets, temples and baths lying around the site.

The Abila site is close to the village of Quwayliba, about 15km north of Irbid. Buses leave from the North bus station in Irbid (170 fils, 25 minutes) for Quwayliba; ask the driver to drop you off at the ruins.

RAMTHA الرمثا

One of the main businesses in this dreary town is smuggling items such as cigarettes and alcohol across the nearby border with Syria. There is no need to linger except to catch onward transport, and there's nowhere to stay so it's best to keep going.

You can get direct transport between Damascus and Irbid or Amman, without stopping in Ramtha. Minibuses and service taxis (both 500 fils, two hours) leave Abdali bus station in Amman for Ramtha, and often go as far as the border, but start early from Amman because most transport has left by 10am. Plenty of minibuses and service taxis shuttle between the border and Ramtha.

See Syria under Land in the Getting There & Away chapter for more information regarding crossing the border to or from Syria.

UMM QAIS (GADARA) أم قيس
☎ 02

In the northwest corner of Jordan are the ruins of another ancient town, Gadara (now called Umm Qais). The ruins are interesting because of the juxtaposition of the ruined Roman city and a relatively intact Ottoman-era village. The site also offers awesome views over the Golan Heights in Syria and the Sea of Galilee (Lake Tiberias) in Israel to the north, and the Jordan Valley to the south.

According to the Bible, it was here that Jesus cast demons out of two men into a herd of pigs (Matthew 8: 28–34), although an alternative site on the eastern shore of Lake Galilee (in Israel) also claims this miracle.

History

The ancient town of Gadara was captured from the Ptolemies by the Seleucids in 198 BC, and then the Jews under Hyrcanus captured it from them in 100 BC. When the Romans (led by Pompey) conquered the east

JERASH & THE NORTH

and the Decapolis was formed, the fortunes of Gadara, taken from the Jews in 63 BC, increased rapidly and building was undertaken on a typically grand scale.

The Nabataeans controlled the trade routes as far north as Damascus. This interference with Rome's interests led Mark Antony to send Herod the Great to conquer them. He failed to do this completely, but did wrest a sizable chunk of territory from them in 31 BC. Herod was given Gadara following a naval victory and he ruled over it until his death in 4 BC – much to the disgruntlement of locals who had tried everything to put him out of favour with Rome. On his death, the city reverted to semi-autonomy as part of the Roman province of Syria.

With the downfall of the Nabataean kingdom in AD 106, Gadara continued to flourish, and was the seat of a bishopric until the 7th century. By the time of the Muslim conquest, however, it was little more than a small village. Throughout the Ottoman period the village was substantially rebuilt.

In 1806, Gadara was 'discovered' by Western explorers and the local inhabitants claim to have formed the first government in Jordan, as well as signing the first agreement with the British in 1920. Excavations did not commence until 1982 when locals were finally repatriated to modern Umm Qais village.

Information

If you enter ancient Gadara (admission JD0.500; open 8am-10pm daily) from the eastern end of the car park, you will get to view the ruins in a roughly chronological order (ie, from the more recent ruins of the Ottoman-era village going back in time as you head west). Apart from anything else, it also ensures a downhill walk.

There are a few signs in English. The brochure about Umm Qais published by the Jordan Tourism Board is useful and printed in German and English; ask at the museum. Umm Qais: Gadara of the Decapolis, published by Al-Kutba (JD3), is ideal for anyone who wants further information. Guides (JD5 per 10 people) are also available at the ticket office in the car park.

There are some toilets in the Government Rest House and the tourist police office is along the laneway from the museum to the Rest House.

The Ruins

Around the eastern entrance from the main road are several tombs, including the **Tomb of Germani** and the **Tomb of Modestus**. About 50m further west, the **Tomb of Chaireas** dates from AD 154.

The first things to see (if you're coming from the east) are the ruins of the **Ottoman-era village** dating from the 18th and 19th

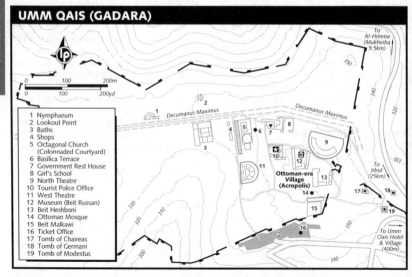

UMM QAIS (GADARA)

0   100   200m
0   100   200yd

To Al-Himma (Mukheiba) 9.5km)

Decumanus Maximus

Decumanus Maximus

To Irbid (25km)

Ottoman-era Village (Acropolis)

To Umm Qais Hotel & Village (400m)

1 Nymphaeum
2 Lookout Point
3 Baths
4 Shops
5 Octagonal Church (Colonnaded Courtyard)
6 Basilica Terrace
7 Government Rest House
8 Girl's School
9 North Theatre
10 Tourist Police Office
11 West Theatre
12 Museum (Beit Russan)
13 Beit Heshboni
14 Ottoman Mosque
15 Beit Malkawi
16 Ticket Office
17 Tomb of Chaireas
18 Tomb of Germani
19 Tomb of Modestus

Columns at the Oval Plaza (Forum), Jerash

South Gate, Jerash

Temple of Artemis, Jerash

Oval Plaza (Forum), Jerash

View of the Jordan Valley and Sea of Galilee (Lake Tiberias), Umm Qais

ANDREW BURKE

MARK DAFFEY

Qala'at ar-Rabad, Ajlun

MARK DAFFEY

Qala'at ar-Rabad, Ajlun

MARK DAFFEY

Octagonal Church ruins, Umm Qais

centuries and also known as the **acropolis**. Inside are two intact houses, **Beit Malkawi** (now used as an office for archaeological groups) and the nearby **Beit Heshboni**. In the southeast corner is the **Ottoman mosque**, and in the far north are the remains of the **girl's school**.

Also in the acropolis, but accessible from the Government Rest House if you follow the signs, is **Beit Russan**, a former residence of an Ottoman governor, and now the **museum** (☎ 7500072, fax 7500071; admission free; open 8am-5pm daily Oct-Apr, 8am-6pm May-Sept). It's set around an elegant and tranquil courtyard. The main mosaic on display (dating from the 4th century and found in one of the tombs) contains the names of early Christian notables and is a highlight, as is the headless, white marble statue of a goddess, which was found sitting in the front row of the west theatre. Exhibits are labelled in English and Arabic throughout.

Northeast of the museum is the **north theatre**, now overgrown and without its original black basalt rocks, which were used by villagers in other constructions. From there, head west along the **decumanus maximus**, the main road that once linked Gadara with other nearby ancient cities such as Abila and Pella, and eventually reached the Mediterranean coast.

West of the Government Rest House (see Places to Stay & Eat later in this chapter) is the **basilica terrace** complex, about 95m by 35m. The western section housed a row of **shops** (the shells of which remain), but the most interesting remains are the 16th-century **octagonal church**, also known as the **colonnaded courtyard**, recognisable by its unusual eight-sided base.

To the south is the well-restored and brooding **west theatre**, which once seated about 3000 people. Like the north theatre, it was also made from black basalt. West along the *decumanus maximus* are the overgrown **baths**. Built in the 4th century, there was an impressive complex of fountains, statues and baths, but little remains after the various earthquakes. Almost opposite is the decrepit **nymphaeum**.

The *decumanus maximus* continues west for another 1km or so, leading to some ruins of limited interest, including **baths**, **mausoleums** and **gates**. Most are beyond repair or unexcavated.

Places to Stay & Eat

Umm Qais Hotel (☎ 7500080, fax 7242313; singles with shared/private bath JD6/8, doubles JD12/16) is a comfortable place on the main street of the modern village, about 400m west of the ruins. The rooms are clean, quiet and sunny and the management is friendly. It also has a small **restaurant**.

A few basic **eateries** are scattered around the village; otherwise come prepared for a **picnic** in the ruins or down the hillside.

The **Government Rest House** (☎ 7500555, fax 7500059; mains from JD2; open 10am-9pm daily), inside the ruins, is a pleasant place to linger with tables commanding spectacular views over the Golan Heights and Lake Tiberias. The menu is generally expensive (a mixed grill costs JD4), but the service is good.

Getting There & Away

Umm Qais village, and the ruins a few hundred metres to the west, are about 25km northwest of Irbid, and about 110km north of Amman. Minibuses leave Irbid's North bus station (250 fils, 45 minutes) on a regular basis. There's no direct transport from Amman.

AL-HIMMA (MUKHEIBA)

Al-Himma hot springs in the village of Mukheiba are literally a stone's throw from the Golan Heights, which is occupied by the Israelis. In contrast to the bare, steeply rising plateau of the Golan to the north, the area is lush, although it can get very hot in summer. The springs, which reach about 33°C, were famous in Roman times for their health-giving properties and are still used today.

Mukheiba is a pleasant village and the springs are worth a day trip from Irbid or you can stay overnight. The place is overrun with local tourists (mostly young men) on Friday, although the hills are more pleasant at this time with hundreds of picnicking families.

Hot Springs

The public baths complex run by the **Jordanian Hot Springs Company** (☎ 7500505) has separate bathing times for men and women; these change regularly. The complex is generally open from 2pm to 8pm daily (earlier on Friday and later if demand is high). Entrance to the village in low/high season costs JD0.500/1 and there's a further

JD0.500/1 charge to use the baths, which are on the right as you enter the village.

Places to Stay & Eat
The **chalets** (☎ 7500505) overlooking the public baths cost JD9 per person and are good value, although a little noisy when the baths are busy. **Apartments** suitable for families cost JD27.

Sah al-Noum Hotel *(singles/doubles with bath, fan & breakfast JD10/12)* has simple and bright rooms, although some are cleaner than others. There's a large, shady restaurant out the back (also open to nonguests), and the manager has access to a lovely private bathing area nearby. The hotel is signposted at the fork in the road near the public baths.

Jordan Hema Restaurant *(☎ 7500512; meals from JD2.500, large beer JD1.750; open 9am-8pm)* overlooks the public baths.

Getting There & Away
Mukheiba is about 10km north of Umm Qais, down the hill towards the Golan via a very scenic road. There are reasonably regular minibuses (100 fils) between Mukheiba and Umm Qais on most days, with plenty on Friday. Direct minibuses from Irbid's North station (350 fils, one hour) also pass along the main street of Umm Qais. If you're there on Friday, hitching is easy, although some families stop en route for a picnic.

The village is well signposted throughout northern Jordan. Make sure you bring your passport as there's a military checkpoint just past the turn-off to the Umm Qais ruins. This is also a good place to hitch a ride.

SHUNEH ASH-SHAMALIYYEH (NORTH SHUNA)   شونه الشمالية
☎ 02
This junction town boasts another **hot springs** complex *(admission JD1; open 8am-9pm daily)*. Irbid locals say the springs are cleaner than those at Al-Himma and they're cheaper, but they're not as well set up.

There are simple **chalets** *(☎ 6587189; chalet JD25 for 4 persons)* in the complex, as well as a shady **restaurant**, although the sulphur smell can be a little overpowering.

Shuneh ash-Shamaliyyeh is accessible by minibus from Irbid (West bus station) and has connections to anywhere along the Jordan Valley road (Highway 65), including Al-Mashari'a (for Pella) and Deir Alla.

PELLA (TAQABAT FAHL)   بيلا
☎ 02
In the midst of the Jordan Valley are the ruins of the ancient city of Pella (known locally as Taqabat Fahl), one of the ten cities of the Decapolis (see the boxed text 'The Decapolis' in the Amman chapter). Although not as spectacular as Jerash, Pella is far more important to archaeologists because it has revealed evidence of life from the Stone Age through to medieval Islamic ruins.

Many of the ruins are spread out and in need of excavation, so some walking and imagination is required to get the most from the site. That said, the setting is superb and there are some fine views over the Jordan Valley.

History
Pella was inhabited as early as 5000 BC, and Egyptian texts make reference to it in the 2nd millennium BC.

Pella really only flourished during the Greek and Roman periods. The Jews largely destroyed Pella in 83 BC because the inhabitants were not inclined to adopt the customs of their conquerors. It was to Pella that Christians fled persecution from the Roman army in Jerusalem in the 2nd century AD.

The city reached its peak during the Byzantine era, and by AD 451 Pella had its own bishop. The population at this time may have been as high as 25,000. The defeat of the Byzantines by the invading Islamic armies near Pella in 635 was quickly followed by the knockout blow at the Battle of Yarmouk (near modern Mukheiba) the next year.

Until the massive earthquake that shook the whole region in 747, Pella continued to prosper under the Umayyads. Archaeological finds show that even after the earthquake the city remained inhabited on a modest scale. The Mamluks occupied it in the 13th and 14th centuries, but afterwards Pella was virtually abandoned.

Information
The site *(admission free)* is officially open 8am to 6pm daily, but if the main gate is closed, you can enter via the Rest House on the hill.

Anyone with a specific interest should buy *Pella*, published by Al-Kutba (JD3) and available in major bookshops around Jordan.

The Ruins

At the base of the main mound (on your right as you enter through the main gate) are the limited remains of a **Roman gate** to the city. Atop the hill are the ruins of an **Umayyad settlement**, which consisted of shops, residences and storehouses. The small, square **Mamluk mosque** to the west dates from 14th century. Carved into the south side of the hill is the recently excavated **Canaanite temple**, which was constructed in around 1270 BC and was dedicated to the Canaanite god Baal.

The main structure, and indeed one of the better preserved of the ruins at Pella, is the Byzantine **civic complex church** (or **middle church**), which was built atop an earlier Roman civic complex in the 5th century AD and modified several times in the subsequent two centuries. Adjacent is the **Odeon** (a small theatre for musical performances). It once held 400 spectators, but you'll need considerable imagination to picture this now. Just east of the civic complex church are the low-lying remains of a Roman **nymphaeum**.

Up the hill to the southeast is the 5th-century **east church**, which is in a lovely setting. From there a trail leads down into Wadi Malawi and then climbs **Tell al-Husn** (note the remains of tombs cut into the hillside), atop which are the stones of a **Byzantine fort** and **Roman temple**. There are good views of the Jordan Valley from here.

Outside the main site, there are the ruins of a small **Abbasid settlement** about 200m north of the main entrance. There are also a few limited **Palaeolithic ruins** (4km) and **Roman baths** and a **rock bridge** (3km) reached via the road past the turn-off to the Rest House. Also, ask at the Rest House how to get to the rubble of a **Hellenistic temple** high on the hill to the southeast; from there, Jerusalem is visible on a clear day.

Places to Stay & Eat

Pella Countryside Hotel (☎ 0795 574145, fax 6560899; singles/doubles JD12/15) has a lovely family feel and a nice outlook towards the ruins. The owner's garden has the national flower of Jordan, the black iris, through late winter and into spring. The three rooms are well kept and it's well signposted on the road to the site. It's a good place to kick back for a few days and the family can arrange picnics in the surrounding hills.

PELLA (TAQABAT FAHL)

1 Pella Park
2 West Church
3 Canaanite Temple
4 Mamluk Mosque
5 Umayyad Settlement
6 Roman Gate
7 Main Entrance
8 Abbasid Settlement
9 Cemetery
10 East Cemetery
11 Pella Rest House
12 East Church
13 Nymphaeum (Baths)
14 Civic Complex Church (Middle Church)
15 Odeon (Theatre)
16 Byzantine Fort; Roman Temple

Pella Rest House (☎ 0795 574145, fax 6560899; meals JD5 plus drinks) commands exceptional views over Pella and the Jordan Valley; Israel is visible to the right of the communications towers, the West Bank to the left. Chicken and fresh fish (from the Jordan River) are the order of the day and the food is good.

Pella Park (☎ 6560856) is a fairly bleak place and you'll pay JD1 per person (plus JD1 per vehicle) to enter – not worth it as the swimming pools are tiny. They do a few simple meals as well.

There is nowhere to stay in Al-Mashari'a, the village on the main road closest to Pella, but there are plenty of shops and cheap **restaurants** if you're waiting for transport. For changing money there's a Housing Bank.

Getting There & Away

From Irbid's West bus station minibuses go to Al-Mashari'a (350 fils, 45 minutes). They also run the length of the Jordan Valley road (Highway 65) between Shuneh ash-Shamaliyyeh (North Shuna) and Shuneh al-Janubiyyeh (South Shuna) and stop at Al-Mashari'a. There is no direct transport from Amman. Pella is a steep 2km walk up from the signposted turn-off, which can be punishing in summer and not particularly scenic. Minibuses (200 fils) run reasonably regularly up to the main entrance of Pella.

JERASH & THE NORTH

The Jordan Valley

Forming a part of the Great Rift Valley of Africa, the fertile valley of the Jordan River was of considerable significance in biblical times and is now the food bowl of Jordan.

The hot dry summers and short mild winters make for ideal growing conditions, and (subject to water restrictions) two or three crops are grown every year. Thousands of tonnes of fruit and vegetables are produced annually, with the main crops being tomatoes, cucumbers, melons and citrus fruits. The introduction of portable plastic greenhouses resulted in a sevenfold increase in productivity and this has meant that Jordan can now afford to export large amounts of its produce to neighbouring countries.

The river rises from several sources, mainly the Anti-Lebanon Range in Syria, and flows down into the Sea of Galilee (Lake Tiberias), 212m below sea level, before draining into the Dead Sea. The actual length of the river is 360km, but as the crow flies the distance between its source and the Dead Sea is only 200km.

In this valley some 10,000 years ago, people first started to plant crops and abandon their nomadic lifestyle for permanent settlements. Villages were built, primitive irrigation schemes were undertaken and by 3000 BC produce from the valley was being exported to neighbouring regions. The river is also highly revered by Christians because Jesus was baptised by John the Baptist in its waters.

Since 1948, the Jordan River has marked the boundary between Jordan Israel and the Palestinian Territories, from the Sea of Galilee to the Yarbis River. From there to the Dead Sea marked the 1967 cease-fire line between the two countries; it now marks the continuation of the official frontier with the Palestinian Territories.

During the 1967 war with Israel, Jordan lost the land it had annexed in 1950, the area known as the West Bank. The population on the east bank of the valley dwindled from 60,000 before the war to 5000 by 1971. During the 1970s, new roads and fully serviced villages were built and the population has now soared to over 100,000.

DEIR ALLA   دير علا

Deir Alla, 35km north of Shuneh al-Janubiyyeh (South Shuna) was first settled in the 3rd century BC but was later abandoned. After the Islamic invasion in the 7th century AD, it served as a cemetery for nearby villages. The site is of some minor historical significance for scholars but, unless you're one of them, there's little reason to visit as there's nothing much to see. The site can be combined with Pella in a day trip from Irbid or Ajlun. A notice board at the base of the ruins has some limited explanations, or you could ask at the Antiquities Office across the road. Minibuses run along the Jordan Valley road and pass right by the ruins.

Eastern Jordan

To the east of Amman, the stony desert rolls on to Iraq and Saudi Arabia. The region is cut by the Trans Arabia Pipeline and the highway to Iraq; if not for these, eastern Jordan would probably be left alone to the Bedouin.

Apart from the transport junction towns of Azraq, Mafraq, Zarqa and Safawi, there are no towns to speak of. The main attractions for visitors are the castles and forts, collectively known as the desert castles, which dot the inhospitable landscape, and the Azraq and Shaumari wildlife reserves. Public transport is limited in eastern Jordan, so travelling around in a chartered taxi, organised tour or rented car is a popular and often necessary alternative.

ZARQA
الزرقاء
pop 700,000
The third largest city in Jordan (after Amman and Irbid) is Zarqa, now virtually part of the urban sprawl of northern Amman. There is nothing to see or do, or anywhere to stay in the city, but anyone travelling around eastern and northern Jordan may end up in Zarqa waiting for onward transport.

There are two terminals for buses, minibuses and service taxis. All forms of transport from Raghadan and Abdali bus stations in Amman (about 200 fils, 30 minutes), and places near Amman such as Salt and Madaba, use the New (Amman) station. From the Old station in Zarqa, there is public transport to smaller villages in the region, such as Hallabat (for Qasr al-Hallabat and Hammam as-Sarah), Mafraq and Azraq. Minibuses travel between the two terminals in Zarqa every few minutes.

MAFRAQ
المفرق
Despite appearances on some maps, Mafraq is much smaller than Zarqa. There is nothing to see and nowhere to stay, but travellers heading to eastern Jordan may need to go there for onward transport.

Like Zarqa, Mafraq has two terminals for buses, minibuses and service taxis. The larger Bedouin station has minibuses and service taxis to most places, including Abdali and Raghadan bus stations in Amman (250 fils, one hour), Salt, Zarqa, Madaba,

Highlights

- **Umm al-Jimal** – these basalt ruins are worth exploring for their remote setting
- **Qasr al-Azraq** – the most accessible, and one of the more interesting, desert castles with a link to the enigmatic TE Lawrence
- **Qusayr Amra** – one of the best-preserved desert castles is plastered with wonderful – and risqué – frescoes and is a Unesco World Heritage site
- **Qasr Kharana** – seemingly lost in the middle of the desert, this mighty two-storey fort has been well restored

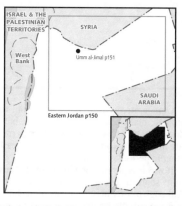

Umm al-Jimal, Deir al-Kahf (for Qasr Deir al-Kahf) and Ar-Ruwayshid (for Qasr Burqu). From the Fellahin station, buses, minibuses and service taxis go to places in northern Jordan, such as Jerash, Irbid, Ramtha and Jabir on the border with Syria.

UMM AL-JIMAL
أم الجمال
Umm al-Jimal (Mother of Camels) has been described as eerie rather than spectacular – there are no grand temples or theatres like those in Jerash. Much of what remains at this large site (800m by 500m) is unpretentious urban architecture; over 150 simple buildings, including 128 houses and 15 churches, have been identified and named.

EASTERN JORDAN

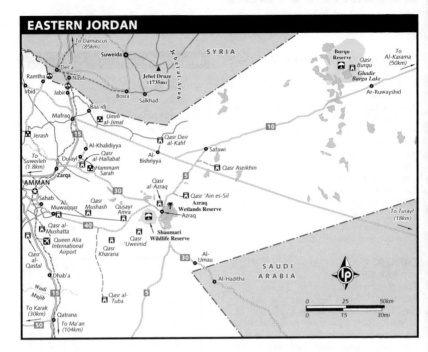

EASTERN JORDAN

Comparatively little is known about the strange, black city of Umm al-Jimal, but it does provide a fascinating insight into rural life during the Roman, Byzantine and early Islamic periods.

It was prosperous for a long time because of its sophisticated method of storing water. Although mostly in ruins, many of the buildings are still discernible because, compared to others, the city was rarely looted and vandalised, and superior materials were used in its construction – Umm al-Jimal is notable for the 'cobelling' method of constructing roofs from large bricks of black basalt.

History

Umm al-Jimal was probably founded in the 1st century BC by the Nabataeans, but was quickly taken over by the Romans, who used it as part of their defensive line. Roads led north to Bosra (in present-day Syria) and southwest to Philadelphia (modern Amman). Because it served as an important trading station for Bedouins and passing caravans, the city prospered. The city grew during the Byzantine period; churches were constructed and Roman buildings were demilitarised.

The boom time was in the early Islamic period when this thriving agricultural city boasted about 3000 inhabitants. However, Umm al-Jimal declined soon after the invasion by the Sassanians from Persia in the early 7th century AD; the city's death knell was sounded by an earthquake in 747. The ruins were occupied by Druze refugees fleeing persecution in Syria early in the 20th century, and used as an outpost by French soldiers during WWI.

Information

It's a good idea to allow several hours to explore the **ruins** *(admission free; open daylight hrs daily)*. Visit early in the morning, or late in the afternoon, when the light shines dramatically on the black basalt and it's not too hot (there is little shade).

For more details about the site, pick up the booklet *Umm el-Jimal* (JD3), published by Al-Kutba and available at most major bookshops in Amman and Aqaba.

Things to See

The large structure just past the southern entrance is the **barracks**, built by the Romans.

The two towers were added about 100 years later and, like the castle at Azraq, it has a basalt door that still functions. The **barracks chapel** was added to the east of the Barracks during the Byzantine period (around the 5th century). About 150m to the left (west) of the Barracks is what some archaeologists believe is a **Nabataean temple**, because of the altar in the middle.

About 100m north of the barracks is the **numerianos church**, one of several decrepit ruins of Byzantine churches. Another 100m to the northeast is the **double church**, a wonderful structure that has been renovated and extended several times over the centuries. About 80m to the right (east) is **house XVII**, with elaborate gates and an arch leading to a courtyard; it was presumably built by a wealthy man. A few metres to the south is the **sheikh's house**, which is notable for its expansive courtyard, stables and stairways.

About 150m north of the double church is the **main reservoir**, one of several oval-shaped water storage facilities around the city. Less than 100m to the left (southwest) is **house XIII**, originally a stable for domestic goats and sheep, and later renovated and used as a residence by Druze settlers.

To the west (about 100m) is the **cathedral**, built in about AD 556, but now mostly in ruins. The **praetorium** (military headquarters) is less than 100m to the southwest. Built in the late 2nd century AD by the Romans, it was extended by the Byzantines, and features a triple doorway.

About 200m to the north is the **west church**, easily identifiable with its four arches and Byzantine crosses.

Getting There & Away

Umm al-Jimal is only about 10km from the Syrian border, and about 20km east of Mafraq. With an early start, it is possible to day trip from Amman by public transport. From the Abdali or Raghadan bus stations in Amman, catch a bus or minibus to Bedouin station in Mafraq (possibly with a connection in Zarqa), and from Mafraq catch another minibus to Umm al-Jimal (200 fils, 30 minutes).

If you're driving, head east of Mafraq along Highway 10 towards Safawi, and look for the turn-off heading north to Umm al-Jimal. If you have chartered a taxi from Amman for a day trip around the desert cas-

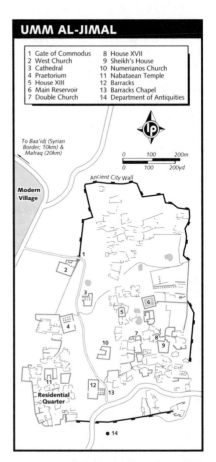

UMM AL-JIMAL

1	Gate of Commodus	8	House XVII
2	West Church	9	Sheikh's House
3	Cathedral	10	Numerianos Church
4	Praetorium	11	Nabataean Temple
5	House XIII	12	Barracks
6	Main Reservoir	13	Barracks Chapel
7	Double Church	14	Department of Antiquities

To Baa'idj (Syrian Border; 10km) & Mafraq (20km)

0   100   200m
0   100   200yd

Ancient City Wall

Modern Village

Residential Quarter

tles, it is possible to include Umm al-Jimal on the itinerary for a little extra (maybe JD5) – but start early to fit it all in.

BURQU   بورقو

Similar in design and purpose to some of the other desert castles is **Qasr Burqu**. It was originally built in the 3rd century AD by the Romans, became a monastery during the Byzantine period, and was restored by the Umayyads in about AD 700.

The castle is not worth visiting as such, and is certainly too difficult to reach to be a part of a day trip around the desert castles. It's the remote location of the castle on the edge of the **Ghadir Burqu** lake, and the apparent incongruity of the lake in the harsh desert, which makes this place so special.

The lake is home to a number of bird species (such as finch, stork and pelican) that come to roost because the water level rarely changes, even in summer. The lake also hosts wildflowers and animals such as gazelle, fox and hyena.

The place is so unique and precious that the Royal Society for the Conservation of Nature (RSCN) hopes to establish Burqu as a protected reserve. Contact the RSCN in Amman before heading to Burqu as permission may be required.

Getting There & Away

The good news for the flora and fauna, and the bad news for visitors, is that Burqu is only accessible by 4WD – and with a guide. The lake and castle are about 25km northwest of Ar-Ruwayshid, which is on the road from Mafraq to the Iraqi border. Although public transport is available between Mafraq and Ar-Ruwayshid, there is no chance of even hitching north of the highway to Burqu, and the access road to Burqu is very rough.

AZRAQ الأزرق
☎ 05

The oasis town of Azraq (which means 'blue' in Arabic) lies 103km east of Amman. Once an important meeting of trade routes, it performs a similar function today although the camels have been replaced by trucks. It forms a junction of roads heading northeast to Safawi and Iraq, and southeast to Saudi Arabia. As such, the town itself is fairly unattractive and the roads are dominated by large transport and diesel fumes.

Azraq was once one of the very few sources of water in the region. It is also home to Qasr al-Azraq (see Desert Castles later in this chapter).

Orientation & Information

Azraq is divided in two, and is located either side of the T-junction of Highway 5 and the highway from Amman. Azraq al-Janubi (South Azraq) stretches about 1km south of the junction, while Azraq ash-Shomali (North Azraq, where the castle is located) starts about 5km to the north

Azraq al-Janubi is basically a truckstop, with restaurants, cafés and mechanics. Although it's far less appealing than Azraq ash-Shomali, the southern end has the only budget hotel, cheap restaurants, money-

changers and private telephone agencies. The post office is in Azraq ash-Shomali.

Azraq Wetland Reserve
حديقة الأزرق المبللة

The Azraq Basin lies mostly in Jordan, and comprises huge areas of mudflats, pools and marshlands. Before some of this was declared an 'internationally important wetland' in 1977 the wetlands suffered appalling ecological damage (see the boxed text 'What Happened to the Wetlands?').

The RSCN has now taken control of the wetlands and has established a small (12 sq km) reserve. Until more water is pumped into the wetlands to attract the birds, there will be little to see, but it is easy to reach and can be combined with a trip to the desert castles and Shaumari Reserve.

Information A new **visitor centre**, run by the RSCN, marks the entrance to the reserve (☎ 3835017; admission JD3, combination ticket with Shaumari Reserve JD4; open 9am-sunset daily). It contains an informative interpretation room, an education room (to raise awareness of the wetlands plight and for the training of guides) and an RSCN Nature Shop.

Wildlife The RSCN estimates that about 300 species of resident and migratory birds still use the wetlands. They include raptor, several species of lark, desert wheatear, trumpeter finch, eagle, plover and duck. A few buffalos enjoy the marshy environs, and there are some semiwild horses about, and jackals and jerbils at night. The best time to see birdlife is winter (December to February) and early spring (March and April), although the raptors arrive in May.

A pathway that takes 30 minutes to walk has been constructed through the reserve, and is ideal for **bird-watching**, although serious birding enthusiasts can take much longer. Visible from the path are also some small **ruins** of Umayyad buildings.

Places to Stay

Zoubi Hotel (singles/doubles with bath JD10/ 20) is the only budget accommodation. The rooms are comfortable, some with charming old-fashioned furniture. It's located behind the Refa'i Restaurant in Azraq al-Janubi, about 800m south of the T-junction.

What Happened to the Wetlands?

The Azraq Basin was originally 12,710 sq km (an area larger than Lebanon). Excavations clearly indicate that it was a popular place to live thousands of years ago and once supported roaming herds of animals, including elephant, cheetah, lion and hippo.

But the wetlands have become an ecological disaster. Extraction of the water from the wetlands to the developing cities of Amman and Irbid started in the late 1960s. Some of the water was 'fossil water' – around 10,000 years old – and was being replaced less than half as quickly as it was being pumped out. Experts believe that 3000 cubic metres of water filled the wetlands every year about 40 years ago. The figure plummeted to a catastrophic 10 cubic metres per year in 1980, and by 1991 the wetlands had dried up completely. A generation ago there was surface water, but in the 1990s the water level dropped to over 10m below the ground. At this time, salt water seeped into the wetlands, making the water unpalatable for wildlife, and hopeless for drinking and irrigation.

The effect on wildlife has been devastating. It was once a staging post for migratory birds en route from Europe to sub-Saharan Africa, but a simple statistic tells the tale: on 2 February 1967 there were 347,000 birds present in the wetlands; on 2 February 2000, there were just 1200 birds. The wetlands were also home to a species of killifish (aphanius sirhani), a small fish of only 4cm to 5cm in length and found nowhere in the world outside Azraq. Believed extinct in the late 1990s, a few somehow survived and the RSCN is trying to ensure the killifish population is again able to grow.

Despite efforts in the 1960s to declare the Azraq wetlands a protected national reserve, it was not until 1977 that the RSCN finally established the Azraq Wetland Reserve.

Since 1994, serious funding and commitment from the United Nations Development Program (UNDP), Jordanian government and RSCN has successfully halted the pumping of water from the wetlands to urban centres. Around 1.5 million cubic metres of fresh water is now being pumped back into the wetlands every year by the Jordanian Ministry of Water, an ongoing process which, it is hoped, will enable 10% of the wetlands to be restored, thereby decreasing salinity and attracting wildlife again to the region. It is estimated, however, that more than 500 illegal wells still exist in the area.

Azraq Resthouse (☎ 3834006, fax 383 5215; singles/doubles/triples with bath & breakfast JD17.500/21.500/28.500) is surprisingly good value with very tidy and comfortable rooms; some are quite spacious. They come with satellite TV and there's a pleasant swimming pool. The turn-off is about 2km north of the T-junction, from where it's a further 1.5km to the resthouse.

Azraq Lodge (☎ 3835017; singles/doubles with bath JD15/22 plus 13% tax) is run by the RSCN. The rooms are tidy but a little bare and uninspiring. Nonetheless, it's a friendly place where meals are available and staff can arrange lunch boxes if you're exploring the Azraq Wetland or Shaumari Reserve. There are 20% discounts available to students.

Places to Eat

A bunch of small eateries lines the 1km stretch of road south of the T-junction. The best are arguably **Turkey Restaurant**, **Cave Restaurant** and **Refa'i Restaurant**, although you could pretty much take your pick.

Azraq Palace Restaurant (open buffets JD6; open 8am-11pm daily) is probably the best place to eat in town. The setting is pleasant and the food (mainly local dishes such as maqlubbeh and mensaf) is tasty. The buffet runs most days from noon to 4pm and 6 to 11pm. At other times, there is an à la carte menu. The restaurant also serves alcohol, which attracts Saudis from across the border.

Azraq Resthouse (see Places to Stay; starters 500 fils-JD2, mains JD3-7; open 8am-11pm daily) has a sterile dining room and overpriced food.

Getting There & Away

Minibuses (650 fils, 1½ hours) travel between the post office (north of the castle in Azraq ash-Shomali) and the Old Station in Zarqa, which is well connected to Amman and Irbid. Minibuses run up and down the road along northern and southern Azraq in search of passengers before hitting the highway to Zarqa. Use this minibus to travel between the two parts of Azraq.

EASTERN JORDAN

SHAUMARI RESERVE حديقة شوماري

Shaumari Reserve was established in 1975 and was the first of its kind in Jordan. Its aim was to reintroduce wildlife that had disappeared from the region, most notably the Arabian oryx (see the boxed text 'Saving the Arabian Oryx'). Despite poaching and natural predators, four species of wildlife have flourished, a testament to RSCN efforts.

The small (22 sq km) Shaumari Reserve is not the place to go to see wildlife roaming the plains unhindered – the animals are kept in large enclosures – but it is worth a visit to see some of the region's most endangered wildlife and the environmentally significant work being done by the RSCN.

Information

At the entrance to the reserve *(admission JD3, combination ticket with Azraq Wetland Reserve JD4; open 8am-4pm daily)* is a shop selling RSCN products. To the right as you pass through the gate is the **nature centre** detailing the fight to save the oryx. Further in is a small **picnic area** with a **children's playground**, which leads to the **observation tower** from which animals can be seen. If you want to get closer, take the 'Oryx Safari' (JD10 for up to 10 people, 45 minutes) that goes through the oryx enclosure in a truck.

Wildlife

Shaumari is home to four main types of wildlife: the Arabian oryx (87 now in the reserve); the blue-necked and red-necked ostrich (40), which was long ago hunted to extinction in the wild in Jordan; the Sabgutu Rosa and Dorcas gazelles (six); and the Persian onager or wild ass (seven).

Nearly 250 species of bird have been identified, including raptor, golden eagle and Egyptian vulture. The best time of year to see birds and wildlife is spring (March to May) and early winter (December).

Places to Stay & Eat

No camping is allowed inside the reserve, but with permission (easy to obtain) from RSCN staff, you can pitch your **tent** opposite

---

Saving the Arabian Oryx

The last time the Arabian oryx was seen in the wild in Jordan was in 1920 when hunting drove the animal to extinction. In 1972, the Arabian oryx was declared extinct in the wild anywhere in the world. The nine lonely oryxes left in captivity were pooled and taken to the Arizona Zoo for a breeding programme. They became known as the 'World Oryx Herd'.

In 1978, four male and four female oryxes were transported to Jordan and three more were sent from Qatar the following year. In 1979, the first calf, Dusha, was born and Jordan's oryx began the precarious road to recovery. By 1983, there were 31 oryxes in Shaumari and they were released into the large enclosures. Since that time, they have been treated as wild animals to facilitate their eventual release into the wild

The Arabian oryx is a herbivore, and, although its white coat had traditionally offered camouflage in the searing heat of the desert, it was also highly prized by hunters, as were its long curved horns, thereby precipitating its near extinction. Oryxes live in herds – even in the enclosures of Shaumari there are two or three small herds. Every two to three years, younger males challenge the leader of the herd for dominance, locking horns in a battle in which the loser often dies.

Adapted well to their desert environment, oryxes once had an uncanny ability to sense rain on the wind. One herd is recorded as having travelled up to 155km, led by a dominant female, to rain. In times of drought, oryxes have been known to survive 22 months without water, obtaining moisture from plants and leaves. In Shaumari, according to the RSCN, a whole year's rain is just enough to get your feet wet so the oryxes here are provided with water.

Most oryx calves are born in winter with an 8½-month gestation period. Mothers leave the herd just prior to birth to make a small nest, before returning to the herd two or three months after the birth of the calf (which can be up to 5kg in weight). Oryxes have a life span of about 20 years.

In a significant landmark for environmentalists the world over, a small group of oryxes was reintroduced into the wild in the Wadi Rum Protected Area in 2002 – a small, tentative step in what is hoped will be the recovery of the wild oryx in Jordan.

the entrance and use the toilets and drinking water for free. There are no showers and you'd need to be self-sufficient with food as the nearest restaurants are in Azraq.

Getting There & Away
Shaumari is well signposted on the road from Azraq south to the Saudi border. From the T-junction in Azraq, the turn-off is 5km to the south, while the small road to the reserve runs for a further 5km; this road into the reserve is paved until the final 1km, and is easily traversable by non-4WD vehicles. It is relatively easy to charter a taxi to the reserve from Azraq, but make sure you arrange for the driver to wait, unless you want to hike 5km back to the main road.

Desert Castles

A string of buildings (pavilions, caravanserais, hunting lodges, forts) and ruins – known collectively (if a little erroneously) as the desert castles – lies in the desert of eastern Jordan. Most were built, or taken over and adapted, by the Damascus-based Umayyads in the late 7th and early 8th centuries. Two castles, Azraq and Al-Hallabat, date from Roman times and excavations of others indicate Nabataean occupation.

There are various theories about their use. The early Arab rulers were still Bedouin at heart and their love of the desert probably led them to build (or take over) these pleasure palaces, which appear to have been surrounded by artificial oases teeming with wild game and orchards. They pursued their pastimes of hawking, hunting and horse-racing for a few weeks each year. The evenings were apparently spent in excessive festivities with plenty of wine, women, poetry and song. They also served as staging posts for pilgrims travelling to Mecca.

Some historians say that only here did the caliphs (Islamic rulers) feel comfortable about flouting the Quran. Others have suggested that they came to avoid epidemics in the big cities or even to maintain links with, and power over, the Bedouin, the bedrock of their support in the conquered lands.

Information
Some of the castles are locked, so you may have to find the caretaker. If he opens any

door especially for you (or provides a commentary), a tip (about 500 fils) is obligatory. The five main castles listed below (except Qasr al-Mushatta) have useful explanations inside their entrances.

Before setting off, make sure you pick up a free copy of the excellent *Desert Castles* brochure, published by the Jordan Tourism Board (JTB) and available at the JTB office in Amman. If you want more information about the castles, pick up the small *The Desert Castles*, published by Al-Kutba (JD3) and available from the larger bookshops around Jordan.

Organised Tours
Jumping on an organised tour of the desert castles from Amman makes a lot of sense, and is one of the few times when an independent traveller on a tight budget will probably have to bite the bullet and pay for a tour.

Tours can be arranged at the Cliff, Venecia, Bdeiwi and Farah hotels in Amman among others. These hotels charge about JD40 per vehicle (holding four or five passengers) per day. You're unlikely to get a better deal by negotiating directly with the driver of a service taxi or private taxi in Amman, and regular taxi drivers may not speak English or know the way.

Getting Around
The five castles which most visitors see are Qasr al-Hallabat (with nearby Hammam as-Sarah), Qasr al-Azraq, Qusayr Amra, Qasr Kharana and Qasr al-Mushatta. Most people on day trips in rented or chartered vehicles from Amman visit the castles in this order (ie, clockwise from Amman) but they can, of course, be visited in the reverse order.

These five castles can be visited quickly in a hectic half day, but it's best to allow a full day for a leisurely drive, a visit to Azraq Wetland and/or Shaumari Reserves and lunch in Azraq. If you start really early (and pay more), it's possible to fit in Umm al-Jimal also.

If you have rented a car for a few days to tour around Jordan, consider renting it for an extra day for a jaunt around the castles and reserves. If driving from Amman, head east of Raghadan bus station towards Zarqa, and follow the signs to Azraq or the individual castles. If you can't afford to rent a car or charter a taxi for the day, or you want to spend more time looking around, base yourself in Azraq town, and use public transport, hitch or charter a vehicle from there.

Public Transport & Hitching With the exception of Qasr al-Mushatta, it is feasible to visit the other four main castles in one day using a combination of public transport and hitching. However, it is very important to note that only the castles at Hallabat and Azraq are accessible by public transport.

QASR AL-HALLABAT
قصر الحلابات

This first stop for many visitors on a day trip from Amman is not necessarily the most interesting, so this could be missed if you're pushed for time.

The caretaker lives in a tent at the entrance, and will open up the castle (for a small tip, of course). It's a good place to watch the sunset, so if you have your own transport, and don't mind driving back to Amman in the dark, try to finish at Qasr al-Hallabat late in the afternoon.

History

The *qasr* was originally a Roman fort during the reign of Caracalla (AD 198–217), a defence against raiding desert tribes, although there's evidence that Trajan before him established a post on the site of a Nabataean emplacement. In the 6th century, it was renovated and became a Byzantine monastery, and was abandoned during the Sassanian invasion from Persia in the early 7th century. About 100 years later, the Umayyads strengthened the fort, and the hedonistic caliph Walid II converted it into a pleasure palace. It once featured baths, with frescoes and mosaics, mosques, forts and reservoirs.

Things to See

Today, the ruins are a jumble of crumbling walls and fallen stones, with only two buildings of much interest.

The square **Umayyad fort** was built of black basalt and a lighter shade of limestone. The fort once contained four large towers, and was three storeys high. In the northwest corner are the ruins of the smaller original **Roman fort** on which the Umayyad fort was apparently built.

Just east of the fort is the rectangular **mosque**, built in the 8th century. Three walls

are still standing, and there's a restored and discernible mihrab (niche facing Mecca) in the south wall.

Getting There & Away

Qasr al-Hallabat is in the village of Hallabat, and is one of the few castles that can be easily visited by public transport. Hallabat has a few basic shops selling food and cold drinks, but has no restaurants or places to stay.

From Amman (Abdali or Raghadan bus stations), take a minibus to the New (Amman) station in Zarqa, another minibus to the Old station in Zarqa, and another to Hallabat village (250 fils, 45 minutes). The minibus drives past Hammam as-Sarah, and can drop you off (ask the driver) at the turn-off.

HAMMAM AS-SARAH
حمام الصرح

Hammam as-Sarah *(Desert Baths; open 24 hrs)* is a tiny bathhouse and hunting lodge built by the Umayyads, and was officially part of the complex at Qasr al-Hallabat. Built from limestone, the building has been well restored over the years, and you can see the channels that were once used for the hot water and steam. Outside the main building is a **well**, nearly 20m deep, and the remains of a **mosque** are nearby.

It's along the main road to Hallabat village, about 4km east of Qasr al-Hallabat.

QASR AL-AZRAQ
قصر الأزرق

Azraq's is the most accessible desert castle, and one of the more interesting. Comparatively little is known about its history and there's been relatively little excavation and renovation. For most visitors, the attraction is the historical link to TE Lawrence.

History

Greek and Latin inscriptions date earlier constructions on the site to around AD 300 – during the reign of the Romans. The building was renovated in the Byzantine period, and the Umayyad caliph Walid II used it for hunting, and as a military base. It was again substantially rebuilt in 1237 by the Ayyubids, and the Ottoman Turks stationed a garrison there in the 16th century.

It is most famous because TE Lawrence and Sherif Hussein bin Ali based themselves there in the winter of 1917, during the Arab

Revolt against the Turks. Lawrence set up his quarters in the room above the southern entrance, while his men used other areas of the fort and covered the gaping holes in the roof with palm branches and clay. They were holed up here for months in crowded conditions with little shelter from the intense cold. Much of the building collapsed in an earthquake in 1927.

Information

If the fort (admission free; open daylight hrs daily) is crawling with tour buses, the caretaker may be trawling for a healthy 'donation' (500 fils is enough).

Things to See

This large building was constructed out of black basalt stone, and was originally three storeys high. The main **entrance** (to the south) is a single massive slab of basalt. Lawrence describes in his book *The Seven Pillars of Wisdom* how it 'went shut with a clang and crash that made tremble the west wall of the castle'. Some of the **paving stones** inside the door have small indentations, carved by former gatekeepers who played an old board game using pebbles to pass the time.

Above the entrance is **Lawrence's Room**. Opposite the entrance, and just to the left, are the remains of a small **altar**, built in the 3rd century AD by the Romans. In the middle of the expansive **courtyard** is a small **mosque**, facing Mecca. It dates to the Ayyubid period (early 13th century), but was built on the ruins of a Byzantine church. In the northeast corner of the courtyard, a hole with stairs leads down to a **well**, full of water until about 20 years ago. In the northwest corner are the ruins of the **prison**.

The northern sections are residential areas with barely discernible ruins of a **kitchen** and **dining room**, and nearby **storerooms** and **stables**. The **tower** in the western wall is the most spectacular, and features another huge **door** made of basalt.

Getting There & Away

Qasr al-Azraq is easy to reach from Amman by public transport. The castle is situated in Azraq ash-Shomali (northern Azraq), about 5km north of the T-junction at the end of the highway from Amman. See the Azraq section earlier in this chapter for details about travelling to and around Azraq, and for information about places to stay and eat.

QUSAYR AMRA

قصر عمرا

Heading back towards Amman along Highway 30, a turn-off leads to Highway 40 and Qusayr (Little Castle) Amra. It is one the best preserved of the desert buildings of the Umayyads; the attractions are the rooms plastered with fascinating frescoes covering some 350 sq m. It was part of a greater complex that served as a caravanserai, with baths and a hunting lodge, possibly in existence before the arrival of the Umayyads.

History

Although historians are undecided, the general consensus is that the building was constructed during the reign of Umayyad caliph Walid I (AD 705–15), who also built the Umayyad Mosque in Damascus. A Spanish team of archaeologists began excavations in the mid-1970s; the frescoes have been restored with the assistance of governments and private institutions from Austria, France and Spain. The building is now a Unesco World Heritage Site.

Information

Entrance to the complex (admission free; open 7am-7.30pm May-Sept, 8am-4.30pm Oct-Apr) is through the excellent **visitor centre** where you may have to ask for the key to the main building with the frescoes. The centre has a relief map of the site and some detailed descriptions of the site's history and the frescoes. The visitor centre also has some public toilets.

Things to See

The entrance of the main building opens immediately to the **audience hall**, where meetings, parties, exhibitions and meals were held. It contains most of the **frescoes**.

A small doorway leads to the left through three small rooms, all part of the baths: the **apodyterium** (changing room); the **tepidarium**, where warm water was offered and warm air circulated beneath the floor; and the domed **calidarium**, which had hot water.

The floors of the two rooms at the back of the main hall bear a modest layer of **mosaics**, but these are hard to see without a torch (flashlight).

The Frescoes of Qusayr Amra

The information boards in the visitor centre at Qusayr Amra assure the visitor that: 'None of the paintings of Qusayr Amra portray scenes of unbridled loose-living or carryings-on'. Given the context of early Islam's prohibition of any illustrations of living beings, it's difficult to agree.

Just how far the boundaries were pushed is evident on the western wall of the audience hall, where there is a depiction of a nude woman bathing. Some historians speculate that she may have been modelled on the favourite concubine of the ruler of Amra. The more your eyes roam the walls within, the more this particular theme becomes apparent.

In the same room, to the left of the nude, stand six great rulers, of whom four have been identified – Caesar, a Byzantine emperor; the Visigoth king, Roderick; the Persian emperor, Chosroes; and the Negus of Abyssinia. The fresco either implies that the present Umayyad ruler was their equal or better, or it is simply a pictorial list of Islam's enemies. Also visible are: a reclining woman representing Victory; peacocks; wrestlers; angels; garden scenes; hunting scenes with wild onagers being driven into a trap; more nude bathing scenes; athletes; and panels depicting craftsmen completing the frescoes.

In the baths section of the building, there are representations of Eros, three busts representing the three ages of man (childhood, youth and old age), more nudes, and pastoral scenes. The highlight, however, is arguably the Dome of Heaven in the calidarium upon which is depicted a map of the northern hemisphere sky accompanied by the signs of the zodiac – one of the earliest known attempt to represent the universe on anything other than a flat surface.

And the purpose of all these paintings? Some Islamic scholars blame the Byzantines, others mumble about rogue rulers who were not true to Islam. But most admit privately that it seems as though the rulers were simply enjoying themselves.

Outside, a few metres north of the main building, is a partially restored 40m-deep stone **well**. It was built to supply water for the baths, and for passing caravans.

Getting There & Away

Qusayr Amra is on the main road and hard to miss, but also impossible to reach by public transport. It's on the right (north) side of the road, 25km southwest of the junctions of Highways 30 and 40. From Azraq, get a minibus towards Zarqa as far as the junction, then hitch. You can charter a taxi from Azraq and combine it with a visit to Qasr Kharana.

QASR KHARANA

قصر الكرانه

Stuck in the middle of a treeless plain, this mighty two-storey edifice clearly looks like a fortress, but historians are divided; the narrow windows were probably for air and light rather than for shooting arrows, and it probably wasn't a caravanserai, because it wasn't located on any popular trade route. The most recent supposition is that it was a meeting room for Umayyad rulers and local Bedouin.

Although small (35 sq m), the castle has been nicely restored and is worth visiting despite its comparative inaccessibility.

History

A painted inscription above one of the doors on the upper floor mentions the date AD 710, which is when it was probably renovated extensively by the Umayyads. The presence of stones with Greek inscriptions in the main entrance suggests it was built on the site of a Roman or Byzantine building, possibly as a private residence.

Information

If the building is closed (*admission free; open daylight hrs daily*), find someone from the tent in the grounds, or the souvenir stall, to open it up.

Things to See

About 60 rooms surround the **courtyard** inside the castle. The long rooms either side of the arched **entrance** were used as **stables**, and in the centre of the courtyard was a **basin** for collecting rainwater.

Make sure you climb to the top levels along one of the elegant **stairways**, passing en route some **rooms with vaulted ceilings**. Most of the rooms in the upper levels are decorated with well-restored **carved plaster medallions**, set around the top of the walls. Stairs in the southeast and southwest corners lead to the 2nd floor and the roof, from which there are great **views** of the stark landscape – although the nearby highway and power station spoil the ambience somewhat.

Getting There & Away
This castle is 16km further west along Highway 40 from Qusayr Amra. Like Qusayr Amra, it can't be missed from the highway, but can't be reached by public transport. Either hitch from Azraq or Amman, or charter a vehicle from Azraq and combine it with a visit to Qusayr Amra.

QASR AL-MUSHATTA
قصر المشتى

Of the five major desert castles, Qasr al-Mushatta (Winter Palace) is the most difficult and time consuming to reach. After a day visiting the other four, some visitors choose to miss this one.

However, the ruins are extensive and fun to wander around. Many pieces have disappeared over the years, ending up in museums around the world; the elaborate carving on the facade was shipped off to Berlin (it's now in the Pergamum Museum) after the palace was 'given' to Kaiser Wilhelm in 1903 by Sultan Abd al-Hamid of Turkey.

History
Qasr al-Mushatta was planned as the biggest and most lavish of all the Umayyad castles, but it was never finished. It was probably started in about AD 743, under caliph Walid II (who intended to establish a city in the area). He was later assassinated by angry labourers, many of whose colleagues had died during the construction of Qasr al-Mushatta because of a lack of water in the area, so building was never completed.

Information
Although a caretaker hangs around the site (*admission free; open daylight hrs daily*), there's nothing to open or close, so no tip is required. Because the castle is located near sensitive areas – primarily the airport – make sure you have your passport ready to show the guards along the way.

Things to See
There isn't a lot to see because the castle was looted, and partially destroyed by earthquakes, so only the walls of incomplete buildings can be seen, and most of the columns and towers have fallen down. There are some fine square **columns** and decorative stonework on the facades.

To the right from the entrance are the ruins of a **mosque**, with its obvious mihrab. In the northern sections are the remains of an **audience hall** and **residences**; the existing pieces provide some idea of how it must have once looked. One unusual feature of the site is that the vaults were made from burnt bricks (an uncommon material in buildings of this style) rather than black basalt.

Getting There & Away
Qasr al-Mushatta is impossible to reach by public transport or hitching. It's also badly signposted, and involves going through at least two military checkpoints. If you're driving from Amman, head towards the Queen Alia airport, turn left (east) off the Desert Highway to the airport, then turn right at the roundabout by the Alia Gateway Hotel. Follow the road for about 12km around the perimeter of the airport, then turn right just before the third, and largest, checkpoint.

One alternative is to charter a taxi from the airport – not a bad idea if you have a long wait for a flight.

OTHER CASTLES
There are numerous other castles in eastern Jordan, and just south of Amman, but they are mostly in ruins and of interest only to archaeologists; they're often impossible to reach by public transport and sometimes only accessible by 4WD.

Qasr 'Ain es-Sil
قصر عين السيل

This is not really a castle or palace but a farmhouse built by the Umayyads, possibly over the fortifications of a Roman building. It is small (17 sq m), and was built from basalt brick. There are some ruins of a **courtyard** (flanked by seven rooms) **equipment** for making bread and olive oil, and some **baths**.

It is located just off the main road through Azraq ash-Shomali (northern Azraq), and only about 2km from Qasr al-Azraq.

Qasr Aseikhin
قصر الشيخين

This small Roman fort, built from basalt in the 3rd century over the ruins of a 1st-century Nabataean building, has great **views** from the hilltop, but nothing else to justify a detour. It's about 22km northeast of Azraq ash-Shomali, and only accessible by 4WD. Go along the road north of Qasr al-Azraq for about 15km, and follow the signs to the fort.

Qasr Deir al-Kahf   قصر دير الكهف

Deir al-Kahf (Monastery of Caves) is another Roman fort, built in the 4th century, also from black basalt. The ruins are more extensive than some others (which makes it more interesting), but it is still very difficult to reach. There is an access road north of Highway 10, or look for the signs along the back roads east of Umm al-Jimal.

Qasr Mushash   قصر موشاش

This large (2 sq km) Umayyad settlement is mostly in ruins. The highlights are the remains of the **palace**, a large **courtyard** surrounded by a dozen rooms, the **baths** and **cisterns**, and **walls** built to protect against possible flooding. It's only accessible by 4WD. Look for the sign along Highway 40.

Qasr al-Muwaqqar   قصر الموقر

This former caravanserai was built in the Umayyad period, but the ruins are so decrepit that it's not worth bothering to find. There are some remains of **reservoirs**, **Kufic inscriptions** and **columns**, but little else to see; the most interesting item, a 10m stone tower with Kufic inscriptions, is now in the National Archaeological Museum in Amman. The **views** are wonderful, however.

The ruins are located about 2km north of Highway 40.

Qasr al-Qastal   قصر القسطل

This ruined Umayyad settlement was ornately renovated by the Mamluks in the 13th century AD, but very little remains. The main building still standing is the 68-sq-m **palace**, but there are ruins of an **Islamic cemetery** and **baths** nearby. It is located just to the west of the Desert Highway, before the turn-off to the airport, but is poorly signposted.

Qasr al-Tuba   قصر التوبة

This is one of the most impressive of the lesser-known castles, but is also the most difficult to reach. It was erected by the Umayyad caliph Walid II in about AD 743, but (like Qasr al-Mushatta) it was never finished after he was assassinated. The castle was probably going to be a caravanserai, and is unusual because it's made out of bricks.

The castle is only accessible by 4WD along a poorly signed dirt track (35km) west of the Desert Highway, or an unsigned dirt track south (50km) of Highway 40. Because the roads are so difficult to find and follow, a knowledgeable guide is recommended.

Qasr 'Uweinid   قصر عويند

This Roman military fort was built in the 3rd century AD to protect the source of Wadi as-Sarhan (now in Saudi Arabia), but was abandoned less than 100 years later. It is only accessible by 4WD, and is about 15km southwest of Azraq al-Janubi (southern Azraq) – look for the turn-off along the road towards Shaumari Reserve.

Qusayr Amra, eastern Jordan

Qasr al-Azraq, eastern Jordan

Blue-necked ostriches, Shaumari Wildlife Reserve

Azraq Wetlands Reserve, Azraq

Gazelles, Shaumari Wildlife Reserve

King's Highway

The King's Highway – known in Arabic as At-Tariq as-Sultani (Road of the Sultan) – is of great historical and religious significance. It has been used by the Israelites, Nabataeans travelling to and from Petra, Christian pilgrims going to Moses' memorial at Mt Nebo, and Muslim pilgrims heading to and from Mecca.

Of Jordan's three highways running from north to south, the King's Highway is the most interesting and picturesque with a host of attractions on or just off the road, including Madaba, Karak, Dana Nature Reserve, Shobak and on to Petra. The road traverses the majestic Wadi Mujib valley, the 'Grand Canyon of Jordan'. Unfortunately, Wadi Mujib is the reason why public transport along this road can be difficult.

Getting Around

Public transport along the King's Highway is neither frequent nor complete, with the stretch between Dhiban and Ariha devoid of any regular public transport. Hitching can be a good way to get around, but be prepared for long waits on deserted stretches.

Rental Car & Private Taxi Renting a car between Amman and Aqaba via the King's Highway is easily the best way to explore the region. With an early start from Madaba, it's possible to travel to Wadi Musa (for Petra) in one long day, with brief visits to Mt Nebo, Mukawir, Umm ar-Rasas, Karak, Dana Nature Reserve and Shobak castle. Most travellers prefer to break up the journey with an overnight stop in Dana or Karak.

Chartering a taxi is also possible for the same journey. If you do so, rent the taxi only as far as Karak – onward public transport is regular from there.

Public Transport & Hitching Travelling all the way along the King's Highway from Amman to Wadi Musa is a heady mixture of minibuses, hitching and chartered taxis. To explore all of the sites covered in this chapter by such methods, you would need up to a week. A summary of the main options is listed here; more information is included in the relevant Getting There & Away sections throughout the chapter.

Highlights

- **Madaba** – this town is renowned for its extensive mosaics and is an alternative base to Amman
- **Mukawir** – Herod's castle of Machaerus offers spectacular views over the Dead Sea and good hiking down to the hot springs of Hammamat Ma'in
- **Wadi Mujib Valley** – a portion of this vast and beautiful valley is a protected reserve
- **Karak** – this old Crusader town is dominated by a magnificent castle
- **Dana Nature Reserve** – this stunning reserve is a fine combination of eco-tourism, wonderful hiking and a 15th-century stone village
- **Shobak** – this Crusader castle offers great views of a desolate landscape, and is much quieter than Jordan's other attractions
- **Mt Nebo** – the site where Moses looked out over the Promised Land affords panoramic views across the Dead Sea

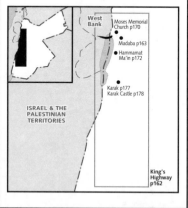

Amman to Madaba Take the regular minibus.

Madaba to Karak The best option is the minibus organised by the hotels in Madaba (minimum of three passengers). It goes from Madaba to Petra with stops in Wadi Mujib and Karak. The Farah

161

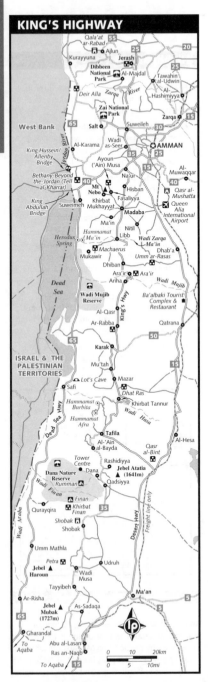

KING'S HIGHWAY

Hotel organises a similar service from Amman. The only alternative is to take a regular minibus from Madaba to Dhiban, charter a taxi to Ariha, then take a minibus to Karak.

Karak to Dana Nature Reserve Take a minibus from Karak to Tafila, and another to Qadsiyya (for Dana) or Shobak village.

Dana Nature Reserve to Wadi Musa (near Petra) Public transport south of Qadsiyya (near Dana) and Shobak village is infrequent, so you may need to take an irregular minibus to Ma'an and then another to Wadi Musa. Hitching is also possible.

MADABA   مأدبا
☎ 05

This easy-going town is best known for its superb and historically significant Byzantine-era mosaics. The town has a strong sense of its unique history, making it a major stop on the tourist trail. Madaba is the most important Christian centre in Jordan, and has long been an example of religious tolerance, a place where the call to prayer from the mosque coexists with church bells; Muslims make up two-thirds of the population, and Christians one-third.

Worth considering as an alternative to Amman as a place to stay, Madaba is far more compact, has some excellent hotels and restaurants, and is less than an hour by regular public transport from the capital. It is also possible to come straight from Queen Alia International Airport, bypassing Amman altogether. Madaba is a good base for exploring the Dead Sea, Bethany-Beyond-the-Jordan (Jesus' baptism site) and other sites such as Mt Nebo, Mukawir (Machaerus) and Hammamat Ma'in.

History

The biblical Moabite town of Medeba was one of the towns divided among the 12 tribes of Israel. It's also mentioned on the famous Meshe Stele raised in about 850 BC by the Moabite king Mesha (see the boxed text 'A Stele at Twice the Price' later in this chapter).

By 165 BC the Ammonites were in control of Madaba; about 45 years later it was taken by Hyrcanus I of Israel, and then promised to the Nabataeans by Hyrcanus II in return for helping him recover Jerusalem. Under the Romans from AD 106, Madaba became a prosperous provincial town with the usual colonnaded streets and impressive public buildings. The prosperity continued during the Byzantine period up until the Sassanian invasion from Persia in AD 614, and most of the mosaics in Madaba date from this period.

The town was eventually abandoned for about 1100 years after a devastating earthquake in AD 747. In the late 19th century, 2000 Christians from Karak migrated to Madaba after a bloody dispute with Karak's Muslims and within their community. They found the mosaics when they started digging foundations for houses. News that a mosaic map of the Holy Land had been found in St George's Church in Madaba reached Europe in 1897, leading to a flurry of exploratory activity that continues to this day.

Orientation

The central, older and most interesting part of Madaba is easy to get around, and there is no reason to venture into the suburbs. The centre of town is St George's Church, and many facilities are located around this area and north towards Al-Mouhafada Circle. All streets are clearly labelled in English, and most major intersections have brown signs pointing to the major attractions.

Information

Tourist Office The **visitor centre** (☎ 325 3536; open 8am-5pm Oct-Apr, 8am-7pm May-Sept) is on Abu Bakr as-Seddiq St, adjacent to the Madaba Mosaic School. There is a moderately helpful information office with a few brochures, toilets, a handy car park and a small showroom with old photos of Madaba; look especially for the 1924 photo of a much smaller Madaba.

It's also worth visiting the **National Society for the Preservation of Madaba and its Suburbs** (☎ 3244679), on Hussein bin Ali St in front of the Burnt Palace, if you have an interest in what's being done to preserve Madaba's architectural and cultural heritage (see the boxed text 'Long Name; Good Cause' later in this chapter). The **Ministry of Tourism & Antiquities** (☎/fax 3245527; e tourism@mota.gov.jo) has an office above the Burnt Palace and also has information about Madaba's preservation efforts.

Guides If you want to get the most from your stay in Madaba, it can be worthwhile to hire a guide. One English-speaking guide who comes highly recommended is Osamah

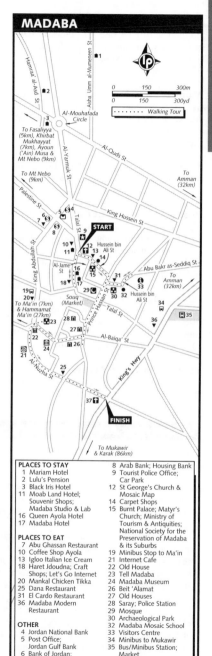

PLACES TO STAY
1 Mariam Hotel
2 Lulu's Pension
3 Black Iris Hotel
11 Moab Land Hotel; Souvenir Shops; Madaba Studio & Lab
16 Queen Ayola Hotel
17 Madaba Hotel

PLACES TO EAT
7 Abu Ghassan Restaurant
10 Coffee Shop Ayola
13 Igloo Italian Ice Cream
18 Haret Jdoudna; Craft Shops; Let's Go Internet
20 Mankal Chicken Tikka
25 Dana Restaurant
31 El Cardo Restaurant
36 Madaba Modern Restaurant

OTHER
4 Jordan National Bank
5 Post Office; Jordan Gulf Bank
6 Bank of Jordan; Minibus Stop to Fasaliyya
8 Arab Bank; Housing Bank
9 Tourist Police Office; Car Park
12 St George's Church & Mosaic Map
14 Carpet Shops
15 Burnt Palace; Matyr's Church; Ministry of Tourism & Antiquities; National Society for the Preservation of Madaba & its Suburbs
19 Minibus Stop to Ma'in
21 Internet Cafe
22 Old House
23 Tell Madaba
24 Madaba Museum
26 Beit 'Alamat
27 Old Houses
28 Saray; Police Station
29 Mosque
30 Archaeological Park
32 Madaba Mosaic School
33 Visitors Centre
34 Minibus to Mukawir
35 Bus/Minibus Station; Market
37 Church of the Apostles

Twal (☎ 0795 5575989; [e] osamast@hotmail .com). The official rate for guides is JD40 per full day, but this is a matter for negotiation depending on your means and the size of the group.

Money Several banks can change cash and travellers cheques, including the Bank of Jordan on the corner of Palestine and King Abdullah Streets, Jordan Gulf Bank near the post office, and the Jordan National Bank on the corner of King Abdullah and Talal Streets. The Arab Bank (Visa and MasterCard) and Housing Bank (Visa) on Palestine St have ATMs.

Post & Communications The post office (open 8am-5pm daily) on Palestine St is small but reliable. Long-distance telephone calls can be made from inside.

Some business cards and brochures still list the local area code for Madaba as 08, but all telephones and faxes in Madaba and surrounding districts have an area code of 05. Madaba's old telephone numbers were also only six digits. If you come across a six digit number, simply replace the '5' with '32' (ie, 543678 becomes 3243678).

Email & Internet Access There are at least eight Internet cafés in Madaba. Among the better ones are **Internet Café** (open 10am-2am daily; access per hour 750 fils) on

Al-Nuzha St, and **Let's Go Internet Café** (JD1 per hour), which was to move to the Haret Jdoudna complex (see Places to Eat later in this chapter) soon after we visited.

Photography & Film Most souvenir shops around town sell film. One of the better places for developing is **Madaba Studio & Lab** (☎ 3245932) near the Moab Land Hotel on Talal St. They charge JD3.500 to develop a roll of 36-print film, and sell standard ASA100 print film (from JD2.500 for 36 photos), slide film (JD7 including developing) and video cartridges (from JD5). It's open from 8am to 9.30pm daily.

Emergency There is a **tourist police office** (☎ 191) along Talal St, just north of St George's Church.

Books & Maps The map in this book will be sufficient for most visitors, but those staying more than a few days may wish to pick up the *Tourist Map of Madaba* (JD2), published by the Royal Jordanian Geographic Centre, which lists all sites and street names in English, and also includes handy maps of Dhiban, Ma'in and Hammamat Ma'in. It's available in a few bookshops in Amman.

The brochure *Madaba and Mount Nebo*, published by the Jordan Tourism Board (JTB), provides a brief but satisfactory explanation of the attractions in Madaba,

---

Meandering Around Madaba

Madaba is compact so all the main attractions can be easily visited on foot. More details about the major sites are mentioned in the text. Allow about two hours, longer if you want to spend more time admiring the mosaics.

The obvious place to start is **St George's Church**, with its **mosaic map**. From there, head south along Talal St and visit the complex of restaurants and craft shops in **Haret Jdoudna**, a wonderfully restored example of traditional Madaba architecture. Return north along Talal St, and then turn right (southeast) along Hussein bin Ali St. This takes you to the **Burnt Palace** and **Martyrs Church**. Further down the hill, at the end of Hussein bin Ali St, turn right (southwest) into Prince Hassan St, then immediately left to reach the **Archaeological Park**. Next door is the **Madaba Mosaic School** and then the **Madaba Visitors Centre**. Return to Prince Hassan St and head up the hill, passing the solid **Saray** on the hill and some decaying but elegant **old houses** to the right (west). Turning right (west) along Al-Baiqa' St is **Beit 'Alamat** to the left (south); some men are probably playing cards directly opposite.

Down an alley running left (south) off Al-Baiqa' St is the entrance to the **Madaba Museum**. Continue further west along Al-Baiqa' St to the junction with An-Nuzha St where there are some more **old houses**. Around 50m northeast of the junction, above an open patch of ground, are the ruins of **Tell Madaba**. An-Nuzha St then leads south and then southwest, taking you to the junction of the King's Highway, where the **Church of the Apostles** stands.

although the map is poor. The brochure is printed in English, French, Italian, German and Arabic, and is available at tourist offices and, usually, the visitor centre. The JTB also publishes several smaller brochures: *Madaba Archaeological Park* (although most of this information is included in *Madaba and Mount Nebo*); *Madaba Mosaic Map*, which has slightly more detailed information about the mosaics in St George's Church; and the excellent *Mount Nebo* (see Around Madaba later in this chapter).

If you need more information about the mosaics and other historical buildings in Madaba, pick up the definitive but weighty *Madaba: Cultural Heritage* (around JD22) published by the American Center of Oriental Research. Much cheaper and more portable is *Mosaic Map of Madaba* by Herbert Donner. The best is the pocket-sized and affordable *Madaba, Mt Nebo* published by Al-Kutba (JD3 to JD5). Most books and maps relevant to Madaba are available at the souvenir shops in the streets around St George's Church.

Entrance Fees
A combined ticket to the Archaeological Park, Madaba Museum and Church of the Apostles costs JD1/2 in low/high season. It's not possible to purchase cheaper tickets for the individual sites if you only want to visit one.

St George's Church & Mosaic Map
This 19th-century Greek Orthodox Church *(Talal St; admission JD1; open 7am-6pm Sat & Mon-Thur, 10.30am-6pm Fri & Sun)* was built over a Byzantine Church.

Unearthed in 1884, the mosaic on the church floor was a clear map with 157 captions (in Greek) of all major biblical sites from Lebanon to Egypt, and down to the Mediterranean – including obvious references to the Nile River, the Dead Sea and, in the middle, Jerusalem and the Church of the Holy Sepulchre. The mosaic was constructed in AD 560, and was originally around 25m long (some experts claim 15m is more accurate) and 6m wide. It once contained more than two million pieces. Only one-third of the original mosaic has survived.

The map itself, while of enormous historical significance, can be difficult to take in with all its fragments. It's definitely worth seeing, but you need to take your time to get the map's bearing.

On Friday and Sunday morning, the church opens at 7am for mass at which visitors are welcome, but viewing the map at these times is not permitted.

Archaeological Park
Some careful restoration and excavation in the early 1990s led to the creation of the Archaeological Park *(☎ 3246681; Hussein bin Ali St; admission low/high season combined ticket JD1/2; open 8am-5pm Oct-Apr, 8am-7pm May-Sept)*, a collection of ruins as well as mosaics from the Madaba area.

To the left as you enter, and elsewhere around the small complex, are displays of mosaics from around Madaba. Look especially for the Hall of Seasons (found under a house in Madaba town); a mosaic from the baths at Herod's castle at Machaerus (1st century BC and claimed to be the oldest mosaic unearthed in Jordan); the upper mosaic from the church at Massuh (10km north of Madaba); and the mosaic from the Church of the Acropolis in Ma'in.

The large roofed structure in front of you as you enter contains the most impressive mosaics on the site. On the north side of the area under the roof is **Hippolytus Hall**, built in the early 6th century. The original structure had rooms around a central courtyard; its purpose is unclear. The corners of the floor have decorations depicting the four seasons, and elsewhere there are pictures of flowers and birds, scenes from the classic Oedipal tragedy of Phaedre and Hippolytus, and portraits of the goddess Aphrodite looking none too pleased with a baby Adonis.

Under the same roof is the **Church of the Virgin Mary**, which was also built in the 6th century and uncovered in 1887. The mosaic on the floor, thought to date from AD 767, is a masterpiece of geometric design.

Between the two churches lie the well-preserved remains of the **Roman Road** which ran east to west between the Roman city gates and was lined with columns. West of the road is the **Church of the Prophet Elias**, which was constructed in AD 608, but the surviving mosaics are not as eye-catching and sometimes poorly lit.

The displays are well labelled in English and a clear map just past the ticket booth indicates the location of each of the exhibits. The park sometimes shuts early (around 4pm) on Friday.

Church of the Apostles

This church (*Al-Nuzha St; admission in low/high season JD1/2 combined ticket; open 8am-5pm Oct-Apr, 8am-7pm May-Sept*) contains a remarkable mosaic dedicated to the 12 apostles, although it can be difficult to get a sense of its overall splendour. The mosaic was created in AD 568 and is one of the few instances where the mosaicist Salomios put his name to his work. The central portion shows Thalassa, a woman who represents the sea, surrounded by fish and some nasty marine creatures. In the same mosaic are representations of less threatening native animals and birds, flowers and fruits.

Burnt Palace & Martyrs Church

The Burnt Palace (*Hussein bin Ali St; admission free; open 8am-5pm Oct-Apr, 8am-7pm May-Sept*) was a late-6th-century luxury private mansion destroyed by fire and earthquake in around AD 749. It contains more mosaics and there are walkways throughout for viewing the site. The **east wing** (down the steps to the left as you enter) contains some good hunting mosaics, while the **west wing's** highlight is the image of a lion attacking a bull. A fragment of a four seasons mosaic is all that remains of the **north wing**. On the site is the continuation of the ancient **Roman road**, which once connected with the road in the Archaeological Park, as well as the 6th-century **Martyrs Church**, which was destroyed in the 8th century. The site requires more imagination than the other sites around town.

Madaba Museum

The Madaba Museum (*☎ 3244056; Al-Baiqa' St; admission low/high season combined ticket JD1/2; open 8am-5pm Oct-Apr, 8am-7pm May-Sept*) was created from several old Madaba houses. It contains the **Folklore Museum**, with jewellery, traditional costumes and a copy of the Mesha Stele (see the boxed text 'A Stele at Twice the Price' later in this chapter). The most interesting mosaics are the **Byzantine Mosaic**; the **Mosaic of the Paradise**; and the ones dating back to the 6th century in the room marked **Traditional House of Madaba**.

Watch out also for the mosaic representing Bacchus, the god of wine. Local legend has it that a local woman, offended by the beautiful young (naked) female body in the mosaic, destroyed it, but decided against defacing the naked male figure. The museum also features artefacts from Umm ar-Rasas and Machaerus castle near Mukawir (see Around Madaba later in this chapter).

There are plans to move the museum to another old Madaba house nearby, provided the current occupants (the police) can find suitable accommodation elsewhere.

Madaba Mosaic School

The Madaba Mosaic School (*☎ 3240723, fax 3240759; admission free; open 8am-3pm Sat-Thur*) was set up in 1992 by the Jordanian Government with help from the Italian Government and is the only school of its kind in the Middle East. Its primary aims are to train Jordanian artists in the production and restoration of mosaics, spread awareness of mosaics in Jordan and to actively preserve mosaics throughout the country. Its restoration work is evident in the Archaeological Park, the Church of the Apostles and at Khirbat Mukhayyat.

The school consists of a workshop, which includes a superb reproduction of the mosaic map in St George's Church; it's displayed on the wall, making it easier to photograph. There is also a library where most of the books are in Italian. This is an active school so all visitors should first visit the administration office staff (turn left about 10m after passing through the gate) who are usually happy to show visitors around, although the classrooms are understandably off-limits.

Old Houses

There are dozens of old Madaba houses around town in varying stages of disrepair. The **Saray**, high on the hill above (west of) Prince Hassan St, used to be the office of the local Ottoman administration and now functions as a police station. Constructed in 1896, it's a suitably solid stone structure with attractive arched windows, best appreciated with the semicircular steps and iron balcony when facing the entrance. The second storey was added in 1922.

Not far away and sadly decrepit is the two-storey **Beit 'Alamat**. Built between 1913 and 1922, it also has some fine arched

Making Mosaics

Mosaics are traditionally made from tiny squares called *tesserae*, chipped from larger rocks. The tessarae are naturally coloured, and carefully laid on a thick coating of wet lime. Unlike the mosaics found in some other countries (eg, Italy), mosaics found in and around Madaba were made for the floor, and were hardy enough to withstand anything – except massive earthquakes.

The larger mosaics found in and around Madaba required painstaking effort and great skill, taking months or years to complete. As a result, they were only created for wealthier citizens who could afford them, and for important buildings (particularly churches). For some reason, very few of the artists signed their names on the mosaics, possibly because so many people were involved over many years, although other names are often listed, such as the people who helped to pay for the mosaic and clergy in the church.

Designs were fairly standard, and featured scenes from everyday life such as animals, fish, plants and people; activities such as hunting; and various religious events or mythological gods and goddesses. Most were enhanced with intricate edges.

windows and a long iron balcony. There are tentative plans for restoration of the house, which, if completed, would make it one of Madaba's finest.

Tell Madaba

This important archaeological site in the heart of Madaba is still under excavation. Like many sites around Madaba, it was discovered by accident by a local when he started digging the foundations for his house. It contains a **Byzantine crypt** (the right arch if you're looking from Talal St); the remains of **Umayyad baths** (the four arches to the left of the crypt, including the remains of water pipes in the wall); and **Umayyad houses** (atop the hill). Of most significance is the **Iron Age wall** or fortification, the largest of its kind in Jordan and visible from above the arch on the top level.

To get the most from this site you'll need a trained eye. It's open to the public but please tread carefully as much remains to be excavated.

Places to Stay

Madaba has an excellent range of hotels and all are within easy walking distance of Madaba's main sites. All prices include breakfast.

Madaba Hotel (☎/fax 3240643; Al-Jame St; singles/doubles from JD10/16) has tidy if unexciting rooms. It also has a Bedouin tent on the roof where you can sleep for JD3 per person.

Queen Ayola Hotel (☎/fax 3244087; Talal St; singles/doubles from JD10/16) is also decent value, although if you can afford a few dinars more, there's better elsewhere. The rooms are well kept.

Lulu's Pension (☎ 3243678, fax 3247617; Hamraa' al-Asd St; singles/doubles/triples with shared bath JD10/20/30, doubles with private bath & balcony JD25) has a lovely family feel, the rooms are very comfortable and the welcome is warm. You can also set up a tent in the garden for JD5.

Mariam Hotel (☎/fax 3251529; e mh@go .com.jo; Aisha Umm al-Mumeneen St; singles/ doubles JD18/22) is perhaps the best place to stay in town with spotless rooms and bathrooms, some of the most comfortable beds in Jordan, and Charl, the super-friendly owner. It's located in a quiet residential district, two blocks northeast of the Al-Mouhafada Circle, but within easy walking distance of the town centre. They hotel also offers 15% discounts to Lonely Planet readers, making it excellent value. Staff also organise transport south along the King's Highway to Petra (see Getting There & Away later in this chapter).

Black Iris Hotel (☎/fax 3250171; Al-Mouhafada Circle; singles/doubles JD15/20) is another classy place with very reasonable prices. It also comes warmly recommended by readers. The stylish rooms, some overlooking a pleasant garden, have spotless bathrooms and some are very spacious; they serve good breakfasts. It's easy to spot from Al-Mouhafada Circle.

Moab Land Hotel (☎/fax 3251318; Talal St; singles/doubles without balcony JD15/20, doubles with balcony JD25, suite JD30) is directly opposite St George's Church. It's an attractive, clean and airy place, staff are friendly and the location is excellent.

Places to Eat

Most of Madaba's restaurants serve alcohol and there are liquor stores dotted around the town.

Madaba Modern Restaurant (*King's High-way; meals around JD2; open 8am-11pm daily*) is the best of the cheap eateries near the bus/minibus station. Typical of its genre, the food owes a lot to a preoccupation with chicken, hummus and salad.

Abu Ghassan Restaurant (*King Abdullah St; meals around JD2.200; open 7am-midnight daily*) is similar and is popular with locals for its *fuul*. Its food does get mixed reviews from readers, however.

Mankal Chicken Tikka (☎ 3244633; *King Abdullah St; meals around JD1.500; open 9am-midnight daily*) is a friendly place that specialises in chicken meals that are ample and reasonably priced.

Coffee Shop Ayola (☎ 3251843; *Talal St; snacks around JD1; open 8am-11pm daily*), almost opposite St George's Church, is a charming relaxed place too small to attract large tour groups. It serves delicious toasted sandwiches (JD1), all types of coffee (500 fils to JD1), tea (500 fils) and cans of cold beer (JD1.500). It's also a good place to spend time with a nargileh.

Dana Restaurant (☎ 3245749, fax 324 5452; *Al-Nuzha St; starters 500 fils-JD2, mains JD2-5; open 9am-11pm daily*) is not far from the Church of the Apostles. The atmosphere is pleasant and they serve open buffets (JD6) as well as à la carte meals, although the food can be patchy.

El Cardo Restaurant (☎ 3251006, fax 325 1007; *Hussein bin Ali St; starters JD1-2, mains JD4-7; open 8am-midnight daily*), opposite the Archaeological Park, serves pricey but good local and international dishes such as pepper steak and barbecued lamb (around JD4). It also does a range of sandwiches (from JD1.500). A large bottle of Amstel costs JD3. The decor is attractive and the service good.

Haret Jdoudna (☎ 3248650; *Talal St; starters from JD1, mains JD3.500-7, pizzas from JD2.500; open 9am-midnight daily*) is a charming complex of craft shops (see Shopping later in this chapter) and places to eat, all set in one of Madaba's restored old houses. The classy **restaurant** upstairs serves delicious food though the service can border on the indifferent. Downstairs is a more informal **café** where you can enjoy good pizzas either indoors or in the pleasant courtyard where there's sometimes live music. There's also a small bar.

Igloo Italian Ice Cream (*Hussein bin Ali St; open 10am-8pm Sat-Thur, 2pm-8pm Fri*) serves good Italian ice cream from 400 fils plus 100 fils for topping.

Shopping

Madaba is famous for its colourful rugs, which can be bought around town, especially between the entrance to the Burnt Palace and St George's Church, although much of what's on offer comes from elsewhere. The souvenir shops in the same area sell a range of other souvenirs.

Next to the entrance to the Burnt Palace, the **National Society for the Preservation of Madaba and its Suburbs** (☎ 3244679) has a necessarily long sign and friendly staff (see the boxed text 'Long Name; Good Cause').

The craft shops in the **Haret Jdoudna** complex (☎ 3248650; *Talal St; open 9am-9pm daily*) have a classy and extensive range of items on offer, including jewellery, books, clothing, mosaics, furniture, textiles and ceramics. Some of the items come from the collection of the Noor Al Hussein Foundation (see Shopping in the Facts for the Visitor chapter) whose profits support community projects around Jordan. There's also a workshop downstairs.

Getting There & Away

The grotty bus/minibus station-cum-market is just off the King's Highway, a few minutes' walk down from the town centre.

To/From the Airport If you want to bypass the bustle of Amman, it's possible to reach Madaba from Queen Alia International Airport, although there is no public transport. Private taxis cost around JD12,

---

Long Name; Good Cause

The National Society for the Preservation of Madaba and its Suburbs (☎ 3244679) began in 1992, and now boasts a membership of over 150. It aims to preserve Madaba's heritage, with a particular focus on protecting the architectural and historical integrity of the old houses around town. It is partly funded by the American Center for Oriental Research in Amman, and by the sale of maps, books and souvenirs from its shop next to the entrance to the Burnt Palace.

but most hotels in Madaba will pick you up from the airport for JD7 if you notify them in advance.

To/From Amman From Raghadan, Wahadat and, less often, Abdali bus stations in Amman, there are regular buses and minibuses (270 fils, one hour) throughout the day for Madaba. The minibuses leave less frequently from Madaba in the evening and you should make your departure no later than 9pm, or earlier on Friday.

To/From the Dead Sea Minibuses also leave from the Madaba bus/minibus station to South Shuna (350 fils, 45 minutes), from where another minibus for Suweimeh (250 fils, 30 minutes) should take you right to the door of the Dead Sea Rest House. Returning to Madaba, you'll need to take a minibus (before 5pm) for Amman and ask the driver to let you out just before Na'ur, from where a minibus will take you to Madaba (total of JD1.250, 1½ hours).

South Along the King's Highway Public transport along the King's Highway is diabolical and, across Wadi Mujib between Dhiban and Ariha, nonexistent. The only worthwhile option is to take the service organised by the Mariam Hotel (you don't have to be staying there). Leaving at 10am, it goes to Petra (arriving around 6pm), with stops at Wadi Mujib for photos, and an hour in Karak. You can get off at Dana, but you'll have to pay the full fare. The service requires a minimum of three people (the hotels ring around Madaba to find other passengers) and costs JD12 per person.

The only alternative is to take a minibus to Dhiban (250 fils, 45 minutes) and then charter a taxi across to Ariha.

To/From Elsewhere It is possible to travel to Karak on a daily minibus (JD1.500, two hours) from the main bus/minibus station, although it travels via the less interesting Desert Highway. The bus, which leaves sometime after 6am, is the university bus for Mu'tah, but it stops at (or near) the minibus station in Karak. Be aware, however, that although this minibus claims to run daily, it often doesn't operate when the university is on holidays so check the day before you want to travel.

From near or in the bus/minibus station in Madaba, minibuses go to Mukawir (for Machaerus castle; 350 fils, one hour) several times throughout the day, the last at around 5pm. For Hammamat Ma'in, public transport is severely limited. At the time of writing, the Mercure Ma'in Resort had begun running a service from Madaba to Hammamat Ma'in every morning at 10am and returning at 6pm; ask at the Mariam hotel in Madaba for the prevailing cost and departure point. You might be able to get on the bus that ferries employees to the springs (around 7.30am). Otherwise, a private taxi will cost at least JD15 for a return journey including an hour's waiting time.

See the Around Madaba section which follows for details of getting to and from Mt Nebo.

Getting Around
If you're laden with bags, private taxis are plentiful; from the bus/minibus station to the centre of town shouldn't cost more than JD1.

AROUND MADABA
There are several attractions around Madaba, but most (with the exception of Mt Nebo and Mukawir) are difficult to reach by public transport. If you don't have time to wait around for infrequent minibuses, consider chartering a taxi in Madaba. A half-day trip (around JD20 to JD25) could take in Mt Nebo, Khirbat Mukhayyat, Ayoun Musa and Hammamat Ma'in. A full day (around JD35) could also take in Mukawir, Umm ar-Rasas and Wadi Mujib, with a possible drop-off in Ariha (for the minibus to Karak).

With the completion of a new road connecting Mt Nebo with the Dead Sea, it is possible to visit Mt Nebo, the Dead Sea and Bethany (the site of Jesus' baptism) in a long day, returning to Madaba in the evening, although you'd have to hitch the 6km to/from Bethany.

Mt Nebo
Mt Nebo is where Moses is said to have seen the Promised Land, a land he was himself forbidden to enter. He died and was later buried in the area, although the exact location of the burial site is the subject of conjecture. The site flickered briefly into the international spotlight with the visit of Pope John Paul II in 2000.

Mt Nebo features several peaks including Siyagha ('monastery' in Aramaic), on which the Moses Memorial Church was built. It's a pleasant side trip from Madaba, just 9km away, and some readers rate the mosaics here as better than those at Madaba. Aside from its religious significance, Mt Nebo commands sweeping views.

Information The entrance to the complex *(admission 500 fils; open 7am-5am daily Oct-Apr, 7am-7pm May-Sept)* is clearly visible on the Madaba to Dead Sea road. It costs 250 fils to park your car in the parking area across the road. Next to the entrance are some toilets (250 fils) and there's a permanent tourist police presence.

The hefty *Town of Nebo* by Fr Sylvestre J Salter and Fr Bellarmiro Bagatti also details other Christian sites in Jordan and is a good reference. More portable and affordable (JD4) is *Mount Nebo* by Michelle Piccirillo. Both are usually available inside the church. The two brochures published by the Jordan Tourism Board – *Madaba and Mt Nebo* and especially *Mount Nebo* – are very informative and available at the tourist office in Madaba.

For food, head about 500m back along the road to Madaba where there are a few restaurants including the recommended **Siyagha Restaurant** (☎ 3250226).

Moses Memorial Church The existence of the church was first reported by a Roman nun, Etheria, in about AD 393. This original church was quite modest with three apses and was only a fraction of the size of what you see today. One of the baptistry chapels with a mosaic was added in 530 and the main basilica was completed in 597. It was during this time that a large Byzantine monastery was built surrounding the church.

The Franciscan brothers bought the site in the 1930s, and excavated most of the ruins of the church and the monastery, as well as reconstructing much of the **basilica**, which is the site's main attraction. The huge mosaic on the floor is yet another quite remarkable work of patient artistry, with scenes of wine-making and hunting, and an assortment of animals, such as panthers, bears, foxes, ze-buses and lions. The mosaic measures about 9m by 3m, and is very well preserved as are the others dotted around the sanctuary.

There is little else to see around the complex except the ruins of part of the original monastery. From the **lookout** at the back (west) of the **courtyard**, the views across the valleys to the Dead Sea, Jericho and Jerusalem, just 46km away, are superb, but they're often concealed by the haze and pollution. A direction finder points you in the right direction. Nearby, a huge **bronze memorial** symbolises the suffering and

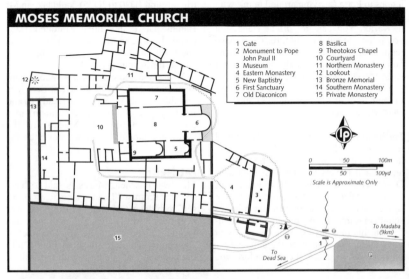

MOSES MEMORIAL CHURCH

1 Gate	8 Basilica
2 Monument to Pope	9 Theotokos Chapel
John Paul II	10 Courtyard
3 Museum	11 Northern Monastery
4 Eastern Monastery	12 Lookout
5 New Baptistry	13 Bronze Memorial
6 First Sanctuary	14 Southern Monastery
7 Old Diaconicon	15 Private Monastery

0   50   100m
0   50   100yd
Scale is Approximate Only

To Madaba
(9km)

To
Dead Sea

death of Jesus on the cross and the serpent that 'Moses lifted up'. There is also a **museum** between the entrance path and the church, but it had yet to open when we were there. It contains numerous artefacts from the Roman and Byzantine eras, including a mosaic cross.

Some of the complex is part of a functioning monastery and is, therefore, off-limits to visitors.

Getting There & Away From Madaba, minibuses (250 fils, 15 minutes) to South Shuneh leave from the bus/minibus station and pass right by the main gate of Mt Nebo.

A return trip in a private taxi from Madaba, with about 30 minutes to look around, shouldn't cost more than JD4 per vehicle.

Khirbat Mukhayyat خربة مخيط
Near the village of Khirbat Mukhayyat, the original site of Mt Nebo village, is the **Church of SS Lot and Procopius**, originally built in the late 6th century AD. Inside this unremarkable building is a remarkable **mosaic**, with representations of daily activities, such as agriculture and wine-making. The church is kept closed so you'll need to find the gatekeeper (who lives only a few hundred metres away) to open it for you – a 500 fils tip is appreciated.

On top of a nearby hill lie the obvious ruins of the **Church of St George**. Built in AD 536, very little of the church remains. The countryside is appealing and pleasant for short **hikes**.

The turn-off to Khirbat Mukhayyat is well signposted, about 3km to the left (south) before reaching the church complex at Mt Nebo. A good road leads into the village, but the road to the Church of SS Lot and Procopius is rough and steep. There is no regular public transport to the village or the churches and hitching requires patience. If you have chartered a taxi to Mt Nebo, pay a little more (around JD2 extra) for a side trip to Khirbat Mukhayyat.

Ayoun ('Ain) Musa عين موسى
Ayoun Musa ('Spring of Moses') is one of two places where the great man is believed to have obtained water by striking a rock – see the special section 'Biblical Jordan' in the Facts About Jordan chapter. There's little to see except low-lying **ruins** of a couple

of churches, but the countryside is charming and there are **hiking** opportunities.

The obvious turn-off to the right (north) is about 1km before the church at Mt Nebo and opposite some restaurants and souvenir shops. There is no public transport to the site, and hitching is almost impossible. A trip can be combined with a visit to Mt Nebo by chartered taxi, although the road to Ayoun Musa is often treacherous and taxi drivers are reluctant to go along this road unless given substantial financial incentive.

Hammamat Ma'in
☎ 05 حمامات معن (معن الزرقاء)
About 60 thermal springs have been discovered in the area south and west of Madaba. The therapeutic values of the most famous, Hammamat Ma'in, have been enjoyed by luminaries such as Herod the Great. The water is hot (at least 45°C), and contains potassium, magnesium and calcium, among other minerals.

Information The complex at Hammamat Ma'in was taken over by the French Mercure group in 2000 and the site has been redeveloped with a luxury hotel and spa centre. The gate to the complex (*admission JD7 per person, JD5 per vehicle; open 6am-midnight daily*) is on the road down from Madaba and is impossible to miss or avoid. While it's a lot to pay, the aim is to limit the number of visitors to preserve the fragile ecological balance of the valley. Day-trippers are welcome to use (free of charge after paying the entrance fee) the Roman baths, the family pool at the base of the waterfall closest to the entrance, and the swimming pool.

Visitors are not allowed to bring food and drink into the complex.

Springs, Pools and Baths There are two main baths open to the public. The Roman baths have clean indoor hot baths (separate for men and women) and are open as long as the gate is open (although you wouldn't want to drive back up the steep road to Madaba after dark).

There is also a small **family pool** beneath a **waterfall** which is one of the first signs to the right as you come down the hill from the gate. In general this pool is restricted to women, families or couples, although this is often not enforced. The water is over 60°C

HAMMAMAT MA'IN

1 Deserted Houses
2 Mosque
3 Mercure Ma'in Spa Resort; Shallal Restaurant
4 Public Swimming Pools, Restaurant & Bar (all in same complex)
5 Family Pool
6 The Chalets
7 Roman Baths
8 Small Snack Shop
9 Entrance (Ticket Gate)

To Ma'in (20km) & Madaba (27km)

Wadi Zarqa Ma'in

Approximate Scale

when it leaves its underground spring but is closer to 50°C by the time it tumbles down the rock. There is a small cave behind the cascading water.

There is also a large, clean cold-water **swimming pool** (not open October to April) that often closes around 4pm. There is a larger **waterfall** immediately to the right (north) of the hotel that is very picturesque, but visitors are discouraged from climbing up to it because the path can be treacherous.

Spa Complex Although it's part of the Mercure Resort, day-trippers and those staying at the chalets are welcome to pamper themselves in this very professionally run complex. Treatments include Dead Sea mud-wrapping, jet showers, hydrotherapy treatment, underwater jet massages, Jacuzzis, massages, hydrojet beds and beauty treatments. Most of the services last between 10 and 30 minutes and individually cost between JD8 and JD14 (beauty facials JD22 to JD30). Alternatively you can buy a two-day pass for JD60 and package deals are offered where you get four different treatments for between JD32 and JD35. There are both men and women among the highly trained staff. It's not cheap but is a wonderful splurge.

Hiking It used to be possible to hike from the springs down the steep gorge to Herodus Spring on the Dead Sea Highway. Such trails are now strictly controlled by the Mercure Resort, which charges for a guide and provisions (JD28 for two people including return car journey back to the springs). If you plan to do this, it's a good idea to phone ahead to make the necessary arrangements. There are other trails up the valley; ask at the resort for details and rates.

Places to Stay & Eat There are two options inside the complex, both of which are administered by the staff of the Mercure Hotel, although the chalets are not accredited to the French chain.

The **chalets** (☎ 3245500, fax 3245550; singles/doubles with bathroom JD24/35, day rates JD15/24) are next to the first waterfall and family pool, and are fairly uninspiring but the cheapest you'll get in Hammamat Ma'in.

Mercure Ma'in Spa Resort (☎ 3245500, fax 3245550; e H2174@accor-hotels.com; singles/doubles from US$132/149) has everything you'd want from a luxury spa resort with supremely comfortable rooms and a superb, tranquil setting. There is a private swimming pool overlooking the valley.

For meals, your only option is the **Shallal Restaurant** in the Mercure Resort, which looks out onto the main waterfall. Expect to pay at least JD5 for a meal and usually more. There are (sometimes) snacks and soft drinks available next to the Roman baths.

Getting There & Away Although just 4km from the Dead Sea Highway, the only access road is from Madaba, 27km to the northeast. If you're driving, the last stretch of road into Hammamat Ma'in is very scenic, but it's steep, so use a very low gear.

Bus/Minibus From Amman, the JETT bus company has buses (JD4.500 return, two hours) between Hammamat Ma'in and Amman on Friday. It is possible to leave Amman in the morning (8am), spend the day at the springs, and return on the 5pm bus back to the capital. Minibuses from Amman's Wahadat or Abdali stations only go as far as Ma'in.

From Madaba, minibuses regularly go to Ma'in village (200 fils, 15 minutes), but the driver will only go down the steep road to Hammamat Ma'in if there is sufficient demand or financial incentive from passengers. More likely, you'll have to hitch from Ma'in, and traffic is light. You might be able to get on the bus that ferries employees to the springs (around 7.30am) – ask your hotel or at the minibus station in Madaba for details.

Taxi A chartered private taxi from Madaba will cost about JD15 for a return journey, including around an hour's waiting time at the springs. Ask around the hotels in Madaba to see if you can share the cost of a taxi ride. Remember that if your taxi enters the gate (from where it's a 300m walk down the hill to the start of the complex), you'll have to fork out JD5 for the car to enter.

Hitching Hitching is easiest on Friday, although the springs can be uncomfortably crowded.

Mukawir (Machaerus)
☎ 05   مكور (ماشيروس)

Just beyond the village of Mukawir is the spectacular 700m-high hilltop perch of Machaerus, the castle of Herod the Great. The ruins themselves are of minor interest, but the setting is breathtaking and commands great **views** out over the impossibly steep surrounding hills and the Dead Sea. Most days you'll even have the place to yourself.

The hill was first fortified in about 100 BC, and expanded by Herod the Great in 30 BC. Machaerus is renowned as the place where John the Baptist was beheaded by Herod Antipas, the successor to Herod the Great – see the special section 'Biblical Jordan' in the Facts About Jordan chapter.

There is nowhere to stay in Mukawir and only a few basic grocery stores, so bring your own provisions.

Castle Machaerus is known to the locals as Qala'at al-Meshneq (Gallows Castle).

From the car park, a stone staircase leads down to the main path. Shortly after the path starts to climb, a small path leads around the main hill to the right. It leads past a number of **caves**, one of which is said to be where the gruesome execution took place, although it's not labelled. You take this path at your

peril as it's uneven, often covered with loose stones, narrow and it's hundreds of sheer metres to the valley floor below.

The main landscaped path is much safer (though quite steep in patches) and winds all the way up to the castle. At the top, the modest ruins are unlabelled. The reconstructed columns mark the site of Herod Antipas' **palace** and you should also be able to make out the low-lying remains of the **baths** and defensive **walls**. The reason to make the climb, however, is for some of the best views in Jordan, down plunging valleys to the Dead Sea and off in the distance to Jerusalem.

The castle is about 2km past the village and easy to spot.

Hiking This is a great area for hiking, with plenty of shepherds' trails snaking along the valley walls. One particularly worthwhile track leads steeply down the west side of the castle hill from the top and along a ridge line towards the Dead Sea. The views are magnificent. You must exercise extreme caution if taking any of these trails as the terrain falls steeply away and many paths are only for the surefooted. Women should also never hike alone. It's possible to follow the shepherds' trails (or the graded future road) down to the hot springs at Hammamat Ma'in (although remember that you may be hit for the entry fee of JD5 on arrival).

Bani Hamida Centre At the end of the village, and the start of the road to the castle, is a women's co-operative, the weaving centre and gallery run by the Bani Hamida Center (see the boxed text 'The Bani Hamida Story'). Visitors are always welcome to look around the small showroom (open 8am to 3pm Sunday to Thursday) where some of the fine woven products are on sale. The women who run it speak little English but are keen to help and show how the weaving is done. They also have a display video which shows many of the skills used by the women who work as part of the co-operative.

Getting There & Away From outside the bus/minibus station in Madaba, minibuses (350 fils, one hour) go to the village of Mukawir, via Libb, four or five times a day (the last around 5pm).

Unless you've chartered a taxi from Madaba, you'll probably need to walk the

The Bani Hamida Story

One of the several organisations in Jordan that sell handicrafts to fund local community development projects (see Shopping in the Facts for the Visitor chapter) is Bani Hamida, named after a group of people who settled in the remote village of Mukawir.

Created under the auspices of the Save the Children Fund, with the continuing assistance of the Canadian and US governments and now administered by the Jordan River Valley Foundation, the Weaving Project Center & Gallery was established in Mukawir. Its aims included reviving traditional weaving practices, raising money for the development of villages in the area and improving the independence of local women. The project now employs over 1500 women who work in the gallery at Mukawir, or at home in one of the 12 nearby villages.

Some of the items made and available for sale in Mukawir and the Jordan River Valley Foundation shop in Amman include pottery, baskets, jewellery, rugs, cushions and bags. Some of the items are created using traditional looms, and are coloured with natural dyes.

remaining 2km (downhill most of the way) to the castle. Otherwise, your minibus driver may, if you ask nicely and sweeten the request with a tip, take you the extra distance. Traffic between the castle car park and the village borders on the nonexistent. The best way to visit is in your own car, allowing you to take as long as you want to explore the surrounding hills and even pause for a picnic.

Umm ar-Rasas   أم الرصاص

Umm ar-Rasas is thought to be the village of Kastron Mefaa, mentioned in the Bible as a Roman military outpost.

A shed hangs over the ruins of the **Church of St Stephen** *(admission free; open daylight hours)*, one of four churches in the original village. Inside the shed are some marvellous **mosaics** dating back to about AD 785. The main mosaic clearly shows hunting, fishing and agriculture, scenes of daily life such as boys enjoying a boat ride, and the names of those who helped pay for the mosaic. The edges of the mosaic are particularly decorative.

If the shed is locked, ask around for the key *(miftah)* and/or caretaker.

Close by are the limited ruins of **Kastron Mefaa** village, none of which are labelled or signposted. About 1.5km north of the ruins is a 15m **stone tower**, the purpose of which baffles archaeologists because there are no stairs inside but several windows at the top.

Getting There & Away A few minibuses go directly to Umm ar-Rasas, via Nitil, from the bus/minibus station in Madaba. Alternatively, catch anything going to Dhiban, and hitch a ride from there. The best option is to charter a private taxi from the obvious turn-off at the roundabout in the middle of Dhiban, but the taxi drivers can demand as much as JD5/7 one way/return, including waiting time. Umm ar-Rasas is also accessible from the Desert Highway by private or chartered vehicle.

Inside the village, the shed and ruins are not signposted. The shed is about 400m behind the post office; take any path from either side of the post office. The post office is 500m north of a T-junction at the road between the King's and Desert Highways and the signposted road leading north to Nitil.

WADI MUJIB   وادي مجيب

Stretching across Jordan from the Desert Highway to the Dead Sea (covering a distance of over 70km) is the vast and beautiful Wadi Mujib, sometimes known as the 'Grand Canyon of Jordan'. Aside from being spectacular, it is also significant as the historic boundary between the ancient Amorites (to the north) and the Moabites (to the south), as mentioned in the Bible. Moses is also believed to have walked through the Wadi Mujib valley.

The valley, which is about 1km deep and over 4km from one edge to the other, is definitely worth seeing even if you don't intend going further south to Karak along the King's Highway. The bottom of the valley where the road cuts through is a huge construction site where a dam is being built with an expected completion date of 2006.

Wadi Mujib Reserve
حديقة وادي مجيب الوطنية

The Wadi Mujib valley is now part of the vast Wadi Mujib Reserve (215 sq km) which drops from an altitude of 900m above sea level to 400m below sea level. It was established by the Royal Society for the

Conservation of Nature (RSCN) for the captive breeding of the Nubian ibex (which will eventually be reintroduced into the wild). It's possible to visit the breeding centre with advance permission from the RSCN. The organisation is also seeking to stamp out illegal hunting by local Bedouin tribes. Overgrazing by goats and demands for licenses by mining companies are perennial threats to the valley's ecosystems.

Geological formations include limestone, basalt and sandstone, and the reserve supports a surprising variety of over 400 species of plants (including rare orchids), 186 species of birds and 250 animal species. The wildlife includes, apart from the Nubian ibex, the Syrian wolf, striped hyena, caracal and Blandford's fox. It is also a staging post for migratory birds travelling between Africa and Europe.

Hiking

All permits for hiking and camping must be prearranged with the RSCN in Amman – see National Parks in the Facts About Jordan chapter for details. There is no access into the reserve without a permit.

The RSCN, which was expected to open a visitor centre at the Wadi Mujib Reserve in mid-2003, allows hiking along only three trails in the reserve. These are:

Mujib Circuit Trail (five to six hours) – from 3km south of the Mujib Bridge, a difficult trail leads up into the reserve ending in the Mujib Gorge with good chances of seeing wildlife

Mujib Lower Trail (one to two hours) – from Mujib Bridge, you pass interesting geological formations and swimming opportunities

Wadi Mujib Trail (eight to nine hours, 18km) – this challenging but rewarding trail leads through the mountains from the King's Highway to the Dead Sea

Compulsory guides are available from the RSCN, but the region is extremely hot and dry in summer, so avoid hiking then.

Places to Stay

With permission from the RSCN, camping is allowed at **Wadi Mujib Campsite**, near the King's Highway, and **Radas Campsite**, closer to the Dead Sea Highway. The campsites are only open in summer (1 April to 15 October) and access costs around JD10 per person per night.

A Stele at Twice the Price

The original Mesha Stele was found by a missionary at Dhiban in 1868. It was a major discovery because it not only provided historical detail of the battles between the Moabites and the kings of Israel, but was also the earliest example of Hebrew script to be unearthed. After surviving intact from about 850 BC (when it was raised by King Mesha of Moab to let everyone know of his successes against Israel) to AD 1868, it came to a rather unfortunate end.

After finding the stele, the missionary reported it to Charles Clermont-Ganneau at the French consulate in Jerusalem who then saw it, made a mould of it and went back to Jerusalem to raise the money which he had offered the locals for it. While he was away, the local families argued over who was going to get the money and some of the discontented lit a fire under the stone and then poured water over it, causing it to shatter. Although most pieces were recovered, inevitably some were lost. The remnants were gathered together and shipped off to France, and the reconstructed stone is now on display in the Louvre in Paris. Copies can be seen in the museums at Amman, Madaba and Karak.

Dhiban ضبان

Dhiban is the last town you'll pass through (if coming from the north) before you begin the descent down into Wadi Mujib. Once the powerful town of Dibon, the capital of an empire carved out by King Mesha in the 9th century BC, Dhiban is where the Mesha Stele was discovered. There is nothing left of the ancient city, but the small, friendly village is still an important junction for transport to Umm ar-Rasas and Ariha; it has a few dismal **eateries**.

About 3km down (south) from Dhiban is an awesome **lookout** over Wadi Mujib. To admire the views without crossing the valley, walk (or charter a taxi) to the lookout from Dhiban.

Ariha أريحا
☎ 03

This is the first village you'll reach as you climb up the southern wall of Wadi Mujib, although the village is about 2.5km beyond the top of the climb on the road to Karak.

At the point where you'll start to breathe easy after negotiating the perilous climb, you'll see the strategically placed **Trajan Rest House** (☎ 2310295; *bed in shared room JD3*), which is also signed as 'Trajan Restaurant'. The restaurant only serves open buffets for tour groups but you can get hot and cold drinks and breakfast here. The accommodation is basic and has curtains for doors. It's a good place to hitch a ride down into the valley.

Getting There & Away
Dhiban is where almost all transport south of Madaba stops. At the moment, the only way to cross the mighty Wadi Mujib from Dhiban to Ariha (about 30km) is to charter a taxi for JD5/10 return. Finding a taxi in Ariha is a lot harder. Bargain hard and be wary of drivers claiming extra payment for cleaning the car afterwards. Hitching is possible, but expect a long wait; make sure your ride doesn't end at the construction site at the bottom of the valley.

If you're travelling in your own car, the sealed road down the north wall of the valley is excellent and easy to negotiate. The steep road up the north side has a number of switchbacks and requires strong nerves and plenty of concentration and patience. The surface has deteriorated (loose stones abound) and you'll share the road with heavy trucks going to and from the construction site. Use as low a gear as possible.

KARAK الكرك
☎ 03
The ancient Crusader stronghold of Karak is 900m above sea level, and lies within the walls of the old city. The fortified castle that dominates the town was a place of legend in the battles between the Crusaders or Franks and the Islamic armies of Saladin (Salah ad-Din). Now among the most famous, the castle at Karak was just one in a long line built by the Crusaders stretching from Aqaba in the south to Turkey in the north.

Often ignored by travellers speeding south towards Wadi Rum, Petra and Aqaba, Karak is worth the effort to get here.

History
Karak lies on the route that ancient caravans travelled from Egypt to Syria in the time of the biblical kings, and was also used by the Greeks and Romans. The city is mentioned several times in the Bible as Kir, Kir Moab and Kir Heres, and later emerges as a Roman provincial town, Characmoba. The city also features on the famous mosaic in St George's Church in Madaba.

The arrival of the Crusaders launched the city back into prominence and the Crusader king Baldwin I of Jerusalem had the castle built in AD 1142. Even today, its commanding position and strategic value are obvious and it also stands midway between Shobak and Jerusalem. It became the capital of the Crusader district of Oultrejourdain and, with the taxes levied on passing caravans and food grown in the district, helped Jerusalem prosper.

The castle was passed on to the de Milly family and through marriage fell into the hands of Renauld de Chatillon who delighted in torturing prisoners and throwing them off the walls into the valley 450m below; he even went to the trouble of having a wooden box fastened over their heads so they wouldn't lose consciousness before hitting the ground. Hated by Saladin for his treachery, de Chatillon had arrived from France in 1148 to take part in the Crusades and from Karak he was able to control the trade routes to Egypt and Mecca, thereby severely disrupting the supply lines of the Islamic armies.

A Chivalrous Siege

In the winter of AD 1183, a gathering of all the important Frankish (Crusader) nobles took place in Karak. They came to celebrate a carefully choreographed wedding, organised as a means of reconciling quarrelling Frankish factions. Saladin, the leader of the Islamic armies, seized on the opportunity and captured the town but met stiffer resistance at the castle. With the assault under way, legend has it that the wedding celebrations within continued unabated. Lady Stephanie, the heiress of Karak, sent out some of the wedding dishes for Saladin. Saladin in turn asked in which section of the castle the young couple were celebrating their wedding night and ordered that this part of the castle was not to be bombarded – a symbol of the chivalry that characterised many of the battles at the time. Saladin's armies withdrew when Frankish reinforcements were sent from across the hills from Jerusalem.

Wadi Mujib

Bronze Memorial, Mt Nebo

King's Highway, Wadi Mujib

Mosaic, Madaba

Crusader castle, Karak

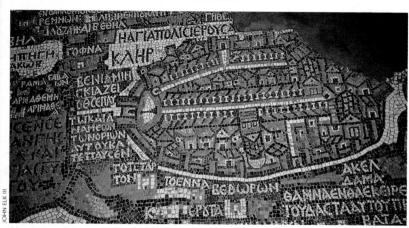

Mosaic map, St George's Church, Madaba

Moses Memorial Church, Mt Nebo

Mosaic, Madaba

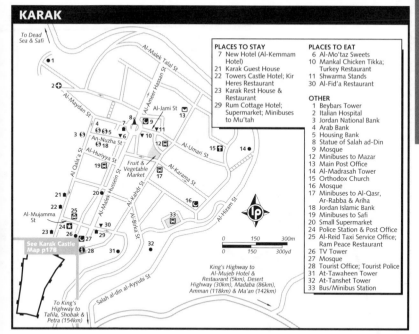

KARAK

To Dead
Sea & Safi

Al-Malek Talal St

Al-Amrer Hassan St

Al-Jami St

Al-Maydan St

An-Nuzha St

Al-Huriyya St

Al-Qala'a St

Al-Malek Hussein St

Al-Kahdr St

Al-Birka St

Al-Umari St

Al-Karama St

Al-Hizam St

Al-Mujamma St

Fruit & Vegetable Market

See Karak Castle Map p178

King's Highway to Tafila, Shobak & Petra (154km)

Salah al-din al-Ayyubi St

King's Highway to
Al-Mujeb Hotel &
Restaurant (5km), Desert
Highway (30km), Madaba (86km),
Amman (118km) & Ma'an (142km)

0   150   300m
0   150   300yd

PLACES TO STAY
7 New Hotel (Al-Kemmam Hotel)
21 Karak Guest House
22 Towers Castle Hotel; Kir Heres Restaurant
23 Karak Rest House & Restaurant
29 Rum Cottage Hotel; Supermarket; Minibuses to Mu'tah

PLACES TO EAT
6 Al-Mo'taz Sweets
10 Mankal Chicken Tikka; Turkey Restaurant
11 Shwarma Stands
30 Al-Fid'a Restaurant

OTHER
1 Beybars Tower
2 Italian Hospital
3 Jordan National Bank
4 Arab Bank
5 Housing Bank
8 Statue of Salah ad-Din
9 Mosque
12 Minibuses to Mazar
13 Main Post Office
14 Al-Madrasah Tower
15 Orthodox Church
16 Mosque
17 Minibuses to Al-Qasr, Ar-Rabba & Ariha
18 Jordan Islamic Bank
19 Minibuses to Safi
20 Small Supermarket
24 Police Station & Post Office
25 Al-Reid Taxi Service Office; Ram Peace Restaurant
26 TV Tower
27 Mosque
28 Tourist Office; Tourist Police
31 At-Tawaheen Tower
32 At-Tanshet Tower
33 Bus/Minibus Station

De Chatillon was later executed for thievery, and the castle finally fell to the armies of Saladin (the Ayyubids) after an eight-month siege dubbed the Battle of Hattin in 1188.

The Mamluk sultan Beybars strengthened the fortress, deepened the moat and added the lower courtyard in the 13th century, but three towers collapsed in an earthquake in AD 1293. Little more is known of the castle until the 1880s, when local fighting compelled the Christians of Karak to flee north to Madaba and Ma'in; peace was only restored after thousands of Turkish troops were stationed in the town.

Orientation & Information

The old city of Karak is easy to get around, although none of the streets are signposted. If you get disoriented, use the huge TV tower near the castle as a landmark. The modern town centre is around the statue of Saladin. The area near the entrance to the castle has recently been redeveloped and it's in the surrounding streets that you'll find most of the hotels and restaurants.

The new **tourist office** (☎ 2351150, fax 2354263; open 8am-3pm Sat-Thur) is of lim-

ited use and overlooks the eastern wall of the castle. It can be reached either from the castle gate or from the small road running south from Al-Mujamma St. As part of the same complex and about 75m to the east, a new **visitor centre** was nearing completion when we visited.

If you need to change money, look no further than An-Nuzha St, a small block south of the Saladin roundabout. There are at least four banks that change money, and most have an ATM for Visa and MasterCard.

The **tourist police** (☎ 191) have an office next door to the tourist office. The well-equipped **Italian Hospital** is on Al-Maydan St. The main **post office** is along Al-Khadr St in the lower (northern) part of town.

Karak Castle

Information The gate to the castle (admission low/high season 500 fils/JD1; open 8am-5.30pm daily) is reached from the western end of Al-Mujamma St and past the Karak Rest House. Even if you're not staying at the Rest House, it's worth stopping by the lobby where there's an impressive relief display of the castle as it stood in its original form.

KARAK CASTLE

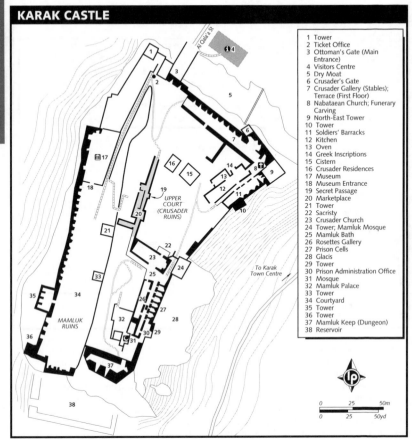

1 Tower
2 Ticket Office
3 Ottoman's Gate (Main Entrance)
4 Visitors Centre
5 Dry Moat
6 Crusader's Gate
7 Crusader Gallery (Stables); Terrace (First Floor)
8 Nabataean Church; Funerary Carving
9 North-East Tower
10 Tower
11 Soldiers' Barracks
12 Kitchen
13 Oven
14 Greek Inscriptions
15 Cistern
16 Crusader Residences
17 Museum
18 Museum Entrance
19 Secret Passage
20 Marketplace
21 Tower
22 Sacristy
23 Crusader Church
24 Tower; Mamluk Mosque
25 Mamluk Bath
26 Rosettes Gallery
27 Prison Cells
28 Glacis
29 Tower
30 Prison Administration Office
31 Mosque
32 Mamluk Palace
33 Tower
34 Courtyard
35 Tower
36 Tower
37 Mamluk Keep (Dungeon)
38 Reservoir

UPPER COURT (CRUSADER RUINS)

MAMLUK RUINS

To Karak Town Centre

0   25   50m
0   25   50yd

Throughout the castle are informative display boards with detailed descriptions of the history and function of each structure. It's worth bringing a torch (flashlight) to explore the darker regions, and some doorways are quite low so watch your head. Reconstruction and excavation work within the castle is ongoing and the museum was being redeveloped when we visited.

Things to See The main entrance, known as **Ottoman's Gate**, is at the end of a short bridge over the dry moat. The old entrance or **Crusader's Gate** was once reached via a wooden bridge, 50m to the east, but has not yet been opened to the public.

From Ottoman's Gate, head past the **ticket office** and take the path leading up to the left.

Resist the temptation to head into the vaulted corridor straight ahead and instead follow the path that leads hard left (north). The long chamber you enter to the right is known as the **Crusader Gallery** or **stables**.

Near the far end of the gallery, you can see down to the Crusader's Gate through an opening in the wall. Those entering the castle did so via a narrow winding passage (separated from the Crusader Gallery by a wall). This is typical of Crusader castles, ensuring the entrance could be easily defended as it was not possible to enter the castle in large numbers. Where the passage enters the end of the gallery is an area sometimes known as the **Nabataean Church**. On the north wall, is a (now headless) **carved figure** which local legend claims to be Saladin, but which actually dates from the 2nd century AD and is believed by scholars to be a Nabataean funerary carving. A small staircase leads up to the site of the **northeast tower**; watch your step.

From the carving, a long passageway leads southwest. Along the left side were the **soldier's barracks** with small holes for light, walls of limestone and straw and a few Byzantine **rock inscriptions** on the walls. Across the corridor is the **kitchen**, which contains large round stones used for grinding olives and huge storage areas for oil and wheat. In a dark tunnel (only visible with a torch) are some **Greek inscriptions** of unknown meaning. A door from the kitchen leads to the right (west) to the huge **oven**.

Continuing southwest along the main passage, you leave the cool, covered area and emerge into the light. Down to the left is the plunging **glacis**, the dizzyingly steep rocky slope that prevented invaders from climbing up to the castle and prisoners from climbing down. This is where Renauld de Chatillon also delighted in expelling undesirables (see History earlier in this chapter).

If you turn hard right (west then northwest), you'll enter the overgrown **upper court**, which has a large **cistern** and the largely unexcavated remains of what are believed to have been the domestic **residences** of the castle. At the northern end of the castle is the **terrace**, directly above the Crusader Gallery, which affords fine views over the castle and down to the moat. Above the far (southern) end of the castle rises **Umm al-Thallaja** (Hill of Snows), which posed the greatest threat to the castle's defences during times of siege. To the west is the village of **Al-Shabiya**, which was once called Al-Ifranj because many Crusaders (Franks) settled here after the fall of the castle.

Returning to where you emerged from the long corridor, head southwest. On the left is a **tower** and what is believed to have been a **Mamluk mosque**. On the right is the castle's main **Crusader church** with a **sacristy** down the stairs to the right (north). Note how in this lowered room there are arrow slits in the walls suggesting that this originally formed part of the castle's outer wall.

If you continue to the southern end of the castle, you'll find yourself in front of the impressive, reconstructed **Mamluk keep**. Because it faces Umm al-Thallaja, it was

here that the defences were strongest, with arrow slits on all four levels and a crenellated section at the top. The keep was built from 1260 by the Mamluk sultan Beybars.

From the keep walk northwest, around to the stairs which lead down to the **Mamluk palace**, which was built for Sultan al-Nasir Muhammad in 1311 using earlier Crusader materials. The **reception hall** is a variation of the classic Islamic design of four *iwans* or chambers off the main hall; on two sides are barrel-vaulted rooms. On the west side was the **mosque**, which was probably restricted to palace notables, with the clearly visible mihrab facing Mecca.

Before continuing, pause near the top of the stairs for some good **views** down Wadi Karak, towards what is believed to be the site of the condemned cities of Sodom and Gomorrah (see the boxed text 'In Search of Sodom' later in this chapter). Return to the main Crusader church; immediately south some stairs lead down. Two corridors run off to the southwest. The left (east) corridor leads past seven **prison cells** and at the southern end was the **prison administration office**. The right (west) passage leads from the foot of the stairs through the **Rosettes Gallery**, named after the carved rosette at the foot of the stairs.

If you're game, take the third passage, which is very dark and leads northwest, roughly underneath the church. The corridor turns right (north) and you emerge into the better-lit areas of the delightful **marketplace** with various **shops** and **cellars** feeding off it. In one of the rooms to the right (east), but only visible with a torch, is believed to be an unexcavated **secret passage** used during sieges to reach a room full of food and water.

At the northern end of the market, the path leads back to the entrance (also the exit) or you can detour to the southwest down the hill to the **Mamluk ruins** which were being extensively reconstructed when we were there.

Places to Stay

New Hotel (☎ 2351942; Al-Maydan St; bed in shared room JD2), also known as Al-Kemmam Hotel, is the cheapest place and the only one in the modern town centre. Guests can use the kitchen and the shared bathrooms aren't bad.

Rum Cottage Hotel (☎ 2351351, fax 235 3789; Al-Mujamma St; singles/doubles with bath JD5/10) isn't bad value, with reasonable rooms, although they can be noisy and the hot water is patchy. Breakfast costs an extra JD2.500 per person.

Towers Castle Hotel (☎ 0795 470800, fax 2354293; Al-Qala'a St; singles/doubles with shared bath JD10/12, with private bath JD12/16) is quieter and the rooms are large, bright and clean. Prices include breakfast.

Karak Rest House (☎ 2351148, fax 235 3148; Al-Qala'a St; singles/doubles/triples with bath & breakfast 15 Feb-15 May JD18/30/37, other times JD15/25/30) is next to the main entrance of the castle. Most of the good rooms have outstanding views, as well as a minibar and clean bathroom.

Karak Guest House (☎ 2355564; Al-Qala'a St; singles/doubles with bath, breakfast & dinner JD15/24) is run by the Rest House and is similarly good value with the same facilities and views.

Al-Mujeb Hotel (☎ 2386090, fax 238 6091; King's Highway; singles/doubles with bath & breakfast JD20/30) has the best rooms in Karak with satellite TV and fridge and staff are attentive. It is, however, a long way (around 6km) from the castle and is inconvenient without your own vehicle.

Places to Eat

Most restaurants are near the castle on Al-Mujamma St or near the statue of Saladin in the modern town.

Ram Peace Restaurant (☎ 0795 470800; Al-Mujamma St; mains JD1.500-3; open 8am-10pm daily), next to Al-Reid Taxi Service office, is friendly but the local food is better than the Western variations.

Al-Fid'a Restaurant (Al-Mujamma St; meals JD3; open 8am-midnight daily) is a popular place and excellent value with main course, dips and salad for a decent price. The service is good and the atmosphere pleasant.

Karak Rest House (see Places to Stay; meals JD6; open noon-4pm & 7pm-11pm daily) has a nice restaurant with reasonable food and superb views down Wadi Karak.

Kir Heres Restaurant (☎ 0795 640264, fax 2355595; Al-Qala'a St; starters JD1-2.500, mains JD4.850-6.250; open 9am-10pm daily), in the same building as the Towers Castle

Hotel, is a welcome addition to the Karak culinary scene. Though expensive, it has good food and service and a pleasant ambience. Dishes include pepper steak (JD6.250) and come with salad and vegetables.

Mankal Chicken Tikka (☎ 2351500; Al-Umari St; starters from 300 fils, mains JD1.500; open 10am-10pm daily) has a limited menu of Indian food; the dining area is a bit claustrophobic.

Turkey Restaurant (☎ 0795 730431; Al-Umari St; mains JD1.500; open 7am-9.30pm daily), next door, does roast chicken and hummus among other standard local fare.

Al-Mujeb Hotel (see Places to Stay; meals from JD5; open noon-10pm daily) is good if you're staying at the hotel, but a bit far away otherwise.

Al-Mo'taz Sweets (☎ 2353388; An-Nuzha St; open 8am-10pm daily) is one of the better places in town for those with a sweet tooth, serving a range of pastries and sweets.

There are some cheap shwarma stands in the streets around the statue of Salah ad-Din, particularly east along Al-Umari St.

Getting There & Away

As with anywhere along the King's Highway, Karak can be difficult but not impossible to reach by public transport – see the relevant section of the Amman chapter, and Madaba section earlier in this chapter.

The bus/minibus station is in the lower, southeastern part of the old city, and the entrance is at a T-junction opposite a mosque.

Minibus From the bus/minibus station in Karak, minibuses go to Amman's Wahadat station (850 fils, two hours) via the Desert Highway on a semiregular basis. Minibuses also run every hour or so along the King's Highway from Karak to Tafila (700 fils, 1½ hours), the best place for connections to Qadsiyya (for Dana Nature Reserve) and Shobak. To Wadi Musa (for Petra), take a minibus to Ma'an (JD1.350, two hours), which leaves three times a day (around 7am and either side of lunchtime) and travels via the Desert Highway. Minibuses to Aqaba (JD1.850, three hours) travel via the Dead Sea Highway about four times a day.

Minibuses along the King's Highway to Al-Qasr, Ar-Rabba, Ariha, Mu'tah and to Safi on the Dead Sea Highway depart from various places in town (as indicated on the map). At the time of research, however, many of Karak's roads were being resurfaced and these departure points had changed temporarily. Check at the tourist office, your hotel or the minibus station for the current locations.

Chartered Taxi From Amman it's possible (with considerable bargaining) to charter a taxi all the way to Karak via the Desert Highway for about JD18 one way. From Amman via the King's Highway, with a few stops in Wadi Mujib and Madaba, expect to pay at least JD22.

From Karak, taxi fares are higher. There is only one taxi company, **Al-Reid Taxi Service** (☎ 2352297) on Al-Mujamma St, making negotiating difficult. Quoted one-way prices include Amman (JD30), Petra (JD40) and Madaba (JD25).

Getting Around
The old city of Karak consists of narrow one-way streets, which are usually congested with traffic and often devoid of taxis. If you're driving, study the map carefully to make sure that you negotiate the one-way system without too many arguments.

AROUND KARAK
Dead Sea البحر الميت
Regular minibuses from Karak go to the phosphate-mining town of Safi, from where it's about a 3km walk to a stretch of water.

Lot's Cave كهف لوط
One of the few places to visit along the southwestern side of Jordan is Lot's Cave where Lot and his daughters took refuge (see the special section 'Biblical Jordan' in the Facts About Jordan chapter and the boxed text 'In Search of Sodom' for more details). The cave is on top of a hill offering views of the Dead Sea, and nearby there's a small Byzantine church and what is purported to be the 'pillar of salt' referred to in the Bible.

The site is signposted from the Dead Sea Highway, and private or chartered vehicles can drive almost to the cave. If you're relying on public transport or hitching, be prepared for a long (3km) steep and hot walk up the hill from the highway. Ask at the building at the start of the road (1km east of the highway), because staff may be able to find you a vehicle to the top.

In Search of Sodom

There's nothing new in the assumption that the world's naughtiest town lay somewhere around the southern end of the Dead Sea, but a team of British geologists believe that they have found the key to its precise location. An area of the Dead Sea close to the modern town of Safi produced bitumen, a saleable item in those days and probably the 'slime pits' referred to in the Old Testament. The geologists think Sodom, and neighbouring Gomorrah, could not have been far away, since the inhabitants would have made their money from the bitumen. If they're right, the site has been under water off the east bank of the sea since biblical times.

The Book of Genesis outlines God's displeasure at the locals' behaviour, and so 'the Lord rained upon Sodom and upon Gomorrah brimstone and fire...and he overthrew those cities, and all the plain, and all the inhabitants of the cities, and that which grew upon the ground...' Fanciful legends of a fevered biblical imagination? Not necessarily. The whole area is located on a fault line, and it would not have been the first time that such a zone has been simply swallowed up when the ground collapsed in a kind of massive implosion, also known as 'liquefaction', or collapse of the soil. The observer reporting for the Book of Genesis may well have been describing a terrible natural disaster, although whether it was caused by the wrath of God cannot be scientifically proven.

Ar-Rabba عرابه
The holy and historical city of Ar-Rabba came under the rule of King Mesha (9th century BC), and Alexander the Great (mid-4th century BC) as well as the Nabataeans (from the 2nd century BC to the 2nd century AD).

At the northern end of the small town are the **ruins** of a Roman temple, with two niches that contained statues of the Roman emperors Diocletian and Maximian, and other Roman and Byzantine buildings. None of the ruins are signposted or labelled in any language.

The ruins are permanently open, free to enter and located to the east of the main road. Ar-Rabba is easily accessible by minibus from Karak.

Mu'tah مؤته
☎ 03

Mu'tah is a nondescript town that boasts one of the best and most popular universities in Jordan. **Mu'tah University** is near the King's Highway, which detours around the university and continues on to Tafila.

Mu'tah is also famous as the location of a battle in AD 632 (some historians say 629), when Byzantine forces defeated the Muslims (who turned the tables four years later). At the main junction in the south of Mu'tah, you'll find a **monument** that commemorates the battle. Along the main road through town on a roundabout, there is also an impressive **mosque** complex containing the **tombs** of some of the Prophet Mohammed's companions. These tombs are often visited by pilgrims.

Getting There & Away Minibuses regularly link Karak with Mu'tah. From Madaba, try the daily university minibus (JD1.500, two hours) from the main bus/minibus station, which travels via the Desert Highway. Be aware, however, that it often doesn't operate during the university holidays so check the day before you want to travel.

HAMMAMAT BURBITA & HAMMAMAT AFRA
حمامات عفرا / حمامات بربيتا

Hammamat Burbita and Hammamat Afra are two thermal hot springs near Wadi Hasa, but the springs and baths at Hammamat Ma'in, not far from Madaba, are better (although they're more expensive). Women are likely to feel uncomfortable at these two hot springs if local men are around in any numbers.

The two springs are signposted about 23km north of Tafila; from the turn-off it's about 13km to Burbita, a green patch at the base of a wadi with a small uninviting rock pool and makeshift galvanised iron roof. Another 6km further on, the road ends at Hammamat Afra, a more beautiful spot favoured by Jordanians on Friday.

There is no public transport to either spot. If you're driving, signposting is confusing and you'll need to ask directions along the way. A chartered taxi from Tafila to Afra will cost around JD12 return, including waiting time.

TAFILA الطفيله
☎ 03

Tafila is a busy market centre and transport junction. There is nothing to see, except the very decrepit ruins of a **Crusader castle**, which is sometimes closed to visitors. It was in Tafila that one of the Prophet Mohammed's emissaries was beheaded, leading to the military conquest by the Islamic armies from AD 632.

Places to Stay & Eat
Afra Hotel *(singles/doubles with shared bath JD5/7)* is the only place to stay and is very drab.

Plenty of cheap places sell felafel and shwarma around town. **Adom Resthouse**, at the southern end of Tafila on the highway to Dana Nature Reserve, is about the best place to eat (around JD4 per person).

Getting There & Away
Minibuses from Karak (500 fils, one hour) go along a back route off the King's Highway, and cross Wadi Hasa which has some superb scenery. There are also direct minibuses to/from Wahadat station in Amman (JD1, 2½ hours) via the Desert Highway; Aqaba (JD1.200, 2½ hours) via the Dead Sea Highway; Ma'an (JD1, one hour) via the Desert Highway; and just down the King's Highway to Shobak and Qadsiyya (for Dana Nature Reserve; 350 fils, 30 minutes).

DANA NATURE RESERVE
☎ 03 حديقة دانا الطبيعية

Dana Nature Reserve (also signed as Dana Wildlife Reserve) is one of Jordan's hidden gems. It also represents an impressive eco-tourism project. Most of the reserve is only accessible on foot. Down off the King's Highway, and the main entrance to the reserve, is the charming 15th-century stone village of **Dana**, which clings to a precipice overlooking the valley and commands exceptional views. It's a great place to spend a few days hiking and relaxing.

The reserve includes a variety of terrain, including peaks over 1500m high and the sandstone cliffs of Wadi Dana which lead to the Dead Sea about 14km to the west. The escarpments and valleys protect a surprisingly diverse ecosystem, including about 600 species of plants (from citrus trees and desert shrubs to tropical acacias), about 200 species of birds, and over 40 species of mammals (of which 25 are endangered), including ibex, mountain gazelle, sand cat, red fox and wolf.

There are almost 100 archaeological sites at the reserve. Of most interest to archaeologists are the ruins of **Khirbat Finan**, copper mines mentioned in the Bible and dating back to at least the 4th century BC. For other visitors, there's little to see except the ruins of a few bridges, churches, cemeteries and hundreds of caves where the copper was mined. The hills still contain copper, but despite intense lobbying from mining companies, the Jordanian government has agreed not to allow mining in the reserve.

The reserve was taken over by the RSCN in 1993 and was the first of its kind in Jordan – an attempt to promote ecotourism, protect wildlife and improve the lives of local villagers all at once. The reserve directly or indirectly employs over 40 locals, and income from tourism has helped to develop Dana village and provide education about environmental issues in local schools. Villagers also make excellent local crafts that are sold by the RSCN under the brand name Wadi Dana. The items are available at the RSCN shops in Dana, Amman and Azraq.

Information

The **visitor centre** (☎ 2270497, fax 2270499; **e** dhana@rscn.org.jo, **w** www.rscn.org.jo; open 8am-8pm daily) is in the guest house complex in Dana village. The centre includes an RSCN shop, craft workshops and a food drying centre for making organic food. It is also the place to book accommodation (see Places to Stay) as well as obtain further information about the reserve, its hiking trails and arrange a guide (JD33.900 for a full day). The staff at the centre are knowledgeable, enthusiastic and friendly, and you sense a genuine commitment to the cause.

Hiking

There are at least 15 trails for exploring the area. The visitor centre has explanations and (usually) maps for each hike; some require a guide. For all hiking in the area you must register at the visitor centre where they'll tell you if a guide is required. The main trail down to the Finan campsite and on to the Dead Sea doesn't require a guide. The major, longer trails on offer include:

Rummam Campground to Dana village (three hours) – takes you past dramatic wadi escarpments and through terraced gardens

Dana to Finan (14km, four to five hours) – the most popular trail, it takes you downhill all the way (although it's uphill on the way back) with the magnificent scenery of Wadi Dana along the way

Finan to Barra via Wadi Hamra (16km, six to eight hours) – a challenging uphill trail, passing an oasis with hot spring en route

Finan to Shobak (two days) – takes you past ancient copper mines and includes an ascent through the beautiful Wadi Ghuweir

Finan to Petra (three days) – follows the trail to Shobak and continues on to Petra

If you book in advance, it's also possible to arrange guided theme tours, which include the Bedouin Tour, as well as walks based around the copper mines, archaeological sites, local crafts and birdwatching.

Places to Stay & Eat

There are two campsites run by the RSCN and bookings should be made in advance. They're expensive (rates decrease if there is more than one person) but wonderful places to camp.

Rummam Campground (per person JD18.540) can be reached via a turn-off on the King's Highway around 5km north of Qadsiyya.

Finan Campground (per person JD18.540) on the valley floor was closed when we visited because the RSCN had plans to build a new 'eco-lodge' on the site. It was expected to open in autumn 2003 – check at the visitor centre. The campground is only accessible on foot or by 4WD (with permission from the RSCN).

There are also three small hotels in Dana village that should suit most budgets.

Dana Tower Hotel (**e** dana_tower2@hot mail.com; singles/doubles JD5/10) occupies a prime location although they don't seem to have made best use of the splendid views. That said, it's a welcoming place and the rustic rooms are well kept. Meals are available for JD3 per person.

Sons of Dana and Al-Qadisiyya Cooperative for Tourism (☎ 2270537; **e** sdq@nets .com.jo; singles/doubles with breakfast JD8/ 16) also has very tidy rooms and is another friendly, well-run place. Meals cost JD4 per person.

Dana Guest House (☎ 2270497, fax 227 0499; e dhana@rscn.org.jo; doubles without balcony JD25.750, doubles/triples with balcony JD36.050/46.350, single occupancy JD25.750) is highly recommended and fantastic value if you can afford it. The rooms are very comfortable and those with balcony have breathtaking views. A great place for a splurge.

Getting There & Away

The easiest way to get here by public transport is from Tafila. Minibuses run reasonably often throughout the day from Tafila to Qadsiyya (350 fils, 30 minutes). The turn-off to Dana village (the faded sign simply says 'Dana Hotel') is just north of Qadsiyya; from here it's a 2.5km (downhill) walk to Dana village. If you hitch, be prepared to wait. If you're chartering a taxi in Karak, expect to pay around JD15 one way. From Ma'an to the south, an irregular minibus (700 fils, 1½ hours) should go to Qadsiyya en route to Tafila, but check before boarding.

If you're driving from Tafila or Karak, the first signpost you'll see off to the right (west) only goes to the Rummam Campground – it's better to continue on to the turn-off just before Qadsiyya.

SHOBAK   شوبك

Shobak Castle is another renowned Crusader fortress. Because it's some distance from the nearest town, it has more of a lonely sentinel aspect than Karak, and perhaps for this reason some readers prefer it to the more frequented Karak Castle.

History & Information

Shobak, formerly called Mons Realis (Montreal), was built by the Crusader king Baldwin I in AD 1115. It withstood numerous attacks from the armies of Saladin before succumbing in 1189. It was later occupied in the 14th century by the Mamluks, who built over many of the Crusader buildings.

Built on a small knoll right at the edge of a plateau and overlooking a number of wadis, the castle (admission free; open daylight hours) is especially imposing when seen from a distance. Restoration work is ongoing and hopefully this will include some signs explaining the castle's various elements. In the meantime, the old caretaker (who lives on the site) shows visitors around (a tip is appreciated) and he does remarkably well with just a few words of English. The castle is best visited in a clockwise direction and it's a good idea to bring a torch (flashlight) for exploring the castle's many dark corners.

Shobak Castle

As you climb up from the entrance, there are some **wells** on the left. Soon after passing these, you'll see the reconstructed **church**, one of two in the castle, down to the left (south). It has an elegant apse supported by two smaller alcoves. The room leading off to the west was the **baptistry**; on the north wall there are traces of water channels leading from above.

Returning back to the main path, turn left (west). After you pass under the arches, a door leads you right (north) into the extensive **market**. If you take the path to the left of the door, some 365 steps lead down into a **secret passageway** to a **well** – especially useful during sieges; tread carefully and use a torch. Heading west, after about 50m you pass a large two-storey building with archways, built by the Crusaders but adapted by the Mamluks as a **school**.

At the northern end of the castle is the semicircular **keep** with four arrow slits for defending the castle. Outside and to the east, dark steps lead down to the **prison**. If heading to the northeast corner of the castle, you can see **Quranic inscriptions**, possibly dating from the time of Saladin, carved in Kufic script around the outside of the keep. Heading south along the eastern perimeter, you'll soon pass the entrance to the **court of Baldwin I**, which has been partly reconstructed; see if you can tell which of the stones are originals. At the south end of the court is an alcove where Renauld de Chatillon was executed. The court was later used as a **Mamluk school**.

Continuing south, you'll pass some **baths** on the right (west). Off to the east (east) is a reconstructed **Mamluk watchtower**. Just past the tower is the second **church**. On a room to the left (north) as you enter, you can see above a door in the east wall a weathered carving of a **Crusader cross**. In the church proper, the arches have been reconstructed and from here you can see more **Kufic inscriptions** on the wall of the watchtower.

Beneath the church are the **catacombs**, which contain more Islamic tablets, some

Christian carvings, large spherical rocks used in catapults and what is said to be Saladin's very simple throne. From the catacombs, the path leads back down to the gate.

Hiking
Although they're not marked, trails head south from Shobak through the hills, past ancient stands of oak to Siq Barid (Little Petra). It is also possible to hike between Shobak and Dana Nature Reserve (see the Dana section earlier in this chapter for details).

Places to Stay & Eat
There is nowhere to stay in Shobak village but the **Shobak Castle Campground** *(JD5 per person)* is signposted both from the village and the castle. It's in a tranquil spot with nice views, although it can get cold at night.

There are a few **grocery stores** and **cheap restaurants** in Shobak village.

Getting There & Away
Occasional minibuses link Shobak village with Amman's Wahadat station (JD1.500, 2½ hours), Aqaba and Karak. Some of the minibuses travelling between Wadi Musa and Ma'an pass through Shobak. There are also minibuses between Shobak and Tafila (800 fils, one hour).

If you're driving, there are two well-signposted roads from the King's Highway to the castle and there are signs from Shobak village. Otherwise, from Shobak village to the castle, you'll have to charter a taxi (up to JD5 return including waiting time; around 3km). The road up to the tiny car park is very narrow.

Petra

بترا

Petra is the sort of place that usually exists only in the imagination and is one place where seeing is indeed believing.

If you can only go to one place in Jordan, make it Petra. Hewn from a towering rock wall, the imposing facades of its great buildings and tombs are an enduring testament to the vision of the Nabataean ancients. The Nabataeans – Arabs who dominated the Trans-Jordan area and controlled the frankincense trade routes of the region in pre-Roman times – chose as their city a place concealed from the outside world and made it into one of the Middle East's most memorable sites.

Much of Petra's fascination comes from its setting on the edge of Wadi Araba, a landscape of sheer and rugged sandstone hills. Access to Petra is through As-Siq, a narrow winding cleft in the rock anything from 2m wide to 200m deep. Almost as spectacular as the monuments themselves are the countless geological shades and swirls formed over the centuries in the rock. Petra is often called the 'Rose City' and, although this describes one of its most enchanting moods, it hardly does justice to the extraordinarily beautiful range of colours that turn Petra from deep, rusty red to almost golden, interlaced with grey, yellow and every shade in between depending on the angle of the sun. Sadly, the soft sandstone is being eroded by wind, water and salt (see the boxed text 'Saving the Siq' later in this chapter).

Few buildings in Petra (which means 'rock' in Greek) are freestanding; the bulk are cut into the rock. Until the mid-1980s, many of these caves were home to the local Bedouin, who have since been moved to new 'villages' to the north – an arrangement many are less than happy with. However, a handful of families still pitch their black goat-hair tents inside Petra, or live in the caves. The Bedouin make their money from drink and souvenir stands, and by selling handicrafts and other artefacts – usually scraps of distinctive pottery and 'old' coins.

The best time to visit Petra is from mid-October to the end of November, and late January to the end of May. This avoids the coldest, wettest (when floods are possible) and hottest times of the year.

Highlights

- **As-Siq** – this dramatic, long and narrow gorge links the outside world with the ancient city
- **The Treasury** – Al-Khazneh, as it's locally known, is arguably Petra's most spectacular, and the most photographed sight in Jordan
- **Royal Tombs** – these towering tombs offer great views of the old city centre
- **The Monastery** - Al-Deir, as it's locally known, is bigger than and just as impressive as the Treasury with some wonderful scenery in the vicinity
- **Siq Barid** – Little Petra, as it's sometimes known, is less dramatic than Petra itself, but is nonetheless a lovely spot
- **Petra by Night** – Exploring As-Siq and the Treasury by candlelight is an unforgettable experience and one that evokes an atmosphere of what Petra once must have been like

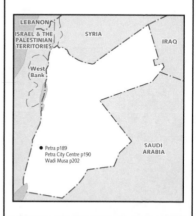

HISTORY

Excavations in the 1950s unearthed a Neolithic village at Al-Beidha, just to the north of Petra, which dates from about 7000 BC. This puts it in the same league as Jericho on the West Bank as one of the earliest known farming communities in the Middle East.

Between that period and the Iron Age (from 1200 BC), when the area was the home of the Edomites, nothing is known. The Edomite capital Sela (mentioned in the Bible) was thought to have been on top of Umm al-Biyara (see the relevant section under Hiking later in this chapter), although the actual site of Sela may lie to the north, about 10km south of Tafila.

The Nabataeans were a nomadic tribe from western Arabia who settled in the area around the 6th century BC. They soon became rich, first by plundering and then by levying tolls on the trade caravans traversing the area under their control. The most lucrative of these trades was frankincense being transported from the southern Arabian peninsula towards Turkey and beyond. The Seleucid ruler Antigonus, who came to power in Babylonia when Alexander the Great's empire was parcelled up, rode against the Nabataeans in 312 BC and attacked one day when all the men were away. His men killed many women and children and took valuable silver and spices. The Nabataeans retaliated immediately, killing all but 50 of the 4000 raiders. Antigonus tried once more to storm Petra but his forces were driven off.

The Nabataeans never really possessed an 'empire' in the common military and administrative sense of the word; instead, from about 200 BC, they established a 'zone of influence' that stretched to Syria and Rome. As the Nabataean territory expanded, more caravan routes came under their control and their wealth increased accordingly. It was principally this, rather than territorial acquisition, that motivated them.

The Roman general Pompey, having conquered Syria and Palestine in 63 BC, tried to exert control over Nabataean territory, but the Nabataean king, Aretas III, was able to buy off the Roman forces and remain independent. Nonetheless, Rome exerted a cultural influence and the buildings and coinage of the period reflect the Graeco-Roman style.

The Nabataeans weren't so lucky when they chose to side with the Parthians in the latter's war with the Romans, finding themselves obliged to pay Rome heavy tribute after the defeat of the Parthians. When the Nabataeans fell behind in paying the tribute, they were invaded twice by Herod the Great. The second attack, in 31 BC, saw him gain control of a large slice of territory.

By the time of the Nabataean King Rabbel II, the Nabataeans had lost much of their commercial power – Palmyra to the north was presenting increasing competition as the major trade route, and sea trade routes had begun to become important. Finally in AD 106, the Romans took Petra and set about imposing the usual plan: a colonnaded street, baths, and so on.

During the Byzantine period, a bishopric was created in Petra and a number of Nabataean buildings were altered for Christian use. By the time of the Muslim invasion in the 7th century, Petra had passed into obscurity and the only activity in the next 500 years was in the 12th century when the Crusaders moved in briefly and built a fort.

From then until the early 19th century, Petra was a forgotten outpost, known only to local Bedouin. These descendants of the Nabataeans were reluctant to reveal its existence because they feared (perhaps, not without reason) that the influx of foreigners might interfere with their livelihood. Finally in 1812, a young Swiss explorer, JL Burckhardt, ended Petra's blissful isolation.

INFORMATION
What to Bring

Don't underestimate the size of Petra and the heat in summer. Always take a good hat, sturdy footwear, plenty of rolls of film and, especially in summer, lots of water. Some mosquito repellent is also a good idea.

Equip yourself with supplies before entering Petra, where food and drink are expensive (a large mineral water costs JD1.500). You can easily find picnic provisions (albeit limited) in the bakeries and supermarkets of Wadi Musa, and some hotels will arrange picnic packs (though these can be pricey).

Tourist Offices

The first stop for all visitors should be the **Petra visitor centre** (☎ 2156020, fax 215 6060; open 6am-9pm daily), just before the entrance. It houses a helpful information counter and toilets. There is also an auditorium where an informative two-hour video (in English) on Petra and its history is shown. Staff seem happy to play it at any time if you ask at the information counter. There's also a 20-minute video that is shown every night at 8pm, but only when there are sufficient tourists in town.

PETRA

PETRA

'Ibrahim' Burckhardt

Johann Ludwig (also known as Jean Louis) Burckhardt was born in Switzerland in 1784. To assist with what was seen in those days as a dangerous sponsored journey around the Middle East and Africa, he was taught Arabic and learned to eat, sleep and behave like a Bedouin. He lived in Aleppo (Syria) for two years, converted to Islam and lived under the alias of Ibrahim bin Abdullah.

In 1812, while en route from Damascus to Cairo, he visited Jerash, Amman, Karak and Shobak. On the way, he heard locals tell of some fantastic ruins hidden in the mountains of Wadi Musa valley, but the people of the region were suspicious of outsiders. To make the detour, he had to think of a ploy so that suspicions were not raised by his guide and porters, as he explained in his posthumously published journal, *Travels in Syria and the Holy Land:*

I, therefore, pretended to have made a vow to have slaughtered a goat in honour of Haroun (Aaron), whose tomb I knew was situated at the extremity of the valley, and by this stratagem I thought that I should have the means of seeing the valley on the way to the tomb.

He was able to examine, albeit very briefly, a couple of sites including the Treasury (Al-Khazneh) and the Urn Tomb, and reported that 'it seems very probable that the ruins at Wadi Musa are those of ancient Petra', concluding that:

the situation and beauty of which are calculated to make an extraordinary impression upon the traveller, after having transversed...such a gloomy and almost subterranean passage (As-Siq)...it is one of the most elegant remains of antiquity existing.

Burckhardt later explored Egypt and Mecca, but contracted fatal dysentery in 1817. He died at only 33 years old, and is buried in the Islamic Cemetery in Cairo.

The information counter is also the place to arrange **guides** *(English, French, Spanish & Arabic; JD8 for 2½ hours or JD35 for a full day including either the Monastery or High Place of Sacrifice)*. For details about horses and other four-legged forms of transport through Petra, see Horse, Donkey & Camel later in this chapter. If there's sufficient demand, **helicopter rides** *(US$60 for between 20 minutes and one hour)* over the ancient city can be arranged – it's a spectacular (if intrusive for other visitors) way to see Petra.

The **Petra Regional Authority** (see the boxed text 'Petra & Tourism'), on a road above the Police roundabout in Wadi Musa, is a local development coordinating agency. It's not a tourist office, but staff are generally happy to help anyone with specific enquiries about the development of Petra and Wadi Musa.

Books & Maps

Very little in Petra is signposted or captioned so a map and guidebook are essential. For most visitors planning to see the major sights over one or two days, this book will be more than sufficient.

The *Petra: The Rose-Red City* brochure, published by the Jordan Tourism Board, has an easy-to-read map, a few explanations and useful photos that help identify certain places. Try to get one before coming to Petra as the visitor centre often runs out.

There are plenty of souvenir books about Petra, such as *Petra* by Iain Browning. They may be nice for a coffee table at home, but are too big to lug around Petra. One of the best guidebooks, *Petra: A Travellers Guide* by Rosalyn Maqsood, includes lots of history and culture, and describes several hikes. *Petra: The Rose-Red City*, by Christian Auge & Jean-Marie Dentzer (Thames & Hudson), is excellent, especially on Petra's historical context. The same authors have published (in French) *Cite des Caravanes*. There's a chapter on hiking in Petra in Tony Howard & Di Taylor's *Jordan – Walks, Treks, Climbs & Canyons*. These books are generally available at shops and stalls around Wadi Musa and Petra (including the shops around the visitor centre). For reconstructions of how Petra's monuments once appeared, *Jordan, Past & Present – Petra, Jerash, Amman*, published by Vision, isn't bad.

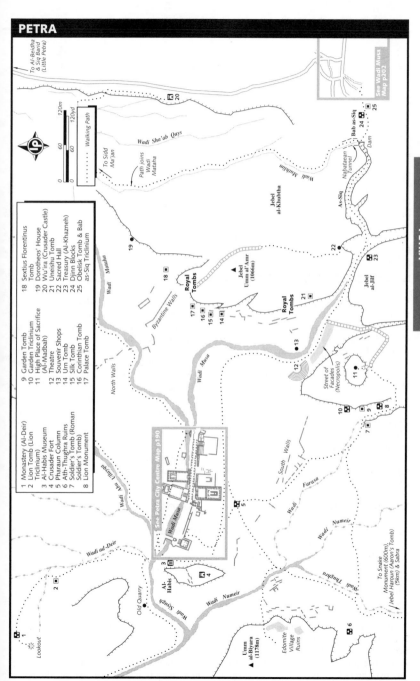

PETRA

1 Monastery (Al-Deir)
2 Lion Tomb (Lion Triclinium)
3 Al-Habis Museum
4 Crusader Fort
5 Pharaun Column
6 Ath-Thughra Ruins
7 Soldier's Tomb (Roman Soldier's Tomb)
8 Lion Monument
9 Garden Tomb
10 Garden Triclinium
11 High Place of Sacrifice (Al-Madbah)
12 Theatre
13 Souvenir Shops
14 Urn Tomb
15 Silk Tomb
16 Corinthian Tomb
17 Palace Tomb
18 Sextius Florentinus Tomb
19 Dorotheos' House
20 Wu'ira (Crusader Castle)
21 Uneishu Tomb
22 Sacred Hall
23 Treasury (Al-Khazneh)
24 Djinn Blocks
25 Obelisk Tomb & Bab as-Siq Triclinium

To Al-Beidha & Siq Barid (Little Petra)

See Wadi Musa Map p207

Walking Path

Wadi Sha'ab Qays

To Sidd Ma'jan

Path joins Wadi Mataha

As-Siq

Nabataean Tunnel

Bab as-Siq

Dam

Wadi Muthlim

Jebel al-Khubtha

Jebel Umm al'Amr (1060m)

Royal Tombs

Royal Tombs

Jebel al-Jilif

Street of Facades (Necropolis)

Wadi Madbah

Byzantine Walls

North Walls

Wadi Musa

South Walls

Wadi Farasa

Wadi Numeir

See Petra City Centre Map p190

Wadi Musa

Abu Ullayqa

Wadi ad-Deir

Old Quarry

Lookout

Al-Habis

Wadi Siyagh

Wadi Numeir

Umm al-Biyara (1178m)

Edomite Village Ruins

Wadi Thughra

To Snake Monument (600m), Jebel Haroun (Aaron's Tomb) (5km) & Sabra

PETRA

0   60   120m
0   60   120yd

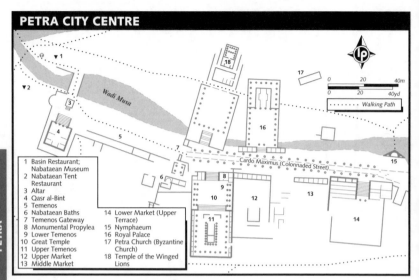

PETRA CITY CENTRE

1 Basin Restaurant;
   Nabataean Museum
2 Nabataean Tent
   Restaurant
3 Altar
4 Qasr al-Bint
5 Temenos
6 Nabataean Baths
7 Temenos Gateway
8 Monumental Propylea
9 Lower Temenos
10 Great Temple
11 Upper Temenos
12 Upper Market
13 Middle Market
14 Lower Market (Upper
   Terrace)
15 Nymphaeum
16 Royal Palace
17 Petra Church (Byzantine
   Church)
18 Temple of the Winged
   Lions

If you plan to hike long distances in Petra without a guide, a more detailed map is required. The best currently available is the Royal Jordanian Geographic Centre's contoured (1:5000) map, published as *The Tourist map of Petra* and the *Map of Petra*. These maps are usually available at bookshops in Wadi Musa and at the small stand next to the Nabataean Museum.

Toilets
There are toilets at the visitor centre; opposite the theatre; and at the back of Qasr al-Bint. If at all possible, avoid going to the toilet elsewhere as it spoils it for the people coming after you, especially the locals.

Entering Petra
If you're coming down the hill from Wadi Musa, take the right fork to the west opposite the Mövenpick Hotel. This road leads to the visitor centre where the **ticket office** (☎ 2156020; *open 6am-4.30pm daily Oct-Apr, 6am-5.30pm daily May-Sept*) is located. Although tickets are not sold after the times specified above, you can remain in Petra after this time, usually until sunset.

At the time of research, entry fees for Petra were in a state of flux; their future depends on the number of tourists visiting Petra. The official rates are JD21/26/31 for one/two/three-day passes. When we visited,

these rates had been reduced by 50% to JD10.500/13/15.500. It was not clear how long these prices, and a further 50% discount for students, would continue. Bring your international student card in case and ask at the ticket office. Multiday tickets are nontransferable and signatures are checked. Children under 15 years old get in free.

If you're contemplating trying to enter Petra without paying: don't. Apart from the fact that tickets are checked and fines of up to JD100 can be levied, it's worth remembering that the ongoing preservation of Petra and the livelihood of many local people depend on the income from tourists. It may be a lot of money, but it's worth it.

Planning
It's vital to plan your trip around Petra properly to make efficient use of your time (see the boxed text 'Suggested Itineraries'). If you're on an organised tour you will have little choice, but independent travellers should start their exploration early. The tour buses start arriving before 9am and the enchanting *siq* (gorge) is best experienced in quietness and away from large crowds. If you want to see the Treasury bathed in sunlight, you can enter Petra early, visit a few other sites such as the High Place of Sacrifice and Theatre, and then return at around 9am. The monastery is at its best in the late afternoon.

THE ANCIENT CITY OF PETRA

There are over 800 registered sites in Petra, including some 500 tombs, but the best things to see are easy to reach. From the gate, an 800m path heads downhill through an area called **Bab as-Siq** (Gateway to the Siq).

Djinn Blocks

Just past the entrance are three enormous monuments, known as the Djinn (Spirit) Blocks, built by the Nabataeans. Their exact functions remain a mystery, but they could have been tombs, or built as dedications to their god, Dushara.

Obelisk Tomb & Bab as-Siq Triclinium

Further along the path are four pyramidal obelisks, built as funerary symbols by the Nabataeans in the 1st century BC. The eroded human figure at the top, along with the four obelisks, is believed to represent the five people buried in the tomb. Underneath is a Nabataean triclinium (dining room), with its three small chambers, where feasts were probably held to commemorate the dead. The carved columns flanking the entrance give a sense of the original facade, while the Doric frieze above the door is also worth a look. Inside, the horseshoe-shaped bench is all that remains.

As-Siq

The 1.2km *siq* starts at an obvious bridge, which is, in fact, part of a new dam. The dam was built in 1963, on top of one built by the Nabataeans in about AD 50, to stop water from Wadi Musa river flowing through As-Siq. To the right (north), Wadi Muthlim heads invitingly through a Nabataean tunnel – the start (or finish) of a great hike (see Hiking later in this chapter).

The entrance to As-Siq was once topped by an arch that was built by the Nabataeans. It survived until the late 19th century, and some remains can be seen at the entrance to As-Siq.

The *siq* often narrows to about 5m (at some points to just 2m) wide, and the walls tower up to 200m overhead. The original channels cut into the walls to bring water into Petra are visible, and in some places the 2000-year-old terracotta pipes are still in place. In Roman times, the path was paved and one section is still intact.

As-Siq is not a canyon (a gorge carved out by water), but is actually one block that has been rent apart by tectonic forces,

---

Petra & Tourism

Petra is overwhelmingly the major attraction for visitors to Jordan, and is visited by about 300,000 people a year (more than 3000 a day in peak periods!), although any instability in the region leads to a drop in tourist numbers. Entrance fees to Petra are also a significant source of revenue for the government: over JD6.4 million (about US$9 million) was collected in 1997; by contrast, Jerash generated just JD851,313 (about US$1.2 million).

All revenue from entrance fees goes to the Jordanian treasury, but only about 25% filters back to the **Petra Regional Authority** (☎ 2157092, fax 2157091; e prc@amra.nic.gov.jo). This money is not necessarily used for restoration, so grants from organisations such as the World Bank are vital. Established in 1966, the Petra Regional Authority is responsible for developing tourism in an area of some 853 sq km, of which 264 sq km have been designated as an 'Archaeological Park'. Among the stated aims of the authority are 'environmental protection' and 'growth and management of sustainable forms of tourism'. It's also involved in an urgently needed urban development plan for the towns of Wadi Musa and Tayyibeh, and the scenic road between both places.

More concerned with the direct environmental and ecological future of Petra is the **Petra National Trust** (PNT; ☎ 06-5930338, fax 5932115; e enquiries@petranationaltrust.com, w www.petra nationaltrust.com). The PNT is an independent non-governmental organisation that aims to 'preserve the environment, antiquities and cultural heritage of the Petra region'. Established in 1989, the PNT helps the Petra Regional Authority to identify problems. It's also involved in training guides, staff and rangers; studying the impact of damage to Petra from erosion and tourism; reducing the number of drink and souvenir stalls in Petra (but finding other avenues of income for stall owners); and creating better, dedicated walking trails.

PETRA

Suggested Itineraries

Almost everything in Petra is a highlight in itself, and the combined effect of the ancient city is truly astonishing. There are, however, some specific sites which should not be missed. These include the Treasury, High Place of Sacrifice, the Street of Facades, Theatre, Royal Tombs and the Monastery. Don't restrict yourself to these, but on no account miss them.

If your time is limited, you may wish to follow these suggestions:

Half-Day (about five hours) You will have little time to explore much, so concentrate on As-Siq; the Treasury (Al-Khazneh); the Theatre; the Royal Tombs; everything along the Colonnaded Street; the temples and churches just south and north of the Colonnaded Street; and the Nabataean Museum.

One Day (about eight hours) One day is really the minimum time needed to do Petra any justice. Try not to rush around in one day if you have time to visit for two: pay the extra for a two-day ticket and explore the site more slowly and thoroughly. In one day, explore the places mentioned above, and allow time for a walk up to the Monastery and to the High Place of Sacrifice, or above the Treasury on Jebel al-Khubtha, if you have any remaining time and energy.

Two Days This is an ideal amount of time, and allows leisurely exploration, hikes to more remote areas, and a long lunch on one or both days. On the first day, allow time to visit the places mentioned under 'Half-Day', and climb to the Monastery. On the second day, detour as far as you want up Wadi Muthlim and Wadi Siyagh for some different landscapes away from the masses; climb to the High Place of Sacrifice from the Theatre and go back to the city centre (or vice versa); and hike above the Treasury on Jebel al-Khubtha.

Three Days A three-day ticket allows a free extra day (ie, four days) and plenty of time to explore the sites and hike off the beaten track. For the first two days, follow the itinerary listed earlier. On the third and/or fourth days, hike to Jebel Haroun, via Snake Monument; hike between the dam (at the entrance to As-Siq) and the Nymphaeum, along Wadi Muthlim and Wadi Mataha; and allow some time to explore Siq Barid (Little Petra) and the ruins of Al-Beidha village.

evinced at various points where the grain of the rock on one side matches the other.

Further along, the walls close in still further, and at times almost meet overhead, shutting out the light and seemingly the sound as well. As-Siq can seem to continue forever, and the sense of anticipation as you look around each corner for your first glimpse of the Treasury (Al-Khazneh) is a wonderful introduction to the ancient city and its magic.

Apart from concealing Petra from the outside world, As-Siq also served as a passageway for religious processions.

Treasury (Al-Khazneh)

Tucked away in such a confined space, the Treasury (known locally as Al-Khazneh) is protected from the ravages of the elements, and it is here that most visitors fall in love with Petra. The facade is an astonishing piece of craftsmanship, with the sophistication, symmetry and grandeur of the carving enough to take away the breath of first-time visitors. Its scale is also a source of wonder, as surprising as it is imposing, and this overall impression is the one which dominates.

As you pause to look, the individual details become more apparent. Atop the six columns at ground level are floral capitals, while the pediment (triangular) depicts a gorgon's head emerging from the surrounding flora. The carved figures alongside horses on the ground level derive from classical mythology. On the top level are two winged Victories in the sunken niches, with four more figures of unknown origin alongside. The central figure above the entrance pediment is the source of much speculation; most scholars believe it to be an assimilation of the Egyptian goddess Isis and the Nabataean goddess Al-'Uzza.

Although carved out of the solid iron-laden sandstone to serve as a tomb for the Nabataean king Aretas III, the Treasury gets its name from the story that pirates hid their treasure here (in the urn in the middle of the second level). Some locals clearly believed this tale because the 3.5m-high urn is pock-marked by rifle shots, the results of vain attempts to break open the solid-rock urn.

The date of the Treasury's construction has also been a subject of debate, and estimates range from 100 BC to AD 200.

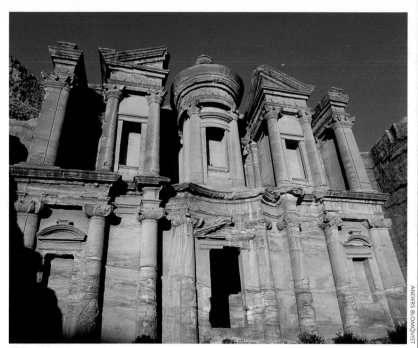

Al-Deir (The Monastery), Petra

Camel, Petra

Guards, the Treasury, Petra

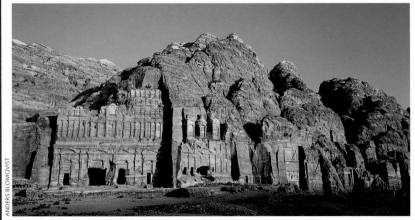

Ruined tombs, Jebel al-Khubtha, Petra

Urn Tomb, Petra

Garden Triclinium, Petra

As with all the rock-hewn monuments in Petra, it's the facade that captivates; the interior is just an unadorned square hall with a smaller room at the back. The Treasury, which is 43m high and about 30m wide, is at its most photogenic in full sunlight between about 9am and 11am (depending on the season; it's also pretty late in the afternoon when the rock glows.

From the Treasury, the *siq* turns off to the right (northwest), and diagonally opposite is a **sacred hall**, which may have had ritual connections with the Treasury.

Street of Facades

Heading towards the centre of the city, and just before the Theatre, are over 40 tombs and houses built by the Nabataeans, but with a definite style reminiscent of the Assyrians. Colloquially called the Street of Facades, its tombs are similar to the hundred or more all around Petra, but are certainly the most accessible. It's easy to forget about these when the majestic Theatre comes into view, but the tombs are worth exploring.

Theatre

Probably built by the Nabataeans in the 1st century BC, the captivatingly weathered Theatre was cut out of rock, slicing through many caves and tombs in the process. The seating area *(cavea)* had an original capacity of about 3000 in 45 rows of seats, with three horizontal sections separated by two corridors. The orchestra section was carved from the rock, but the backdrop to the stage or *frons scaenae* (which is no longer intact) was constructed (as opposed to carved) in three storeys with niches and columns overlaid by marble. The performers made their entrance through one of three entrances, the outlines of which are still partially visible.

The Theatre was renovated and enlarged (to hold about 8500) by the Romans soon after they arrived in AD 106. To make room for the upper seating tiers, they demolished a number of tombs. Under the stage floor were storerooms and a slot through which a curtain could be lowered at the start of a performance. From near the slot, an almost-complete statue of Hercules was recovered.

The Theatre was badly damaged by an earthquake in AD 363, and parts of it were then removed to help build other structures in Petra.

Saving the Siq

As-Siq, which runs along the dry Wadi Musa river bed, is under constant threat for three very different reasons. First, thousands of people visit every day (see the boxed text 'Petra & Tourism' earlier in this chapter), and walk up and down it at least twice (and, sometimes, vandalise it). Second, flash floods are not uncommon in winter, and have caused serious damage (and deaths) in the recent past.

Finally, the Nabataeans built sophisticated hydraulic systems to divert flood waters from along As-Siq to other wadis, and for irrigation and storage. After centuries of neglect, erosion and earthquakes, these are ironically causing serious damage to As-Siq and various monuments because their bases are now often in underground water, loaded with salt that works its way up the walls and destroys the sandstone. The damage to the Treasury (Al-Khazneh) is the most worrying.

Various foreign governments and non-governmental organisations are busy undertaking surveys, and some urgently needed restoration of the Nabataean hydraulic system has started. The main benefactor is the Swiss government, which feels some kindred spirit with Petra because the 'discoverer' of Petra, Burckhardt (see the boxed text "Ibrahim' Burckhardt' earlier in this chapter), was born in Switzerland.

High Place of Sacrifice (Al-Madbah)

The most accessible of the many sacrificial places high in the mountains is called the High Place of Sacrifice, known locally as Al-Madbah (Altar). Located on top of Jebel Madbah, the altars are fairly unimpressive, but the views of the city to the northwest, Wadi Musa village to the east and the shrine on top of Jebel Haroun to the far southwest are superb. About 50m down (north) over the rocks from the High Place are more staggering views, this time of the Royal Tombs.

The steps to the High Place, which start about 200m before (tzo the southeast of) the Theatre just past a couple of souvenir stands, are fairly obvious, but not signposted. The climb up takes about 45 minutes, and is better in the early morning when the sun is behind you. It's marginally easier than the steps up to the Monastery, but is

PETRA

Nabataean Religious Processions

Some historians speculate that the primary function of As-Siq was akin to the ancient Graeco-Roman Sacred Way. Some of the most important rituals of Petra's spiritual life began as a procession through the narrow canyon, while it also represented the endpoint of a pilgrimage by Nabataean pilgrims. Many of the wall niches that are still visible today along As-Siq's walls used to hold figures of the Nabataean god, Dushara. Some were carved and constructed by the city authorities, while others probably took the form of an act of religious obeisance by a wealthy individual. These small sacred sites served as touchstones of the sacred for pilgrims and priests, offering them a link to the more ornate temples, tombs and sanctuaries in the city's heart, reminding them that they were leaving the outside world, and on the threshold of what was for many a holy city.

still steep and taxing at times. Donkey owners will implore you to ride one of their poor animals for a negotiable JD5/7 (one way/return).

As you near the summit, the trail leads straight ahead into a flatter valley. While you may wish to explore this area, the High Place is to the right (take the right fork at the rubble of a stone building). At the top, pass the two **obelisks** dedicated to the Nabataean gods, Dushara and Al-'Uzza; the altars are further along to the north and at the highest point in the immediate area. The top of the ridge was levelled to make a platform, and large depressions with drains show where the blood of sacrificial animals flowed out.

You can return the same way (ie, back along the steps and finishing near the Theatre), but if you have the energy it's better to go back via Wadi Farasa and on to the city centre, or southwest towards Snake Monument and/or Jebel Haroun. See Hiking later in this chapter for more details about hiking to and from the High Place of Sacrifice.

Royal Tombs

The Wadi Musa river bed widens out after the Theatre. To the right (north), carved into the face of Jebel al-Khubtha, are the impressive burial places known collectively as the 'Royal Tombs'.

The first (and most southern) is **Uneishu Tomb**, dedicated to a member of the Nabataean elite. It's virtually opposite the Theatre, and easy to miss because most visitors head to the other main tombs.

Urn Tomb, recognisable by the enormous urn on top of the pediment, is accessible by stairs. It has an open terrace over a double layer of vaults, probably built in about AD 70 for King Malichos II or Aretas IV. Above

the four half-columns was an architrave with four figures representing deities. The room inside is enormous, measuring 18m by 20m, and the patterns in the rock are striking. It's difficult to imagine how the smooth walls, sharp corners and three small chambers at the top were carved out with such precision. A Greek inscription on the back wall details how the building was used as a Byzantine church in the mid-5th century.

Further up (north) is **Silk Tomb**, which is the most unimpressive of the group in terms of the surviving state of its carvings, due in large part to earthquake damage. It is, however, noteworthy for the stunning pink, white and yellow colouring of the rocks.

Corinthian Tomb is something of a hybrid with elements of both Hellenistic and Nabataean influences. The portico on the lower level of the tomb is distinctively local in origin, while the upper decorative features are more Hellenistic in style. The top level is reminiscent of Al-Khazneh. The tomb gets its name from the Corinthian capitals adorned with floral motifs. By no means the most ornate of the Royal Tombs – it has suffered centuries of exposure to the elements – it's nonetheless worthy of a visit.

Palace Tomb is a delightful three-storey imitation of a Roman or Hellenistic palace, and one of the largest and most recent monuments in Petra. Its facade is thought to owe more to ornamental flourishes rather than religious significance. The two central doorways are topped by triangular pediments, while the two on either side have arched pediments. The doors lead into typically simple funerary chambers. The eighteen columns on the upper level are the most distinctive and visually arresting elements of the tomb. The top left corner is built – rather than cut out –

of stone because the rock face didn't extend far enough to complete the facade.

A few hundred metres further around (northeast) is **Sextius Florentinus Tomb**, built in AD 130 for a Roman governor whose exploits are regaled in an inscription above the entrance. This tomb is often neglected, but it is worth the short walk. Narrower than those to the southwest, it has some dazzling rock colourings and the gorgon's head in the centre of the facade above the columns is eroded, but it is still possible to distinguish the vine tendrils emanating from the head. The horned capitals suggest that the Roman adaptation of Nabataean architecture retained key influences from earlier periods. Unlike many of the other tombs, the interior is worth a look for the clearly discernible *loculi* or graves, with five carved from the back wall and three on the right as you enter.

There is plenty of room here for wider exploration of more photogenic tombs, and other temples and religious sites in the area. If you have the time and energy, a track between the Palace and Sextius Florentinus tombs leads to a wonderful position above the Treasury – see Hiking later in this chapter for details.

The Tombs of Petra

There are more ancient tombs dotted around the Petra area than any other type of structure and they are certainly among the most compelling of the ancient city's monuments. The size and design of the tombs depended in large part on the social status and financial resources of the deceased. Simple cave-like rooms marked the final resting place of ordinary citizens. Others belonging to what was probably Petra's upper-middle class are quite large (such as those along the Street of Facades), but with quite simple and austere exterior decoration. The ornate facades of the Royal Tombs, the high point of Nabataean funerary architecture, mark the burial site of the city's nobles and royalty. The dead were buried in graves (*loculi*) carved from the walls inside the tomb while the exterior decoration symbolised the soul (and even the presence of the deceased). Sometimes orchards and porticoes surrounded the tombs and all but the most simple contained banqueting halls where funerals and commemorative feasts were held.

Colonnaded Street

Further west along Wadi Musa is the Colonnaded Street, where a few columns have been re-erected and the slopes of the hills either side are littered with the debris of the city centre.

Built in about AD 106 (around the same time that a similar street in Jerash was built), over the remains of another thoroughfare built by the Nabataeans, the Colonnaded Street follows the standard Roman pattern of an east–west *decumanus*. What is puzzling is the lack of evidence of a *cardo*, or north–south axis, which traditionally was always the main street. Columns of sandstone lined the carriageway (around 6m wide) and they were in many places covered with marble, while the shops which lined either side were entered through covered porticoes.

At the start of the Colonnaded Street is the **Nymphaeum**, or public fountain dedicated to the Nymphs. It was probably here that the waters from As-Siq were channelled. Typical of its kind, it is thought to have had a large semicircular niche with statues and fountains. Little can be seen today; it's really only recognisable by the huge tree, a welcome respite from the endless sun in summer. It was probably built in the 2nd century AD.

On the left (south) of the colonnaded street are the limited remains of the market area, archaeologically divided into **Lower Market** (also known as the Upper Terrace), **Middle Market** and **Upper Market**. Further up on the right (north) are the unrecognisable ruins of the **Royal Palace**.

The street finishes at the **Temenos Gateway**, built in the 2nd century AD with three arches, wooden doors and towers. It marked the entrance to the *temenos*, or courtyard, of the Qasr al-Bint, marking the movement from the commercial areas of the city to the sacred area of the temple. Its design is reminiscent of Roman triumphal arches throughout the empire, although with Nabataean traces, such as the floral capital atop at least one column. Look closely for the few floral friezes which remain to suggest that this was once a very grand structure. Opposite (south) are the decrepit ruins of **Nabataean baths**.

Great Temple

Excavations of the Great Temple have been underway since 1993 and have yielded impressive results. It was built as a major

PETRA

Leaving Petra with a Smile

Petra is no different to popular tourist sites the world over, where tourists are a magnet for all kinds of local competitive spirit. Scams are refreshingly rare, but many travellers still find the hard sell that can pursue you during your stay (and which you'll most likely encounter soon after you arrive in Wadi Musa) a little wearying. The main target of touts and others with souvenirs or services to sell are the large tour groups; independent travellers are much more likely to enjoy the solitude of their visit.

While the constant requests to buy can be an irritant, it need not spoil your stay in this truly remarkable place. For a start, it's worth remembering that you are passing through the traditional land of the Bedouin and the overwhelming majority of traders are doing nothing more than trying to make a living in what is a very competitive market; after the downturn in tourist numbers after 2001, some Jordanian tourism employees had not been paid for two months. Once you break down the barrier with a smile (even if you don't intend to buy anything), you'll find almost all will reciprocate in kind. Sadly, the disdain of a minority of tourists towards the locals makes it easy to see why large visitor numbers can irretrievably alter the traditional hospitality of a place.

You'll also find that some local have a mischievous sense of humour, with camels being offered as 'air-conditioned taxis' and at least one inventive young woman offering handicrafts with the words 'Look for free and buy for money or look for money and buy for free'. Most of all, remember that the local Bedouin are as much a part of Petra as the monuments carved from the rock.

Nabataean temple in the 1st century BC, and despite being badly damaged by an earthquake not long after, was in use (albeit in a different form) until the late Byzantine period. The first set of stairs was marked with a monumental *propylea* (gateway) while the courtyard at the top of the first stairs was the lower *temenos* (sacred area), flanked on the east and west sides by a triple colonnade; some columns have been reconstructed. On the upper level was the temple's sacred enclosure with four huge columns at the entrance. The temple was once 18m high, and the enclosure was 40m by 28m. The interior was covered with red and white stucco work.

Qasr al-Bint

One of the few free-standing structures in Petra, this temple was built in around 30 BC by the Nabataeans, adapted to the cult of Roman emperors and destroyed in about the 3rd century AD. Despite the name given by local Bedouins – Qasr al-Bint al-Pharaun (Castle of the Pharaoh's Daughter) – it was almost certainly built as a dedication to the Nabataean god, Dushara, and was one of the most important temples in the ancient city. In its original form, it stood 23m high and had marble staircases, imposing columns topped with floral capitals, a raised platform for worship, and ornate plaster and stone reliefs and friezes, small traces of which are still evident. It may have been used for the worship

of the goddess Al-'Uzza, in addition to Dushara. The sacrificial altar, once overlaid with marble, indicates that it was probably the main place of worship in the Nabataean city and its location at street level suggests that the whole precinct (and not just the temple interior) was considered sacred.

Temple of the Winged Lions

The newly excavated Temple of the Winged Lions is named after the carved lions that topped the capitals of the columns. The temple was built in about AD 27, and dedicated to the fertility goddess, Atargatis, who was the partner to the main male god, Dushara, although some scholars speculate that the goddess Al-'Uzza may also have been worshipped here.

This was a very important temple, and had a colonnaded entry with arches and porticoes that extended down to and across the wadi at the bottom. Fragments of decorative stone and plaster found on the site, and now on display in the Nabataean Museum, suggest that both the temple and entry were handsomely decorated. The area is partially fenced off, but is easy to reach. Although there's not much to see, the **views** are nice.

Petra Church

An unmistakable awning covers the remains of the Petra Church (also known as the Byzantine Church). The church was originally built by the Nabataeans, and then redesigned and expanded by the Romans. It eventually burned down, and was then destroyed by various earthquakes, before being lovingly restored by the American Center of Oriental Research in Amman.

Inside the church are some exquisite **mosaics** on the floor, created in the Byzantine period. Ask someone there to open the **baptistry** at the back for a quick look around. A helpful map and explanations in English are located inside the church.

Al-Habis

Beyond the Qasr al-Bint is the small hill of Al-Habis (Prison). Steps lead up the face of Al-Habis to **Al-Habis Museum** *(open 8am-4pm daily)*. The museum, which has a tiny collection of artefacts, is inside a cave tomb, and is probably not worth the climb unless you want more views. A trail goes past the museum for 100m or so, and overlooks Wadi Siyagh, but then becomes dangerous. (It is possible to walk along Wadi Siyagh, however: see Hiking later in this chapter.)

On top of Al-Habis are the limited ruins of a small **Crusader fort**, built in the 12th century AD as a lookout. The path (an easy 15 minutes) to the fort starts at the southern end of Al-Habis hill; look for the signs, or ask directions. The ruins are not impressive, but the **views** of the city centre certainly are.

Monastery (Al-Deir)

Similar in design to the Treasury, the spectacular Monastery (known locally as Al-Deir) is far bigger (50m wide and 45m high) and just as impressive. Built in the 3rd century BC, probably as a Nabataean temple, it has crosses carved on its inside walls that suggest the Monastery was used as a church in Byzantine times. Similar in design but larger than Al-Khazneh, it has towering columns and a large urn flanked by two half pediments. The three-dimensional aspect of the upper level beautifully complements the lower facade and this element is thought to be derived from Hellenistic influences. The courtyard in front of Al-Deir was once surrounded by columns and was probably used for sacred ceremonies.

Opposite the Monastery there's a strategically placed drinks stall in a cave with a row of seats outside where you can sit and contemplate the majestic sight. Up past the drinks stand, and a few minutes further up the rocks, are stunning **views** of Wadi Musa village to the southeast; Wadi Araba, which stretches from the Dead Sea to Aqaba, to the west; and the peak of Jebel Haroun, topped by a small white shrine, to the south.

It was once possible to climb up a steep trail to a point above the Monastery, but this is currently not allowed for the sake of preserving the Monastery itself as well as tourists – one visitor fell to her death a few years ago. There are tourist police in attendance to prevent you from making the dangerous ascent.

The climb to the Monastery takes about one hour, and is best started in mid-afternoon when there is welcome shade along the way and the Monastery is at its most photogenic. The spectacular ancient rock-cut path of more than 800 steps is easy to follow (but steep and taxing at times), and is a spectacle of weird and wonderfully tortured stone. If you really don't want to walk, donkeys (with a guide) can be hired for about JD3/5 one way/return.

The start of the trail to the Monastery is not signposted, but is reasonably obvious. It starts from behind (to the northwest of) the Basin Restaurant and Nabataean Museum. If in doubt, ask locals – or look for weary hikers coming down.

The path to the Monastery passes the **Lion Tomb** (Lion Triclinium) set in a small gully. The two lions that lent the tomb its name are weather-beaten, but can still be made out, facing each other at the base of the monument.

Nabataean Museum

In the same building as the Basin Restaurant, this museum *(open 8am-4pm daily)* has a small but interesting display of artefacts from the region. The historical explanations in English are comprehensive, and will help most visitors better understand the history of Petra. A shop inside the main building sells detailed maps of the area.

PETRA BY NIGHT

'Petra by Night' can be one of Petra's highlights, a magical way to see the old city by candlelight. The walk starts from the Petra visitor centre at 8pm on Monday and Thursday nights (it sometimes doesn't run when tourist numbers are low), and lasts two hours, taking you along As-Siq (which is specially lined with candles) as far as the Treasury, where traditional Bedouin music is played and mint tea is served. There are often performances of Bedouin storytelling.

Tickets cost JD12 (children under 12 are free), and are available from a few travel agencies in town or from the information counter inside the Petra visitor centre. Remember that if you don't already have an entrance ticket for Monday or Thursday, you may have to pay the JD20 (one-day) entrance fee, *plus* JD12.

HIKING

Anyone with enough energy, time and enthusiasm, who wants to get away from the crowds, see some stunning landscapes, explore unexcavated tombs and temples and, perhaps, meet some Bedouin villagers, should go hiking.

Guides can be hired from the information counter just inside the Petra visitor centre (see Tourist Offices earlier in this chapter for details of prices and available languages). A guide is essential for Umm al-Biyara and Sabra and recommended for Jebel Haroun. For longer hikes, organise a reliable (but expensive) guide at the visitor centre one day in advance; or try to find a cheaper (and possibly less reliable) guide inside Petra.

A list of a few popular and accessible hikes around Petra follows. None of them is too strenuous or involves camping overnight (which is not allowed anyway). Serious hikers should also pick up one of the hiking maps mentioned in Books & Maps under Information earlier in this chapter. Please note that the approximate hiking times do not include the time needed to explore the site and/or linger to admire the views.

Wadi Siyagh

One trail starts to the northwest of Al-Habis hill (across the dry riverbed) and goes along Wadi Siyagh. Once a suburban area of Petra, the wadi and the nearby slopes have unexcavated tombs and residences to explore. The main attractions are the shady trees and water pools (and even waterfalls in the winter) along the wadi. In spring, the flowers are beautiful. Anywhere along Wadi Siyagh, and away from the noisy museum/restaurant area and past the quarry, is a great place for a picnic or a nap in the sun.

The trail along Wadi Siyagh is easy to follow, but becomes a bit rough in parts. Just go as far as you want, but remember that you must come back the same way. Do not walk along the wadi if rain is imminent because flash floods are a real possibility.

Qasr al-Bint to High Place of Sacrifice, via Wadi Farasa

This is a two-hour return trip. Most people head to the High Place of Sacrifice from the steps near the Theatre, but it's possible to start from near the city centre. From behind the Qasr al-Bint, go up the obvious path for about 300m to a four-way junction at the Pharaun Column. The walking trail heads uphill to the High Place, via Wadi Farasa. It's best to start in the early morning.

The trail up the steps from near the Theatre to the High Place, and back down to the Qasr al-Bint, via Wadi Farasa, is far easier to follow.

High Place of Sacrifice to Qasr al-Bint, via Wadi Farasa

The trip to the Qasr al-Bint from the High Place of Sacrifice takes one hour one way; add an extra 40 minutes if you go via Wadi Farasa. Refer to the High Place of Sacrifice section earlier in this chapter for information about getting to the High Place along the steps starting near the Theatre.

As you face the drinks stand from the top of the path, a trail to the left (west) heads down to Wadi Farasa (Butterfly Valley). The start of the trail is not immediately obvious, so look for the helpful piles of stones indicating the trail, or ask for directions at the drinks stand.

On the way down is the **Lion Monument**, where water used to run down the rock from above and out of the lion's mouth. The lion is about 5m long and 2.5m high. A stone **altar** diagonally opposite suggests the fountain had some religious function. The steps wind further down the side of the cliff to the **Garden Tomb**, which archaeologists believe was probably a temple. To the right (east), are the remains of a high wall, part of what was once a water reservoir.

A little further down on the left (west) is the **Soldier's Tomb** (also known as the Roman Soldier's Tomb), named for the statue over the door. Almost opposite (east) is the **Garden Triclinium**, a hall used for feasts after the dead were placed in the Soldier's Tomb. The hall is unique in Petra because of the decorations on the interior walls.

A few minutes further down is a gorge and the path then flattens out and follows Wadi Farasa, the site of ancient rubbish dumps, and ends up at the **Pharaun Column**, the only surviving column of another Nabataean temple. If you're disoriented, the pale-green roof over the Petra Church, north of the Colonnaded Street, is a good landmark for the direction you need to head. At the start of Wadi Farasa, a trail of sorts heads west towards Snake Monument.

Snake Monument

The trip from the High Place of Sacrifice to the Snake Monument and back to Qasr al-Bint takes three hours, or 2½ hours return from Qasr al-Bint. The curled stone on a rock pedestal that faintly resembles a snake is not that exciting, but there's a chance to meet Bedouin villagers.

The trail at the (southern) end of Wadi Farasa (if coming from the High Place of Sacrifice) is not obvious. If you have a map and a sense of direction, head left (west) as soon as the trail heads into a gorge past the **Garden Triclinium**; continue west, and then southwest, past a Bedouin village to the left (south); and then down Wadi Thughra for another 45 minutes. Another Bedouin settlement with a large, brown tent marks the spot where the **Snake Monument** can be seen. From there, return to Qasr al-Bint.

In fact, it's far easier to reach the Snake Monument from Qasr al-Bint. Head up the obvious path behind Qasr al-Bint until you reach the Pharaun Column; take the middle (vehicular) path down to the Snake Monument (the path to the left heads up to the High Place of Sacrifice, and the third, to the far right, goes nowhere interesting). The sign near the Pharaun Column warns not to go further without a guide, but the Snake Monument is easy to reach on foot. Follow the obvious vehicular path; the Bedouin village and monument is another 15 minutes' walk southwest from the end of this path.

Umm al-Biyara

The return trip from Qasr al-Bint to Umm al-Biyara (Mother of Cisterns) takes about three hours return. Umm al-Biyara is a mountain (1178m) to the southwest of the city centre.

On top may have been the Edomite capital of Sela, from where the Judaean king Amaziah (who ruled from 796 to 781 BC) threw 10,000 prisoners to their deaths over the precipice – although the actual site is possibly further north and not far from Tafila.

The mountain does have the ruins of a 7th-century-BC **Edomite village** on top, and many unexcavated **tombs** along the eastern cliffs. The **views** over the city centre and the surrounding area are probably the best you will see in Petra.

The trek to the top is tough going. The trail starts behind Qasr al-Bint, and initially follows Wadi Thughra (ie, along the road towards the Snake Monument from Pharaun Column). The path up the rock face starts from next to the largest of the rock-cut tombs on the southeast face. Climb the rock-strewn gully to the left of this tomb for 50m. Look for, and keep following, the original path cut into the rocks. At times the steps have completely eroded away and are dangerous.

A guide is strongly recommended. Start the hike in the mid-afternoon when most of the path is in shade.

Jebel Haroun

This trip from Qasr al-Bint to Jebel Haroun via the Snake Monument takes around six hours return. Jebel Haroun (1350m) is thought to be Mt Hor from the Bible where Aaron, brother of Moses, is believed to be buried. The small, white shrine on top of Jebel Haroun, which can be seen from Wadi Musa village and even the Dead Sea, was built in the 14th century, apparently over Aaron's tomb. There are some excavations of a religious complex underway nearby. The views towards the monastery and Dead Sea are worth the effort of getting here, as one reader discovered.

The path passes Bedu settlements and from the top of the mountain the 360° views to Petra's Deir and the Dead Sea rift are stunning...the walk from/to the entrance of Petra is about three hours each way...a total of about 18km return. The track is easy to find even without a guide. My kids found four different species of lizards at the top, including some big ones.

Jeroen Peters

The trail to Jebel Haroun starts at the Pharaun Column, and goes past the Snake Monument. Just continue to the southwest towards the obvious white shrine (which can look deceptively close); the trail is not steep until the last bit. At the bottom of the mountain, find the caretaker if you want to see inside the shrine. A guide is recommended, or go on a donkey (with a guide) from Qasr al-Bint or even the High Place of Sacrifice.

Sabra

This trip from Qasr al-Bint to Sabra takes five hours return. South of the Snake Monument are the remains of the Nabataean village, Sabra, with some ruins of walls, temples, bridges and a theatre. A guide is needed to even find the trail from Snake Monument.

Wadi Muthlim & Wadi Mataha to the Nymphaeum

This trip can take three hours one way. At the eastern entrance to the *siq* is a dam. Only a few metres north is an incredible Nabataean tunnel, which leads to a small and beautiful *siq* along Wadi Muthlim.

At the point where Wadi Muthlim finishes and reaches **Sidd Ma'jan**, it's possible to head east and then south along Wadi Sh'ab Qays to near the **Wu'ira Crusader Castle** (see Around Petra later in this chapter); tourist police are always on the lookout here for anyone trying to get into Petra without paying. It's hard to get your bearings in this part of Petra, and getting lost is a real possibility.

It's far better to head west along Sidd Ma'jan, which soon leads into Wadi Mataha. Along this wadi is **Dorotheos' House**, the interesting ruins of a number of residences. Wadi Mataha continues west, and then southwest, and eventually meets the Wadi Musa river bed at the Nymphaeum.

Some parts of the trail are tricky, and may be impassable if it's been raining. There is a genuine possibility of flash floods along Wadi Muthlim, because the dam at the start of the *siq* diverts water down this wadi. Do not start this trek if it's raining, or is likely to.

Above the Treasury

This trip takes 1¼ hours return from the Palace Tomb. An obvious set of steep steps commences about 150m northeast of the Palace Tomb. The climb takes about 20 minutes and leads to the top of a ridge affording wonderful views. Start this hike in the mid-afternoon when some parts are in the shade.

If you continue south along a less obvious dirt path at the end of the steps for another 15 minutes, and then down a small ravine, you'll come to a dramatic position about 200m above the Treasury, with fantastic (but incomplete) views of the mighty edifice; watch your step. You may have the place to yourself (there's not even a drink stand in sight), and the only noise you can hear is the echo of the people marvelling at the Treasury below. It is easy to get disoriented while finding the path back to the top of the steps, so look out for landmarks.

HORSE, DONKEY & CAMEL

Horses with guides can only be rented for JD7 for the 800m stretch between the main entrance and the start of As-Siq. It costs around JD20 for a two-hour horse ride around the surrounding hills. The price can be negotiated down to as little as JD2 going back up to the entrance (which some weary visitors gladly pay).

Horses and **carriages** with guides are only allowed between the main entrance and the Treasury (2km). These are officially for the disabled and elderly, but are often rented by tired hikers. They cost JD20 (return) for a two-person carriage.

Donkeys with guides are also available all around Petra for negotiable prices. They can go almost to the top of the Monastery (about JD3 one way), and all the way to the High Place of Sacrifice (about JD5 one way), and can be rented for trips as far as Snake Monument and Jebel Haroun. Leading donkeys is a genuine occupation for local Bedouin, but animal lovers may think twice about hiring one of these poor animals to climb the incredibly steep and narrow paths to the Monastery or High Place.

Camel rides are more for the novelty value, and are available for short rides and photographs near the Theatre and Qasr al-Bint. A trip between Qasr al-Bint and the Treasury, for example, costs about JD7.

If you see any animal being cruelly treated, please report it to the Brooke Hospital for Animals.

PLACES TO EAT

At the western end of the Colonnaded Street, near Qasr al-Bint, two restaurants offer similar all-you-can-eat buffets (if there are enough tourists) or set meals (at other times).

Brooke Hospital for Animals

Just to the left of the main entrance to Petra is a large expanse of ground dotted with horses. At the back is the **Princess Alia Horse Clinic** (☎ 2156379, fax 2156437), affiliated with the London-based **Brooke Hospital for Animals** (W www.brooke-hospital.org.uk), which has a number of animal hospitals in Egypt, Pakistan and India.

Founded in 1987, the clinic in Petra aims 'to improve the condition and wellbeing of working equine animals'. It cares for abused horses; educates locals and children in the area about the treatment of animals; provides free preventive measures against disease; and operates mobile clinics to remote regions. It also provides sun shelters and water troughs for horses, and gives (second-hand) saddles and other equipment to owners of working animals. Over 20,000 horses, and 250 other animals, were treated by staff in 1997.

If you see a genuine case of any animal being badly treated (rather than being worked hard) – and remember that a large proportion of any mistreatment is done by tourists – please ring the number (operating 24 hours a day) listed earlier. (See Treatment of Animals under Society & Conduct in the Facts about Jordan chapter for more information.)

While the staff at the clinic are friendly, they're not interested in being a 'tourist attraction', but anyone with a genuine interest in their work – and, especially, anyone wishing to make a donation – can visit the clinic any day between 8am and 3pm.

The upmarket **Basin Restaurant** is run by the Crown Plaza Resort and meals (or buffets) cost JD8. It's expensive but servings are large and the food is good.

Nabataean Tent Restaurant is more informal and charges JD6.

Throughout the site, including at the High Place of Sacrifice and the Monastery, stalls sell cold drinks, bottled water and some basic foodstuffs as well as souvenirs. Prices are high.

Restaurants and shops in Petra stay open during Ramadan, but please be discreet when eating, drinking or smoking in front of locals.

Around Petra

The village of Wadi Musa is the transport and accommodation hub for Petra, as well as other attractions in the vicinity that are well worth seeing if you have more time (and energy).

Getting to some of the places near Petra by public transport is difficult. Some hotels and travel agencies in Wadi Musa can arrange a tour to take in some – and even all – of the places listed later in this chapter from about JD10 per person (minimum of four people). During quiet periods, however, you will invariably have to find other passengers to share the cost. If there are enough

of you, it may work out cheaper (and certainly more flexible) to charter a service or private taxi for the day, although negotiations with taxi drivers around Wadi Musa can be a frustrating experience.

WADI MUSA   وادي موسى
☎ 03

The village that has sprung up around Petra is Wadi Musa (Moses' River). It's a mass of hotels, restaurants and shops stretching about 5km down from 'Ain Musa to the main entrance of Petra. The village centre, with its shops, restaurants and hotels, is little more than three streets, while most hotels are strung out along the main road.

Many locals are aware of tourists flocking to Petra with big wallets and little time. The touts can be tiresome, although usually only when you arrive in town laden with bags. After the signing of Jordan's peace agreement with Israel in 1994, Wadi Musa became a boom tourist town, transformed almost overnight from a small town with few visitors to a sprawling and competitive place. It's worth remembering that the traditional Bedouin society of Wadi Musa was suddenly overrun by visitors laden with cash. Large numbers of Israelis began to visit, along with other tourists, encouraged by moves towards peace in the region. Some locals have coped with this better than others – see the boxed text 'Warning' under Places to Stay.

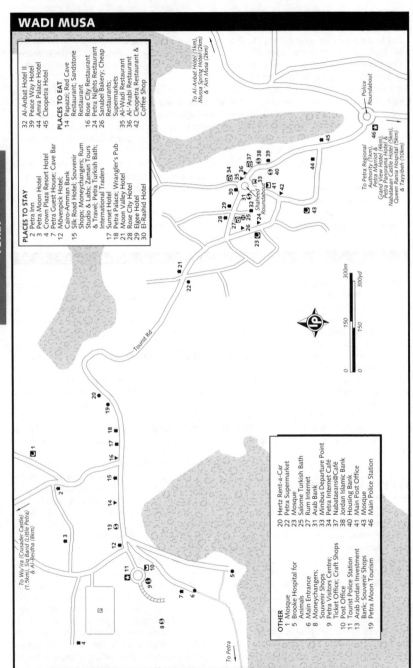

WADI MUSA

PLACES TO STAY
2 Petra Inn
3 Petra Moon Hotel
4 Crown Plaza Resort Hotel
7 Petra Guest House; Cave Bar
12 Mövenpick Hotel;
   Cairo-Amman Bank
15 Silk Road Hotel; Souvenir
   Shops; Moneychangers; Rum
   Studio & Labs; Zaman Tours
   & Travel; Petra Turkish Bath;
   International Traders
17 Sunset Hotel
18 Petra Palace; Wrangler's Pub
21 Moon Valley Hotel
28 Rose City Hotel
29 Elgee Hotel
30 El-Rashid Hotel

32 Al-Anbat Hotel II
39 Peace Way Hotel
44 Amra Palace Hotel
45 Cleopetra Hotel

PLACES TO EAT
14 Papazzi; Red Cave
   Restaurant; Sandstone
   Restaurant
16 Rose City Restaurant
24 Petra Nights Restaurant
26 Sanabel Bakery; Cheap
   Restaurants;
   Supermarkets
35 Al-Wadi Restaurant
36 Al-Arabi Restaurant
42 Cleopetra Restaurant &
   Coffee Shop

OTHER
1 Mosque
5 Brooke Hospital for
   Animals
6 Main Entrance
8 Moneychangers;
   Souvenir Shops
9 Petra Visitors Centre;
   Ticket Office; Craft Shops
10 Post Office
11 Tourist Police Station
13 Arab Jordan Investment
   Bank; Souvenir Shops
19 Petra Moon Tourism

20 Hertz Rent-a-Car
22 Petra Supermarket
23 Mosque
25 Salome Turkish Bath
27 Rum Internet
31 Arab Bank
33 Minibus Departure Point
34 Petra Internet Café
37 Nabataeans@Café
38 Jordan Islamic Bank
40 Housing Bank
41 Main Post Office
43 Mosque
46 Main Police Station

To Wu'ira (Crusader Castle)
(1.5km), Siq Barid (Little Petra)
& Al-Beidha (8km)

Tourist Rd

To Petra

To Al-Anbat Hotel (1km),
Musa Spring Hotel (2km)
& Ain Musa (2km)

Police
Roundabout

To Petra Regional
Authority (1km),
Petra Marriot &
Grand View Hotel (4km),
Petra Panorama Hotel &
Nabataean Castle Hotel (5km),
Queen Rania Hospital (5km)
& Tayibeh (10km)

Shaheed
Roundabout

0   150   300m
0   150   300yd

Sadly, in the aftermath of September 11 and with the escalation of hostilities between Israel and the Palestinians, visitor numbers to Petra have plummeted and one of the Middle East's most extraordinary sites can be eerily empty.

Orientation

'Wadi Musa' refers to everywhere between 'Ain Musa and the entrance to Petra. The obvious village centre is around the Shaheed roundabout; most transport leaves from here, and it's where you'll find the cheapest places to eat. It shouldn't cost more than JD1 for a taxi ride to most places around the village. The main road doesn't really have a name, but some locals call it Tourist Road for obvious reasons.

Information

Tourist Offices The best source of information is the Petra visitor centre near the entrance to Petra (see earlier in this chapter). For information about minibuses and other transport, you're better off asking at your hotel or one of the restaurants around the Shaheed roundabout.

Money There are surprisingly few money-changers in Wadi Musa, although many hotels will change money albeit, at a poor rate. It's usually better to change travellers cheques before you come to Petra.

The Housing Bank and Jordan Islamic Bank up from the Shaheed roundabout are good for money changing; both have ATMs. The Arab Bank is down from the roundabout. Closer to the gate into Petra, the Arab Jordan Investment Bank, and the Cairo-Amman Bank in the Mövenpick Hotel, change cash and (usually) travellers cheques with a minimum of fuss. There's also a moneychanger behind the Petra visitor centre. All banks are open from about 8am to 2pm, Sunday to Thursday and (sometimes) 9am to 11am on Friday.

The representative for American Express is **International Traders** (☎ 2157711), in the Silk Road Hotel complex (enter from the main road), but they don't change travellers cheques.

Post & Communications The attraction of using the small post office at the back of the Petra visitor centre is that mail is post-marked 'Petra Tur Office'. It's open 7am to 6pm Saturday to Thursday and sometimes also opens on Friday. Another small post office by the Mussa Spring Hotel ('Ain Musa) is open 8am to 5pm Saturday to Thursday. The main post office in Wadi Musa village is open from 8am to 5pm Saturday to Thursday and, occasionally, Friday morning.

International telephone calls can be made from several private agencies along the main streets of Wadi Musa village for around JD1.500 per minute, and from the Petra Internet Café from about 750 fils. Several booths for Alo telephone cards are located at the entrance to Petra.

The telephone numbers in Wadi Musa are all now seven digits. If you come across a six-digit number, replace the first two digits (often '33') with '215'.

Internet & Email Access The best places for internet in Wadi Musa are the **Petra Internet Café** (☎ 2157264; e alpetra@hotmail .com), just up the hill from the Shaheed roundabout, where it costs JD1.250/2 for 30 minutes/one hour (connections are generally fast); **Rum Internet** (☎ 2157906), down the hill from the roundabout, charges JD1 an hour and is open 24 hours; and **Nabataeans@Café** (☎ 2157411) just up from the roundabout – it also claims to be open 24 hours.

Photography & Film The best place to buy film in Wadi Musa is the Kodak Express outlet, **Rum Studio and Labs** (☎ 2157467), in front of the Silk Road Hotel on the main road. A roll of 36 100ASA Kodak film costs JD3, while for slide you pay JD6.500. To develop and print your photos costs from JD5 for the smallest size, but for slides it takes three days so you're better off doing it in Amman. The outlet is open 8am to 2pm and 3pm to 9.30pm daily.

Bookshops Inside Petra, behind the visitor centre and along the main road through Wadi Musa, souvenir stands sell books about Petra, but everything is more expensive than in Amman. See earlier in this chapter for information about books and maps.

Emergency The high-standard **Queen Rania Hospital**, 5km from the Police roundabout on the road to Tayyibeh, is open for emergencies without referral. Several private physicians have offices in Wadi Musa and are generally open from 9am to 1pm and 4pm to 6pm.

The main **police station** (☎ 191 or ☎ 215 6551) in Wadi Musa is adjacent to the Police roundabout. The **tourist police station** (☎ 2156441), opposite the Petra visitor centre, is open 24 hours. A few tourist police – surprisingly fewer than at other sites around Jordan – can be found lounging around in the shade inside Petra. There are always some stationed near the Monastery.

Turkish Bath

A 'Turkish bath' will ease any aching muscles after walking the trails of Petra. Sadly the two places in town generally only have male attendants. The service includes a steam bath, massage, scrub and 'body conditioning' for JD15. **Petra Turkish Bath** (☎ 2157085; open 10am-11pm daily), in the passage under the Silk Road Hotel (enter from the main road), is closest to the entrance of Petra, although it's not the cleanest place. Most locals prefer **Salome Turkish Bath** (☎ 2147342), near Al-Anbat Hotel II. Some of the upmarket hotels also have Turkish baths at surprisingly reasonable prices.

Places to Stay

Things have changed just a little over the years in Petra. Back in 1908, Macmillan's guide to *Palestine and Syria* had the following advice:

At Petra, there is no sleeping accommodation to be found, and travellers therefore have to bring with them camp equipment, unless they prefer to put up with the inconvenience of sleeping in the Bedwin huts at Elji, half an hour distant from Petra, or spend the night in some of the numerous temples. Such a course cannot be recommended to European travellers, especially if ladies are in the party.

Even as recently as 1991, there were only four official hotels in Petra.

Camping is no longer permitted inside Petra and visitors now have a choice of over 60 hotels in the area.

Prices fluctuate wildly in Petra, depending on the season and amount of business. The high season is generally from March to May and October to February, but even at these times, prices can drop quickly from the official rates when things are quiet, especially if you're staying more than a couple of nights.

Although many hotels offer 'half board' (which includes breakfast and dinner) at a higher rate, you can always obtain a room-only rate if you wish to eat elsewhere.

In winter, make sure there is heating and that it works. Surprisingly few places have fans, and only the more expensive hotels have air-conditioning. The views advertised by some hotels are of Wadi Musa valley, which is attractive, but not of Petra itself.

Places that are some distance from the entrance to Petra will offer free transport to and from the gate (usually once a day in either direction).

One last word: have a good idea of where you want to stay before arriving in town. If you get off the minibus at the Shaheed roundabout in Wadi Musa with a backpack, you'll likely be besieged by persuasive touts so stick to your guns.

Places to Stay – Budget

There's a sameness among many budget places. Most will try to entice you with offers of the *Indiana Jones and the Last Crusade* video and free shuttles to/from Petra. Touts can be persistent and sometimes join the minibus before it arrives in Petra to start

Warning

Women travellers must be aware that allegations of sexual harassment have been made against some (but by no means all) of the budget hotels in the streets around the Shaheed roundabout. These include unwanted intrusions into unlocked rooms, peeping toms and a range of unwanted (and mostly verbal) advances. There have also been allegations of rape made against at least one hotel. Women should exercise great caution at any of the budget hotels and should never travel alone off the beaten track (eg, to Little Petra) with male hotel staff. In particular, we do not recommend the Valentine Inn (formerly Twaissi Inn). Because of the allegations, we have grouped the budget places which we do recommend into those where lone women travellers might feel uncomfortable because most of the clientele is male ('Mostly Men') and those where lone women should experience no difficulties ('Women Welcome').

their sales pitch early. The choice for women is more difficult than elsewhere in Jordan.

Mostly Men Down the hill on the road to Petra, **Moon Valley Hotel** (☎ 2157131 or 2156824; rooftop bed JD2, smaller singles JD7, larger singles/doubles JD10/15) gets good reports from travellers and the more expensive rooms are particularly good value. It's a friendly place and one where the hard sell is refreshingly absent.

Peace Way Hotel (☎/fax 2156963; e peace way@index.com.jo; singles/doubles with bath & breakfast JD10/15) is also good value and the rooms are nice and tidy.

Elgee Hotel (☎ 2156701, fax 2157002; singles/doubles with bath JD10/15), across the road from the Rose City Hotel, is also a good option and the rooms are nice and tidy if uninspiring.

Rose City Hotel (☎ 2156440, fax 215 6448; singles/doubles with breakfast JD8/15) has reasonable rooms and friendly staff. Quieter than most, it's one of the better-value places in the village centre.

Women Welcome In the village of 'Ain Musa, **Mussa Spring Hotel** (☎ 2156310, fax 2156910; e musaspring_hotel@yahoo.co.uk; singles/doubles with shared bath JD6/8, with private bath JD8/10, rooftop bed JD2) is one of the first places you reach at the start of Wadi Musa. It's a pleasant place that's far removed from the clamour of the village centre. It also offers daily free shuttles to/from the gate at Petra 5km away. The rooms are smallish but the restaurant is quite groups.

Al-Anbat Hotel I (☎ 2156265; e alanbath@ joinnet.com.jo; singles/doubles JD8/10) is on the road between 'Ain Musa and Wadi Musa and is excellent value. The rooms, which come with satellite TV, are better than those in many mid-range hotels and there some good views down the wadi. Breakfast costs JD2 and free transport to/from Petra can be arranged.

Cleopatra Hotel (☎/fax 2157090; singles/ doubles with bath & breakfast JD10/14) has reasonable but small rooms, and an extensive range of movies on DVD in the lobby.

Places to Stay – Mid Range

All the room rates for the places listed in this section include private bathroom and breakfast.

El-Rashid Hotel (☎ 2156800, fax 215 6801; e el_rahidhotel@hotmail.com; Shaheed Roundabout; singles/doubles JD12/20) has sterile but spacious and comfortable rooms right in the centre of town. During quiet periods management is happy to negotiate, which may make it accessible for budget travellers.

Sunset Hotel (☎ 2156579, fax 2156950; singles/doubles JD15/20) is handy for the entrance to Petra and has pleasant rooms although some are better than others.

Amra Palace Hotel (☎ 2157070, fax 215 7071; e amrapalace@index.com.jo; singles/ doubles/triples low season JD20/33/35, high season JD25/38/42, including half board) has very comfortable rooms (with satellite TV) that border on the stylish, and rates are often negotiable when things are quiet.

Al-Anbat Hotel II (☎ 2156265, fax 215 6888; e alanbath@joinit.com.jo; singles/ doubles JD11/22) has generally quiet, well-furnished rooms with satellite TV and rates are negotiable, which would make it especially good value in the heart of Wadi Musa.

Petra Moon Hotel (☎/fax 2156220; singles/ doubles JD15/20) is up behind the Mövenpick Hotel and is convenient for the entrance to Petra. The rooms are spacious and comfortable, and the staff helpful. If you are planning to spend more than two nights, the price per night drops dramatically.

Silk Road Hotel (☎ 2157222, fax 215 7244; singles/doubles JD25/35) has lovely rooms and is good mid-range value close to Petra. The restaurant is also good and popular with tour groups.

Petra Inn (☎/fax 2156401; e petra_inn@ hotmail.com; singles/doubles JD25/35) is similarly good value with semiluxurious rooms and a convenient location.

Places to Stay – Top End

At all of the places listed here, there are some surprising bargains to be found when business is quiet.

Petra Palace (☎ 2156723, fax 2156724; e ppwnwm@go.com.jo; singles/doubles US$47/57) is superb value. Some of the luxury rooms open out onto a terrace with a swimming pool and there's a good restaurant and bar.

Crown Plaza Resort Hotel (☎ 2156266, fax 2156977; e cprpetra@nets.jo; singles/ doubles JD90/100 plus taxes) is also close to the gate to Petra and is decent value, particularly if you can get one of the packages where a double costs JD53 including breakfast, dinner and taxes. There's a heated swimming pool, Jacuzzi, sauna, tennis courts, bar and restaurants.

Petra Guest House (☎ 2156266, fax 215 6724; e ppwnwm@go.com.jo; singles/doubles JD60/80) is also owned by the Crown Plaza and sits right above the entrance to Petra.

Mövenpick Hotel (☎ 2157111, fax 215 7112; e hotel.petra@moevenpick.com; singles/doubles with half board JD150/190) is another top-end place close to the gate into Petra. There are four restaurants (which get mixed reports from readers), swimming pool, games room, children's playground and upmarket gift shops.

There are four luxury hotels on the scenic road between Tayyibeh and Wadi Musa.

Nabataean Castle Hotel (☎ 2157201, fax 2157209; e resort.nabataean@moevenpick .com; singles/doubles with half board JD160/ 190) has everything you could want from a five-star hotel with prices to match.

Petra Panorama Hotel (☎ 2157390, fax 215 7389; e panorama@index.com.jo; singles/ doubles/triples JD100/115/135 plus 8% tax), like most of the hotels along this road, has wonderful sunset views and luxurious rooms, as well as a swimming pool.

Petra Marriott (☎ 2156408, fax 2157096; e petramrt@go.com.jo; singles/doubles low season with half board JD45/50, high season JD60/75) is around 4km from the Police roundabout on the road to Tayyibeh and is superb luxury value. There's a swimming pool, restaurants, Turkish bath and even a cinema for (free) use by guests.

Grand View Hotel (☎ 2156871, fax 215 6984; e nzzalco@nets.com.jo; singles/doubles JD40/50) has the usual five-star facilities including swimming pool and games room.

Places to Eat

The main road through Wadi Musa is dotted with **grocery stores** where you can stock up on food, munchies and drinks for Petra, although the selection is fairly uninspiring unless you like processed cheese. Several **fruit and vegetable stalls** are also located in the village.

Sanabel Bakery (☎ 2157925; open 5am-midnight daily), around the corner from Rum Internet, does a delicious range of

Arab sweets and fresh bread that can be handy for a picnic.

Places to Eat – Budget

Most of the cheapest places to eat are in Wadi Musa village. There are a few places offering felafel and shwarma, especially around the Shaheed roundabout and just up from Sanabel bakery.

Al-Wadi Restaurant (☎ 0795 221232; soups 600-900 fils, mains JD1.500-3.500; open 7am-late daily) is one of two good places right on Shaheed roundabout. There's pasta and pizza, as well as a range of vegetarian dishes and local Bedouin specialties. It also does breakfast (around JD1.500) and it's a good place to hang out while waiting for your minibus to leave.

Al-'Arabi Restaurant (☎ 2157661; mains from JD1; open 6am-midnight daily), almost next door, is a bright place with helpful staff and good meals. A large chicken shwarma with salad and hummus costs JD2.500. Repeat customers get a discount.

Cleopetra Restaurant & Coffee Shop (☎ 0795 318775; buffet JD3; open 6am-11pm daily), just south of the Shaheed roundabout, does a few à la carte dishes, and the open buffet with a range of Bedouin specialties is great value. You also get breakfast (600 fils to JD1.500).

Petra Nights Restaurant (☎ 0795 849536; meals from JD2.500; open 6am-11pm daily) is rustic and there's no menu, but the owner's friendly and can cook just about any local dish you desire. The food and rooftop dining area get the thumbs up from readers.

Rose City Restaurant (starters 500 fils-JD1, mains from JD2.750; open 9am-10pm daily) is one of the few budget places near the entrance to Petra. It serves breakfast as well as a limited range of local dishes that consistently get good reports from readers. The service is also good.

Places to Eat – Mid Range

All of the places listed here are down the hill from Wadi Musa village and close to the entrance to Petra.

Papazzi (☎ 2157087; starters JD1, mains JD2-5; open 11am-9.30pm daily) is a Western-style pizza place that does good Italian (thin) or American (thick) pizzas (small from JD2.500) and pasta (around JD2).

Red Cave Restaurant *(☎ 2157799; mains from JD2.500; open 9am-10pm daily)* is cavernous, cool and friendly and the menu has a good selection. The Bedouin *gallayah* comes with lamb or chicken as well as rice, onions and a spicy tomato sauce. For other Bedouin specialties such as mensaf or *maqlubbeh*, about an hour's notice is usually required.

Sandstone Restaurant *(☎ 2157701; mains JD6, starters from 500 fils; open 8.30am-9pm daily)*, next door to Papazzi, is a friendly place with expensive but decent meals. They sometimes do buffets (JD6). Don't be put off by the local men sitting outside in the evening.

Entertainment

There's not a lot to do in the evening, other than recover from aching muscles and plan your next day in Petra. Some hotels organise videos or other entertainment, but only when there are enough takers.

Down the hill, close to the gate to Petra, are two bars that are pricey but have a pleasant atmosphere.

Cave Bar *(☎ 2156266; open 3pm-midnight daily)* is housed in a 2000-year-old Nabataean rock room, next to the entrance to the Petra Guest House (see Places to Stay), behind the visitor centre. It has a classy ambience and the novelty value is high – it's one of the most unusual places you'll ever down a pint. Beers start from JD2.750, spirits from JD4 and cocktails from JD4 and the drinks menu is very extensive. When things are busy it has been known to stay open until 4am.

Wranglers Pub *(☎ 2156723, fax 2156724; open 2pm-midnight daily)*, at Petra Palace, is a trendy place although it's a bit soulless when things are quiet. Prices are similar to those at the Cave Bar.

Shopping

There are plenty of souvenir shops lining the road down to the gate into Petra, as well as tables adorned with jewellery, carvings, coins and pretty rocks set up by local Bedouins around Petra itself. In Petra, the favourite local variation is coloured sand in glass bottles; you can even get them to write your name if you give them time.

The top-end hotels all also have gift shops selling pricey but good-quality handicrafts.

Organised Tours

The most professional agency in Wadi Musa for arranging trips inside Petra and around Jordan (including Wadi Rum and Aqaba) is **Petra Moon Tourism** *(☎ 2156665, fax 215 6666; e eid@petramoon.com, w www.petra moon.com)*, which has an office on the road to Petra; they can also organise camel treks to Wadi Rum. **Zaman Tours & Travel** *(☎/fax 2147722)*, in the same building as the Silk Road Hotel, has also been recommended by readers.

Most of the budget (and a few mid-range and top-end) hotels can also arrange day trips around Petra and further afield.

Getting There & Away

Public transport to and from Wadi Musa is less frequent than you'd expect, given that it's a large village and the number one tourist attraction in Jordan. The unofficial terminal for public transport is the Shaheed roundabout in the upper (eastern) end of Wadi Musa village. Ask at your hotel or at one of the restaurants on the roundabout to check the likely departure times.

JETT Bus The JETT bus company operates three buses a week (on Sunday, Tuesday or Wednesday, and Friday) in both directions (JD6, 3½ hours) between its domestic office in Amman and the main gate to Petra. The bus departs Amman at 6.30am, and leaves from Wadi Musa at around 5pm. For those with limited time, there is a same-day return fare of JD28 fromAmman to Petra, which includes a guide and food but not the entrance fee.

Minibus Most minibuses can drop passengers off anywhere between 'Ain Musa village and the main entrance to Petra, but for departures it's best to wait at Shaheed roundabout. Most minibuses won't leave unless they're at least half full, so be prepared for a wait. Tickets can often be booked the day before.

At least three minibuses travel every day between Amman (Wahadat station) and Wadi Musa (JD1.750, three hours) along the Desert Highway, via Tayyibeh. These buses leave Amman at about 6am, 8am and midday – the departure times from Wadi Musa are changeable so ask around the day before you want to travel.

PETRA

Minibuses leave Wadi Musa for Ma'an (600 fils, 45 minutes) intermittently throughout the day (more often in the morning). From Ma'an, there are connections to Amman, Aqaba and (indirectly) Wadi Rum. Minibuses also leave Wadi Musa for Aqaba (JD3, two hours) at about 6.30am, 8am and 4pm – again, ask around the day before.

For Wadi Rum (JD3, 1½ hours), there is a daily minibus sometime after 6am. You may need to reserve a seat the day before with the driver – ask around the roundabout or your hotel should be able to ring the driver. Alternatively get a minibus to Aqaba, and get off at, and hitch a ride from, the turn-off to Wadi Rum. To Karak, a minibus sometimes leaves at around 8am, but demand is low so it doesn't leave every day. Alternatively, go via Ma'an.

Private Taxi Private (yellow) taxis around Wadi Musa will go anywhere for a price, but negotiation can be an unrewarding process. One-way trips to Little Petra cost about JD10; Wadi Rum or Aqaba, JD30; and Karak, JD40. If you want to travel to Madaba or Amman via the King's Highway, with stops at Karak and possibly Dana or the Dead Sea, expect to pay at least JD80.

Car & Motorcycle Petra and Wadi Musa are well signposted all along the King's and Desert Highways.

Hertz Rent-a-Car (☎ 2156981 or ☎ 0795 914093) has an office in Wadi Musa; it's the first building on your right as you come down the hill towards Petra gate. The cheapest cars cost JD30 per day plus JD10 Collision Damage Waiver (CDW) per day. A 4WD Pajero costs a steep JD100 per day plus JD20 CDW.

The road from Petra to Little Petra has now been extended to rejoin the Wadi Musa to Shobak road and is one of the more scenic alternatives for heading this way. The views are especially nice in the early morning.

Getting Around

The standard, non-negotiable fare anywhere around the central Wadi Musa area is JD1; a little more if you go as far as 'Ain Musa. There are usually plenty of private (yellow) unmetered taxis travelling up and down the main road, especially by late afternoon, looking for weary travellers.

WU'IRA (CRUSADER CASTLE) وعره

Built by the Crusaders in the early 12th century AD, Wu'ira *(admission free; open daylight hours daily)* was abandoned less than 60 years later. A precarious bridge leads to the limited ruins.

Look for the unsigned turn-off, about 1.5km north of the Mövenpick Hotel, and on the left (west) side of the road leading to Siq Barid (Little Petra). See Hiking earlier in this chapter for information about hiking to the castle.

SIQ BARID (LITTLE PETRA) البيد

Siq Barid (The Cold) is colloquially known as Little Petra *(admission free; open daylight hours daily)* although it's nowhere near as dramatic or extensive. The surrounding area is quite picturesque and you're likely to have the place to yourself.

From the car park, an obvious path leads to the 400m-long **siq**, which opens out into larger areas. The first open area has a **temple**, which archaeologists know little about. Four **triclinium** – one on the left and three on the right – are in the second open area, and were probably once used as dining rooms to feed hungry travellers as Siq Barid was something of a minor resupply post on the caravan routes. About 50m further along the *siq* is the **Painted House**, which is another small dining room and is reached by some steps. The badly faded frescoes are on the underside of the interior arch. The room was later used for shelter by local Bedouins whose fires have badly blackened the walls. Cut into the rock opposite the room is a large **cistern**, highlighting the fact that the Romans converted Siq Barid into something of a water storage and resupply point. There are also worn water channels cut into the rock at various points along the walls of the *siq*.

At the end of Siq Barid are some steps. If you climb to the top, there are some **great views**. If you come prepared, you can walk the short distance from here to the ruins of Al-Beidha, or a relatively easy one-hour path to the Monastery (Al-Deir) inside Petra itself. For the latter you must first go to the Petra ticket office and purchase your ticket or get your multi-day ticket stamped. Checks by police in this area are frequent so this is definitely not a way to get into Petra without paying.

As-Siq, Petra

The Treasury, Petra

As-Siq, Petra

Obelisk Tomb and Bab as-Siq Triclinium, Petra

Delivery donkey, Petra

Bedouin guide, Petra

For either hike, it's worth taking along one of the local guides who'll greet you at the car park when you arrive. They can also be moderately useful inside Siq Barid. Prices are negotiable.

Getting There & Away

Prior to the downturn in tourist numbers, a shuttle bus operated between Siq Barid and the village mosque in Wadi Musa (around JD3 return). The bus waits for an hour or two and then takes you back to Wadi Musa. Ask around town (your hotel may try to organise a more expensive tour) or at the visitor centre to see if it's running.

Otherwise, if you can't find a tour to Little Petra being organised by one of the hotels in Wadi Musa, a private taxi will cost about JD10 one way or, if you bargain well, JD15 return including 30 minutes waiting time.

If you're driving, follow the road north of the Mövenpick Hotel and follow the signs to 'Beda' or 'Al-Beidha'. The road twists north through some lovely scenery and past a number of tombs carved into the rock to the west, for 7km. From the fork, take the left road from where it's just under a further 1km to the car park.

Hitching is possible, especially on Friday when local families head out in droves for a picnic.

AL-BEIDHA   البيدا

The ruins of Al-Beidha village date back some 9000 years and, like Jericho, constitute one of the oldest archaeological sites in the Middle East. The remains are worth seeing for this historical significance, but the ruins themselves are fairly unremarkable and require plenty of imagination. There are plans for further excavations, as well as the landscaping of trails and the erection of signposts for visitors.

To get there, follow the trail starting to the left (south) of the entrance to Little Petra for about 20 minutes.

'AIN MUSA   عين موسى

If you arrive in Wadi Musa by public transport from most places, you'll pass a small building (with three white domes) on the right before entering the village which lies 2km downhill. This is not a mosque, but 'Ain Musa (Moses' Spring) where Moses supposedly struck the rock with his staff and water gushed forth to the appreciation of the thirsty masses (see the special section 'Biblical Jordan' for more details).

TAYYIBEH   الطيبه

The scenic road from Wadi Musa to Tayyibeh, about 10km south of Wadi Musa, is spectacular for sunsets and worth driving along at dusk if you have your own vehicle or are able to charter a taxi.

Tayyibeh is the home of **Sofitel Taybat Zaman Hotel & Resort** (*☎ 2150111, fax 215 0101;* **e** *H2818@accor-hotels.com; singles/ doubles US$150/180*), an evocative reconstruction of a traditional stone village with luxurious and spacious rooms, a terrace **restaurant** (*set meal per person US$15*) with superb views (although the food gets mixed reviews), handicraft shops, swimming pool and Turkish bath (JD12 per person). When things are quiet, rates can be negotiable.

Local minibuses (450 fils) from Shaheed roundabout in Wadi Musa village go to Tayyibeh. A taxi will go there for about JD3 one way.

Southern Desert & Aqaba

Jordan's far south is home to two of the country's most popular attractions: Wadi Rum, an enchanting desert landscape of sand and rocks, and Aqaba, which boasts enough diving and snorkelling to satisfy most visitors.

The Desert Highway is the main route between Amman and Aqaba. It passes through monotonous desert for about 300km as far as Ras an-Naqb, from where it winds down off the plateau past the turn-off to Wadi Rum and on to Aqaba. Public buses, minibuses and service taxis between Amman and Aqaba, Petra and Karak all use the Desert Highway. Private buses run by JETT and Trust go via the faster Dead Sea Highway.

QATRANA القطرانه
☎ 03

One of the few towns along the Desert Highway is Qatrana, a couple of kilometres north of the turn-off to Karak. The only reason to stay here is to have a quick look at **Qatrana castle**, built in 1531 by the Ottomans. It has been nicely restored, but nothing is explained. A token effort has been made to fence it off, but it's effectively open to the public and entrance is free.

Qatrana has some uninspiring **eateries** for truckies. Most tourists head for the **Ba'albaki Tourist Complex** (*doubles with bath & breakfast JD32*) about 8km north of Qatrana on the highway. It has souvenir shops and a **restaurant** where buffets cost around JD5.

MA'AN معان
☎ 03

Ma'an has been a transport junction and trading centre for many centuries and is now one of the larger towns and administrative centres in southern Jordan. There's nothing of interest in Ma'an, but the central area is quite pleasant and some travellers may have to stay overnight while waiting for transport to Wadi Rum, Wadi Musa (for Petra) and Aqaba. The people of Ma'an are friendly – probably because they see so few tourists – and there are a couple of decent places to stay and eat. The town is very busy during the haj as it lies on the main route from Jordan and Syria to Mecca in Saudi Arabia.

Highlights

- **Wadi Rum** – this spectacular desert area offers some extraordinary scenery and silent nights under a stunning blanket of stars

- **Camel Treks** – travelling by camel from Wadi Rum to Aqaba or Petra is an interesting alternative to service taxis and minibuses

- **Aqaba** – Jordan's one and only 'resort' has a balmy winter climate and an idyllic setting

- **Diving & Snorkelling** – remarkable marine life and coral are just waiting to be explored off the coast of Aqaba

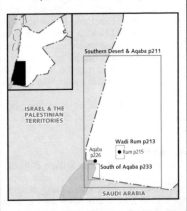

Southern Desert & Aqaba p211

ISRAEL & THE PALESTINIAN TERRITORIES

Wadi Rum p213

Aqaba p226

● Rum p215

South of Aqaba p233

SAUDI ARABIA

Orientation & Information
The main north–south thoroughfare of interest to travellers is King Hussein St, where there are a number of restaurants, and the Arab and Housing Banks, both of which have ATMs. Opposite the Housing Bank is **Horizon Internet Centre** (*☎ 213 1700; e St68@hotmail.com*) where one hour's surfing (fast connections) costs JD1; it's open 9am to 11.30pm Saturday to Thursday and 4pm to 11.30pm on Friday.

Places to Stay & Eat
Kreashan Hotel (*☎ 2132043; Al-Bayyarah St; bed in 3- or 4-bed room JD3, double JD6*),

210

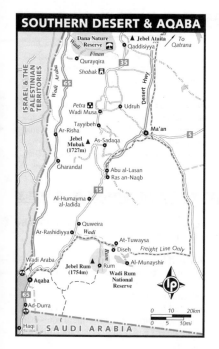

SOUTHERN DESERT & AQABA

also signed as **Krishan Hotel**, has clean, simple and sunny rooms, each with a private balcony, in a central location. The shared bathrooms are clean. It's a small block east of the mosque at the northern end of King Hussein St. The **restaurant** is downstairs *(meals from JD1.500; open 6am-10pm daily)*. It's a friendly place that does the usual fare (including breakfast) but does it well.

Hotel Tabok *(☎ 2132452; singles/doubles JD2/4)*, north of the big roundabout if you're entering the town from the west, has basic but generally clean rooms, although the location is a bit bleak. There is also a seven-bed 'apartment' for JD20.

A similar option, **Shweikh Hotel** *(☎ 213 2427; singles/ doubles JD2/4)* is a little to the south of Hotel Tabok.

There are a number of excellent **restaurants** along King Hussen St which serve good grilled and barbecue chicken for around JD1.500. The **pastry shop** on the corner of King Hussein and Palestine Streets has a huge range of tasty sweet treats. There are also a few **cafés** at the bus station.

Getting There & Away

If you can't get a direct bus to where you want to go in Jordan, chances are that you can find a connection in Ma'an.

The station for buses, minibuses and service taxis is southeast of the centre, an easy 10-minute walk from the Kreashan Hotel. Departures from Ma'an start to get fewer by 2pm and often stop around 5pm.

There are regular minibuses in the morning between Ma'an and Amman's Wahadat bus station (JD1.100, three hours and less frequent service taxis (JD1.200). To Aqaba, minibuses (JD1.500, 80 minutes) and service taxis (JD1.400) are also regular. To Wadi Rum, catch the minibus to Aqaba and hitch a ride from the turn-off. Minibuses to Wadi Musa (for Petra; 600 fils, 45 minutes) leave intermittently in the morning. You could also try a service taxi (JD1.100). To Karak, there are occasional service taxis (JD1.750, two hours) and usually three minibuses (JD1.400) a day.

A chartered taxi to Wadi Musa should cost a negotiable JD7; to Karak or Aqaba, expect to pay JD15.

WADI RUM وادي رم
☎ 03

Wadi Rum offers some of the most extraordinary desert scenery you'll ever see, and is a definite highlight of any visit to Jordan. This area, made famous by the presence of the Arab Revolt and TE Lawrence in the early 20th century, has lost none of its allure and forbidding majesty. Its myriad moods and dramatic colours, dictated by the changing angle of the sun, make for a memorable experience. Unless you're really pushed for time, if at all possible linger for a few days here, slowing down to the timeless rhythm of desert life, enjoying the galaxy of stars overhead at night and the spectacular sunrises and sunsets. Like most deserts, Wadi Rum is as much to be experienced as it is to be seen.

The *jebels* of Wadi Rum completely dominate the small village of Rum, which has a few concrete houses, a school, some shops and the 'Beau Geste' fort, headquarters of the much-photographed Desert Patrol Corps.

The region known as Wadi Rum is actually a series of valleys about 2km wide stretching north to south for about 130km.

SOUTHERN DESERT & AQABA

Desert Patrol

The camel-mounted Desert Patrol was set up to keep dissident tribes in order, and to patrol the border. Today they've exchanged their camels for blue armoured patrol vehicles – with heavy machine guns mounted at the back. They can achieve speeds of over 100km/h through the desert as they pursue their prey (these days drug smugglers near the Saudi border), and occasionally rescue tourists who have lost their way.

The men of the Desert Patrol can be quite a sight in their traditional full-length khaki robes, dagger at the waist, pistol and rifle slung over the shoulder – but mostly they now wear khaki uniforms like anywhere else. Inside the compound, the officer and men on duty (who are not necessarily Bedouin) sit under the shady eucalyptus trees and while away the time entertaining visitors with traditional Arabic coffee and tea and, if you're lucky, stories of their more picaresque predecessors. They still revel in their photogenic nature and will pose for those who sit with them, discuss the inconsequential and pass the time with a tea.

Among the valleys is a desert landscape of sand and rocks, punctuated by towering *jebels* that have eroded into a soft sandstone over a period of up to 50 million years. The valley floors are about 900m above sea level, and the highest peak in Jordan is Jebel Rum (1754m), near the Government Rest House.

Although conveniently and collectively known as 'Bedouin', the major tribe of Wadi Rum is the Huweitat, who claim to be descendants of the Prophet Mohammed. Villagers and nomads throughout the Wadi Rum area number about 5000. The local people are also incredibly friendly, particularly once you get out into the desert, away from the competitive environment of Rum village.

History

Wadi Rum was first possibly mentioned in Ptolemeus' *Geography* as 'Aramaua' and, according to some Islamic scholars, is mentioned in the Quran as 'Ad'. Excavations have confirmed that the area was inhabited between 800 and 600 BC, and was popular with travellers because of the abundance of springs and animals (for hunting). By about the 4th century BC, Wadi Rum was settled by the Nabataeans who built temples and wrote inscriptions on the rocks – many of which can still be seen.

The region is probably more famous because the indefatigable TE Lawrence (see the boxed text 'Lawrence of Arabia' later in this chapter) stayed here in 1917. The serendipitous discovery of a Nabataean temple (behind the Government Rest House) in 1933 again brought Wadi Rum to the attention of the world, but the temple was not completely excavated until 1997 by a team of French archaeologists.

Wildlife

Despite its barren appearance, Wadi Rum is home to a complex ecological system. Dotted among the desert are small plants that are used by the Bedouin for medicinal purposes, and during the infrequent rains parts of the desert can turn into a colourful sea of flowers.

With the extreme heat and lack of water, not many species of animal exist, and sensibly most only venture out at night. If you're really lucky, you may see jackals, wolves, wild goats, the strictly nocturnal Arabian sand cats, and the highly endangered Arabian oryxes, a group of which were released into Wadi Rum in 2002 (see the boxed text 'Saving the Arabian Oryx' in the Eastern Jordan chapter). Rodents such as jerboas and jerbils are more common. A few birds of prey, such as vultures and eagles, as well as more genteel sparrows and larks, can also be found. And watch for scorpions, snakes and the scary (but harmless) camel spiders.

When to Go

The best months to visit are early spring (March and April) and late autumn (October to November). In winter (December to February) it can rain, and snow on the mountains is not uncommon. In the hot season (May to September) daytime temperatures often soar past 40°C. Throughout the year (including summer), however, night-time temperatures can fall to 0°C, so come prepared if you're camping or watching the sunset.

WADI RUM

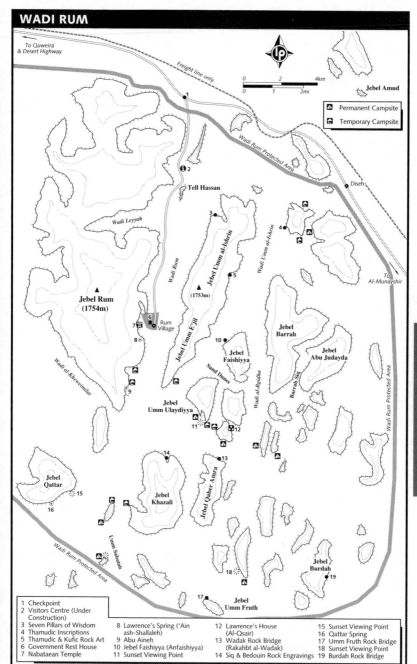

To Quweira
& Desert Highway

Freight line only

Jebel Amud

0   2   4km
0   1   2mi

Wadi Rum Protected Area

Diseh

A Permanent Campsite
C Temporary Campsite

Tell Hassan

Wadi Leyyah

Wadi Rum

Jebel Umm al-Ishrin

Wadi Umm al-Ishrin

Jebel Rum
(1754m)

(1753m)

Jebel Umm E'jil

Rum
Village

To
Al-Munayshir

Wadi al-Khweimilat

Jebel
Barrah

Jebel
Abu Judayda

Jebel
Faishiyya

Sand Dunes

Wadi al-Bqeiha

Barrah Siq

Wadi Rum Protected Area

Jebel
Umm Ulaydiyya

Jebel
Qattar

Jebel
Khazali

Jebel Qaber Amra

Jebel
Burdah

Wadi Rum Protected Area

Umm Sahatah

Jebel
Umm Fruth

1 Checkpoint
2 Visitors Centre (Under
   Construction)
3 Seven Pillars of Wisdom
4 Thamudic Inscriptions
5 Thamudic & Kufic Rock Art
6 Government Rest House
7 Nabataean Temple

8 Lawrence's Spring ('Ain
   ash-Shallaleh)
9 Abu Aineh
10 Jebel Faishiyya (Anfaishiyya)
11 Sunset Viewing Point

12 Lawrence's House
   (Al-Qsair)
13 Wadak Rock Bridge
   (Rakahbt al-Wadak)
14 Siq & Bedouin Rock Engravings

15 Sunset Viewing Point
16 Qattar Spring
17 Umm Fruth Rock Bridge
18 Sunset Viewing Point
19 Burdah Rock Bridge

SOUTHERN DESERT & AQABA

The Bedouin

These desert dwellers, the *bedu* (the name means nomadic), number several hundred thousand, but few can still be regarded as truly nomadic. Most have been crowded out from traditional lands and ways of life by ever-expanding populations and ill-conceived government conceptions of modernity. Some have opted for city life, but most have, voluntarily or otherwise, settled down to cultivate crops.

A few retain the old ways – it is estimated that around 40 families still live a nomadic or semi-nomadic existence in the Wadi Rum area. They camp for a few months at a time in one spot and graze their herds of goats, sheep or camels. When the sparse fodder runs out, it's time to move on again, which also allows the land to regenerate. All over the east and south of the country, you'll see black goat-hair tents (*beit ash-sha'ar* – literally 'house of hair') set up; sometimes just one, often three or four together. Such houses are generally divided into a haram (forbidden area) for women and another section for the men. The men's section is also the public part of the home. Here guests are treated to coffee and sit to discuss the day's events. Most of the family's belongings and stores are kept in the haram (strangers are not permitted inside).

The Bedouin family is a close-knit unit. The women do most of the domestic work, including fetching water, baking bread and weaving clothes. The men are traditionally providers and warriors. There is precious little warring to do these days, and the traditional intertribal raids that for centuries were the staple of everyday Bedouin life are now a memory.

Most of those still living in the desert continue to wear traditional dress, and this includes, for men, a dagger – a symbol of a man's dignity but rarely used in anger now. The women tend to dress in more colourful garb, but rarely do they veil their tattooed faces.

Although camels, once the Bedouin's best friend, are still in evidence, they are now often replaced by the Landrover or Toyota pick-up. Other concessions to modernity are radios (sometimes even TVs), plastic water containers and, occasionally, kerosene stoves.

The Jordanian government provides services such as education, and offers housing to the Bedouin who remain truly nomadic, but both are often passed up in favour of the lifestyle that has served them so well over the centuries.

The Bedouin are renowned for their hospitality and it is part of their creed that no traveller is turned away. This is part of a desert code of survival. Once taken in, a guest will be offered the best of the available food and plenty of tea and coffee. The thinking is simple and based loosely on a principle of reciprocal giving: today you are passing through and they have something to offer; tomorrow they may be passing your camp and you may have food and drink – which you would offer them before having any yourself. Such a code of conduct made it possible for travellers to cross the desert in the knowledge that they had a chance of survival.

One has to wonder, if tourists continue to pass through in ever-growing numbers (and 99 times out of 100 in no danger of expiring on a sand dune), how long outsiders can expect to be regaled with such hospitality, especially where there is no opportunity for reciprocation. After all, the original sense of it has largely been lost. Perhaps the moral for travellers is to be open to such things, but not to deliberately search out the Arab 'hospitality experience', reducing it to a kind of prefab high to be ticked off from the list of tourist excitements claimed as a virtual right. There is a world of difference between the harsh desert existence that engendered this most attractive trait in Arab culture and the rather artificial context in which most of us experience this part of the world today.

Information

Wadi Rum recently came under the management of the Royal Society for the Conservation of Nature (RSCN) and in 1998 the society established the Wadi Rum Protected Area. The project is modelled on similar projects around Jordan – including the highly successful Dana Nature Reserve – and seeks to promote tourism in balance with the imperative to protect fragile ecosystems. As a result, admission to Wadi Rum (*JD2 per person, JD5 per vehicle*) is strictly controlled and all vehicles, camels and guides within Wadi Rum must be arranged either through, or with the approval of, the RSCN.

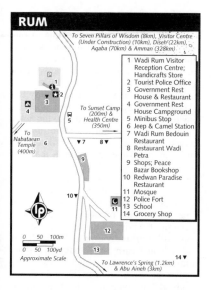

RUM

To Seven Pillars of Wisdom (8km), Visitor Centre
(Under Construction) (10km), Diseh (22km),
Aqaba (70km) & Amman (328km)

To Sunset Camp
(200m) &
Health Centre
(350m)

To
Nabataean
Temple
(400m)

1 Wadi Rum Visitor
Reception Centre;
Handicrafts Store
2 Tourist Police Office
3 Government Rest
House & Restaurant
4 Government Rest
House Campground
5 Minibus Stop
6 Jeep & Camel Station
7 Wadi Rum Bedouin
Restaurant
8 Restaurant Wadi
Petra
9 Shops; Peace
Bazar Bookshop
10 Redwan Paradise
Restaurant
11 Mosque
12 Police Fort
13 School
14 Grocery Shop

0   50   100m
0   50   100yd
Approximate Scale

To Lawrence's Spring (1.2km)
& Abu Aineh (3km)

Until sometime in 2003, the RSCN has a makeshift **visitors reception centre** (☎/fax 2032918; e rum@nets.com.jo) outside the Rest House. The new visitor centre on the road into Rum (about 10km north of the Rest House) was due for completion in 2003.

If you have not pre-arranged a guide (see Guides and Travel Agencies later in this chapter), you will be allocated a guide by the RSCN. Setting off into the desert alone is forbidden. In an effort to preserve the area, only certain campsites are permitted; most visitors come as day trippers so enjoying the solitude is easier than it seems.

The helpful **tourist police** (☎ 2018215) are in a small office in the Rest House complex. The police station (☎ 2017050) in the old police fort will not receive complaints (go to the tourist police), but they will come looking for you if you get lost.

The Bedouin are a conservative people, so please dress appropriately. Loose shorts and tops for men and women are OK around the Rest House and village, but baggy trouser/skirts and modest shirts/blouses will, besides preventing serious sunburn, earn you more respect from the Bedouin, especially out in the desert.

What to Bring Flies during the day can be tiresome and the mosquitos at night (especially if you're sleeping out in the open) can

be voracious, so bring some insect repellent. Also essential are a hat (or Bedouin headgear), sunscreen, sturdy footwear and plenty of water. If you're camping anywhere, including the Rest House, bring a torch (flashlight), a book to read and a padlock (many tents are lockable).

Books & Maps If you plan to do any short hikes and scrambles, pick up a detailed guidebook and map; if you intend to do some serious hiking and rock climbing, organise a guide through the RSCN.

The British climber Tony Howard has spent a lot of time exploring Wadi Rum, and has co-written (with Di Taylor) the excellent and detailed *Treks & Climbs in Wadi Rum* (Cicerone Press). The condensed, pocket-sized and more affordable (JD3 to JD5) version of this is called *Walks & Scrambles in Rum*, and is published by Al-Kutba. Treks and climbs around Wadi Rum are also mentioned in Howard and Taylor's *Jordan – Walks, Treks, Climbs & Canyons*. These books are available at some bookshops throughout Jordan and (normally) at the Peace Bazar Bookshop in Rum village, and occasionally from the Rest House.

The Wadi Rum brochure published by the Jordan Tourism Board is colourful and has a map showing the major sites. The 1997 *Map of Rum* is contoured and detailed for a small section of northern Wadi Rum (ie, around Rum village). The most detailed and informative map is *Wadi Rum Tourist Plan*, published by International Traditional Services Corp, but unfortunately it's not widely available in Jordan.

Shopping The Peace Bazar Bookshop in Rum village has some of the titles listed above.

Also worth a visit is the **Handicrafts Store** (☎ 2032918; open 8am-5pm daily), next to the visitors reception centre, which sells items made by local women to whom most of the profits are returned. It also sells a few books about Wadi Rum.

Excursions
For details on reaching many of the sites described here, see the 4WD and Camels sections that follow. Note that in arranging your excursion, the regulated prices relate only to transportation, and do not include food, tents

Wadi Rum Protected Area

In keeping with its efforts to preserve the fragile local environment, the RSCN requires those making excursions into Wadi Rum to follow a few simple rules, regardless of whether you're in a 4WD, astride a camel or hiking.

- All vehicles must stay on the designated tracks
- Hunting is prohibited, as is the collection of any animals, flowers, herbs, rocks, fossils or archaeological artefacts
- No camping or climbing except in official sites set up for this purpose
- Do not damage any trees or graffiti any rocks
- Do not collect firewood or make fires; apart from damaging trees and shrubs, it may also damage the habitat for local animals
- No littering
- Respect the customs and lifestyle of local people and always ask before you take photos

While many of these rules may seem obvious, the scourge of graffiti and cigarette butts (especially at the sunset sites), as well as damage to rock art and safety bolts left on the *jebels* by climbers, are just a few reminders of where tourists have been, risking lasting environmental damage as well as spoiling it for everyone else, not least the local Bedouin. As the RSCN motto says: 'Leave nothing but footprints, take nothing but memories'.

and blankets. These are a matter for negotiation with your guide and can cost as much as JD35 per person per day (JD20 per person for a group of five); it often includes an extra vehicle to transport these items to your campsite each day. If you have your own sleeping bag, tent and have arranged your own provisions in advance, all you should have to pay is the cost of your four-wheeled or four-legged vehicle.

Short Excursions Most of the attractions around Wadi Rum can be reached in a 4WD vehicle, on a camel or by hiking. Anyone with less money, time and energy can see a few things on foot in the vicinity of the Government Rest House.

On a small hill about 400m behind (southwest of) the Rest House (follow the

telephone poles) are the limited ruins of a 1st-century BC **Nabataean temple**. An interesting explanation (in English and French) of the temple and its excavation is on a wall inside the Rest House. Near the temple are some **inscriptions** by hunters and nomads dating back to the 2nd century BC.

Lawrence's Spring is named after TE Lawrence, who wrote about it in the *Seven Pillars of Wisdom*, but it's more properly known locally as 'Ain ash-Shallaleh. It's fairly unimpressive compared to the other sights of Wadi Rum. Head south from the Rest House and follow the eastern side of Jebel Rum for 1.2km. From the obvious water tank at ground level, a 20-minute scramble up some rocks (follow the line of green shrubs) brings you to a small pleasant pool with startling **views** to Jebel Khazali and beyond. Nearby are **Nabataean inscriptions**, as well as some written by camel drivers of the Saudi Arabian Thamud tribe.

About 3km south of the Rest House, and past Lawrence's Spring, is **Abu Aineh**, which has another spring and temporary camp site for tour groups. To get there, keep following the eastern side of Jebel Rum.

Long Excursions Most of the major attractions, nicer landscapes and better rock formations are further away from Rum village.

The following major sites are the ones featured in the RSCN's itineraries; vehicles, camels and guides can be hired for them. The walking, driving or riding distance from the Rest House in Rum village is included in brackets.

Barrah Siq (14km) This long (about 5km) *siq* is worth exploring, but be very careful if it's raining or rain is imminent; flash floods are possible
Burdah Rock Bridge (19km) This is a narrow piece of rock precariously perched about 80m above the ground. It can be climbed (up the western side) without gear by anyone who has experience in rock climbing (one climber fell to his death here in 1999).
Jebel Faishiyya/Anfaishiyya (10km) It boasts the best Nabataean and Thamudic inscriptions in Wadi Rum, but they're probably of more interest to archaeologists than ordinary travellers
Jebel Khazali (7km) This superb and serene spot has some welcome shade. The narrow *siq* can be explored on foot for about 150m until some you reach some rocks, which can only be surmounted by rope.

Wadi Rum Protected Area

Hejaz Railway, Wadi Rum

Bedouin tent camp, Wadi Rum

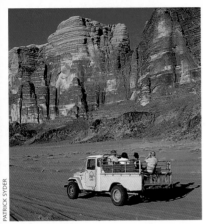

Transport, Wadi Rum

Donkey, Wadi Rum

Sand dunes, Wadi Rum

Camel drivers, Wadi Rum

Lawrence of Arabia

Born in 1888 into a wealthy English family, Thomas Edward Lawrence ('TE' to his friends) studied archaeology, which led him to undertake excavations in Syria and Palestine in 1909 and 1910. With the outbreak of WWI, Lawrence became an intelligence agent in Cairo. Supporting the cause of the Arab Revolt and manifesting his own hostility towards French politics in Syria, Colonel Lawrence favoured the creation of a Sunni and Arab state.

But was it was the desert revolt of 1917 that stirred the Western imagination and etched his name into legend. At the side of Emir Faisal and with the support of General Allenby, Lawrence and the Arab warriors conquered Aqaba. He entered Damascus in triumph, marking the final defeat of the Ottoman Turks. Syria then became a joint Arab–English state, although not the independent one many Arabs had fought for (and been promised).

He has been widely credited in the West as the reason for this important victory over the Turks, often to the chagrin of Arabs, whose soldiers numbered around 100,000, of whom 10,000 were killed. By all accounts, Lawrence, never the most humble of men, did little to alter the perception that he was the figure most responsible for victory.

Returning to England, Lawrence defended his ideas at the Paris Peace Conference and served as the special interpreter of the Hashemites. It was at this time that he started his principal work, *The Seven Pillars of Wisdom*, which recounts his adventures. He apparently wrote it twice, because he lost the first manuscript in a train station in London.

In 1921, he was sent to Trans-Jordan to help Emir Abdullah formulate the foundations of the new state. He later left this position and enrolled in 1922 with the Royal Air Force (RAF), under the assumed name of Ross, first as a pilot, and then as a simple mechanic.

In 1927 he left on a mission to India but returned home because of rumours that he had encouraged an uprising of Afghan tribes. He left the RAF in February 1935 and died on 19 May after a motorcycle accident.

Lawrence's House/Al-Qsair (9km) This is little more than a heap of bricks, apparently once part of a house occupied by Lawrence, and built on the foundations of a Nabataean temple. The remote location and supreme views of the red sands are the main attraction.

Qattar Spring (8km) This beautiful spring is especially worthwhile during the rainy season and the immediate area offers some short hikes

Sand Dunes/Red Sands (6km) While there are sand dunes in several places around Wadi Rum, this section to which most groups are taken has a small section of beautiful red sand up the slope of Jebel Umm Ulaydiyya. It's a great place for scrambling around and falling over.

Seven Pillars of Wisdom (8km) Named after Lawrence's book, this large rock formation is easy to see and reach from the main road into Wadi Rum, just south of the junction to Diseh. Because it is so accessible, it's not included on the usual tours from Rum village, but can be arranged as an extra. Otherwise, hitch a ride or walk along the main road from the Rest House.

Sunset & Sunrise (11km) Dusk and dawn are the magical (and cooler) times to be in the desert. The best vantage points differ according to the time of year; the most common is Umm Sabatah. Jeep drivers can take you there and

either wait or pick you up later (they are reliable about such things); or arrange a sunset tour which includes a traditional Bedouin dinner for a negotiable price.

Umm Fruth Rock Bridge (13km) This is another small and remote rock bridge that can easily be climbed without gear or a guide

Wadak Rock Bridge/Rakahbt al-Wadak (9km) This rock formation is easier to climb and more accessible than Burdah Rock Bridge, but is not as impressive. The views across the valley are superb.

Guides & Travel Agencies

If you arrive in Wadi Rum as an independent traveller without having pre-arranged a guide, the taxi rank principle applies – you take the next guide/driver on the RSCN's roster. This is perfectly adequate as all the guides on the RSCN list are experienced and, increasingly, well trained.

If, however, you wish to request a specific guide, you are advised to contact the guide in advance and confirm the request with a fax or email to the RSCN. It's possible to simply turn up and request a particular guide, but you run the risk of them not being available and for longer excursions some planning is required on the part of the guide (eg, buying provisions, arranging camels).

Among those guides which we recommend or which have been highly recommended by readers are:

Al-Hillawi Desert Services (☎/fax 2018867, ☎ 0795 940117, e camping@hillawiservices .com, w www.hillawiservices.com) Run by the manager of the Rest House
Aouda Abdillah (☎ 0795 617902, e aodeh25@ yahoo.com, w www.aodeh.de/index.htm)
Attayak Ali (☎/fax 2032651, ☎ 0795 689373) Also one of the registered climbing guides
Attayak Aouda (☎/fax 2035844, ☎ 0795 834736)
Attallah Sweilhin (☎ 2033508, ☎ 077 428449, e attallah_hours@hotmail.com) Also arranges horse trekking
Difallah Ateeg (☎/fax 2019135, ☎ 0795 539956, e difallahz@yahoo.com)
Hussein Suleiman (☎/fax 2019645, ☎ 0795 583763)
Mohammed Sabah Al-Zalabeh (☎/fax 2032961, ☎ 077 427809, e mohammed_rum@yahoo .com, w www.mohammedwadirum.8m.com)
Sabagh Eid (☎/fax 2016238)
Zedane Al-Zalabieh (☎/fax 2032607, ☎ 0795 506417, e zedn_a@yahoo.com)

4WD

Most jeeps seat six people and some of the older ones are pick-ups with bench seats in the back. The official (fixed) rates set by the RSCN, and to which all drivers must adhere, for 4WD excursions are in the boxed text below.

Most of the places listed in Long Excursions earlier in this chapter could be visited,

albeit quickly, in about six hours, but if you pay for the vehicle for the day you should have no problem. Some drivers may, however, be reluctant to visit everywhere you want to go. Make sure you discuss your itinerary with the driver/guide, and the RSCN, before you set out, and if you have any complaints of this kind, make sure you report them to the RSCN when you return to Rum.

It's also important to realise that the maximum times listed above are exaggerated and your journey time may be significantly less. On the negative side of things, refunds for shorter excursions than you expected are not possible. On the positive side, Wadi Rum is best enjoyed if you slow down to the pace of the desert and don't race around in a mad rush. Take your time at each site as you'll still have time to complete the itinerary if you linger for a while to admire the view and soak up the silence.

Better still, if possible, plan to spend at least one night (preferably more) sleeping under stars which is when you'll most appreciate being here.

Camels

If you have the time, travelling around Wadi Rum by camel is highly recommended. Apart from being ecologically sound, it will enable you to experience Wadi Rum as the Bedouin have for centuries and to really appreciate the silent gravitas of the desert.

The official RSCN rates per person per camel are in the boxed text on the following page.

Note that if you take a camel overnight, you will need to negotiate an additional

4WD Excursions in Wadi Rum			
sites	km	maximum time (hrs)	price (JD) per vehicle
Lawrence's Spring	6	½	7
Jebel Khazali	14	1½	15
Sunset sites (via Lawrence's Spring & Jebel Khazali)	22	2	18
Sand dunes (via Lawrence's Spring, Jebel Khazali & Lawrence's House)	26	2	25
Rock Bridge (via Lawrence's Spring, Jebel Khazali & Umm Fruth Rock Bridge)	40	3	32
Barrah Siq (via Lawrence's Spring, Jebel Khazali & Rock Bridge)	50	6	45
Day Hire	open	unlimited	45
Day Vehicle for luggage	-	-	35

Camel Treks in Wadi Rum

sites	km	maximum time (hrs)	price (JD)
Nabataean Temple	1	1	2
Lawrence's Spring	6	2	7
Jebel Khazali	14	4	16
Sunset sites (via Lawrence's Spring & Jebel Khazali)	22	overnight	40
Sand dunes (via Lawrence's Spring, Jebel Khazali & Lawrence's House)	26	5	20
Rock Bridge (via Lawrence's Spring, Jebel Khazali & Umm Fruth Rock Bridge)	40	overnight	40
Day Hire	unlimited	6	20
Day Camel for luggage	-	-	20

price for food, tents and so on (see Excursions earlier in this chapter).

It is also possible to arrange camel excursions from Wadi Rum to Aqaba (three to six nights depending on the route); or to near Wadi Musa (for Petra; about five nights). In addition to the usual JD20 per camel per day rate, you'll need to factor in the necessary provisions, tents (if required), and returning the camels back to Rum.

Horse Trekking

An alternative and memorable mode of four-legged transport through Wadi Rum and surrounding areas is by horse. Expect to pay around JD50 per day. Among the agencies or guides who can organise such an expedition are:

Attallah Sweilhin (☎ 2033508, ☎ 077 428449, |e| attallah_hours@hotmail.com)
Bait Ali (☎ 2016331, fax 2012699, |e| info@ desertexplorer.net, |w| www.desertexplorer.net)

Hiking

For longer excursions, a guide is compulsory – check with the RSCN to see whether you are allowed to venture out alone as these rules were in a state of flux when we visited. One popular hike is a circumambulation of Jebel Rum (eight hours).

Remember that it's very easy to get disoriented; temperatures can be extreme; natural water supplies are not common and sometimes undrinkable; passing traffic is rare; and maps are often inaccurate. Hiking should not be attempted in the hotter months (May to September). That said, if you come prepared (5L water containers

can be bought at the shops in Rum) and notify the RSCN and/or tourist police of your planned route, it can be a wonderful way to see Wadi Rum.

The books by Tony Howard and Di Taylor (see Books & Maps earlier in this chapter) list a number of hikes in the region.

Rock Climbing

Wadi Rum offers some challenging rock climbing, equal to anything in Europe and some climbers believe it to be even better. There's a vast array of climbs right up to French 8 grade. The most accessible and popular climbs are detailed in books written by Tony Howard and Di Taylor (see Books & Maps earlier in this chapter).

While rock climbing is still a nascent industry in Wadi Rum and you'll need to bring your own gear, the situation has improved in recent years. There are at least six accredited climbing guides (contactable through the RSCN), most of whom have been trained in the UK. When arranging a climbing trip, contact the RSCN at least a few days in advance so that equipment and transport can also be organised and prices negotiated. Expect to pay a minimum of JD110 for one to two days' climbing – it may sound expensive but it's not when compared to Europe, and few climbers leave disappointed.

One of the more popular climbs for amateur climbers is up Jebel Rum, because minimal gear is needed and it's close to the Rest House, although a guide is still required to find the best route and to help with the climb. There are also a number of sites north of the road to Diseh.

Organised Tours

Although it's not necessary to do so, you can arrange trips to Wadi Rum through most of the hotels in Wadi Musa, as well as the following agencies:

International Traders (☎ 2013757, fax 2015316, **e** aqaba.office@traders.com.jo) Aqaba. Not really for budget travellers, this agency is expensive but reliable

Peace Way Tours (☎ 2022665, **e** tours@peace way.com) Aqaba. This budget agency gets decidedly mixed reviews from readers

Petra Moon (☎ 2156665, fax 2156666, **e** eid@ petramoon.com) Wadi Musa. Very professional. Check their website at **w** www.petramoon.com

Qutaish & Sons (☎ 2014679, fax 2013882) Aqaba. Another long-standing budget agency although, again, with both positive and negative reports from travellers

Costs start from JD45 per person per day (including transport, food and an overnight stay in the desert) and can rise well above this. Make sure you find out exactly what you're getting for your money, including how many meals are covered by the price.

Places to Stay

Thankfully there is still no hotel in Rum village or anywhere in Wadi Rum, and most of those who stay overnight understandably prefer to sleep out in the desert.

Rum Village There are tents out the back of the **Government Rest House** (☎ 2018867; mattress in 2-person tent JD3 per person), but they're only recommended if you arrive in Wadi Rum too late to head into the desert. Some of the mattresses are very thin. You do have access to the toilets and hot showers in the Rest House, as well as a communal Bedouin tent in which to relax. The tents are lockable so bring a small padlock as the site is open to the car park and has little security. Always keep your valuables with you.

It's also possible to find a bed with a family in Rum village. The only organised arrangement is through the **Restaurant Wadi Petra** (☎/fax 2019135, ☎ 0795 539956; **e** di fallahz@yahoo.com; mattress JD2 per person).

There is also the excellent **Sunset Camp** (☎/fax 2032961, ☎ 0795 502421; **e** moham med_rum@yahoo.com, **w** www.mohammed wadirum.8m.com; beds in tent JD6-8), next to the phone tower in Rum village.

In the Desert Experiencing the legendary hospitality of the Bedouins and sleeping out under the stars are among the primary reasons for heading out into the desert. Under the RSCN rules, camping is permitted only in certain designated areas (these are marked on the Wadi Rum map).

If you want to sleep out in the open air, remember that it can get very cold at night and mosquitos can be a problem.

Places to Eat

Government Rest House (☎/fax 2018867; starters 600-960 fils, mains JD3.600-8.400 including tax; open 6.30am-10pm daily) is good value. A main dish of kebabs or *shish tawouk*, french fries, and salads and dips costs JD3.600. Sandwiches cost 720 fils to JD1.200, an omelette is JD1.200 and a continental breakfast costs JD3. If there are enough people, open buffets are served for JD6. The Rest House also serves alcohol, and drinking a large Amstel beer (JD2.500) while watching the sun's rays light up Jebel Umm al-Ishrin is a perfect way to finish off a tough day.

Outside the Rest House, **Restaurant Wadi Petra** (☎/fax 2019135; breakfast JD1.500, dinner or lunch JD3; open 6.30am-11pm daily) is an excellent choice. It's clearly visible from the Rest House and the dining area is pleasant.

Along the main road of Rum Village, the **Wadi Rum Bedouin Restaurant** and **Red-wan Paradise** (open 6am-1am daily) serve fairly standard local fare for around JD2.

For those on a tight budget, the small **grocery stores** along the main road through Rum village have canned food, biscuits and mineral water. If you're arranging your own provisions for an excursion into the desert, you'll have greater variety if you stock up elsewhere en route to Wadi Rum.

Getting There & Away

Public transport is limited because Rum village has a small population and many visitors come on tours organised by agencies or hotels from Wadi Musa or Aqaba. All public transport stops in front of the Rest House.

Minibus It's a good idea to check at the visitor centre or Rest House when you arrive in Wadi Rum to check the prevailing departure times.

At the time of research, there was at least one minibus a day to Aqaba (JD1.500, one hour); 7am is the most reliable departure time. From Sunday to Thursday, you should also find one leaving around 12.30pm and possibly again at 3pm, ferrying teachers from the school back to Aqaba. On Friday and Saturday, there is sometimes a minibus around noon. To Wadi Musa (JD3, 1½ hours), there is a daily minibus at 8.30am.

If you want to head to Ma'an, Karak or Amman, the minibuses to either Aqaba or Wadi Musa can drop you along the Desert Highway (750 fils, 20 minutes), where it's easy enough to hail onward transport.

Private Taxi Occasionally taxis hang around the visitor centre and Rest House waiting for a fare back to wherever they came from – normally Aqaba, Wadi Musa or Ma'an. To charter a taxi, count on about JD20 to Aqaba, and JD25 to Wadi Musa or Ma'an. We did, however, meet two travellers who chartered a taxi in Aqaba and paid JD25 for the return journey *including* six hours waiting time.

Hitching Because of the limited public transport to and from Rum village, many travellers (including locals) are forced to hitch – a normal form of transport in this part of Jordan.

The well-signposted turn-off to Wadi Rum is along the Desert Highway, about 5km south of Quweira. From Aqaba, take any minibus heading along the highway and get out at the turn-off (600 fils); from Wadi Musa or other towns to the north, anything headed towards Aqaba will pass the Rum road. Hitching from here may involve an hour or two's waiting time, but traffic is reasonably regular. Drivers sometimes ask up to JD3 for taking you. Alternatively, if you have pre-arranged your excursion through Wadi Rum with a guide, he may come out to pick you up.

DISEH الدسيه

Diseh is northwest of Rum village, about 12km as the vulture flies but 22km by road. Inhabitants and devotees of Wadi Rum insist that Diseh is a very poor cousin. With the changes introduced by the RSCN, Diseh has in some ways indeed become a less attractive option because you cannot enter the Wadi Rum Protected Area direct from Diseh, but must travel via the visitor centre and Rum village. However, you could easily arrange your transport and guide in Diseh and then enter with them through the main entrance. While the scenery is not as spectacular as it is at Wadi Rum, there are some recommended camps in Diseh that have been given the thumbs up from readers and you'll still find yourself sleeping in the silence of what is still a beautiful desert. This can be nice, provided you don't need too many luxuries.

Things to See
The paved road to Diseh from the turn-off to Rum offers a few accessible *jebels* and landscapes, which are easy to explore. Locals will happily (and for a price) drive you out into the desert area north of the railway line. The area is dotted with **Nabataean and Roman dams**, artificial **rock bridges**, **rock carvings** and **inscriptions**. The landscape around **Jebel Amud** is the most interesting.

Places to Stay & Eat
A number of camps in or near Diseh have been recommended by readers. Expect to pay around JD6 for a bed in a communal tent or JD8 for a tent to yourself.

Jabal Rum Camp (☎ 0795 536391; e jabal_rum_camp@yahoo.com) is a large, well-run camp that organises traditional Bedouin performances if there are enough people. Take the Diseh road from the police checkpoint (16km after leaving the Desert Highway) for 3km. Just after the railway crosses the road, a turn-off leads a further 2km to the camp.

North of the railway line is the well-run campsite of **Bait Ali** (☎ 2016331, fax 201 2699; e info@desertexplorer.net, w www.desertexplorer.net; bed in communal tent JD6, bed in private tent JD8). Breakfast costs an additional JD2, and they also arrange horse trekking (see earlier in this chapter).

Safari Camping (☎ 0795 583763; e hussein_rum@yahoo.com) is in Diseh itself and is also a good place to camp.

Palm Camp (☎ 06-5624056, fax 5623670) and **Captain's Camp** (☎ 2016905, ☎ 0795 510432, fax 2016904; e captains@firstnet.com.jo) have also been recommended by readers, as has **Bedouin Meditation Camp** (☎/fax 2032607, ☎ 0795 506417; e zedn_a@yahoo.com).

SOUTHERN DESERT & AQABA

Getting There & Away

You're unlikely to find a minibus or service taxi headed all the way to Diseh, so follow the instructions for getting to Wadi Rum and get out at the turn-off to Diseh (the police checkpoint 16km after leaving the Desert Highway). From there you'll have to hitch (be prepared for quite a wait), or the police may, if you ask nicely, ring ahead to one of the camps, where someone is usually happy to come out and pick you up.

AQABA   العقبة
☎ 03

The balmy winter climate and idyllic setting on the Gulf of Aqaba make this Jordan's aquatic playground. While Amman shivers in winter with temperatures around 5°C and the occasional snowfall, the daytime mercury in Aqaba rarely goes below 20°C and is often quite a few degrees warmer. In summer, however, the weather is uncomfortably hot, with daytime temperatures over 35°C, but it's often made bearable by the sea breezes. It also helps if you enjoy the mandatory siesta between 1pm and 4pm.

Aqaba is popular with Jordanians from the north (forget trying to get a room during holidays such as Eid al-Adha – see Islamic Holidays in the Facts for the Visitor chapter), and with Saudis from across the border. It's also an obvious place to break a journey to/from Israel/Egypt. Diving and snorkelling are Aqaba's main attractions. It's not as extensive as Egypt, but is still a great place to explore the underwater brilliance of the coral-rich gulf. Aqaba is a relaxed place with a good range of hotels and restaurants. The port does mar the view a little and the beaches close to town are fairly unappealing, but it's still a good place to kick back and relax from the rigours of life on the road.

History

Excavations at Tell al-Khalifa, 4km west of central Aqaba and right on the border of Jordan and Israel and the Palestinian Territories, have revealed copper smelters thought to be the site of Ezion Geber as mentioned in the Bible. Smelting was also carried out here from the 10th to 5th centuries BC with ore coming from mines in Wadi Araba.

As trade with southern Arabia and Sheba (present-day Yemen) developed, the area around Aqaba thrived because the great road from Damascus came through, via Amman and Petra, and then headed off west to Egypt and Palestine. The main town was occupied by the Ptolemies from Egypt during the 2nd and 3rd centuries BC, and then the Nabataeans from about the 3rd to the 1st centuries BC. During Roman times it was renamed Aqabat Ayla (Pass of Alia).

At the time of the Muslim invasion in AD 636, there was a church and even a bishop of Ayla. In the 10th century, a Muslim traveller described Aqaba as 'a great city' and a meeting place of pilgrims en route to and from Mecca. In AD 1024, the town was sacked by local tribes and then consigned to a minor historical role after subsequent and devastating earthquakes.

The Crusaders occupied the area in the 12th century and fortified a small island nearby – then called Ile de Graye, but now known as Pharaoh's Island (see the South of Aqaba section later in this chapter). By 1170, both the port and island were in the hands of the Ayyubids, under Saladin. In 1250, the Mamluks took over. By the beginning of the 16th century, the town had been swallowed up by the Ottoman Empire, and lost much of its significance when the main trading area of the region was moved to Baghdad in the middle of the 16th century.

For about 500 years, until the Arab Revolt during WWI, Aqaba remained an insignificant fishing village. Ottoman forces occupying the town were forced to retreat after a raid by the Arabs and TE Lawrence in 1917. From then on, the British used Aqaba as a supply centre from Egypt for the push up through the Trans-Jordan and Palestine regions.

After WWI, the border between Trans-Jordan and Saudi Arabia had still not been defined, so Britain arbitrarily drew a line a few kilometres south of Aqaba. The Saudis disputed the claim but took no action. As the port of Aqaba grew, the limited coastline proved insufficient, so in 1965 King Hussein traded 6000 sq km of Jordanian desert for another 12km of coastline with Saudi Arabia.

Orientation

King Hussein St (also known as the Corniche) is the main axis of Aqaba. It runs more or less north–south along the coast through the centre of town, and follows the Gulf of Aqaba around to the west as far as Israel and the Palestinian Territories, and to the south as far as Saudi Arabia. In the city, a walking path parallels King Hussein St, but it only hugs the coast in small sections because of the private beaches owned by the upmarket hotels, as well as the marina and navy docks.

Most of the charmless urban sprawl in Aqaba is taking place to the north and west of the centre, and the massive port facilities start a few kilometres south of the centre. Consequently, central Aqaba has been spared the worst ravages of development and remains quite pleasant. Most of the budget and mid-range hotels, restaurants, banks and other facilities are clustered together in the bustling city centre, with the more upmarket hotels at the northwestern end of the beach.

Information

Tourist Office The tourist office (☎/fax 2013363) is in the visitor centre at the western end of Prince Mohammed St near the waterfront. Inside the small complex, look for the door marked 'Information'. Staff are friendly enough but offer little more than a limited range of brochures published by the Jordan Tourism Board. The office is open from 7.30am to 2.30pm Sunday to Thursday, although there are plans to open 8am to 8pm daily in the future.

Visa Extensions The police station (☎ 201 2411), opposite the bus station, should be able to help with visa extensions, although there was talk of moving this function to another building nearby when we were there. A three-month extension is usually available on the spot and is free. It's best to go earlier in the day (8am to 3pm). Aqaba is the only reliable place to get your visa extended outside Amman.

Money There are numerous banks around the city. Many are located along the southern side of Al-Hammamat al-Tunisieh St. They include: the Arab Bank, which has an ATM for Visa and MasterCard, near the park; Jordan National Bank on Zahran St; the Housing Bank (with an ATM for Visa and Plus cards) along the Corniche; and the Arab Investment and Jordan Islamic Banks on Al-Hammamat al-Tunisieh St, which have ATMs for Visa and Plus cards. There's also a Housing Bank ATM outside the post office (Visa and Plus cards).

Numerous moneychangers are also dotted around the city centre; many are congregated around the corner of Zahran and Ar-Razi Streets. They're open for far longer than banks, and most change travellers cheques without commission.

The agent for American Express is **International Traders** (☎ 2013757, fax 2015316; e aqaba.office@traders.com.jo) Located on Al-Hammamat al-Tunisieh St, they're open 8.30am to 1pm and 4pm to 7pm Saturday to Thursday, but they don't change travellers cheques.

Tickets for the ferry or fast boat to Egypt (see Sea in the Getting There & Away chapter) must be purchased in US dollars cash if bought at the ferry port, but there are exchange booths at the terminal for this. If you buy a ticket from one of the agencies in town, you can usually pay in dinars.

Post & Communications The **General Post Office** is open from 7.30am to 7pm Saturday to Thursday and 7.30am to 1.30pm on Friday. There is a reasonably efficient poste restante service.

Outside the post office is a gaggle of Alo telephone booths, and several stalls nearby sell telephone cards. Other private telephone agencies are located on the main streets, and some moneychangers also offer telephone services. Note that international calls from Aqaba are up to five times cheaper than in Wadi Rum.

Aqaba telephone numbers now conform with the national seven-digit standard. If you come across an old six-digit number, replace the first '3' with '20' (eg, 313757 becomes 2013757).

DHL (☎ 2012039) has an office on Al-Petra St.

Email & Internet Access Aqaba has a good sprinkling of Internet cafés, most of which charge JD2 although this may come down in the future. Two recommended places are in the building to the southeast of the Aqaba Gulf Hotel on King Hussein St: **Samir Internet Café** (☎ 2033413) has superfast ASDL connections and is open 9am to 11pm daily, and **City Internet** (☎ 2018732) is open 24 hours. You could also try **Salsabeel Internet Café** (☎ 2034044), opposite Gelato Uno (see Places to Eat later in this chapter) and also open 24 hours.

Bookshops Aqaba has two excellent bookshops that sell a range of international newspapers as well as books about Jordan and the region. The **Redwan Bookshop** (☎ 2013704; e redwanbook@firstnet.com.jo), on Zahran St, is one of the best in Jordan with an extensive selection of hard-to-find Jordanian titles, Lonely Planet guidebooks and novels. It's open 8.30am to 12.30pm and 4pm to 9pm daily, and sometimes open at other times and on Friday. **Yamani Library** (☎/fax 2012221), also on Zahran St a few doors to the north, is open 10am to 2.30pm and 5pm to 9.30pm every day and has a good range.

Photography & Film There are numerous photo stores around Aqaba. One of the more reliable ones is **Photo Hagop** (☎ 2012025) on Zahran St. To develop a roll of 36 prints costs JD4.500, while a roll of 36 100ASA print film costs JD2. For slide film, prices start from JD4 and video cartridges cost from JD3.500. It's open 8.30am to 11pm daily.

Electricity In a reminder of Britain's influence in the region, some sockets in Aqaba are of the British variety although many have now been converted to the European two-pin plug. If you plan on using your own electrical appliances, it's worth bringing both kinds of socket just in case.

Laundry Most visitors stay long enough in Aqaba to get some laundry done – especially useful if you've gathered layers of dust and sand from Wadi Rum. Among the better places are **Frindes laundry** (☎ 201 5051; open 8am-1pm & 4pm-10pm Sat-Thur), on Al-Petra St, which charges 200/400/500 fils for socks/shirt/trousers, and **Rana Dry Clean** (open 9am-midnight Sat-Thur) on An-Nahda St, where charges are the same.

Emergency The well-equipped **Princess Haya Hospital** (☎ 2014111) has great views if you're convalescing. It also offers **decompression chambers** (☎ 2014111, ☎ 201 4117), and staff are trained to deal with diving accidents. The most convenient **police station** (☎ 2012411 or ☎ 191) is opposite the bus station on Ar-Reem St.

Dangers & Annoyances Women travellers have reported varying degrees of harassment from local lads on the public beaches. This may even happen on the private beaches belonging to the upmarket hotels, to which you should report anything immediately. On the public beaches, foreign women will feel far more relaxed (but not necessarily more comfortable) wearing loose shirts and baggy shorts. See the later Beaches entry for more details.

Ayla (Old Aqaba)

Along the Corniche, and incongruously squeezed between the marina and the Mövenpick Resort, is the site of old Aqaba, the early medieval port city that bore the name of Ayla. The ruins are limited, but worth a quick look if you're in the area. Helpful noticeboards in English clearly pinpoint items of interest and put the place in some perspective. The site is free to enter, permanently open and easily accessible from the main road.

At the back of the parking space behind the JETT bus office is another small section of the old city, but this is fenced off while excavations continue.

Aqaba Castle (Mamluk Fort)

Aqaba castle (admission in low/high season 500 fils/JD1; open 7am-5pm daily Oct-Apr, 7am-7pm May-Sept), measures around 50m by 50m although it is unusual in having sides of slightly uneven length. It is worth looking around as it has been partially reconstructed and gives some sense of its original form.

The first castle may have been built by the Crusaders in the 13th century, but most scholars attribute its construction to the Mamluks during the reign of the sultan Qansur al-Ghuri (1510–17), as attested by the attractive relief inscriptions in Arabic inside the entrance gate. In one of the eastern rooms off the main courtyard are further inscriptions suggesting that the castle was renovated and enlarged by the Ottomans in 1587 and 1628. In subsequent centuries, the castle was probably used as a khan or caravanserai for travelling pilgrims on their way between their homeland and Mecca. The Ottomans occupied the castle until World War I when, in 1917, the fortress was substantially destroyed by shelling from the British Royal Navy. The Hashemite coat of arms above the main entrance was raised soon afterwards as the Arab Revolt swept through Aqaba.

A helpful map and explanation in English is on a noticeboard in the southwest corner of the courtyard. Please note that tickets must be purchased at the museum (see following) in the visitor centre and entitles you to enter both on the same ticket.

Aqaba Museum (Museum of Aqaba Antiquities)

This small museum *(admission low/high season 500 fils/JD1; open 7am-5pm daily Oct-Apr, 7am-7pm May-Sept)* is inside the visitor centre. The centre and museum were once the home of Sherif Hussein bin Ali – the great-great-grandfather of the present king, Abdullah II – who lived here for a while after WWI.

The collection of artefacts includes coins from Iraq and Egypt, ceramics from the excavations of Ayla (Old Aqaba), 8th-century stone tablets from the Islamic period and some late Byzantine reliefs. All captions are in English and there are some informative descriptions of the items and the archaeological history of the area. The ticket also entitles you to enter the castle.

Beaches

Aqaba promotes itself as a resort (most pictures feature people happily water-skiing and lazing on the beach), but the town itself is not nearly as developed for such activities as it pretends to be. For most of the watersports action and the better beaches, you'll need to head south of town (see South of Aqaba later in the chapter). Even here there is often little shade and public transport is limited.

Now that the Mövenpick Resort has taken over one of the few public beaches, the only free beaches in Aqaba are the stretch of sand (most of which is covered with cafés) between the navy docks and Aqaba castle; and just south of the Mina House Restaurant, which is the safest public beach for women – although it's all relative. These beaches are fairly unattractive.

The beaches run by the upmarket hotels in the northwest part of Aqaba are clean and available to the public, but normally at a cost. The Aquamarina, Radisson SAS and Mövenpick Resort hotels all charge anywhere between JD2.500 and JD10 to use their beaches, but may reduce this if things are quiet and you look presentable.

Glass-Bottom Boats

If you can't go diving or snorkelling, the next best thing is a ride in a glass-bottom boat. The ride is fun, but the amount of fish and coral that can be seen is usually disappointing unless you get away from central Aqaba (where much of the coral has died) and hire the boat for two to three hours. The going rate for a boat (holding about 10 people) is about JD10 per hour, but, with patience, you may be able to negotiate down to around JD5 if business is quiet or competition is fierce (especially on Friday). Ask around the hotels about sharing costs with other travellers, or wait for a boat to fill up.

Most boats line up along the public beach lined with cafés north of the castle.

The glass-bottom boats can also be rented for longer trips if you want to go swimming or snorkelling (bring or rent your own equipment); this is a great day out if you can get a group together. Count on about JD50 per day for a boat holding ten people, or about JD35 for a boat holding six.

Activities

Water Sports Al-Cazar Hotel (Club Murjan), Aquamarina Beach Hotel and Royal Diving Club south of Aqaba are well set up for water sports. Nothing is cheap of course: it's about JD3 for a short burst of water-skiing and JD4 for windsurfing. Another place to ask about jet-skis or expensive yacht trips is around the marina. Locals prefer the more sedate paddle boats, available along the public beach north of Aqaba castle. Any of the dozens of the faster speedboats docked around the Mina House Floating Restaurant can also be rented for very negotiable prices.

It is important to remember that activities such as jet-skis, water-skiing and speedboats are not permitted in the Red Sea Aqaba Marine Park (see the boxed text 'Red Sea Aqaba Marine Park' under South of Aqaba later in this chapter) so must be done out in open water to avoid damaging the fragile coral. The bay around the city centre is usually OK.

Diving & Snorkelling For details of the diving sites along the coast south of town, see South of Aqaba later in this chapter.

It's important to remember that if you dive to any depth, it is dangerous to go to certain altitudes until after six hours have

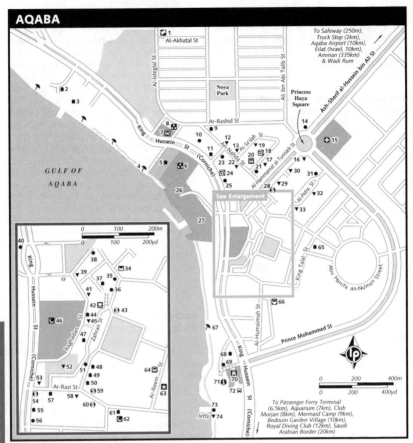

elapsed. This includes the road to Petra and most roads out of Aqaba. Deeper dives require an even longer time period.

Turkish Baths

Aqaba Turkish Baths (☎ 2031605), on King Hussein St, offers the full works – massage, steam bath and scrubbing – for JD8. Readers have highly recommended this place. Women are welcome to attend, but need to make a reservation in advance so that 'special arrangements' (ie, female attendants though this can't be guaranteed) can be found. They're open 9am to 9pm daily.

Places to Stay

Aqaba is a popular place for Jordanian and Saudi tourists in winter (October to March),

but the exact dates of this peak season (and therefore prices) can fluctuate widely on the whim of local hotel staff. People also flock to Aqaba from northern Jordan during long weekends and public holidays, especially around Eid al-Adha (immediately after the haj), for which you'd need to book weeks in advance. At these times, prices may also increase by as much as 30%.

Just about all hotels, including the budget places listed here, have air-conditioning and sometimes a fan. In the summer the air-conditioning is more a necessity than a luxury, and always make sure it's working before forking out any money. In summer, budget travellers may find it cooler to sleep on the roof of their hotel or at one of the camps along the beach south of Aqaba.

AQABA

PLACES TO STAY

2	Radisson SAS Hotel; Coral Bar
3	Aquamarina Beach Hotel; Arab Bank ATM; Nightclub; Diving Club
5	Mövenpick Resort Hotel
9	Al-Cazar Hotel; Al-Cazar Car Rental; Dolphin Bar; Sea Star
11	Aqaba Gulf Hotel
37	Dweikh Hotel 1; Red Sea Hotel; Nairoukh Hotel 1; Amira Hotel
44	Al-Amer Hotel; Al-Shuala Hotel Syrian Palace Restaurant; Al-Tarboosh Restaurant
47	Al-Khouli Hotel; National Restaurant
48	Jordan Flower Hotel
49	Petra Hotel
50	Jerusalem Hotel
55	Nairoukh 2 Hotel; Arab Divers; German Honorary Consulate
57	Crystal Hotel; Romantic Bar
61	Al-Naher al-Khaled Hotel
65	Al-Zatari Hotel
68	Moon Beach Hotel

PLACES TO EAT

12	Chicken Tikka Restaurant; Floka Restaurant
13	Pizza Hut
16	Mr Cool Café
17	Gelato Uno
19	Silk Road Restaurant
22	Chilli House; Captain's Restaurant; Rana Dry Clean
29	Bakery
30	Al-Mohandes Cafeteria
32	Humam Supermarket
33	China Restaurant
39	Ali Baba Restaurant
41	Hani Ali
45	Al-Shami Restaurant; Qutaish & Sons Travel Agency
52	Produce Souq
53	Pearls Fast Food
58	Juice Stands
74	Mina House Floating Restaurant

OTHER

1	Egyptian Consulate
4	Private Beach
6	Ayla (Old Aqaba) Ruins
7	JETT Bus Office
8	Ayla (Old Aqaba) Ruins
10	Oryx Rent-a-Car (Miramar Hotel)
14	Royal Jordanian Airlines Office
15	Princess Haya Hospital
18	Salsabeel Internet Cafe
20	Trust International Transport Bus Office
21	Hertz Car Rental; Coffee Shops
23	Red Sea Diving Centre
24	Samir Internet Cafe; City Internet
25	Aqaba International Dive Centre
26	Marina; Romero Restaurant; Royal Yacht Club of Jordan
27	Navy Docks
28	Arab Investment Bank; Jordan Islamic Bank
31	Frindes Laundry; DHL
34	General Post Office; Telephone Booths; ATM
35	Yamani Library (Bookshop)
36	Redwan Bookshop
38	International Traders (American Express)
40	New Entertainment Complex
42	Al Fardos Coffee Shop
43	Arab Bank
46	Sherif al-Hussein bin Ali Mosque
51	Photo Hagop
54	Housing Bank; Avis Car Rental; Peace Way Tours
56	Aqaba Turkish Baths
59	Jordan National Bank
60	Moneychangers
62	Mosque
63	Police Station
64	Main Bus/Minibus Station
66	Minibus/Service Taxi Station (to Karak & Safi)
67	Public Beach; Cafés; Paddle & Glass-Bottom Boats
69	Jordan Design & Trade Center (Noor al-Hussein Foundation)
70	Aqaba Castle (Mamluk Fort)
71	Visitors Centre; Tourist Office; Aqaba Museum
72	Minibuses (to Ferry Terminal & Saudi Arabia)
73	Speedboat Dock

Places to Stay – Budget

Camping There is little to recommend camping in Aqaba, except the low price and the possibility of a sea breeze in summer. Those south of town are better.

Bedouin Garden Village (☎ 0795 602521; e bedwinjamal@yahoo.com; per person in tent or cabin JD2, half board around JD12) is a wonderful place to stay and has been recommended by lots of readers; it's certainly the best camping option around Aqaba. Located about 10km south of the town centre on the east side of the road, it has straw teepees, Bedouin tents (for sleeping and relaxing) and a pleasant **restaurant**. They cook filling meals (JD6.500 or sandwiches for JD1), can arrange Bedouin music performances in the evenings if there are enough people, and rent out snorkelling gear (JD3 per day). One reader described it as 'one of the most romantic places in Jordan'.

Mermaid Camp (☎ 0795 567761; per person JD2) is another place along the beach south of Aqaba with a laid-back atmosphere, good snorkelling nearby and friendly staff.

Hotels Unless stated otherwise, most places listed here have (non-satellite) TV, air-conditioning and a private bathroom with hot water (not always reliable). Many places don't offer breakfast, and certainly not for the quoted price, but can usually rustle up something simple for around JD1.500. Tariffs in most budget places are negotiable by JD1 to JD3 per person, especially in quieter times.

Three cheapies are next to each other along Zahran St. It's usually possible to sleep in a shared room or on the roof for around JD2 per person.

Jordan Flower Hotel *(singles/doubles with shared bath JD5/8, with private bath JD8/10)* is simple but undoubtedly the best of the three. The rooms are generally clean and the staff friendly.

Petra Hotel *(☎ 2013746; singles/doubles JD5/7)* is OK but the shared bathrooms are very bleak. The view from the roof is wonderful. Women travellers should stay elsewhere.

Jerusalem Hotel *(☎ 2014815; singles/doubles JD5/8)* is probably the most run-down and least welcoming of the three.

Al-Khouli Hotel *(☎ 2030152, fax 2030664; Zahran St; singles/doubles low season from JD8/10, high season JD12/14)* is one of the better places in the area. It's worth paying an extra JD2 for a room with a balcony as these are nicer.

Four slightly more expensive places (and also a step up in quality) are all next door to each other at the northern end of Zahran St. They are located in a quiet off-street courtyard with an open-air teahouse out the front and some rooms have balconies. All are friendly places.

Dweikh Hotel I *(☎ 2012984, fax 2012985; e dweikhhotel@firstnet.com.jo; singles/doubles JD10/15)* has very tidy rooms with the added advantage of satellite TV.

Nairoukh Hotel I *(☎ 2019284, fax 2019285; singles/doubles JD11/18)* is similar to the Dweikh but not quite as good value.

Amira Hotel *(☎ 2018840, fax 2012559; singles/doubles with breakfast JD12/18)* also has decent, quiet rooms which are similar to the other two.

Red Sea Hotel *(☎ 2012156, fax 2022566; e z_72@hotmail.com; singles/doubles start at JD6/10, all rooms have private bath)* is a bit more run-down than the others.

Al-Naher al-Khaled Hotel *(☎ 2012456, fax 2012457; e zv51@hotmail.com; Ar-Razi St; singles/doubles JD14/18)* can easily be negotiated down to JD10/14, which is good value. Management has plans to put satellite TV in the rooms, which are all pleasant, bright and clean.

Al-Amer Hotel *(☎/fax 2014821; Raghadan St; singles/doubles JD12/18)* is excellent upper-budget value with sunny, clean rooms. Ask for one at the front where the views are superb.

Places to Stay – Mid Range

Every place listed here has a fridge, air-conditioning, TV (usually satellite), telephone and hot water. If you can negotiate a lower price, these places are fantastic value and prices include breakfast.

Al-Zatari Hotel *(☎ 2022970, fax 2022974; King Talal St; singles/doubles/triples JD20/28/32)* is highly recommended, with spacious, well-appointed rooms; most have superlative views. The staff are also friendly. It's just a short walk downhill to the town centre.

Nairoukh 2 Hotel *(☎ 2012980, fax 2015749; King Hussein St; singles/doubles in low season JD14/20, in high season from 16/25)* is similarly good value close to the centre with modern rooms, helpful staff and decent views.

Moon Beach Hotel *(☎/fax 2013316/7; e amsaad77@yahoo.com; King Hussein St; singles without seaview JD13, singles/doubles with seaview JD17/30)* is a great new place. It's a stone's throw from the castle and hence removed from (but easy walking distance to) the bustle of central Aqaba. The rooms are lovely and most have great views.

Al-Shuala Hotel *(☎ 2015153, fax 2015160; e shula@firstnet.com.jo; Raghadan St; singles/doubles JD16/24)*, is right in the heart of the action and while the rooms are smaller than some, those on the west side have excellent views.

Crystal Hotel *(☎ 2022001, fax 2022002; Ar-Razi St; singles/doubles JD20/30)* has rooms that are very comfortable and spacious, if a little sterile. The official rates of JD40/55 may return when things get busy – not as good value.

Al-Cazar Hotel *(☎ 2014131, fax 2014133; e alcsea@alcazar.com.jo; An-Nahda St; singles/doubles JD34/54)* has pleasant rooms, a swimming pool, pub, an on-demand DVD cinema with over 200 movies and is professionally run. The quoted rates are rarely asked and significant discounts are possible with negotiation. They also run Club Murjan, a watersports centre (see South of Aqaba later in this chapter) to which guests have free access.

Aquamarina Beach Hotel *(☎ 2016250, fax 2032630; e aquama@go.com.jo; singles/doubles JD40/58)* is comfortable, with a swimming pool, bar and dive centre (see the South of Aqaba section later in this chapter).

The big selling point is that the hotel is located on its own private beach to which guests have access. There's an Arab Bank ATM (for Visa) at the gate.

Places to Stay – Top End
All the top-end places are on King Hussein St in the northwestern part of the city. Tariffs listed here include breakfast, and it's always worth asking about any packages they have on offer. With some genteel negotiation, it's sometimes even possible (but only in low season) to get the Jordanian rates, which would make these places exceptional value.

Aqaba Gulf Hotel (☎ 2016636, fax 2018246; e info@aqabagulf.com; King Hussein St; singles/doubles US$80/100) is excellent if you can get the rate of JD35/45 that is routinely offered when things are quiet. The luxurious rooms, swimming pool, tennis courts, bar, restaurants and service are all you'd expect from a five-star place.

Radisson SAS Hotel (☎ 2012426, fax 201 3426; e aqizh_gm@go.com.jo; King Hussein St; singles/doubles with city view JD60/70, with sea view JD70/80) is typical of this high-quality chain with the added advantage of having its own beach.

Mövenpick Resort Hotel (☎/fax 2034020; e resort.aqaba@moevenpick.com; King Hussein St; singles/doubles JD60/65) is arguably Aqaba's finest with a high-class complex including a private beach.

Places to Eat
Aqaba has a large range of places to eat to suit almost all budgets, and many travellers will welcome the plentiful seafood, although it can be expensive – for the lobster expect to pay JD35.

Places to Eat – Budget
Al-Mohandes Cafeteria (Al-Hammamat al-Tunisieh St; open 7.30am-midnight daily) is a very popular place with locals for cheap and tasty shwarma and felafel in a clean and lively setting.

Pearls Fast Food (☎ 2015057; Ar-Razi St; meals from JD1; open 24 hours) is ideal if you crave a burger (with chips and soft drink for JD1) at 3am, and they also do a range of main dishes for around JD2.300. It's a friendly place and the food is simple but tasty.

Syrian Palace Restaurant (☎/fax 201 4788; Raghadan St; starters under JD1, mains JD2-7; open 10am-midnight daily), next to Al-Amer Hotel, offers good Syrian and Jordanian food at moderate prices. The tables by the window are the best and the service is good if a little slow.

Al-Tarboosh Restaurant (☎ 2018518; Raghadan St; meals around JD1; open 7.30am-midnight daily), next door to the Syrian Palace, does good shwarmas, as well as fine pastries in the room next door; small pastry pizzas with meat or cheese are excellent value at 200 fils apiece.

Al-Shami Restaurant (☎ 2016107; Raghadan St; starters under JD1, mains JD2-6; open 11am-1am daily), in a lane between Raghadan and Zahran streets, is another popular place recommended by readers. The menu (printed in English outside) is quite extensive and the air-conditioned dining area upstairs has good views.

National Restaurant (☎ 2012207; Zahran St; mains from JD2.500; open 7.30am-midnight daily), under Al-Khouli Hotel, is a busy place and deservedly so. The meat and chicken dishes come with salads and hummus, and it's one of the cheapest places around for fish dishes (JD3.250).

Mr Cool Café (Princess Haya Square; meals from JD1; open 7am-midnight daily) offers tasty burgers and salads in a friendly atmosphere.

Chicken Tikka Restaurant (☎ 2013633; An-Nahda St; starters under JD1, mains JD2.500-6; open noon-midnight daily) specialises in Indian food with reasonable chicken tikka (half chicken with fries JD2.500) and chicken tandoori (JD3.250) among the highlights. Fish dishes cost JD6.

Pizza Hut (☎ 2016947; An-Nahda St; open noon-midnight daily) is good value with small pizzas from around JD2 and submarine sandwiches from JD1.500.

Chilli House (☎ 2012435; An-Nahda St; burgers from JD1.500, pastas from JD2; open 11am-1am daily) is one of the better fast-food places around town.

Places to Eat – Mid-Range & Top End
Ali Baba Restaurant (☎ 2013901; Raghadan St; starters under JD1, mains JD3-10; open 8am-midnight daily) draws the crowds for its setting which is pleasant enough, but it's

trading on its past reputation according to many readers. The food is patchy and the service often indifferent.

China Restaurant *(☎ 2014415; Al-Petra St; starters from JD1.100, mains JD1.300-6; open 11.30am-3pm & 6.30-11pm)* is a great Chinese restaurant. The cook is Chinese and his restaurant has long maintained a high standard; it gets numerous repeat visitors. Prices are reasonable. There is a well-stocked bar where a large beer costs from JD1.800 and spirits cost from JD1.500.

Captain's Restaurant *(☎ 2016905; An-Nahda St; starters 600 fils-JD6, mains JD2-7; open 8am-midnight daily)*, near the Chilli House, has a pleasant dining area around the side and the pasta dishes (from JD2) are good value. Seafood starts from JD5.500, which isn't bad. Breakfast is also served (600 fils to JD1.600).

Mina House Floating Restaurant *(☎ 201 2699; starters under JD1, mains from JD3.500; open noon-midnight daily)* is, as the name suggests, in a boat moored south of Aqaba castle. Fish dishes start at JD6.500, which is good considering it is always freshly caught, and not frozen as in some other Aqaba restaurants. The food and service are very good and the setting most pleasant.

Hani Ali *(☎ 2015200; Raghadan St; burgers from JD1.200, other mains JD2.250-6; open 8am-11pm daily)* is a good place for breakfast (JD1 to JD2), a meal or afternoon tea. The fish (from JD5.500) and pasta (from JD2.250) is very reasonably priced and great sweets and ice cream are served for dessert.

Romero Restaurant *(☎ 2022404; starters JD1-2, mains JD3.500-7; open noon-11.30pm daily)*, at the Royal Yacht Club of Jordan in the marina, is a charming but expensive place to watch the sunset and mingle with Aqaba's nouveau riche. There's a good bar.

Floka Restaurant *(☎ 2030860; An-Nahda St; starters JD4.500-6, mains JD5.500-11; open 12.30pm-11.30pm daily)* is an upmarket seafood restaurant that has been recommended by readers.

Silk Road Restaurant *(☎ 2033556; As-Sa'dah St; salads JD1-3, seafood starters from JD6.500, mains JD2.750-12.500; open noon-4pm & 6pm-2am daily)* is one of Aqaba's finest restaurants and has a lovely atmosphere. Pastas and non-seafood main dishes are reasonably priced at JD2.750 to JD4, but it would be a false economy not to try

the delicious seafood. There are three attractive dining areas, and every night at 10pm there is a live belly-dancing performance which you can easily enjoy or escape. There's also an extensive, reasonably priced wine and alcohol list (a draught Amstel costs JD2). This is a great place to blow the budget or for a special occasion.

Self-Catering

A few small **grocery stores** are dotted around central Aqaba, so stock up here if you're heading to Wadi Rum.

The best supermarket is **Humam Supermarket** *(☎ 2015721; Al-Petra St; open 8.30am-2.30pm & 4pm-11pm daily)*. There's also a **Safeway** *(open 8am-midnight daily)* about 750m north of Princess Haya Hospital. The **produce souq**, at the back of the southern end of Raghadan St, is where all manner of meat, chicken, fish, fruit and vegetables can be bought.

The best **bakery** *(open 6am-11pm daily)*, unsigned in any language, is along Al-Hammamat al-Tunisieh St.

Cafés & Ice-cream Parlours

There are **cafés** along the public beach north of the Aqaba castle (where the front row seats of the cafés are so close to the water that you can wet your toes while you whet your whistle). No alcohol is served at these public places.

The **juice stands** on Ar-Razi St are popular places for travellers to hang out at and meet others. **Al-Fardos Coffee Shop,** just off Zahran St and close to the Red Sea Hotel, is a traditional café where local men sip coffee and play backgammon and chess. It has a pleasant outdoor setting, and foreign women are welcome.

To help alleviate heatstroke, head for anywhere that sells ice cream, such as **Mr Cool Café** *(Princess Haya Square)*; **Hani Ali** *(Raghadan St)*, a sugar-addict's paradise of traditional sweets and delicious ice cream; or **Gelato Uno**, off An-Nahda St behind the Hertz car rental office.

Entertainment

Aqaba is not as vibrant for nightlife as you might expect. All the top-end hotels have bars, and most offer 'happy hours'. For example, the Crystal Hotel has the **Romantic Bar. Dolphin Bar** *(Al-Cazar Hotel)* is popular with expats and has pool tables and a friendly atmosphere. **Royal Yacht Club of Jordan**, in the marina, is where the upmarket crowd goes It's a great place to unwind, enjoy the sunset and catch some late afternoon breezes. Large beers cost JD3 and spirits, without mixers, about JD3.

For traditional Arabic dancing, and more modern stuff, head to the **nightclub** in the Aquamarina Beach Hotel. The **Coral Bar** at the Radisson SAS Hotel has a nightclub with an entertaining piano player. There is usually a better ambience in the restaurants that serve alcohol, such as the **Silk Road Restaurant**, where it's fine to linger until late.

A new entertainment complex was due to open on the waterfront soon after we were there. Next to the roundabout in the centre of town where King Hussein Street turns northwest, it is expected to include restaurants, cinemas, amusement parlours and a bar.

Shopping

There are plenty of shops around the centre of Aqaba selling the usual range of tourist souvenirs, such as carpets and bottles of coloured sand. As always, it's worth picking through many of the tacky items to find what you're looking for.

One shop which stands out for its quality is the **Jordan Design & Trade Center** (☎ 201 2601; open 8am-7pm Tues-Thur & Sat-Sun, 8am-2pm & 4pm-7pm Mon & Fri), directly opposite the entrance to the visitor centre and museum. Run by the Noor Al Hussein Foundation (see Shopping in the Facts for the Visitor chapter), profits from the sale of its high-standard products go to support vulnerable communities throughout Jordan. Items include jewellery, wall hangings, woven and embroidered products, basketwear and ceramics.

Getting There & Away

Air Aqaba has Jordan's only commercial airport outside Amman, although it only awakes from its normal slumber when a flight is about to leave or arrive.

Royal Wings, a subsidiary of Royal Jordanian, flies between Aqaba and Amman (JD33.550/67 one way/return, or JD62 for same-day return) at least once every day. Flights leave Amman in the morning, and return from Aqaba in the evening. These flights alternate between Marka airport (in

northeastern Amman) or the larger Queen Alia International Airport (south of the capital) depending on demand.

Royal Wings (☎ 2014474) has an office at Aqaba airport, but it's far more convenient to buy tickets at the **Royal Jordanian** office (☎ 2012403 or 2014477), on Ash-Sherif al-Hussein bin Ali St, where tickets for all Royal Jordanian flights can be bought, confirmed or changed. The Royal Jordanian office is open every day from 9am to 5pm, although it sometimes closes early on Friday.

Bus From Aqaba to Amman, it's worth paying for the comfort and air-conditioning of JETT and Trust private buses, which are also quicker (four hours) because they travel along the Dead Sea Highway, whereas the cheaper public buses (and minibuses) use the Desert Highway (about five hours) and stop to drop off and pick up passengers.

Try to book tickets for JETT or Trust buses at least a day in advance of when you want to travel, and as soon as possible at peak times. Buses for both companies leave from outside their respective offices. As always, check with the company to see whether departure times have changed.

From the **JETT office** (☎ 2015222), on King Hussein St next to the Mövenpick Hotel, buses (JD4.200) run five times daily to Amman with the first at 7am and the last at 5pm.

Trust International Transport (☎ 2032200 or ☎ 2032300), on An-Nahda St, has six daily buses (JD4) to the capital, the first at 7.30am and the last at 6pm. There is also a morning (8.30am) and afternoon (3.30pm) bus to Irbid (JD6, 5½ hours).

Ordinary public buses travel between the main bus/minibus station in Aqaba and Amman's Wahadat station (JD4, five hours) about every hour between 7am and 3pm, sometimes later. **Afneh** (also known as Afana) has services about every hour between 7am and 10pm, to Abdali station in Amman.

To Israel, Trust International Transport has a daily (10am) departure for Tel Aviv (JD21), via Nazareth (JD18) and Haifa (JD18). There's no bus on Saturday.

Minibus To Wadi Musa (for Petra), minibuses (JD3, two hours) leave at around 8.30am, 10.30am, 12.30pm and 1.30pm, but the exact departure times (and number of daily minibuses) depend on the number of passengers going in both directions. Otherwise, get a connection in Ma'an (JD1.500, 80 minutes) for which there are hourly departures throughout the day.

Two minibuses go to Wadi Rum (JD1.500, one hour) at around 6am and 6.30am, ostensibly to ferry teachers to the school there. On Friday there is usually only one minibus a day. At other times, catch a minibus towards Ma'an, disembark at the turn-off to Wadi Rum and then hitch a ride to Rum village from there.

Minibuses to Amman (JD4, five hours) leave hourly throughout the day.

All of the above minibuses leave from the main bus/minibus station on Ar-Reem St. Minibuses to Karak (JD1.850, three hours), via Safi and the Dead Sea Highway, are the exception, leaving from the small station next to the mosque on Al-Humaimah St.

Service Taxi From the main bus/minibus station, service taxis head to Amman (JD5, five hours), but far less regularly than buses and minibuses. To Karak (JD3.250, three hours), they leave from the small station on Al-Humaimah St. Service taxis start lining up at either station at 6am and many have left by 8am so get an early start. Chartering a taxi costs at least JD25 one way to Petra and to Wadi Rum return.

From the main bus/minibus station, service taxis go to the nearby border of Israel and the Palestinian Territories (JD1.250), most often early in the morning. Taxis are normally marked 'Southern Passing Service' and often have the number 8 on the door. Chartering a taxi between central Aqaba and the border costs about JD5. For more information about crossing the southern border to/from Israel and the Palestinian Territories, see the Getting There & Away chapter.

Car Aqaba has several car-rental agencies. If you want to rent a car for any length of time and cover the whole country, there's a greater range of choice. Most Aqaba agencies charge a 'drop fee' (JD25) if you wish to leave the car in Amman or at Queen Alia International Airport – a bit rich as some of the agencies have offices in Amman. However, renting in Aqaba makes some sense as public transport in the south of the country

is less frequent and requires more connections than in the north. Aqaba is also far easier to drive around than Amman.

The prices listed here do not include petrol. It's recommended that you pay the 'collision damage waiver' (where available), which means you pay nothing additional in the case of an accident.

Al-Cazar Hotel (☎ 2014131, fax 2014133, e alc sea@alcazar.com.jo) An-Nahda St. This hotel has a reliable car rental agency that charges from JD25 per day with unlimited kilometres. There is no CDW available, so you pay an excess of JD300 if you have an accident.

Avis (☎ 2022883, e avis@go.com.jo) Housing Bank Centre, King Hussein St. Avis charges from JD25 per day for normal cars with unlimited kilometres and JD60 for 4WDs (usually ordered from Amman). CDW starts from JD7 per day.

Hertz (☎ 2016206, fax 201 6125, e hertz@go .com.jo) An-Nahda St. Charges start from JD35 per day with unlimited kilometres. If you rent the car for less than three days, you pay an additional 7% tax, and if you rent for five days or more it is free to drop the car in Amman; otherwise it's JD25. Strangely, paying the JD10 per day CDW still leaves you with US$100 to pay in the event of an accident.

Oryx Rent-a-Car (☎ 2012133, fax 2018789) Miramar Hotel, King Hussein St. The cheapest cars start from JD20 plus JD5 CDW per day. The 4WDs start from JD65 per day plus JD10 daily CDW. This is one place where it's better to pay in cash rather than credit card.

Hitching If you're hitching a ride to the north, the truck park 3km to the north of the city centre is a good place to start. A service/private taxi there should cost around 500 fils/JD2.

Sea There are two daily boat services to Nuweiba in Egypt. For information about these services, see Sea in the Getting There & Away chapter.

A reliable place that sells tickets for the fast boat in Aqaba is **International Traders** (☎ 2013757, fax 2015316; e aqaba.office@ traders.com.jo). Located on Al-Hammamat al-Tunisieh St, it's open 8.30am to 1pm and 4pm to 7pm Saturday to Thursday and you can pay in dinars (JD22). Alternatively, buy your ticket at the ferry port.

Although some agencies in Aqaba sell tickets for the slow boat (look for a sign advertising the fact in the window), there's no

Royal Diving Club, Aqaba

Jewel fairy basslet

Parrotfish

Coral crab

Coral garden, near Aqaba

Butterfly fish

Forsters hawkfish

Hawksbill sea turtle

need to buy your ticket in advance as they never sell out and you can purchase it at the ferry terminal when departing.

Organised Tours Some travellers prefer to visit Wadi Rum as part of an organised excursion from Aqaba. These can be arranged by many of the hotels, or you can use a tour agency. For an overnight trip (usually 24 hours) to Wadi Rum, costs start from JD45 per person if there are two people, although the per person rate drops significantly if there are more people. Some agencies have been known to take short cuts on food, so make sure you spell out your requirements and find out what you get for your money before handing it over.

Among the more experienced agencies offering tours to Wadi Rum are:

International Traders (☎ 2013757, fax 2015316, e aqaba.office@traders.com.jo) Al-Hammamat al-Tunisieh St. Not really for budget travellers, this agency is also more expensive but similarly reliable.

Peace Way Tours (☎ 2022665; e tours@peace way.com) Housing Bank building on King Hussein St. This agency gets mixed reviews from readers (although it seems to depend on the guide).

Qutaish & Sons (☎ 2014679, fax 2013882) Near Al-Shami Restaurant, off Zahran St. Another long-standing agency although, again, with both positive and negative reports from travellers.

Red Sea Tours Another budget agency in the Jordan Flower Hotel on Zahran St.

Some agencies also organise day trips to Petra (JD40), but this is poor value as your time in Petra will be limited and the price doesn't include entrance fees – it's better to go under your own steam.

Getting Around

To/From the Airport Aqaba airport is about 10km north of town, and close to the border with Israel and the Palestinian Territories. There's no public bus or minibus to the airport, so take a service taxi (600 fils) marked 'Southern Passing Service' or service taxi no 8 from the main bus/minibus station. If there are no service taxis, a private taxi shouldn't cost more than JD3, but will probably cost JD5. Be wary of unscrupulous taxi drivers trying to fleece unsuspecting tourists who have just arrived in Aqaba.

To/From the Ferry Terminal Minibuses leave from near the entrance to Aqaba castle on King Hussein St for the Saudi border and pass the terminal (350 fils) for ferries and the fast boat to Egypt. A private taxi from central Aqaba shouldn't cost more than JD2.

Taxis Hundreds of private (yellow) taxis cruise the streets beeping at any tourist (Jordanian or foreign) who is silly enough to walk around in the heat rather than take an air-conditioned taxi. Taxis are unmetered so prices are entirely negotiable, and the drivers in Aqaba enjoy the sport. Try to get an idea of an approximate fare from one of the locals or your hotel, and of course agree to a price before getting in.

SOUTH OF AQABA

The road south of Aqaba stretches about 18km to the Saudi Arabian border at Ad-Durra. Much of the coastline is taken up by the massive port facilities, but there are a few beaches, as well as some excellent diving and snorkelling spots. A minibus runs intermittently from near Aqaba castle on King Hussein St to the Saudi border.

SOUTHERN DESERT & AQABA

There are plans for a new visitor centre along the road north of the Royal Diving Club and close to the Bedouin Garden Village (see Places to Stay in Aqaba earlier in this chapter). Entrance fees for the marine park may follow on its heels.

Diving & Snorkelling

The northern end of the Gulf of Aqaba enjoys high salinity, and the winds from the north and minimal tides mean the water stays clear. The temperature of the water is warm (an average 22.5°C in winter and 26°C in summer), attracting a vast array of fish, and helping to preserve the coral.

Marine Life The Jordan Royal Ecological Society (☎/fax 06-567 9142; e jreds@nets .com jo) says the gulf has over 110 species of hard coral, 120 species of soft coral and about 1000 species of fish. These include colourful goat fish, leopard flounder, clown fish; various species of butterfly fish, parrot fish, angel fish; the less endearing spiky sea urchin, poisonous stone fish, scorpion fish, sea snakes, jellyfish and moray eels. Green turtles and hermit crabs can also be found.

Books Lonely Planet's *Diving and Snorkeling Guide to The Red Sea* concentrates on sites along the Egyptian coast, but has a detailed section about diving around the Gulf of Aqaba. The major bookshops in Aqaba (see Bookshops) have a good range of books about diving, such as the *Introduction to the Marine Life of Aqaba*. The Redwan Bookshop sells the plastic *Red Sea Fishwatchers Field Guide*, which can be taken underwater to identify species of fish and coral.

Health If you're cut by coral, or stung by a stonefish, see Health in the Facts for the Visitor chapter for advice and remedies. The Princess Haya Hospital in Aqaba is well equipped for diving mishaps, and even has a decompression chamber. The reputable dive centres are equipped with emergency oxygen tanks, a first-aid kit and a mobile phone.

Considerations for Responsible Diving & Snorkelling To help preserve the ecology and beauty of the reefs, please consider the following tips when diving or snorkelling:

- Do not touch or feed fish, and minimise your disturbance of marine animals. In particular, do not ride on the backs of turtles as this causes them great anxiety. Feeding fish may disturb their normal eating habits, encourage aggressive behaviour or be detrimental to their health.
- Do not touch or remove any marine life or coral, dead or alive, from the sea or beach. Dragging equipment across the reef can also do serious damage. Polyps can be damaged by even the gentlest contact. Never stand on coral – instead use a jetty (or boat) to reach the water, even if the coral looks solid and robust. If you must hold onto the reef, only touch exposed rock or dead coral.

Red Sea Aqaba Marine Park

Jordan's only stretch of coastline is the northern part of the Gulf of Aqaba, and it's home to over 300 types of coral and numerous species of fish and marine life. Jordan's only port (and the region's major shipping lane) and resort cause real problems for the fragile marine environment.

In an attempt to halt the damage, the **Red Sea Aqaba Marine Park** (☎ 2019405, fax 2014206) was established in 1997. The park stretches for about 8.5km, from the Marine Science Station to the Royal Diving Club, and extends about 350m offshore and 50m inland. The park contains about 80% of Jordan's public beaches and most of the decent diving and snorkelling spots, so the park managers are trying to find the right balance between promoting tourism and preserving the marine environment.

Local and foreign environmentalists have managed to ban fishing and limit boating in the park, and have established jetties into the sea so that divers and snorkellers can jump into the water rather than wade out over coral from the beach. A visitor centre is planned, and park rangers will ensure that visitors and locals obey the strict environmental protection laws.

The park managers also hope to conduct a public awareness campaign for locals (particularly children) and all divers and snorkellers; lobby the government to enforce local environmental laws; and conduct further research into the damage caused by tourism and pollution. The Marine Science Station, south of Aqaba, is also deeply involved in the preservation of the marine environment.

Safety Guidelines for Diving & Snorkelling

Before embarking on a diving or snorkelling trip, careful consideration should be given to making it a safe, as well as an enjoyable, experience. You should:

- Possess a current diving certification card from a recognised scuba diving instructional agency
- Be sure you're healthy and feel comfortable diving
- Obtain reliable information about physical and environmental conditions at the dive site (eg, from a reputable local dive centre)
- Be aware of local laws, regulations and etiquette about marine life and the environment
- Dive only at sites within your realm of experience; if you can, engage the services of a competent, professionally trained dive instructor or dive master
- Be aware that underwater conditions vary significantly from one region, or even site, to another: seasonal changes can significantly alter any site and dive conditions, which influences the way divers dress for a dive and what diving techniques they use
- Ask about the environmental characteristics that can affect your diving and how local trained divers deal with these considerations

- Be conscious of your fins. Even without contact, the surge from heavy fin strokes near the reef can damage delicate organisms. When treading water in shallow reef areas, take care not to kick up clouds of sand. Settling sand can easily smother the delicate organisms of the reef.
- Do not throw any rubbish into the sea, or leave it on the beach. Plastics in particular are a serious threat to marine life. Turtles can mistake plastic for jellyfish and eat it.
- Ensure that boat anchors are on buoys, and not attached to precious coral, and take care not to ground boats on coral.
- Practise and maintain proper buoyancy control. Major damage can be done by divers descending too fast and colliding with the reef. Make sure you're correctly weighted and your weight belt is positioned so that you stay horizontal. If you haven't dived for a while, have a practice dive in a pool before trying the reef. Be aware that buoyancy can change over the period of an extended trip: initially you may breathe harder and need more weight; a few days later you may breathe more easily and need less weight.
- Resist the temptation to buy coral or shells. Aside from the ecological damage, taking marine souvenirs depletes the beauty of a site and spoils the enjoyment of others – and is illegal in Jordan.

Diving & Snorkelling Sites The coast between Aqaba and the Saudi Arabian border boasts about 30 diving and snorkelling sites. Of these, about 25 can be enjoyed by snorkellers and all but one is accessible from a jetty or beach.

Site names change from time to time, and from one diving agency to another. Several sites have been subdivided and given even more names. Sites are not signposted, nor are they remotely obvious from the road; if you want to dive or snorkel independently you'll have to ask for directions, or take pot luck. Snorkellers will find it far better to pay the extra and use the private beaches run by the Royal Diving Club or Club Murjan.

The following are the more popular sites (listed in order from Aqaba). You can also snorkel at Pharaoh's Island, which is in Egyptian waters; see later in the chapter.

First Bay Offshore from the Marine Science Station, it has good coral gardens for divers at a depth of 8m to 15m

King Abdullah Reef Named after the king (an avid diver) and offshore just north of the Mermaid Camp, it has good visibility and decent but unspectacular coral. It's easily accessible from the beach, and the coral starts about 20m offshore.

Black Rock Offshore from Mermaid Camp, this site boasts diverse species of soft coral and is good for snorkellers

Cedar Pride This ship was deliberately sunk to create a diving site in 1985. It's only 200m offshore, and in water about 20m deep. The wreck is covered with bright, soft coral and is home to schools of colourful fish. The waves can be a bit harrowing at times, however, and the sea urchins can be a pain. Sadly, this is also the site with the most litter.

Japanese Garden Located just south of the Cedar Pride, this site is ideal for snorkellers and has a stunning array of coral

Gorgonian I This reef is probably the best place for snorkelling, although the waves can be difficult. The coral is superb, and there's plenty of marine life and the chance to see sea turtles.

Gorgonian II This is similar in size, accessibility and standard to Gorgonian I, but the coral is not as good; there are numerous moray eels

New Canyon A sunken Russian tank lies 30m offshore and at a depth of just 5m. Further into the sandy canyon, the walls are lined with coral.

Blue Coral This is another sloping reef, with hard and soft coral at shallow depths

Moon Valley Accessible from the beach, about 800m north of, and run by the Royal Diving Club, this sandy area has a sloping reef and a varied, but unremarkable, array of fish and coral. Napoleon fish are often found at greater depths.

Aquarium Not to be confused with the aquarium at the Marine Science Station, this is the name given to the reef accessible from the jetty at the Royal Diving Club. There are enough colourful fish, and soft and hard coral, to impress all divers and snorkellers.

Saudi Border Wall The coral is perfectly preserved, but because it's only about 300m north of the Jordan/Saudi border, divers should take great care – the best sections are not accessible by snorkellers

Diving Centres Most of the dive agencies have offices in Aqaba where you must arrange your equipment and destination. The price per dive invariably decreases the more you do. The most professional agencies include:

Aqaba International Dive Centre (☎/fax 203 1213, |e| diveaqaba@yahoo.com) Off King Hussein St. This popular, friendly and well-equipped centre charges JD17 per dive including transport and all equipment (JD15 if you do two dives on the same day). To do the basic open-water PADI course costs JD200.

Aquamarina Diving Club (☎ 2016250, fax 201 4271, |e| aquama@go.com.jo) King Hussein St. Based at the Aquamarina Beach Hotel, they charge JD32 per dive with full equipment. Each additional dive during the same day is JD17. If performing just a night dive, the cost is JD32 plus equipment (JD15). There must be a minimum of four people for a night dive. The PADI course costs JD280. This is one of the few companies to do boat dives.

Arab Divers (☎ 2031808, fax 2012053, |e| arab divers@hotmail.com) King Hussein St, next to Nairoukh 2 Hotel. This dive company has been highly recommended by a number of readers; they charge JD16 for the first dive with full equipment, JD25 per person per night dive (minimum of two people) and JD210 for the open-water PADI course. They also run other courses and the instructors speak English, German, French and Japanese.

Red Sea Diving Centre (☎ 2022323 or ☎ 2018969, fax 2018969) Off King Hussein St. One of the more long-standing dive centres in Aqaba, they charge about JD24 for two dives (if you have your own equipment, otherwise plus equipment hire) and JD40 for two dives with full equipment.

Royal Diving Club (☎ 2032709, fax 2017097, |e| rdc@jptd.com.jo) Around 12km south of the city centre. In operation since 1986, this experienced company is very professionally run. Charges start from JD14.500 for the first dive (JD26 if two in the same day) plus JD8 per dive for equipment. They charge JD240 for the open-water PADI course and night dives cost JD30, including torch but not including the price of equipment (minimum three people). Talk to them about dive programmes they run for children and people with a disability.

Sea Star (☎ 2014131, fax 2014133, |e| alcsea@ alcazar.com.jo) Based at Al-Cazar Hotel in Aqaba. Each dive with full equipment and dive master accompaniment costs JD30, while rates decrease the more dives you do. They also do night dives with prior notice; check out their website at |w| www.seastar-watersports.com.

Extras All of these diving centres can organise night dives. Camera enthusiasts should note that no dive centres have marine cameras for hire, so bring your own. Other costs include: an underwater torch (flashlight), about JD5 per trip; wetsuits, about JD3.300/6.600 for a short/long one; and fins, about JD1.500.

Diving Courses Most of the diving centres run courses for BSAC, PADI or CMAS. Costs range from about JD25 for a basic one-dive 'introductory' course to between JD170 and JD250 for the open-water PADI course. Other courses include 'advanced diver', 'wreck diver course' and 'dive master'. Courses are often run by Europeans who speak English, French, German and/or Italian.

Snorkelling All of the diving centres mentioned earlier rent out flippers, mask and snorkel for around JD3 per day. Snorkelling gear can also be bought from the Redwan Bookshop (see Bookshops in the Aqaba section).

If you have your own gear and want to go snorkelling away from the beach, ask the diving agencies about the cost of accompanying a scuba-diving trip. The cheapest place to snorkel is Club Murjan (JD4 plus equipment), while the Royal Diving Club charges JD5. If you ask the friendly staff there they will be happy to point out the best spots.

Aquarium المربى المائي

Part of the Marine Science Station complex, the aquarium (☎ 2015145; admission JD2; open 8am-5pm daily) is worth a visit, but probably only if you don't get a chance to go diving or snorkelling. The tanks provide a colourful glimpse of the Gulf of Aqaba's marine life, including coral, moray eels, turtles and the stone fish. There are very few labels in any language. The aquarium is about 7.5km south of central Aqaba, and about 500m south of the passenger terminal for ferries to Egypt.

Club Murjan نادي المرجان

About 1.3km south of the Marine Science Station is Club Murjan, the beach and diving centre run by Al-Cazar Hotel in Aqaba. Guests of the hotel, and divers using the hotel's diving centre, can enjoy the facilities at Club Murjan for no charge, while the public can use the good **beach**, **swimming pool** and toilets/showers during the day for JD4, including return transport from Al-Cazar Hotel. Hire of snorkelling gear costs an extra JD7 per day. Watersports gear such as canoes and paragliders are also normally available. There is a **bar** and **restaurant** on the site.

Tala Bay Development

Just north of the Royal Diving Club and about 11km south of Aqaba is an ambitious development project that won't be anywhere near completed during the life of this book. The plan is for a marina, villas, apartments, golf course, hotels and watersports club, and developers are working closely to ensure that it has minimal impact upon the environmental protections demanded by the Red Sea Aqaba Marine Park. In the meantime, expect to see a vast construction site and more trucks than usual along the road.

Royal Diving Club مركز الغوص الوطني

About 12km south of Aqaba, and close to the Saudi border, is the Royal Diving Club, which is an excellent place for swimming, diving and snorkelling. It has a lovely **swimming pool** and a decent **beach**, where women can feel relaxed. Shade is available.

The entrance fee of JD5 allows guests to use the facilities (ie, beach, pool, sunbed, towel and showers/toilets) and the **restaurant** serves simple snacks, drinks and alcohol. Snorkelling gear costs an extra JD3 per day. Entrance and transport is free for anyone scuba diving with the Royal Diving Club.

The minibus (700 fils one way) provided by the centre picks up guests from outside most hotels in Aqaba at about 9am and returns at about 5pm. You can usually tee up the minibus with one of the hotels, but it's preferable to ring the Royal Diving Club the day before to find out the nearest pick-up point and to make sure they wait for you. A private taxi costs about JD3 one way, but is difficult to arrange going back to Aqaba.

The RDC also has plans for an extension of its facilities, including a hotel.

Pharaoh's Island جزيرة فرعون

This picturesque island is about 15km south of Aqaba, but only a few hundred metres from Taba, in Egypt. It's actually in Egyptian waters, but travelling to or from Egypt this way is not permitted.

Excavations suggest that the island was inhabited as far back as the Bronze Age. The fantastic Crusader **Salah ad-Din Fort** is fun to explore; and there is really good **swimming** and **snorkelling** in the lagoon and **diving** further out which is only accessible by boat.

Top-end (and a few mid-range) hotels can arrange trips to the island for about JD25 per person (depending on the number of passengers), which includes the entrance fee to the island, Egyptian visa, lunch and transport – but boats only leave when there are enough passengers (about ten) to make the trip feasible. Two days notice is often required to allow time for the visas to be processed.

Language

Arabic is Jordan's official language. English is also widely spoken but any effort to communicate with the locals in their own language will be well rewarded. No matter how far off the mark your pronunciation or grammar might be, you'll often get the response (usually with a big smile): 'Ah, you speak Arabic very well!'.

Learning a few basics for day-to-day travelling doesn't take long at all, but to master the complexities of Arabic would take years of consistent study. The whole issue is complicated by the differences between Classical Arabic (*fus-ha*), its modern descendant MSA (Modern Standard Arabic) and regional dialects. The classical tongue is the language of the Quran and Arabic poetry of centuries past. For long it remained static, but in order to survive it had to adapt to change, and the result is more or less MSA, the common language of the press, radio and educated discourse. It is as close to a lingua franca (a common language) as the Arab world comes, and is generally understood, if not always well spoken, right across the Arab world – from Baghdad to Casablanca. An educated Iraqi would have no trouble shooting the breeze about world politics with a similarly educated Moroccan, but might have considerably more difficulty ordering lunch.

Fortunately, the spoken dialects of Jordan are not too distant from MSA. For outsiders trying to learn Arabic, the most frustrating element nevertheless remains understanding the spoken language. There is virtually no written material to refer to for back-up, and acquisition of MSA in the first place is itself a long-term investment. An esoteric argument flows back and forth about the relative merits of learning MSA first (and so perhaps having to wait some time before being able to communicate adequately with people in the street) or focusing your efforts on a dialect. If all this gives you a headache now, you'll have some inkling of why so few non-Arabs, or non-Muslims, embark on a study of the language.

Pronunciation

Pronunciation of Arabic can be tongue-tying for someone unfamiliar with the intonation and combination of sounds. Pronounce the transliterated words slowly and clearly.

This language guide should help, but bear in mind that the myriad rules governing pronunciation and vowel use are too extensive to be covered here.

Vowels

Technically, there are three long and three short vowels in Arabic. The reality is a little different, with local dialect and varying consonant combinations affecting their pronunciation. This is the case throughout the Arabic-speaking world. More like five short and five long vowels can be identified:

a   as the 'a' in 'had'
e   as the 'e' in 'bet'
i   as the 'i' in 'hit'
o   as the 'o' in 'hot'
u   as the 'oo' in 'book'

A macron over a vowel indicates that the vowel has a long sound:

ā   as the 'a' in 'father'
ī   as the 'e' in 'ear', only softer
ū   as the 'oo' in 'food'

Consonants

Pronunciation for all Arabic consonants is covered in the alphabet table on the following page. Note that when double consonants occur in transliterations, both are pronounced. For example, *al-Hammam* (toilet/bath), is pronounced 'al-ham-mam'.

Other Sounds

Arabic has two sounds that are very tricky for non-Arabs to produce, the 'ayn and the glottal stop. The letter 'ayn represents a sound with no English equivalent that comes even close. It is similar to the glottal stop (which is not actually represented in the alphabet) but the muscles at the back of the throat are gagged more forcefully – it has been described as the sound of someone being strangled. In many transliteration systems 'ayn is represented by an opening quotation mark, and the glottal stop by a closing quotation mark. To make the transliterations in this language guide (and throughout the rest of the book) easier to use, we have not

The Standard Arabic Alphabet

Final	Medial	Initial	Alone	Transliteration	Pronunciation
ﺎ			ا	ā	as the 'a' in 'father'
ـب	ـبـ	بـ	ب	b	as in 'bet'
ـت	ـتـ	تـ	ت	t	as in 'ten'
ـث	ـثـ	ثـ	ث	th	as in 'thin'
ـج	ـجـ	جـ	ج	g	as in 'go'
ـح	ـحـ	حـ	ح	H	a strongly whispered 'h', like a sigh of relief
ـخ	ـخـ	خـ	خ	kh	as the 'ch' in Scottish *loch*
ـد			د	d	as in 'dim'
ـذ			ذ	dh	as the 'th' in 'this'
ـر			ر	r	a rolled 'r', as in the Spanish word *caro*
ـز			ز	z	as in 'zip'
ـس	ـسـ	سـ	س	s	as in 'so', never as in 'wisdom'
ـش	ـشـ	شـ	ش	sh	as in 'ship'
ـص	ـصـ	صـ	ص	ṣ	emphatic 's'
ـض	ـضـ	ضـ	ض	ḍ	emphatic 'd'
ـط	ـطـ	طـ	ط	ṭ	emphatic 't'
ـظ	ـظـ	ظـ	ظ	ẓ	emphatic 'z'
ـع	ـعـ	عـ	ع	'	the Arabic letter 'ayn; pronounce as a glottal stop – like the closing of the throat before saying 'Oh-oh!' (see Other Sounds on p.238)
ـغ	ـغـ	غـ	غ	gh	a guttural sound like Parisian 'r'
ـف	ـفـ	فـ	ف	f	as in 'far'
ـق	ـقـ	قـ	ق	q	a strongly guttural 'k' sound; in Egyptian Arabic often pronounced as a glottal stop
ـك	ـكـ	كـ	ك	k	as in 'king'
ـل	ـلـ	لـ	ل	l	as in 'lamb'
ـم	ـمـ	مـ	م	m	as in 'me'
ـن	ـنـ	نـ	ن	n	as in 'name'
ـه	ـهـ	هـ	ه	h	as in 'ham'
ـو			و	w	as in 'wet'; or
				ū	long, as the 'oo' on 'food'; or
				aw	as the 'ow' in 'how'
ـي	ـيـ	يـ	ي	y	as in 'yes'; or
				ī	as the 'e' in 'ear', only softer; or
				ay	as the 'y' in 'by' or as the 'ay' in 'way'

Vowels Not all Arabic vowel sounds are represented in the alphabet. See Pronunciation on p. 238.

Emphatic Consonants Emphatic consonants are similar to their nonemphatic counterparts but are pronounced with greater tension in the tongue and throat.

distinguished between the glottal stop and the 'ayn, using the closing quotation mark to represent both sounds. You'll find that Arabic speakers will still understand you.

Transliteration

It's worth noting here that transliteration from the Arabic script into English – or any other language for that matter – is at best an approximate science.

The presence of sounds unknown in European languages and the fact that the script is 'incomplete' (most vowels are not written) combine to make it nearly impossible to settle on one universally accepted method of transliteration. A wide variety of spellings is therefore possible for words when they appear in the Roman alphabet – and that goes for places and people's names as well.

The whole thing is further complicated by the wide variety of dialects and the imaginative ideas Arabs themselves often have on appropriate spelling in, say, English (and words spelt one way in Jordan may look very different in Syria, which has strong French influences). Not even the most venerable of western Arabists have been able to come up with a satisfactory solution.

While striving to reflect the language as closely as possible and aiming at consistency, this book generally spells place, street and hotel names and the like as the locals have done. Don't be surprised if you come across several versions of the same thing.

Pronouns

I	ana
you	inta (m)/inti (f)
he	huwa
she	hiyya

The Transliteration Dilemma

TE Lawrence, when asked by his publishers to clarify 'inconsistencies in the spelling of proper names' in *Seven Pillars of Wisdom* – his account of the Arab Revolt in WWI – wrote back:

'Arabic names won't go into English. There are some 'scientific systems' of transliteration, helpful to people who know enough Arabic not to need helping, but a washout for the world. I spell my names anyhow, to show what rot the systems are.'

we	naHnu/eHna (some-
	times pronounced niHna in Jordan
you	ento
they	humma

Greetings & Civilities

Arabs place great importance on civility and it's rare to see any interaction between people that doesn't begin with profuse greetings, inquiries into the other's health and other niceties.

Arabic greetings are more formal than in English and there's a reciprocal response to each. These sometimes vary slightly, depending on whether you're addressing a man or a woman. A simple encounter can become a drawn-out affair, with neither side wanting to be the one to put a halt to the stream of greetings and well-wishing. As an *ajnabi* (foreigner), you're not expected to know all the ins and outs, but if you come up with the right expression at the appropriate moment they'll love it.

The most common greeting is *salām aleikum* (peace be upon you), to which the correct reply is *wa aleikum as-salām* (and upon you be peace). If you get invited to a birthday celebration or are around for any of the big holidays, the common greeting is *kul sana wa intum bi-khīr* (I wish you well for the coming year).

After having a bath or shower, you will often hear people say to you *na'iman*, which roughly means 'heavenly' and boils down to an observation along the lines of 'nice and clean now, huh'.

Arrival in one piece is always something to be grateful for. Passengers will often be greeted with *al-Hamdu lillah al as-salāma* – 'thank God for your safe arrival'.

Hi.	marHaba
Hello.	ahlan wa sahlan or
	just ahlan (Welcome)
Hello. (response)	ahlan bēk
Goodbye.	ma'a salāma/
	Allah ma'ak
Good morning.	sabaH al-khayr
Good morning. (response)	sabaH 'an-nūr
Good evening.	masa' al-khayr
Good evening. (response)	masa' 'an-nūr
Good night.	tisbaH 'ala khayr
Good night. (response)	wa inta min ahalu

Useful Words & Phrases

Yes.	*aiwa/na'am*
Yeah.	*ay*
No.	*la*
Please. (request)	*min fadlak* (m)/ *min fadlik* (f) (can also be used to get somebody's attention)
Please. (formal)	*law samaHt* (m)/ *law samaHti* (f)
Please. (come in)	*tafaddal* (m)/ *tafaddali* (f)/ *tafaddalū* (pl)
Thank you.	*shukran*
Thank you very much.	*shukran jazīlan*
You're welcome.	*'afwan/ahlan*
Pardon/Excuse me.	*'afwan*
Sorry!	*āsif!*
No problem.	*mish mushkila/ mū mushkila* (in Jordan the *mish* is sometimes said as *mu*)
Never mind.	*maalesh*
Just a moment.	*laHza*
Congratulations!	*mabrouk!*

Small Talk

Questions like 'Is the bus coming?' or 'Will the bank be open later?' generally elicit the inevitable response: *in sha' Allah* – 'God willing' – an expression you'll hear over and over again. Another common one is *ma sha' Allah* – 'God's will be done' – sometimes a useful answer to probing questions about why you're not married yet.

How are you?	*kayf Hālak?* (m)/ *kayf Hālik?* (f)
How are you?	*shlonak?* (m)/ *shlonik?* (f)
Fine.	*al-Hamdu lillah* (lit: Thanks be to God)
What's your name?	*shu-ismak?* (m)/ *shu-ismik?* (f)
My name is ...	*ismi ...*
Pleased to meet you. (departing)	*furṣa sa'ida*
Nice to meet you.	*tasharrafna* (lit: you honour us)
Where are you from?	*min wayn inta?*
I'm from ...	*ana men ...*
Australia	*ustrālya*
Canada	*kanada*
Europe	*oropa*
Japan	*yaban*
New Zealand	*nyu zīlanda*
South Africa	*afrika el janubiya*
the USA	*amerka*

Are you married?	*inta mutajawwiz?* (m)/ *inti mutajawwiza?* (f)
Not yet.	*mesh Halla*
How old are you?	*adīsh 'amrak?/ kam sana 'andak?*
I'm 20 years old.	*'andī 'ashrīn sana*
I'm a student.	*ana tālib* (m)/ *ana tāliba* (f)
I'm a tourist.	*ana sa'iH* (m)/ *ana sa'iHa* (f)
Do you like ...?	*inta batHib?*
I like ...	*ana baHib ...* (m)/ *ana uHib...* (f)
I don't like ...	*ana ma baHib ...* (m)/ *ana lā uHib ...* (f)

Language Difficulties

Do you speak English?	*bitiHki inglīzi?/ Hal tatakallam(i) inglīzi?*
I understand.	*afham*
I don't understand.	*ma bifham la afham*
I speak ...	*ana baHki .../ ana atakallam ...*
English	*inglīzi*
French	*faransi*
German	*almāni*
I speak a little Arabic.	*ana behke arabe shway*
I don't speak Arabic.	*ana ma behke arabe*
I want an interpreter.	*urīd mutarjem*
Could you write it down, please?	*mumkin tiktabhu, min fadlak?*
What does this mean?	*shu yā'nī?*
How do you say ... in Arabic?	*kayf taqul ... bil'arabi?*

Getting Around

Where is ...?	*wayn ...?*
airport	*al-maṭār*
bus station	*maHaṭṭat al-bāṣ/ maHaṭṭat al-karaj*
railway station	*maHaṭṭat al-qiṭār*
ticket office	*maktab at-tazākar*

What time does ... leave/arrive?	sa'a kam biyitla'/ biyuṣal ...?
boat/ferry	al-markib/as-safina
bus	al-bāṣ
plane	ṭīyara
train	al-qiṭār

I want to go to ...	ana baddeh rūh ala ...
Which bus goes to ...?	aya otobīs beh rūh ala ...?
Does this bus go to ...?	hal otobīs beh rūh ala ...?
How many buses per day go to ...?	kam otobīs be rūh ben wa'har ...?
How long does the trip take?	kam as-sa'a ar-raHla?
Please tell me when we get to ...	omol mārūf elleh hamma nūsal ...
Stop here, please.	wakef, omal mārūf
Please wait for me.	ntov, omal mārūf
May I sit here?	feneh ekād Hon?

1st class	daraja ūla
2nd class	daraja thāni
ticket	at-tazkarah
to/from	ila/min

Where can I hire a ...?	wayn feneh esta'jer ...?
bicycle	al-'ajila
car	as-sayyāra/ārabeye
motorcycle	motosaikul
guide	ad-dalīl

Directions

How do I get to ...?	kīf būsal ala ...?
Can you show me (on the map)?	wayn (fil kharīṭa)?
How many kilometres?	kam kilometre?

What ... is this?	shū ... hey?
street/road	ash-sharia
village	al-qariyya

on the left	'ala yasār/shimāl
on the right	'ala yamīn
opposite	muqābil
straight ahead	'ala ṭūl/sawa/dugri
at the next corner	tanī zarūb
this way	min hon
here/there	hon/honāk
in front of	amām
near	qarīb
far	ba'īd
north	shimāl
south	junub

east	sharq
west	gharb

Around Town

I'm looking for ...	ana abHath ...
Where is the ...?	wayn ...?
bank	al-maṣraf/al-bank
beach	ash-shāti'
chemist/pharmacy	as-ṣayidiliyya
city/town	al-medīna
city centre	markaz al-medīna
customs	al-jumruk
entrance	ad-dukhūl
exchange office	masref
exit	al-khuruj
hotel	al-funduq
information	isti'lāmāt
market	as-sūq
mosque	al-yamā'/al-masjid
museum	al-matHaf
old city	al-medīna qadīma
passport & immigration office	maktab al-jawazāt wa al-hijra
police	ash-shurṭa
post office	maktab al-barīd
restaurant	al-maṭa'am
telephone office	maktab at-telefon
temple	al-ma'abad
tourist office	maktab as-siyaHa

I want to change ...	baddeh sarref ...
money	maṣāri
travellers cheques	sheket msefrīn

What time does it open/close?	aymata bteftah/ byeftah?
I'd like to make a telephone call.	fene talfen omol mārūf

Paperwork

date of birth	tarīkha al-mūlid
name	ism
nationality	jensīya
passport	jawaz as-safar
permit	tasrīH
place of birth	makan al-mūlid
visa	sima

Accommodation

I'd like to book a ...	feneh ehjuz ...
Do you have a ...?	fī ...?
(cheap) room	ghurfa (rkīsa)
single room	ghurfa mufrada
double room	ghurfa bi sarīrayn

for one night	la leile waHde
for two nights	leiltēn
May I see it?	mumkin atfarraj-ha?
It's very noisy/ dirty.	fi khēr dajeh/waṣaq
How much is it per person?	qad aysh li kul waHid?
How much is it per night?	adeh bel leil?
Where is the bathroom?	wayn al-Hammam?
We're leaving today.	eHna musafirīn al-youm

address	al-'anwān
air-conditioning	kondishon
blanket	al-baṭāniyya
camp site	mukhaym
electricity	kahraba
hotel	funduq
hot water	mai Harra/sākhina
key	al-miftaH
manager	al-mudīr
shower	dūsh
soap	sabūn
toilet	twalet/mirhad

Shopping

Where can I buy ...?	wayn feneh eshtereh ...?
What is this?	shu hadha?
How much?	qad aysh/bikam?
How many?	kam waHid?
How much money?	kam masāri/fulūs?
That's too expensive.	mayda ghalī khēr
Is there ...?	fi ...?
There isn't (any).	ma fi
May I look at it?	feneh etallā 'alaya?

chemist/pharmacy	farmasiya
laundry	gaṣīl
market	sūq
newsagents	maktaba

big	kabīr
bigger	akbar
cheap	rakhīs
cheaper	arkhas
closed	maghlūq/musakkar
expensive	ghāli
money	al-fulūs/al-maṣaari
open	maftūH
small/smaller	ṣaghīr/as-ghar

Time & Date

What's the time?	as-sā'a kam?
When?	matā/emta?
now	Halla'
after	bādayn
on time	al waket
early	bakīr
late	ma'qar
daily	kil youm
today	al-youm
tomorrow	bukra/ghadan
day after tomorrow	ba'ad bukra
yesterday	imbārih/ams
minute	daqīqa
hour	sā'a
day	youm
week	usbū'
month	shahr
year	sana
morning	soubeh
afternoon	bād deher
evening	massa
night	leil

Monday	al-itnein
Tuesday	at-talata
Wednesday	al-arbi'a
Thursday	al-khamīs
Friday	al-jum'a
Saturday	as-sabt
Sunday	al-aHad

Months

The Islamic year has 12 lunar months and is 11 days shorter than the western (Gregorian) calendar, so important Muslim dates will fall 11 days earlier each (western) year. There are two Gregorian calendars in use in the Arab world. In Egypt and westwards, the months have virtually the same names as in English (January is yanāyir, October is octobir and so on), but in Jordan, Syria and eastwards, the names are quite different. Talking about, say, June as 'month six' is the easiest solution, but for the sake of completeness, the months from January are:

January	kanūn ath-thani
February	shubāt
March	azār
April	nisān
May	ayyār
June	Huzayrān
July	tammūz
August	'āb

Numbers

Arabic numerals are simple to learn and, unlike the written language, run from left to right. Pay attention to the order of the words in numbers from 21 to 99.

0	٠	şifr
1	١	waHid
2	٢	itnayn/tintayn
3	٣	talāta
4	٤	arba'a
5	٥	khamsa
6	٦	sitta
7	٧	saba'a
8	٨	tamanya
9	٩	tis'a
10	١٠	'ashara
11	١١	Hid-'ashr
12	١٢	itn-'ashr
13	١٣	talat-'ashr
14	١٤	arba'at-'ashr
15	١٥	khamast-'ashr
16	١٦	sitt-'ashr
17	١٧	saba'at-'ashr
18	١٨	tamant-'ashr
19	١٩	tisa'at-'ashr
20	٢٠	'ashrīn
21	٢١	waHid wa 'ashrīn
22	٢٢	itnein wa ashrīn
30	٣٠	talātīn
40	٤٠	'arba'īn
50	٥٠	khamsīn
60	٦٠	sittīn
70	٧٠	saba'īn
80	٨٠	tamanīn
90	٩٠	tis'īn
100	١٠٠	mia
101	١٠١	mia wa waHid
200	٢٠٠	miatayn
300	٣٠٠	talāta mia
1000	١٠٠٠	alf
2000	٢٠٠٠	alfayn
3000	٣٠٠٠	talāt-alaf

Ordinal Numbers

first	awal
second	tanī
third	talet
fourth	rabeh
fifth	khames

September	aylūl
October	tishrīn al-awal
November	tishrīn ath-thani
December	kānūn al-awal

Emergencies

Help me!	sā'idūnī!
I'm sick.	ana marīd (m)/
	ana marīda (f)
Go away!	imshi!
doctor	duktūr/tabīb
hospital	al-mustash-fa
police	ash-shurta/al-bolis

The Hejira months, too, have their own names:

1st	MoHarram
2nd	Safar
3rd	Rabi' al-Awal
4th	Rabei ath-Thāni
5th	Jumāda al-Awal
6th	Jumāda al-Akhira
7th	Rajab
8th	Shaban
9th	Ramadan
10th	Shawwal
11th	Zuul-Qeda
12th	Zuul-Hijja

FOOD

I'm hungry/thirsty.	ana ju'ān/aţshān
What is this?	ma hādha?/
	shu hādha?
I'd like ...	bheb ...
Another ... please.	... waHid kamān, min fadlak

breakfast	al-fuţūr
dinner	al-'ashā
food	al-akl
grocery store	al-mahal/al-baqaliyya
hot/cold	harr/bārid
lunch	al-ghada
restaurant	al-maţ'am
set menu	tabak

Soup

soup	shurba
lentil soup	shurbat al-'adas

Vegetables

vegetables	khadrawat
cabbage	kharoum
carrot	jazar
cauliflower	arnabīţ
cucumber	khiyār

eggplant	*bazinjan*	banana	*moz*
garlic	*tum*	date	*tamr*
green bean	*fasūliya*	fig	*tīn*
lentils	*'adas*	grape	*'inab*
lettuce	*khass*	lemon	*limūn*
okra	*bāmiya*	lime	*limūn Hamḍ*
onion	*baṣal*	orange	*burtuqāl*
peas	*bisīla*	pomegranate	*rummān*
potato	*baṭāṭa*	watermelon	*baṭṭīkh*
salad	*salata*		
tomato	*banadura*		
turnip	*lift*		

Drinks

		milk	*halīb*
		mineral water	*maya at-ta'abiyya*
		sour milk drink	*ayran*
		water	*mayy*

Meats

meat	*laHm*
camel	*laHm jamal*
chicken	*farūj*
kidney	*kelāwi*
lamb	*laHm ḍānī*
liver	*kibda*

Miscellaneous

bread	*khobz/a'aish*
butter	*zibda*
cheese	*jibna*
egg	*beid*
pepper	*filfil*
salt	*milH*
sugar	*sukar*
yoghurt	*laban*

Fruit

fruit	*fawaka*
apple	*tufaH*
apricot	*mish-mish*

Glossary

This glossary is a list of Arabic (A) words commonly used in Jordan, plus some archaeological (arch) terms and abbreviations.

abu (A) – 'father of...'
agal (A) – black headropes used to hold a *keffiyah* in place
agora (arch) – open space for commerce and politics
'ain (ayoun) (A) – spring or well
Alo – private telephone company that runs Jordan's telephone service
amir (A) – see emir
arak – alcoholic spirit
Ayyubids – the dynasty founded by Salah ad-Din (Saladin) in Egypt in 1169

bab (abwab) (A) – gate
beit (A) – house
beit ash-sha'ar (A) – goat-hair Bedouin tent
benzin 'adi (A) – regular petrol
bin (A) – 'son of...'; see also *ibn*
burj (A) – tower

caliph (A) – Islamic ruler
caravanserai – large inn enclosing a courtyard, providing accommodation and a marketplace for caravans
cardo maximus (arch) – Roman main street, from north to south

Decapolis – literally 'ten cities'; this term refers to a number of ancient cities in the Roman Empire, including Amman and Jerash
decumanus (arch) – Roman main street, from east to west
deir (A) – monastery
duwaar (A) – circle

Eid al-Fitr (A) – Festival of Breaking the Fast, celebrated throughout the Islamic world at the end of *Ramadan*
emir (A) – Islamic ruler, leader, military commander or governor; literally 'prince'

haj (A) – the pilgrimage to Mecca
haji (A) – one who has made the haj
hammam(at) (A) – natural hot springs; sometimes refers to a Turkish steam bath, and toilet or shower

haram (A) – forbidden area
hejab (A) – woman's head scarf
HKJ – Hashemite Kingdom of Jordan, the country's official name

IAF – Islamic Action Front, the largest political party in Jordan
ibn (A) – 'son of...'; see also *bin*
il-balad (A) – 'downtown', the centre of town
imam (A) – religious leader
intifada – ongoing Palestinian uprising against Israeli authorities in the West Bank, Gaza and East Jerusalem that started in December 1987
iwan (A) – vaulted hall opening into a central court

jalabiyya (A) – man's full-length robe
janub(iyyeh) – south(ern)
jebel (A) – hill or mountain
JETT – Jordan Express Travel & Tourism, the major private bus company in Jordan
jezira (A) – island
jisr (A) – bridge
JTB – Jordan Tourism Board

keffiyah (A) – chequered scarf worn by Arab men
khal min ar-rasas (A) – unleaded petrol
khirbat (A) – ruins of an ancient village
khutba (A) – Islamic sermon
Kufic (A) – a type of highly stylised old Arabic script

madrassa (A) – theological college that is associated with a mosque; also a school
Majlis al-Umma (A)– Jordan's National Assembly
malek (A) – king
malekah (A) – queen
Mamluks – literally 'slaves'; this slave and soldier class was characterised by seemingly unending blood-letting and intrigue for the succession
masjid (A) – mosque
medina (A) – old walled centre of any Islamic city
midan (A) – town or town square
mihrab (A) – niche in the wall of a mosque that indicates the direction of Mecca
minaret (A) – tower on top of a mosque

minbar (A) – pulpit in a mosque
MSA – Modern Standard Arabic
muezzin (A) – mosque official who calls the faithful to prayer five times a day, often from the *minaret*
muhafaza(t) (A) – governorate(s)
mumtaz (A) – 'super' petrol or '1st class' (especially on trains); literally 'excellent'

nargileh (A) – water pipe used mainly by men to smoke tobacco
necropolis (arch) – cemetery
NGO – nongovernmental organisation
nymphaeum (arch) – literally 'temple of the Nymphs'; a place with baths, fountains and pools

oud (A) – Arabic lute

PLO – Palestine Liberation Organisation
PNC – Palestine National Council
PNT – Petra National Trust
PRA – Petra Regional Authority
praetorium (arch) – military headquarters
propylaeum (arch) – grand entrance to a temple or palace

qala'at – (A) castle or fort
qasr (A) – castle or palace
qibla (A) – direction of Mecca
Quran (A) – holy book of Islam
qusayr (A) – small castle or palace

rababa (A) – traditional single-string Bedouin instrument
Ramadan (A) – Muslim month of fasting

ras (A) – cape, point or headland
RDC – Royal Diving Club (near Aqaba)
RSCN – Royal Society for the Conservation of Nature

servees – service taxi
shamal(iyyeh) (A) – north(ern)
sheikh (A) – officer of the mosque or venerated religious scholar
sherif (A) – descendent of the Prophet Mohammed (through his daughter, Fatima); general title for Islamic ruler
sidd (A) – dam
siq (A) – gorge or canyon
souq (A) – market
stele – stone or wooden commemorative slab or column decorated with inscriptions or figures

tell (A) – ancient mound created by centuries of urban rebuilding
temenos (arch) – a sacred courtyard or similar enclosure
tetrapylon (arch) – an archway with four entrances
Trans-Jordan – Jordan's original name
triclinium (arch) – dining room

Umayyads – first great dynasty of Arab Muslim rulers
umm (A) – 'mother of ...'
UNRWA – United Nations Relief and Works Agency

wadi (A) – valley or river bed formed by watercourse, dry except after heavy rainfall

Thanks

Many thanks to the travellers who used the last edition and wrote to us with helpful hints, useful advice and interesting anecdotes:

Rob Abbott, Krystyna Adamek, Barry Aitken, Salim Akbar, Karl Alexanderson, Zahid Ali, Danny Allen, Wahid Arsalan, Bastian Asmus, Fatima Awwad, Steve Bailey, Dr Keith Barnard, Geoff Barton, Joan Batychi, Luca Belis, Brian Benson, Kemal Berberoglu, Alain Bertallo, Sophie Berteau, Tim Bewer, Sheila Bharat, Sam Birch, Sherry Blankenship, Roger Blesa, Alison & Bryan Bluck, Thomas Bocquet, Arthur Borges, Sally Bothroyd, Thomas Breitmeier, Melinda Brenton, Eric Brouwer, Charles Brown, Caroline & Pirmin Buchhaupt, Belinda Buitenhek, Mr Burns, Steffan Bush, Holly Byrne, Andrew Cameron, Elizabeth Campbell, Jack Campbell, Graham Cansdale, Vinod Chandra, Samuel Charache, David Chaudoir, Tan Kwang Cheak, Tibor Cinkler, Mark Conrod, Katie Cooke, Lara Cooke, David & Astrid Cooksey, Ian Cooper, Lisa Cozzetti, Andrew Craig, Bob Cromwell, Margaret Cronin, Neil Crooks, Linton Cull, Willem De Poorter, Peter Debruyne, Fiona Dent, Sarita Dev, Bronwyn, Hughes & Jamie Doman, Linda Dufour, Josef Dulac, Andy Dunbar, Regina Dunford, Julie Durand, Roland W Earl, Bruce Elliott, Antonio Elorza, Iliya Englin, Tracy Fenn, Susan Fielding, Mark Forkgen, Tobias Fox, Susan Fraser, Marie Brodeur Gelinas, Bernhard Gerber, Rita Ghanem, John Giba, Wynand Goyarts, Daniel Groeber, Michelle Groenvelt, Agnes Grundeken, Peder Gustafsson, Pamela Hagedorn, Matthew Hanning, Graham Harman, Jeffrey Harrison, Lutz Heide, Alfred Heuperman, Markus Heyme, Linda Hicking, C Hoad, Patrick Holian, Jeff Hopkins, Sharon Humphrey, Ruth Hutson, Jouni Hytönen, Paul Inman, M Jackson, Mary Jackson, Christian Jacob, Andreas Jens Jahrow, Juliette Jeffries, Maria Jesus de Lope, Esther Jilovsky, Johan & Diewertje Jol, Jan Joosten, Jack Jordan, Catherine Junor, Nazima Kadir, Jesse Kalisher, A Kamberg, Viktor Kaposi, Gina & Mark-Matthijs Kattenberg, Len Keating, J Keith Mercer, Maurits Kelder, Allan Kelly, Chrisof Kemper, G Kennedy, Jo Kennedy, Cathie Kerr, Hala Khalaf, Bob Kieckhefer, Karen Killalea, Derek Kim, Volker Kintrup, Klaus Kirchner, Peter Klein, Ross Klein, Paul Koetsawang, Koe Kok Hau, Andrzej Komorowski, Rina Kor, Peter Koutsoukos, Yan Lachat, Baylor Lancaster, Jeri Lang, Anne & Ted

Last, Espen Lauritzen, Bryce Leckie, Jill Ledger, Stephen-Andrew Lee, Dieter Lehmann, Jean Francois Lemay, Robert Leutheuser, Henry YM Lim, John Lindberg, David Liu, Zhiyu Liu, Clare Loveday, Roger Low Puay Hwa, Janine Lucas, Marc Luetolf, Jurgen Maerschand, Tommy Malmspren, Dorothy Mares, Leone Marsdon, Nick Massey, Bob Maysmor, Mark McCabe, Margaret McDonnell, Cliff McKeen, Nicky McLean, Peter Meaker, Thorsten Meier, Fernando Mesa, Thomas Moeller-Nielson, Gavin Mooney, Jo-Ann Morris, Mariella Mosler, Szabolcs Mosonyi, Hal Mozer, Miles Murdoch, Andrea Mussi, Margaret Nash, Giovanni Neri, Michell Nicklin, Katharina Nickoleit, Alex & Diane Nikolic, Sibren Oosterhaven, Brendan O'Regan, Mary Margaret Page, Chris Paget, GL & MJ Palm, Meritxell Pijoan Parellada, Kim Parker, Norman Parker, Dr Janos Patai, David Patel, Shane Peckham, H Pedersen, TL Peirce, David Perry, Jeroem & Maria Peters, Wendy Peters, Sean Plamondon, Patricia Pogonatos, Jose Pras, Therese Quin, Karolina Racova, Elizabeth Raymont, Thomas Reber, Justin Reed, Ken Reed, Miriam Reichmuth, Jon Reimer, Bandi Irisz Reka, Emerson Roberts, Christina Rogers, Darren Ross, Jean-Pierre Roy, Kolja Sadowski, Joan Schlegel, Tim Schmith, Katya Schodts, E Schotman, Rahel Schultz, Peter Serne, Susie Shinaco, Erica Sigmon, Giovanni Silvestro, Olga Simkova, Khaldoun Sinno, Betania SL, Jan & Hetty Smalheer, Rebecca Smith, Fenwick Snowdon, Herman E Spivey, Arne Stapnes, Jim Stephenson, Kay Stern, Walter Stielstra, Joan Stokes, Dan Sturgis, S Sumpton, Megan Sutton, Zvi Teff, Chad Thomson, David Thornforst, Hilvert Timmer, Jos Trappeniers, Bev & John Treacy, Stephanie Truesdell, Eleana Tsocas, Max & Eva Tsolakis, Greg Tuck, Catherine Turnbull, Andrew Turner, Fran Turner, Fabio Umehara, Martine van Dusseldorp, Joeri van Meenen, Geeske van Mierlo, Peter van Nederpelt, Bart van Rooij, Muriel Vander Donckt, Levente Varhelyi, Balint Vaszilievits-Somjen, Yasmina Volet, Jan Vorsselmans, Arno Waal, Suraj Wagh, Frank Wannenwetsch, Michael Ward, Jenny Wardall, Arme T Warmington, Crystal Water, Felix Weber, Sarah Whitson, John Wilkes, Sandra Wilkinson, Kristy Williams, Frank & Irma Wilson, Benny Wong, Jennifer Woo, Peter Woodbury, Steve Woodruff, Boris Worrall, Adam Wozniak, Kim Wroblewski, CH & WB Yee, Simon Young, T Yousuff, Martin Zissell

LONELY PLANET

You already know that Lonely Planet produces more than this one guidebook, but you might not be aware of the other products we have on this region. Here is a selection of titles that you may want to check out as well:

Middle East
ISBN 1 86450 349 1
US$24.99 • UK£14.99

Greece
ISBN 1 86450 334 3
US$19.99 • UK£12.99

Iran
ISBN 0 86442 756 5
US$21.99 • UK£13.99

Lebanon
ISBN 1 86450 190 1
US$16.99 • UK£10.99

Turkey
ISBN 1 74059 362 6
US$24.99 • UK£14.99

Libya
ISBN 0 86442 699 2
US$16.99 • UK£11.99

Tunisia
ISBN 1 86450 185 5
US$16.99 • UK£10.99

Morocco
ISBN 1 74059 361 8
US$21.99 • UK£13.99

Syria
ISBN 0 86442 747 6
US$17.95 • UK£11.99

Egypt
ISBN 1 86450 298 3
US$19.99 • UK£12.99

Available wherever books are sold

LONELY PLANET

Guides by Region

onely Planet is known worldwide for publishing practical, reliable and no-nonsense travel information in our guides and on our Web site. The Lonely Planet list covers just about every accessible part of the world. Currently there are 16 series: Travel guides, Shoestring guides, Condensed guides, Phrasebooks, Read This First, Healthy Travel, Walking guides, Cycling guides, Watching Wildlife guides, Pisces Diving & Snorkeling guides, City Maps, Road Atlases, Out to Eat, World Food, Journeys travel literature and Pictorials.

AFRICA Africa on a shoestring • Botswana • Cairo • Cairo City Map • Cape Town • Cape Town City Map • East Africa • Egypt • Egyptian Arabic phrasebook • Ethiopia, Eritrea & Djibouti • Ethiopian Amharic phrasebook • The Gambia & Senegal • Healthy Travel Africa • Kenya • Malawi • Morocco • Moroccan Arabic phrasebook • Mozambique • Namibia • Read This First: Africa • South Africa, Lesotho & Swaziland • Southern Africa • Southern Africa Road Atlas • Swahili phrasebook • Tanzania, Zanzibar & Pemba • Trekking in East Africa • Tunisia • Watching Wildlife East Africa • Watching Wildlife Southern Africa • West Africa • World Food Morocco • Zambia • Zimbabwe, Botswana & Namibia
Travel Literature: Mali Blues: Traveling to an African Beat • The Rainbird: A Central African Journey • Songs to an African Sunset: A Zimbabwean Story

AUSTRALIA & THE PACIFIC Aboriginal Australia & the Torres Strait Islands •Auckland • Australia • Australian phrasebook • Australia Road Atlas • Cycling Australia • Cycling New Zealand • Fiji • Fijian phrasebook • Healthy Travel Australia, NZ & the Pacific • Islands of Australia's Great Barrier Reef • Melbourne • Melbourne City Map • Micronesia • New Caledonia • New South Wales • New Zealand • Northern Territory • Outback Australia • Out to Eat – Melbourne • Out to Eat – Sydney • Papua New Guinea • Pidgin phrasebook • Queensland • Rarotonga & the Cook Islands • Samoa • Solomon Islands • South Australia • South Pacific • South Pacific phrasebook • Sydney • Sydney City Map • Sydney Condensed • Tahiti & French Polynesia • Tasmania • Tonga • Tramping in New Zealand • Vanuatu • Victoria • Walking in Australia • Watching Wildlife Australia • Western Australia
Travel Literature: Islands in the Clouds: Travels in the Highlands of New Guinea • Kiwi Tracks: A New Zealand Journey • Sean & David's Long Drive

CENTRAL AMERICA & THE CARIBBEAN Bahamas, Turks & Caicos • Baja California • Belize, Guatemala & Yucatán • Bermuda • Central America on a shoestring • Costa Rica • Costa Rica Spanish phrasebook • Cuba • Cycling Cuba • Dominican Republic & Haiti • Eastern Caribbean • Guatemala • Havana • Healthy Travel Central & South America • Jamaica • Mexico • Mexico City • Panama • Puerto Rico • Read This First: Central & South America • Virgin Islands • World Food Caribbean • World Food Mexico • Yucatán
Travel Literature: Green Dreams: Travels in Central America

EUROPE Amsterdam • Amsterdam City Map • Amsterdam Condensed • Andalucía • Athens • Austria • Baltic States phrasebook • Barcelona • Barcelona City Map • Belgium & Luxembourg • Berlin • Berlin City Map • Britain • British phrasebook • Brussels, Bruges & Antwerp • Brussels City Map • Budapest • Budapest City Map • Canary Islands • Catalunya & the Costa Brava • Central Europe • Central Europe phrasebook • Copenhagen • Corfu & the Ionians • Corsica • Crete • Crete Condensed • Croatia • Cycling Britain • Cycling France • Cyprus • Czech & Slovak Republics • Czech phrasebook • Denmark • Dublin • Dublin City Map • Dublin Condensed • Eastern Europe • Eastern Europe phrasebook • Edinburgh • Edinburgh City Map • England • Estonia, Latvia & Lithuania • Europe on a shoestring • Europe phrasebook • Finland • Florence • Florence City Map • France • Frankfurt City Map • Frankfurt Condensed • French phrasebook • Georgia, Armenia & Azerbaijan • Germany • German phrasebook • Greece • Greek Islands • Greek phrasebook • Hungary • Iceland, Greenland & the Faroe Islands • Ireland • Italian phrasebook • Italy • Kraków • Lisbon • The Loire • London • London City Map • London Condensed • Madrid • Madrid City Map • Malta • Mediterranean Europe • Milan, Turin & Genoa • Moscow • Munich • Netherlands • Normandy • Norway • Out to Eat – London • Out to Eat – Paris • Paris • Paris City Map • Paris Condensed • Poland • Polish phrasebook • Portugal • Portuguese phrasebook • Prague • Prague City Map • Provence & the Côte d'Azur • Read This First: Europe • Rhodes & the Dodecanese • Romania & Moldova • Rome • Rome City Map • Rome Condensed • Russia, Ukraine & Belarus • Russian phrasebook • Scandinavian & Baltic Europe • Scandinavian phrasebook • Scotland • Sicily • Slovenia • South-West France • Spain • Spanish phrasebook • Stockholm • St Petersburg • St Petersburg City Map • Sweden • Switzerland • Tuscany • Ukrainian phrasebook • Venice • Vienna • Wales • Walking in Britain • Walking in France • Walking in Ireland • Walking in Italy • Walking in Scotland • Walking in Spain • Walking in Switzerland • Western Europe • World Food France • World Food Greece • World Food Ireland • World Food Italy • World Food Spain **Travel Literature:** After Yugoslavia • Love and War in the Apennines • The Olive Grove: Travels in Greece • On the Shores of the Mediterranean • Round Ireland in Low Gear • A Small Place in Italy

Mail Order

Lonely Planet products are distributed worldwide. They are also available by mail order from Lonely Planet, so if you have difficulty finding a title please write to us. North and South American residents should write to 150 Linden St, Oakland, CA 94607, USA; European and African residents should write to 10a Spring Place, London NW5 3BH, UK; and residents of other countries to Locked Bag 1, Footscray, Victoria 3011, Australia.

INDIAN SUBCONTINENT & THE INDIAN OCEAN Bangladesh • Bengali phrasebook • Bhutan • Delhi • Goa • Healthy Travel Asia & India • Hindi & Urdu phrasebook • India • India & Bangladesh City Map • Indian Himalaya • Karakoram Highway • Kathmandu City Map • Kerala • Madagascar • Maldives • Mauritius, Réunion & Seychelles • Mumbai (Bombay) • Nepal • Nepali phrasebook • North India • Pakistan • Rajasthan • Read This First: Asia & India • South India • Sri Lanka • Sri Lanka phrasebook • Tibet • Tibetan phrasebook • Trekking in the Indian Himalaya • Trekking in the Karakoram & Hindukush • Trekking in the Nepal Himalaya • World Food India **Travel Literature**: The Age of Kali: Indian Travels and Encounters • Hello Goodnight: A Life of Goa • In Rajasthan • Maverick in Madagascar • A Season in Heaven: True Tales from the Road to Kathmandu • Shopping for Buddhas • A Short Walk in the Hindu Kush • Slowly Down the Ganges

MIDDLE EAST & CENTRAL ASIA Bahrain, Kuwait & Qatar • Central Asia • Central Asia phrasebook • Dubai • Farsi (Persian) phrasebook • Hebrew phrasebook • Iran • Israel & the Palestinian Territories • Istanbul • Istanbul City Map • Istanbul to Cairo • Istanbul to Kathmandu • Jerusalem • Jerusalem City Map • Jordan • Lebanon • Middle East • Oman & the United Arab Emirates • Syria • Turkey • Turkish phrasebook • World Food Turkey • Yemen **Travel Literature**: Black on Black: Iran Revisited • Breaking Ranks: Turbulent Travels in the Promised Land • The Gates of Damascus • Kingdom of the Film Stars: Journey into Jordan

NORTH AMERICA Alaska • Boston • Boston City Map • Boston Condensed • British Columbia • California & Nevada • California Condensed • Canada • Chicago • Chicago City Map • Chicago Condensed • Florida • Georgia & the Carolinas • Great Lakes • Hawaii • Hiking in Alaska • Hiking in the USA • Honolulu & Oahu City Map • Las Vegas • Los Angeles • Los Angeles City Map • Louisiana & the Deep South • Miami • Miami City Map • Montreal • New England • New Orleans • New Orleans City Map • New York City • New York City City Map • New York City Condensed • New York, New Jersey & Pennsylvania • Oahu • Out to Eat – San Francisco • Pacific Northwest • Rocky Mountains • San Diego & Tijuana • San Francisco • San Francisco City Map • Seattle • Seattle City Map • Southwest • Texas • Toronto • USA • USA phrasebook • Vancouver • Vancouver City Map • Virginia & the Capital Region • Washington, DC • Washington, DC City Map • World Food New Orleans **Travel Literature**: Caught Inside: A Surfer's Year on the California Coast • Drive Thru America

NORTH-EAST ASIA Beijing • Beijing City Map • Cantonese phrasebook • China • Hiking in Japan • Hong Kong & Macau • Hong Kong City Map • Hong Kong Condensed • Japan • Japanese phrasebook • Korea • Korean phrasebook • Kyoto • Mandarin phrasebook • Mongolia • Mongolian phrasebook • Seoul • Shanghai • South-West China • Taiwan • Tokyo • Tokyo Condensed • World Food Hong Kong • World Food Japan **Travel Literature**: In Xanadu: A Quest • Lost Japan

SOUTH AMERICA Argentina, Uruguay & Paraguay • Bolivia • Brazil • Brazilian phrasebook • Buenos Aires • Buenos Aires City Map • Chile & Easter Island • Colombia • Ecuador & the Galapagos Islands • Healthy Travel Central & South America • Latin American Spanish phrasebook • Peru • Quechua phrasebook • Read This First: Central & South America • Rio de Janeiro • Rio de Janeiro City Map • Santiago de Chile • South America on a shoestring • Trekking in the Patagonian Andes • Venezuela **Travel Literature**: Full Circle: A South American Journey

SOUTH-EAST ASIA Bali & Lombok • Bangkok • Bangkok City Map • Burmese phrasebook • Cambodia • Cycling Vietnam, Laos & Cambodia • East Timor phrasebook • Hanoi • Healthy Travel Asia & India • Hill Tribes phrasebook • Ho Chi Minh City (Saigon) • Indonesia • Indonesian phrasebook • Indonesia's Eastern Islands • Java • Lao phrasebook • Laos • Malay phrasebook • Malaysia, Singapore & Brunei • Myanmar (Burma) • Philippines • Pilipino (Tagalog) phrasebook • Read This First: Asia & India • Singapore • Singapore City Map • South-East Asia on a shoestring • South-East Asia phrasebook • Thailand • Thailand's Islands & Beaches • Thailand, Vietnam, Laos & Cambodia Road Atlas • Thai phrasebook • Vietnam • Vietnamese phrasebook • World Food Indonesia • World Food Thailand • World Food Vietnam

ALSO AVAILABLE: Antarctica • The Arctic • The Blue Man: Tales of Travel, Love and Coffee • Brief Encounters: Stories of Love, Sex & Travel • Buddhist Stupas in Asia: The Shape of Perfection • Chasing Rickshaws • The Last Grain Race • Lonely Planet ... On the Edge: Adventurous Escapades from Around the World • Lonely Planet Unpacked • Lonely Planet Unpacked Again • Not the Only Planet: Science Fiction Travel Stories • Ports of Call: A Journey by Sea • Sacred India • Travel Photography: A Guide to Taking Better Pictures • Travel with Children • Tuvalu: Portrait of an Island Nation

Index

Text

Bold indicates maps.

Bold indicates maps.

Boxed Text

Bold indicates maps.

MAP LEGEND

CITY ROUTES

Freeway	Freeway	Unsealed Road
Highway	Primary Road	One Way Street
Road	Secondary Road	Pedestrian Street
Street	Street	Stepped Street
Lane	Lane	Tunnel
	On/Off Ramp	Footbridge

REGIONAL ROUTES

Tollway, Freeway
Primary Road
Secondary Road
Minor Road

BOUNDARIES

International
State
Disputed
Fortified Wall

HYDROGRAPHY

River, Creek
Canal
Lake
Dry Lake; Salt Lake
Spring; Rapids
Waterfalls

TRANSPORT ROUTES & STATIONS

Train
Underground Train
Metro
Tramway
Cable Car, Chairlift
Ferry
Walking Trail
Walking Tour
Path
Pier or Jetty

AREA FEATURES

Building
Park, Gardens
Market
Sports Ground
Beach
Cemetery
Campus
Plaza

POPULATION SYMBOLS

✪ CAPITAL .... National Capital
◉ CAPITAL .... State Capital
● CITY .... City
● Town .... Population Large
● Village .... Population Small
Urban Area

MAP SYMBOLS

■ ....Place to Stay
▼ ....Place to Eat
● .... Point of Interest

☒ Airport	Cinema	Mosque	Pub or Bar
❸ Bank	Dive Site	▲ Mountain	Ruins
↗ Beach	Embassy	Museum	Shopping Centre
Border Crossing	Golf Course	National Park	Synagogue
Bus Terminal	Hospital	One Way Street	Taxi Rank
Camping/Caravan	Internet Cafe	Parking	Telephone
Cave	Lookout	Police Station	Toilet
Church	Monument	Post Office	Tourist Information

Note: not all symbols displayed above appear in this book

LONELY PLANET OFFICES

Australia
Locked Bag 1, Footscray, Victoria 3011
☎ 03 8379 8000 fax 03 8379 8111
email: talk2us@lonelyplanet.com.au

USA
150 Linden St, Oakland, CA 94607
☎ 510 893 8555 TOLL FREE: 800 275 8555
fax 510 893 8572
email: info@lonelyplanet.com

UK
10a Spring Place, London NW5 3BH
☎ 020 7428 4800 fax 020 7428 4828
email: go@lonelyplanet.co.uk

France
1 rue du Dahomey, 75011 Paris
☎ 01 55 25 33 00 fax 01 55 25 33 01
email: bip@lonelyplanet.fr
www.lonelyplanet.fr

World Wide Web: www.lonelyplanet.com *or* AOL keyword: lp
Lonely Planet Images: www.lonelyplanetimages.com